IMPORTANT

You can access the companion Web site for this book on the Internet at:

www.intel.com/intelpress/rpcs

Use the serial number located in the upper-right hand corner of the last page in the book to register your book and access additional material, including the Digital Edition version.

In memory of my grandfather,
who believed in my education and achievements.

— Lauri Minas

Contents

1 Introduction 1
    Goals 1
    Who Should Read this Book 2
    How this Book is Organized 3

2 How Power Became an Issue 11
    Millions of x86 Servers 11
    A Growing Digital World 13
    Higher Performance and Energy Consumption 15
    Exploding Data Storage Requirements 16
    The Denser Digital World 17
    Data Center Heat Rising 19
    How Much Cooling? 20
    Power Availability in Question 22
    Summary 23

3 Power Consumption in Servers 25
    Server Power Usage 26
        Power and Server Form Factor 26
        Power and Heat 27
        How Cooling is Achieved 27
    Server Power Breakdown by Components 31
        Estimating Power Consumption 32

Power and Memory   33
Power Supplies   38
Power and Storage   39
Summary   41

4   Data Center Power Consumption   43

Growth of Power Use in Data Centers   44
Data Center House Load   46
Data Center Efficiency and Power Use   50
   PUC and DCiE Defined   51
Variables that Affect Power Consumption   52
   Power Distribution Systems   57
   Uninterruptable Power Systems   58
   Transformer Losses   61
Power Usage Varies with Data Center Tiers   63
   The Uptime Institute's Classification Tiers   64
Data Center and Power Use Examples   65
Summary   68

5   Power Metrics for Servers   69

Server Power Benchmarks and Metrics   70
Server Power Monitoring Methods   77
   Server Nameplate Values and Derating   77
   CPU Utilization to Estimate Power Usage   79
   Subsystem Power Measurements and System Instrumentation   81
   Power Monitoring and Management Tools   82
   Intel Processor Power Management Technologies and Tools   85
Summary   86

6   Power Metrics for Data Centers   89

The Business of Metrics   90
Amps, Watts, Power, and Energy   92
Energy Metrics: What to Measure and Where   94
   Inventory Assets   94
   Estimate IT Power Consumption   94
   Inventory Business Requirements   95
   Measure Power Consumption   95

    Make Measurement an Ongoing Process 97
  Metrics and Measures 98
    Two Essential Metrics: DCiE and PUE 98
    Estimating DCiE and PUE 99
    Improving DCiE Measurement 101
  Additional Key Metrics 103
  ASHRAE Data and Temperature Measurements 107
  Metrics Measuring Cooling and Air Conditioning
    Efficiency 109
    Tons of Cooling 114
  Data Center Power Management Tools 116
    Power sizing and efficiency calculators 116
    Power Metering and Sizing Tools 117
  Facility Management Systems and Sensors 121
  Summary 123

7 Configuring Energy Efficient Servers 125

  Impacts of a Low Power Server 126
  Components of Energy Efficient Servers 128
    Energy Efficient CPUs 129
    Demand Based Switching 131
    C-States 132
    Reduced Power Memory Configurations 137
    Options for Reduced Power Storage 141
    Data Tiers 142
    Storage Form Factor 143
    Solid-state Memory 145
    Reducing the Amount of Data 146
    Fans: Keeping It Cool with Less Power 149
    Efficient Power Supplies 153
  Configuring OS and Applications for Low Power 157
    Operating System Capabilities 158
    Linux[†] Operating System 160
    Sun OpenSolaris[†] 162
  Optimizing Applications for Reduced Power
    Consumption 162
  Power Impacts of Consolidation and Virtualization 164
  Summary 166
  Case Study Example 168
    Host Europe 168

8   Energy-Efficient Data Center Tuning   171

Tuning Existing Data Centers – Overview of the
    Opportunity   172
Energy Efficiency Tuning of the IT Load   173
    Server Efficiency   175
    Storage Efficiency   176
    Server Virtualization, Consolidation, and Refresh
        Efficiency   179
Cooling Efficiencies   182
    Manage the Airflow   183
    Rack It Up   186
    Tape Up, Baffle and Blank It   188
    Hot and Cold Don't Mix   188
    Look Underfoot   194
    Look Overhead   197
    Concentrate Cooling   197
    Liquid Cooling   199
    Let It Get Hot   200
    Save with Economizers   201
    Cooling Efficiency Summary   203
Power Distribution Efficiency   204
    UPS   206
    Power Distributions Units (PDUs)   207
    Three-Phase Alternating Current Power   208
    Direct Current Distribution (-48V and 400V DC)   209
    Right Sizing the Data Center Design   211
Organization Culture Efficiency   212
Measure and Improve   212
Share and Learn From Industry Partners   217
Summary   217
Customer Examples   220

9   Designing New Energy Efficient Data Centers   227

Investment Considerations   227
IT Load Planning and Capacity Factors   229
    Considerations for Compute Density or Expanding Floor
        Space   231
New Data Centers: Starting With a Plan   233
Container Options   236
Summary   243

Contents **xi**

10 Energy-Efficient Server and PC Management 245
Server Life Cycle Costs: The Complete View 246
Companywide Power Management Plan for PCs 252
Case Study: Intel IT Four-Year Refresh 253
  Synopsis 253
  The Challenge 253
  The Opportunity 254
  The ROI Analysis 255
  Findings 255
  Conclusion 258
Case Study: Intel IT Power Management to the Limit 259
  Synopsis 259
  The Challenge 259
  Analysis 259
  Implementation 262
  Conclusion 263
Server Recycling Services 263
Summary 266

11 Industry Vision and Recommendations 269
Increased Energy Efficient Servers:
  Opportunities for the Computer Industry 270
  Motherboard Components 270
  Platform Power Management 271
  Server Power Supply Improvements 272
  USB Modifications for Increased Energy Efficiency 274
  Controlling the Data Explosion 276
Future Energy Efficiency Standards: Power and Performance
  Metrics 277
Summary 279

Appendix A Energy-Efficient Server Maintenance 281
Server Maintenance to Maintain Energy Efficiency 282
  Procedures and Schedules 282
    Spring Cleaning Keeps Servers Cool 284
    Dusty Add-in Cards Consume More Power 285
  Data and Hard Disk Drive Maintenance 286
    Power Supply Maintenance 287
    Preventive Maintenance: The CMOS and BIOS 288

Operating System Maintenance   288
Database Maintenance   289
Upgrading for Energy Efficiency   292
   Determining When to Upgrade   292
   Memory Upgrades: Lower Power, Better Performance   293
   Increasing Storage with Additional Hard Drives   294
Frequent Problems and Fixes   294
   Troubleshooting Methods   295
   Problem Determination Tips   295
   Troubleshooting the Processor   296
   Troubleshooting Memory   297
   Troubleshooting Hard Disk Drives   297
   Troubleshooting the Power Supply   298
Summary   299

Appendix B   Energy Efficiency Measurement Templates 301
U.S. Department of Energy Templates   301

Appendix C   Resources for Energy Efficiency 307

Appendix D   Performance Per Watt 315
Energy Benefits of Dual-Core Intel® Xeon® Processors   315

References 319

Index 325

Foreword

In 2001, I spoke to the trend toward increasing heat created by microprocessors, and I said that in the years ahead it would not be "business as usual" when fabricating these devices.

With research and innovation in materials science, process technology, and microarchitectures, we at Intel have attacked the thermal problem with significant success. What resulted was a *right-hand turn* to multi-core processing as we entered a new era of Moore's law.

The first era was dominated by the need to understand the materials, physics, and chemistry to make Moore's law work. The second era was about scale and manufacturing efficiency to deliver products in high volume. The right-hand turn has taken us to the new third era, which is all about energy efficient performance.

IT professionals running large data centers have been given a ferocious foursome of challenges that have converged to provide an intense focus on data center efficiency. Rising energy costs are increasing the total cost of ownership (TCO) of the data center center. Simultaneously, the economic environment is not only resisting increments but demanding lower TCO in short order.

Moreover, higher density servers driven by multi-core processors and dense form factors such as server blades are rapidly increasing the rapidly increasing power density in the data center. Finally, eco-technology requirements are now socially expected; they are not just regulatory requirements. This combination of challenges has quickly created a demand for improvements in data center power efficiency. We now need the equivalent right-hand turn at the data center level.

Real-world technical problems are rarely solved by improvements on single dimension. This is especially true when addressing the challenges of minimizing power consumption in a data center. Lauri Minas and Brad Ellison have identified a multitude of loads that contribute to power consumption and have recommended ways to reduce power consumption for each of the loads.

As Minas and Ellison report, Intel continues to make improvements at the processor level, and the performance per Watt ratio is responding favorably. They also point out that, while servers consume the most energy, other systems draw power as well. A thorough analysis of power consumption includes storage systems and network switches.

Perhaps the richest vein in this gold mine of a book is the authors' analysis of emergent power consumption issues at the data center level. With increasing compute density, both power distribution and cooling quickly dominate floor space as limiting factors to the overall capacity of a center.

Minas and Ellison report Intel's modeling of thermal behavior to better understand how cool air should be routed through racks of servers. They provide the necessary metrics to measure power consumption and track year-over-year improvements.

I recommend this book to IT professionals who want a comprehensive treatment of the many dimensions of power usage. I am pleased to see these Intel engineers sharing our experience with our community of customers.

Pat Gelsinger, Senior Vice President and General Manager,
Digital Enterprise Group

Acknowledgments

The authors would like to thank their many colleagues for discussions and content that contributed substantially to this book. Special thanks go out Charles Milo for germinating the concept for this book and providing key content and substantial reviews.

Thanks go to Deva Bodas for his load power content, Derek Collier for his Romley platform power knowledge, Richard Greco for content on system P states and C states, David Filani for his Node Manager content, Sunny Lam for his platform power content, Kevin Bross for his knowledge on DC power, Sunil Saxena for his OS power state knowledge, John Powell for his CPU power state content, Len Brown for his knowledge of Linux[†], Charles Rego for his green IT knowledge, Dave Hilliard for his Windows 2008[†] power management content, and Dave Hill for the volume of content he provided on the latest server power technologies.

Particular thanks go to John Hengeveld and Bob Zak for their superb job as copy editors. We would like to thank David and Susan King for their enthusiasm and support throughout this project. Thanks go to the illustrators who made this book look so interesting—Rick Eberly and Margaret Anderson. And, last but not least, we want to recognize the assistance of the program manager, Stuart Douglas, for making it possible to produce this book.

Lauri Minas would like to thank her daughters, Lisa and Natalie, and fiancé Carey Smith for their patience and encouragement during the many nights and weekends she worked on this book. She would also like to thank Deb Webb, the craziest and best friend anyone could ever have, for giving her the confidence to take on large projects such as this book.

Brad Ellison would like to thank his wife, Linda, and their family for the support, patience and encouragement during the many nights and weekends he spent working on this book. In addition, many thanks are due to friends and colleagues at Intel and elsewhere in the industry for the opportunity to investigate, learn and contribute to the emerging body of data center knowledge.

Chapter 1

Introduction

Genuine beginnings begin within us, even when they are brought to our attention by external opportunities.
—William Throsby Bridges

Is data center power consumption driving you up a wall, limiting your profitability, driving up your support costs or reducing your service levels? This book will help you by providing straight forward methods to reducing power consumption within a data center and in servers. It introduces methodologies and metrics to analyze how servers and data centers consume power and how to optimize their energy efficiency.

The book provides a straight forward treatment to each step in this process, providing background information on electricity, power and server components. It also provides multiple case studies to illustrate power savings potential and points to which new technologies provide the greatest benefit.

Goals

Computation and data storage has a huge value to modern enterprise. This has resulted in the installation of millions of data centers in businesses around the globe. Historically, the cost to power and cool these facilities was small relative to the investment in servers, storage units and other equipment. Today, however, the annual power and cooling costs of typical data centers are almost equal to the cost of the hardware. With current power consumption rates, the EPA predicts data centers face the risk of running out of power for cooling and to keep their servers operating unless something changes.

The primary goal in writing this book was to create a framework in which data centers, large and small, could analyze and reduce their power consumption. Accordingly, this book provides a quantitative approach to understanding energy efficiency within a server and within a data center. We cover best-known methods for power minimization and energy efficiency beginning with the basics of dual in-line memory modules (DIMM) selection, configuring Intel processors with reduced power states, options for constantly spinning disks, power management features in operating systems and other internal components. Then we build on these basics by exploring methods to manage power distribution, cooling and optimize the efficiency in data centers.

We present guidelines on how to monitor and manage the power consumption within data centers are presented in Chapters 4, 6 and 8. Case studies include models for power reduction techniques and performance per watt optimization (Chapters 3, 6, and 7). We've also included recommendations on how to maintain or modify a data center and servers for energy efficiency, even with environments of mixed equipment (Chapters 8 and 9). We use many examples derived from real data center situations to illustrate the concepts presented in the book and the power savings achieved.

Who Should Read this Book

We've written this book with three groups of people in mind. First, Professionals who are IT managers, architects, operating engineers and technicians should use this book as a way to learn about power reduction technologies and the quantitative methods used to analyze data centers. Second, platform architects and design engineers will find the holistic approach of this book beneficial to improving specific server component designs for energy efficiency. Finally, IT professionals will find the book useful as a reference, particularly for its examples of energy efficient data center design and analyses of power costs.

This book is suitable as an advanced undergraduate and graduate reading source for those students and instructors working in the areas of computer engineering, computer systems engineering, and energy efficient systems engineering. Students of MBA programs with a concentration in information technology (IT) will also benefit from understanding our framework.

How this Book is Organized

The book is organized from the bottom up. We start with looking at the lowest level of the data center, that is, with microprocessors and motherboard components, and we move ever upward to explore implications of data center design, with chapters tracing the pathway and providing information not often found gathered together and integrated.

The book is written as a reference guide to allow jumping to specific topics. Each chapter is a self-contained block of information. Data center managers may choose to focus on chapters that address data center power and management—Chapters 4, 6, 8, 9 and 10. IT Technicians who manage computers may benefit from focusing on the chapters on servers—Chapters 3, 5, 7, 10 and 11. Finance or Data center managers who plan to build a new facility would benefit from Chapters 4, 7 and 9. Put together, this book provides a wealth of information on everything related to making a data center energy efficient and keeping it that way.

Chapter 2: Overview of Computing and Data Center Evolutions

Chapter 2 illustrates how the world has become a digital economy with the growth rate of x86 servers doubling in the past few years. During this time, computer performance has grown exponentially, resulting in higher compute power consumption and increasing energy requirements for cooling hot spots in the data center.

Most existing facilities are built to accommodate only 40 to 75 watts per square foot—about a quarter of what would be ideal for today's needs. According to AFCOM's Data Center Institute, power failures and limits on power availability will interrupt data center operations at more than 90 percent of all companies over the next five years. According to a 2006 survey of the Data Center Users' Group (DCUG), a group of influential data center and facility managers formed by Emerson Network Power, "33 percent of respondents expect to run out of power and cooling capacity by the end of 2007, and 96 percent stated they would be out of capacity by 2011." Simply put, data centers are rapidly putting serious pressure on power and cooling capacity for various reasons.

Energy prices are rising, as are the risks of diminishing availability of energy resources. A solution to this challenge will require industry innovation at all levels—from silicon, to racks, to data center cooling systems—to pave the way for continuing, cost-effective IT growth.

Chapter 3: Power Consumption in Servers

To understand how to best reduce the power use within a server, it is good to understand how a server uses power. Chapter 3 discusses the various components of a server and the amount of power consumed. On a basic server system today, CPUs consume the most power, followed by memory, power supply inefficiency, then disks, PCI slots, the motherboard and lastly, the fan and networking interconnects at the low end.

Before the year 2000, servers, on average, drew about 50 watts of electricity; by 2008, they were using up to 250 watts or more. An estimate of power consumption (P) at any specific processor utilization (n%) can be calculated, if power consumption at maximum performance (P_{max}) and at idle (P_{idle}) are known.

Blade servers offer benefits by providing greater processing power in smaller rack space with simplified cabling. As many as 60 blade servers can be placed in a standard height 42U rack. The typical power and cooling demand for this configuration is more than 4,000 Watts compared to a full rack of 1U servers at 2,500 Watts.

Chapter 3 also illustrates how other server components contribute to the overall data center power draw. Memory modules can vary in power from 5W up to 21W per DIMM, for DDR3 and fully buffered DIMM (FB-DIMM) memory technologies. Power supplies are typically profiled for efficiency at a very high load factor of 80 to 90 percent. However, most data centers have a typical load of 10 to 15 percent area, making the power supply efficiency very poor. A basic server with two or four hard disk drives (HDDs) will consume 24W to 48W for storage. By themselves, a few disks do not consume much power. But external storage systems could have hundreds of disks, consuming tremendous amounts of power in the data center.

This chapter closes by reviewing the recent shift to multi-core processor chips which helps to address energy consumption of the processor by adding power management features, reducing frequency in exchange for multiple execution threads and reducing core operating voltage. Server power is trending up, but newer components are being manufactured to run more efficiently.

How this Book is Organized

Chapter 4: How Data Centers Consume Power

Chapter 4 describes how overall power consumption is growing in data center's "house loads" at a rate faster than the power consumption of individual servers. In 2005, electricity consumption by servers in the United States was approximately 0.6 percent of overall production. When the additional load of data center support infrastructure (UPS, cooling systems, lighting, and so forth) is figured in, this number jumps to an estimated 1.2 percent of U.S. production and 0.8 percent globally—the equivalent of five 1000MW power plants and fourteen 1000MW power plants, respectively. The cost: USD 4.5 billion, or about as much as was spent by 5.8 million average households. It is expected that, if current trends do not change, data center power consumption will double again by 2011.

There are many factors and variables that can affect power consumption in data centers. The most significant expenditure of a facility's power budget is usually spent addressing waste heat removal. This chapter includes data that shows how overall power consumption is growing in the data center's house loads at a rate faster than the power consumption of individual servers. The data demonstrates that approximately 38 percent of the total power consumed by a typical data center can be attributed to internal and external cooling system equipment. In this chapter we show how chillers and air management systems are the largest portion of house load. The power distribution system itself can represent approximately 11 percent of the total data center power consumption. In an average data center, as much as 50 to 70 percent of the electricity could power equipment other than compute and storage servers.

Chapter 4 also reviews power impacts from data center design and layout options. Choice of microprocessors and system thermal management tools are directly linked to facility cooling and power use. For example, a 4kW rack of servers generally requires 1 ton of refrigeration and ~500 cfm (cubic feet per minute) of airflow at 20°F. Generating 1 ton of refrigeration takes ¾ - 1¼kW of input power, absent efficiency improvements. Data center Tier classifications, which use redundancy for reliability create significant impacts on power consumption. Understanding the tradeoffs and impacts of various power system design elements is imperative to building highly efficient data centers.

Chapter 5: Server Tools: Methods, Measurements and Metrics

Chapter 5 provides insight into the approach for determining power consumption and energy efficiency in servers. The steps for measuring server power consumption can be approached with several different methods and metrics. Two key metrics are SPECpower_ssj2008 and performance per Watt. This information helps in two aspects; peak power draw is important for guiding the deployment and density of servers to a data center, and average power is the main factor of the power bill.

Server power consumption varies with the server's configuration and usage model. Real-time power monitoring and historical aggregation allows data center managers to see trends in power usage over time and to identify key values such as minimum, typical, and peak usage.

A good benchmark or metric provides a toolset to test and improve server power efficiency. There are many other benchmarks for servers. We cover each of these and identify the type of workloads they best profile to help in selection of the best metrics for your data center. We explain nameplate derating and some of the problems that arise from this method of estimating server power consumption. In addition, we show how to calculate CPU activity. Since the CPU is the manager of I/O subsystems and memory, it is a very simple and useful indicator of power usage. Finally, we survey server power management tools and the latest power management technologies incorporated into Intel processors.

Chapter 6: Data Center Tools: Methods, Measurements and Metrics

Chapter 6 presents methods for determining power consumption efficiency in data centers. The metrics covered enable energy and power consumption benchmarking in order to develop plans to reduce consumption and improve operations. Not only do good metrics help in correctly designing capacity, they also help align the design with the organization's goals. For example, a good ROI metric of power usage should include criteria that is meaningful to the business, such as energy consumption or input/output operations per second (IOPS) per kilowatt, or even revenue per Watt.

Valid measurements and metrics enable IT professionals to examine the correlation between performance/utilization and capital and operating costs. In this chapter we show the top three places to measure power and energy consumption and explain what the measurements define.

There are many competing metrics for measuring power and cooling in data centers. In Chapter 6 we identify the best metrics that are currently used by the industry. We show what they measure, how they are calculated, and how to interpret the results. Metrics covered include the basics of PUE and DCiE, to newer ones such as deployed hardware utilization ratio and layout efficiency. In addition, we cover best metrics and available calculators for sizing and analyzing cooling and power distribution efficiencies.

The quantification of power consumption can assist IT managers in optimizing operations, making new technology selection decisions, or developing capital investment plans. Understanding the different metrics is important so that operators choose the best metrics to support sound decision making and furthering business objectives.

Chapter 7: Configuring an Energy Efficient Server

Chapter 7 discusses how to build or specify a server with reduced power consumption. Improving the energy efficiency of a server can involve simple steps such as updating to the latest processors and BIOS to much more complex changes watt virtualization of the applications and storage. The average server wastes from a third to over half of the power delivered to it. Efficient server technologies and configuration practices can reduce data center power consumption by 20 to 55 percent.

In Chapter 7 we examine new processor technologies and their impact on reducing power consumption. Processor technologies covered include: multiple cores, demand based switching (DBS) dynamic frequency and voltage scaling (P-states) and processor C states.

Server power consumption is about more than the processor. In this section we also provide insight into how to reduce power consumption with the other components that make up a fully configured server. We explain how memory power consumption is heavily dependent upon the quantity, type, vendor, and part number of DIMMs installed. We give rules of thumb for selecting and configuring memory to consume the least amount of power possible and review different options for energy efficient storage and their power impacts. Options that we discuss include establishing tiered storage, virtualizing storage, increasing airflow with small form factor drives, reducing disk demand with data de-duplication and compression, low-powered SSDs mainly for read data to MAID (massive array of idle disks) systems. We define what constitutes an energy efficient fan and cooling system and show how choosing a high efficiency power supply can be the single greatest item to reduce overall system power.

We highlight requirements for the new Energy Star specification along with recommendations for how to select servers that meet the criteria. Finally, we cover energy efficient operating systems and technologies. Included in this section are Windows 2008[†], OpenSolaris[†] and Linux[†] operating systems. We will show how altering the P-state can reduce a server's power consumption at low utilization without limiting any of the performance needed at peak demand levels.

New generations of servers and subsystem components are making significant improvements in reducing power consumption. By selecting the energy efficient subsystem components, not only will the server be energy efficient, but the beneficial impacts will also spread to data center space use, power distribution and cooling systems efficiencies.

Chapter 8: Tuning the Data Center for Power Efficiency

If you want to tune your existing data center(s) to use less energy, this is the chapter for you. Chapter 8 provides tactical information for selection and optimizing efficiency of the house load, infrastructure and IT load components. We use several examples to illustrate how efficient technologies and practices can improve the energy efficiency of servers and data centers. Our models and examples show how the state-of-the-art scenario could reduce electricity use by as much as 45 to 55 percent compared to current trends—efficiency gains that could be realized using today's technologies.

Chapter 8 starts with some simple techniques for improving energy efficiency, such as turning off unused or seldom used servers. From culling the server population, we move on to how to increase storage efficiency by thin provisioning or optimizing SAN infrastructure. We identify the impacts of these and other efficiency measures, including a consolidation program achieved through server refresh and virtualization that can pay for itself within a year.

Following server and storage efficiencies, Chapter 8 covers the fundamentals for improving the thermal environment of data centers. We show how air management is a key part of effective and efficient cooling and one of the greatest opportunities for facilities operators to reduce power consumption. In addition, we offer best-practice design tips for air handler units, rack implementations, cold and hot aisle spacing and orientation, raised floor considerations, and ceiling plenum heights. We show how supplemental liquid cooling directly in racks impacts cooling efficiencies. Finally we review air and water-side economizers to show how a data center can achieve power usage efficiencies approaching 1.0.

Chapter 8 wraps up with efficiency improvements for power distribution systems. It begins with a discussion of how the UPS and PDU conversion losses can impact cooling efficiency. We also review how UPS and PDU systems vary significantly in both technology and efficiency to help you make the best decisions for tuning your data center.

Chapter 9: Designing New Energy Efficient Data Centers

Chapter 9 takes a look at new data center design. Given the life span variation between IT equipment and facility infrastructure, planning for long term energy efficiency is complex. We cover IT load planning in relation to capacity factors and the resulting impact to energy efficiency. Because it is very expensive to modify a facility's infrastructure once it has been built, sufficient spare capacity must be built in to the design to support both immediate (day one) needs as well as projected needs over the lifecycle of the data center.

We present considerations for accommodating capacity via additional compute density or expanding floor space. Many data centers today reach a break-even point at compute or power densities of around 250 Watts per square foot. This section offers benefits and tradeoffs to take into consideration in deciding whether to increase compute density or to expand.

For new data center planning, this chapter provides factors to consider which can help optimize energy efficiency as a component of the plan. The multiple factors that should be assessed to create an energy efficient plan are discussed. We also discuss tradeoffs when selecting power distribution capacity. A review of modular designs is included in this section along with a discussion of how this can help optimize a data center for maximum efficiency and utilization

The last section in this chapter covers use of prefabricated containerized data centers and their energy efficiency benefits.

Chapter 10: Energy Efficient Server and PC Management

This chapter provides examples and case studies on server refresh strategies showing how large data centers operate and manage their servers for increased energy efficiency. The return on investment (ROI) for these case studies will reflect key strategies that not only are energy efficient, but also have a strong financial return.

One case study reviews how Intel IT refreshed 25 percent of their servers in 2008 and has seen almost ~7X improvement in performance per watt. It includes the financial results, including the significant capital spend avoidance that was achieved.

Chapter 11: Industry Vision and Recommendation

We conclude the book by presenting challenges and opportunities for improving energy efficiency in future products as well as exploring opportunities for improving data center analysis methods. As energy efficiency becomes more valuable, developers and system engineers have an opportunity to make increased energy efficiency a primary design objective for future components and systems.

In addition to improving future products, new energy-efficiency standards, measurements and metrics will help universal adoption for a more complete characterization of data center and server energy behavior. This chapter is intended to provide perspectives on what to expect from future products.

Appendix A: Energy Efficient Server Maintenance

Appendix A presents some basics of server maintenance and best-practices to help maintain the energy efficiency state of servers in small offices. The material includes system management, recommended upgrades and server refresh cycles to minimize power consumption. Best known methods and examples illustrate how upgrades keep a server at optimum performance per watt.

Appendix B: Energy Efficiency Measurement Templates

Appendix B contains templates from the Department of Energy that can assist in profiling a data center and developing benchmark measurements as covered in Chapter 6.

Appendix C: Energy Efficiency Web Sites and References

Appendix C contains a list of organizations and their web sites that focus on energy efficiency, including technologies, specifications, education and information. It is not exhaustive but rather is intended to help the reader begin the journey of exploration into the rapidly changing world of data center and server energy efficiency best practices.

Appendix D: Performance per Watt

Appendix D explains the energy benefits provided by Dual-Core Intel® Xeon® Processors.

Chapter 2

How Power Became an Issue

I think there is a world market for maybe five computers.
—Thomas Watson

This chapter shows how the amount of energy consumed by data centers has doubled in recent years and is projected to increase drastically if changes are not made. Several forces are responsible for this. The growth of computing has resulted in thousands of data centers around the world housing millions of x86 servers. The volume of data is exploding, along with application demand for increased performance in servers. As technology advances, newer process technologies shrink transistors enabling computing density increases, and denser computing dissipates more heat, requiring more cooling. All this adds up to increasing power consumption for data centers.

Millions of x86 Servers

Computing has evolved from hundreds of mainframes to thousands of distributed midrange computers to the millions of x86 servers that are found in just about all businesses now. Ever changing servers have derived new capabilities from ever smaller and faster transistors and ever denser systems. More servers not only consume more power, but the increased system densities increase system heat and required cooling.

Large enterprises have their hands full supporting thousands of x86 servers with multiple operating systems and their applications, all drawing more power, with no end in sight.

Historically, the cost of power and cooling in facilities has been relatively small compared to the cost of hardware. Today, however, the annual costs of the facility, server power, server cooling, capital investment, depreciation, and operating costs, are almost equal to the cost of the hardware. Soon, depending on where the data center is located, this will no longer be true. As illustrated in Figure 2.1, in high utility rate areas, such as Europe or the northeast part of the United States, the cost of the utilities to support a single x86 server will exceed the server cost in less than three years.

According to the U.S. Environmental Protection Agency (EPA), the amount of energy consumed by data centers doubled between 2000 and 2006. Keeping up with this forecasted IT electricity demand will require building ten new 1,000MW coal or nuclear fired power plants within five years. Today's data centers face the risk of running out of power for cooling and keeping their servers operating.

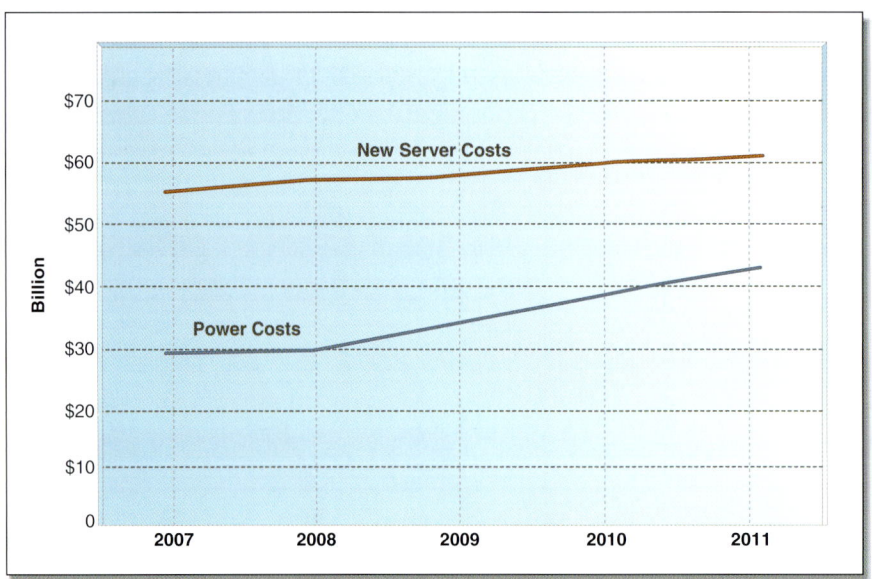

Figure 2.1 Power Cost v Server Cost, 2007-2011

Source: IDC White Paper, The Diverse and Exploding Digital Universe, Sponsored by EMC. March, 2008

The EPA (*www.epa.gov*) also forecasts that power failures and brownouts could affect as much as 90 percent of the data centers in the United States in the next decade.

A Growing Digital World

Most of our world's economy is digital. Information Technology (IT) is an increasingly important factor in the growth of businesses today. This growth in value of computing in businesses results in millions of data centers around the globe. Many large corporations have multiple data centers in several continents to keep their business running 24/7.

Some examples of how computing has permeated different types of businesses include:

- Health care moving to electronic medical records
- Manufacturing utilizing global networked organizations
- Online banking as banks migrate away from paper-based business models
- Financial services based on digital transactions
- Online insurance networked with repair shops and police departments
- Retail moving toward real-time inventories and supply chain management
- Transportation utilizing global positioning system (GPS) navigation and radio-frequency identification (RFID) tracking

As a result of this growing value of computing, many data centers now house hundreds or thousands of servers, storage arrays, and network equipment.

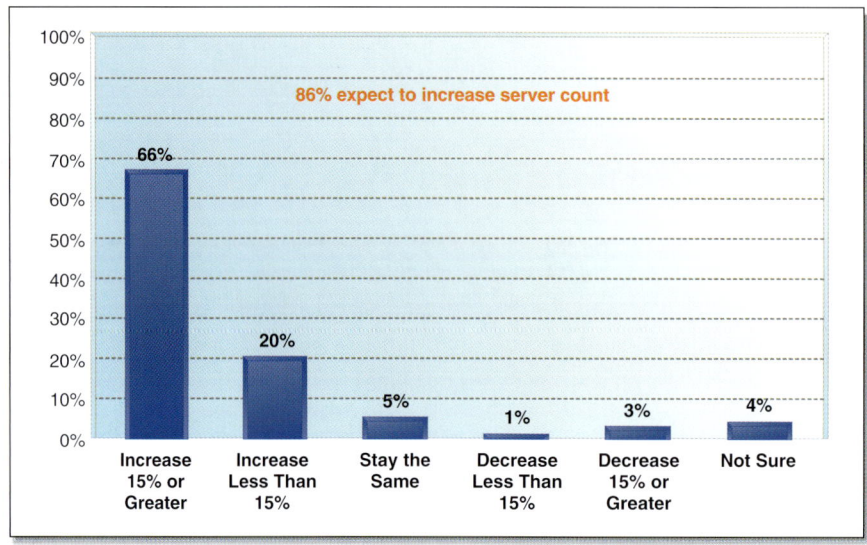

Figure 2.2 Change in Server Requirements
Source: Filani et al., 2008

As Figure 2.2 illustrates, continued growth in the number of servers is expected, as companies increasingly look to computing for efficiency and productivity increases. Worldwide, total server numbers have increased approximately 150 times in less than a decade. During that same period, average compute power per server has increased by a factor of 10, and smaller form factors have packed that power into much smaller spaces.

By 2006, x86 servers were responsible for the majority (68 percent) of the electricity used by U.S. servers and related IT equipment such as storage devices and network equipment. These x86 servers also experienced the greatest growth in energy use among all server classes, more than doubling from 2000 to 2006 at a compound annual growth rate (CAGR) of 17 percent. A February 2008 press release from IDC reported that in 2007 worldwide x86 unit shipments grew 8.3 percent to 7.6 million units and that unit shipment growth is accelerating each year (IDC 2008). Infrastructure systems, including the power delivery and cooling that are necessary to support the operation of IT equipment, also consumed a significant amount of energy, comprising 50 percent of total annual electricity use by IT data centers.

Higher Performance and Energy Consumption

Electricity prices have been on the rise, but the real culprit driving increasing energy costs is the insatiable demand for computing horsepower. Computer performance has grown exponentially for decades, driven by a combination of improvements in manufacturing technologies and architectural innovations. Performance increases that are being achieved by packing more transistors operating at higher speeds into processors are also increasing overall energy consumption.

An example of this increase in computing performance is the next-generation Intel® Core™ micro-architecture built with Intel® 45nm high-K metal gate silicon technology. With roughly twice the density of Intel® 65nm technology, Intel's 45nm packs about double the number of transistors into the same silicon space. That's more than 400 million transistors for dual-core processors and more than 800 million for quad-core server processors. Intel's 45nm technology enables great performance leaps, with up to a 50-percent larger L2 cache. Intel's 45nm technology packs 820 million transistors into the Intel® Xeon® processor 5400 series. Compare this with the previous generation Intel Xeon processor 5300 series, which had 582 million transistors.

To understand how small a transistor is with 45nm technology, consider the following. The original transistor built by Bell Labs in 1947 could be held in your hand, while hundreds of Intel's new 45nm transistors can fit on the surface of a single red blood cell. A 45nm transistor can switch on and off approximately 300 billion times a second. A beam of light travels less than a tenth of an inch during the time it takes a 45nm transistor to switch on and off.

45 nanometers (nm) in perspective

A nail	20,000,000 nm
A human hair	90,000 nm
Ragweed pollen	20,000 nm
Bacteria	2,000 nm
Intel 45 nm transistor	**45 nm**
Rhinovirus	20 nm
A silicon atom	0.24

This new transistor breakthrough allows Intel to continue delivering record-breaking server processor speeds and performance well into the future. The Quad-Core Intel Xeon processor can boost performance up to 1.5x over previous generation dual-core processors. Compare that with the Intel® Pentium® 4, which consumed about 83 Watts at full power. Then consider that the Pentium 4 represented a 319 percent increase in power consumption over its predecessor, which had a maximum power consumption of 26 Watts. These advances are, in turn, driving increases in power consumption by servers and switches.

Exploding Data Storage Requirements

Data is the essence of businesses and computing. As businesses and their computing environments have grown, so has the data and required storage to support the business. The emergence of the digital economy has yielded thousands of data centers and millions of servers. The increase in data and storage requirements has driven rapid growth in storage servers, storage area networks, network-attached storage, and external hard disk drive (HDD) arrays, all technologies using increasing amounts of power as their capacities and the data grow.

From punch cards 300 years ago (Jacquard loom) to UNIVAC1 tapes in 1950 to optical disks of today, storage has always been a key component of data centers. Today, in addition to their storage needs generated by business processes, U.S. companies are increasingly subject to regulations that require the long term collection and storage of digital data (Warmenhoven 2005). The most well-known of these regulations in the United States is the Sarbanes-Oxley Act, which requires long-term storage of financial information and email messages. Similarly, the U.S. Health Insurance Portability and Accountability Act (HIPAA) caused the establishment of national standards for electronic health care transactions and a demand to modernize the storage of health information to improve both access to and security for massive quantities of sensitive electronic information over the next few years. Such new requirements multiply the existing need for electronic data backups, archiving, and disaster preparedness in data centers. In some industries, it is estimated that the number of records that must be retained is growing at a CAGR of 50 percent or greater.

These trends not only require a growing number of storage servers, arrays, and storage networks, but they also require that the data be hosted in highly reliable data centers with sufficient capacity to meet peak and growing loads. This increase in infrastructure results in increased energy consumption and cooling. Tables 2.1 and 2.2 highlight how energy consumption in data centers has grown with respect to storage and network infrastructure equipment.

Table 2.1 Estimated Energy Use of Network Equipment, 2000 – 2006 (billion kWh/year)
Source: EPA, 2007

Network Location	2000	2001	2002	2003	2004	2005	2006
Server closet	0.07	0.09	0.11	0.13	0.15	0.17	0.19
Server room	0.22	0.27	0.32	0.37	0.44	0.51	0.57
Localized data center	0.25	0.30	0.34	0.39	0.44	0.50	0.56
Mid-tier data center	0.22	0.27	0.31	0.35	0.40	0.45	0.50
Enterprise-class data center	0.60	0.71	0.77	0.85	0.95	1.06	1.15
Total	1.36	1.64	1.85	2.08	2.38	2.70	2.97

Table 2.2 Estimated Energy Use of Network Equipment, 2000 – 2006
Source: EPA, 2007

Estimated Energy Use (billion kWh/year) of Network Equipment, 2000 to 2006							
Network Location	2000	2001	2002	2003	2004	2005	2006
Server closet	0.07	0.09	0.11	0.13	0.15	0.17	0.19
Server room	0.22	0.27	0.32	0.37	0.44	0.51	0.57
Localized data center	0.25	0.30	0.34	0.39	0.44	0.50	0.56
Mid-tier data center	0.22	0.27	0.31	0.35	0.40	0.45	0.50
Enterprise-class data center	0.60	0.71	0.77	0.85	0.95	1.06	1.15
Total	1.36	1.64	1.85	2.08	2.38	2.70	2.97

The Denser Digital World

Another trend that drives up the use of power in data centers is the increase in server density. As facility managers try to squeeze more computing power into less space, the energy consumption of a single rack of servers increases. In an attempt to reduce operations management, IT managers are consolidating and adopting higher density computer systems.

The fastest growing type of server in data centers is the blade server. Many data centers are replacing older, larger pedestal servers with racks of blade servers. In a July, 2008 press release, Gartner projected a CAGR of 19 percent for blade shipments from 2007 through 2012, making blades the fastest growing segment of the server market. Blades generate the most heat per square foot. Blade servers can have more than a fivefold increase in power density compared to the average 10kW/rack systems.

While the blade server market is growing fast, it is not the bulk of the x86 server market yet. According to the Gartner press release, blade servers account for 10 percent of shipments today. However, the effect that blades have on data center thermal management is significant. In a January 2009 survey of IT decision makers conducted by Ziff Davis Enterprise, publisher of *eWEEK*, 43 percent of companies report that their server consolidation initiatives or blade servers created hot spots that cannot be managed with ambient (room-level) cooling strategies (eWeek, 2009). These hot spots are more than an inconvenience; as a nearly identical percentage of survey respondents indicated that air conditioning and power management are the most critical areas of concern when an enterprise undergoes a data center consolidation project.

Table 2.3 Effects of Creating High-Density Data Centers
Source:V. Turner, 2008

Factors	Average Watt/Square Foot	Average kW/Rack	Megawatts Consumed	Annual Utility Costs
Year 2003	40	2	4	USD 288,000
Year 2005	80	4	8	USD 576,000
Year 2007	240	15	24	USD 1,700,000
Year 2010	500	30	50	USD 3.600,000

As shown in Table 2.3, increases in computer system power consumption—and the resulting increases in heat generation—have been occurring for years. The IDC data highlights the effects of next generation, high density data centers. The average kW usage per rack is epecting to increase more than 15 times. Wattage per square foot will evolve from a planned/designed for average of 40 Watts per square foot up to 500 Watts. These effects and the resulting costs are not nominal.

Another effect of high density data centers is the resulting increase in heat generation. Traditional approaches to data center cooling have consistently been able to scale to meet these increases. However, as Table 2.3 shows, the new blade densities are testing the limits of traditional cooling systems. A rack that held an average of 7 servers 10 years ago holds between 20 and 22 today, and servers that used to consume an

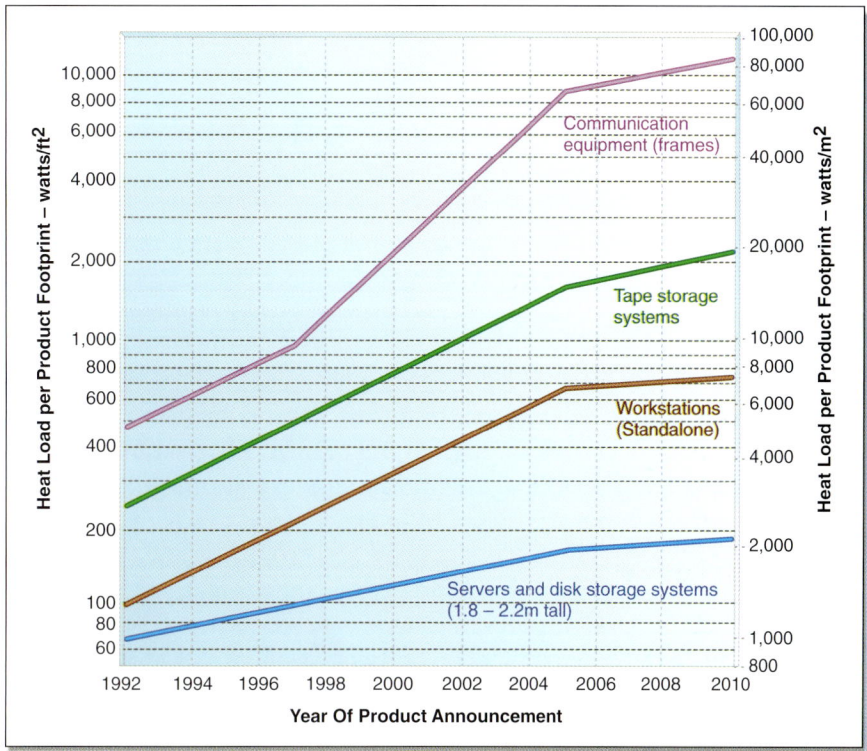

Figure 2.3 Product Heat Density Trends, 1992-2010
Source: The Uptime Institute, 2003.

average of 100 Watts of power now consume an average of 400 Watts. A July, 2008 University of California, San Diego study reports that energy usage per compute server rack has been growing from approximately 2 kW per rack in 2000 to an estimated 30 kW per rack in 2010 (e! Science, 2008). Denser racks generating increased heat require greater amounts of energy, both for operating and for cooling.

Data Center Heat Rising

With the increased use of racks of blades and 1U servers, companies are starting to become aware of the problem of thermal management. As manufacturing shrinks, and architecture innovations have led to increased server performance, we are seeing energy use increase as well. More circuits means more energy. Energy can be neither created nor destroyed; when you add energy to a system, it has to go somewhere—and it does, in the form of heat. Managing the heat is more difficult with dense equipment, but it is critical because hot spots cause reliability issues and shorten equipment life.

Not only do hot spots reduce reliability; they also increase costs. The rated power consumption of a typical server is estimated to have increased by a factor of 10 over the past 10 years. Such increased power densities can lead to a greater probability of thermal failure, impacting the availability of these systems. Additional cooling is required to avoid thermal failure, leading to an increase in operational cooling costs. For example, a 30,000 square foot 10MW data center can easily spend USD 2 to 5 million for the cooling infrastructure. On average, every Watt of power consumed with compute and storage servers needs an additional 0.5 to 1W of power to operate the cooling system (ASHRAE 2005b).

Heat densities of data center equipment are projected to continue to rise throughout this decade. Rack densities above 3 to 4kW are now becoming common. This density appears to be the threshold at which current approaches to cooling reach their practical limits. Increases in capabilities and performance are expected to drive power densities even higher in the years ahead. The biggest impact of this trend will be the requirement of additional energy to keep thermals in a safe, reliable range. While most data centers are likely to be able to provide sufficient electrical power, it does create a risk if there are temporary brownouts or limited energy to provide sufficient air circulation and air cooling capacity.

How Much Cooling?

Despite the attention that's starting to be focused on power and thermal management, it is clear that much work remains to be done. Data center planners are only beginning to obtain and recognize measurements and data to help deal with increased server densities. Many planners don't know their complete heating and cooling requirements, much less how to accurately measure them. *Watts per square foot* is a key measure of power and heat distribution that can help a data center planner break down a room into hot and cool zones. However, most businesses don't know the current planned level of Watts per square foot in their data center. This information is available, or could be calculated, but for many businesses, it's not yet top-of-mind.

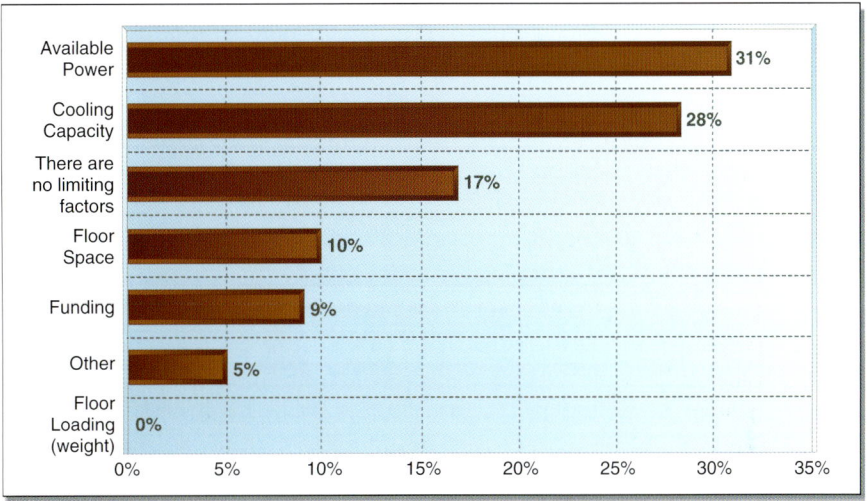

Figure 2.4 Factors Limiting Data Center Growth
Source: Filani et al., 2008

As the computer industry has been packing more processing power into a smaller footprint over the years, there is a common misconception that power consumption and heat generation are shrinking along with server size. This is not the case.

Just as many data center managers and planners do not measure their power and cooling, many also do not have energy strategies. As these new dense servers become installed alongside previous generation systems, they create hot zones within the data center that cannot be effectively managed using traditional approaches to cooling. New strategies and technologies must be implemented to provide the cooling high-density systems require for reliable operation.

The impact of these density and performance increases was not anticipated when most of today's data centers, infrastructure equipment, and operational practices were designed. Most existing facilities are built to accommodate only 40 to 75 Watts per square foot—about a quarter of what would be ideal for today's needs. The current cooling technologies and strategies were designed over 30 years ago. In many cases, IT and facilities managers are not even sure if their facilities will operate as expected, as they are only now being tested at their design limits. For all these reasons, power and cooling can be a limiting factor in keeping up with the business data center needs, as Figure 2.4 illustrates.

Power Availability in Question

With respect to energy usage, large data centers more closely resemble industrial facilities than commercial buildings. In fact, data centers can be more than 40 times as energy intensive as conventional office buildings (Greenberg et al., 2006). The increasing power density poses significant challenges in routing the large amounts of power needed per rack for future systems. Even if the cooling problem can be solved for future higher density systems, it is likely that delivering current to these configurations will reach the power delivery limits of most data centers. Furthermore, some speculate that future increases in power densities will be difficult to address purely at a facilities level.

According to AFCOM's Data Center Institute (AFCOM 2006), power failures and limits on power availability will interrupt data center operations at more than 90 percent of all companies over the next five years. While most data center managers feel they have adequate power today, they also recognize that they will need much more power within 24 months or less. Also, recent stories in the trade media indicate that executives outside of the IT community are becoming increasingly aware of the costs of data center power consumption. It's clear that the days of energy spending as an unexamined cost of doing business are over.

Given the trends of rising global energy prices and projected digital data growth at roughly 40 percent annually, this isn't only a matter of addressing the IT budget; it also becomes the challenge of diminishing availability of energy resources. The Uptime Institute performed a study of 19 computer rooms with more than 200,000 square feet of floor space and found that more than 60 percent of their capacity had been wasted because of poorly designed airflow and layouts. According to a 2006 survey of the Data Center User's Group (DCUG), a group of influential data center and facility managers formed by Emerson Network Power, "33 percent of respondents expect to run out of power and cooling capacity by the end of 2007, and 96 percent stated they would be out of capacity by 2011." Simply put, data centers are rapidly putting serious pressure on power and cooling capacity for a variety reasons.

Clearly, a huge financial opportunity exists for improving data center efficiency and reducing energy consumption. Beyond power delivery and cooling, increased energy consumption also has an environmental impact (for example, 4 millions ton of annual carbon dioxide emissions), and environmental agencies worldwide, such as Energy Star and Japan's Top Runner Program, are considering standards to regulate server and data center power. Many companies are starting to report their greenhouse gas emissions as part of their corporate responsibility initiatives, and government agencies are striving to meet specific energy use goals. Energy-intensive data centers can become a significant portion of an organization's energy use and greenhouse gas emissions, and thus challenge an organization's ability to meet these targets.

Heat waves and energy brownouts plus the threat of energy loss expose corporate data centers to areas of risk that were taken lightly in years past. With reserve electric capacity declining in the United States, power availability issues will likely continue to grow. Unlike improvements in the computing industry for price and performance efficiencies, the energy industry pricing model consistently increases the price per unit (kWh) annually, and this will continue to place increasing pressure on energy consumption reduction for businesses of all sizes.

Summary

As the world has become a digital economy, companies have grown large data centers with thousands of x86 servers. The growth rate of x86 servers has been doubling in the past few years. During this time, computer performance has grown exponentially, driven by customer demand and enabled by industry improvements in manufacturing technologies and architectural innovations. However, with denser computing comes higher power consumption and the need for more energy to cool hot spots in the data center.

At the current pace, the cost of energy has become a huge concern and will surpass the costs of the entire computer systems for many businesses in a few years. Some are approaching that point already. Energy prices are rising, as are the risks of diminishing availability of energy resources. Limited power to a data center could cause unmanaged hot spots and system reliability issues. A solution to this challenge will require industry innovation on an ongoing basis and at all levels—from silicon, to racks, to data centers—to pave the way for continuing, cost-effective IT growth.

Chapter 3

Power Consumption in Servers

Energy consumption matters both to our environment and our economy.
—John Baldacci

Capabilities of servers and their power consumption have increased over time. Multiply the power that servers consume by the number of servers in use today, and power consumption emerges as a significant expense for many companies.

This chapter explains how servers consume electrical power. It provides a foundation for later discussions concerning how to build and use servers that consume less power. The main power consumers in a server are the processors and memory. Server processors are capping and controlling their power usage, but the amount of memory used in a server is growing and, with that growth, more power is consumed by memory.

Other, smaller consumers of power within a server include the hard disk drives, PCI-e slots, and I/O connectors. Today's power supplies are very inefficient and waste power both at the wall socket and when converting AC power to DC. When servers are in operation, the entire chassis will heat up. This is especially true for dense blade and 1U servers. Cooling is then required to keep the components at a safe operating temperature. This cooling takes additional power, but it is critical to server reliablity.

Server Power Usage

As data centers and volumes of servers have grown, so has the overall amount of electricity consumed. Electricity used by servers doubled between 2000 and 2005, from 12 billion to 23 billion kilowatt hours. This was due to the increase in the number of servers installed in data centers and because of the required cooling equipment and infrastructure (Koomey, 2008).

Individual servers are consuming increasing amounts of electricity over time. Before the year 2000, servers on average drew about 50 Watts of electricity. By 2008, they were averaging up to 250 Watts. As more data centers switch to higher density server form factors, the power consumption will increase at a faster rate. Analysts have forecasted that if the current trend is not abated, then the power to run servers will be equal to or greater than the server cost.

Due to these trends, it is important to understand how a server uses and consumes power. When replacing or upgrading a server, it is possible to specify energy efficient improvements.

Power and Server Form Factor

Power use varies with the server's form factor. In the x86 server market, there are four basic server form factors:

- Pedestal servers
- 2U server rack servers
- 1U rack servers
- Blade servers

Where floor space is restricted, and increasing computing capacity is a goal, many data centers take advantage of rack servers or blade servers rather than pedestal servers.

Servers, routers, and many other data center infrastructure devices are designed to mount in steel racks that are 19 inches wide. For rack servers, the height of the server is stated in multiples of U, when 1U equals 1.75 inches. The U value identifies the form factor. Most common are 1U and 2U servers.

Power consumption is a function of the server's individual form factor, the heat and thermal environment related to that configuration, and the workload being processed. Workloads are increasing across all server types due to increases in server processing performance, and thus become another trend increasing power consumption on servers.

Power and Heat

Much of the electrical energy that goes into a computer gets turned into heat. The amount of heat generated by an integrated circuit is a function of the efficiency of the component's design, the technology used in its manufacturing process, and the frequency and voltage at which the circuits operate. Energy is required to remove heat from a server or from a data center packed with servers.

Computer subsystems such as memory subsystems and power supplies, and especially large server components, generate vast amounts of heat during operation. This heat must be dissipated to keep the components within their safe operating temperaturesbecause overheated parts will generally have a shorter maximum lifespan. Shorter component lifespan can produce sporadic problems, system freezes, or even system crashes.

In addition to server component heat generation, extra cooling is necessary when parts of the server are run at higher voltages or frequencies than specified. This is called over-clocking. Over-clocking a server results in increased performance, but italso generates a greater amount of heat.

How Cooling is Achieved

Server manufacturers use several methods to cool components. Two common methods are the use of heat sinks to increase the surface area that dissipates the heat and the use of fans to speed up the exchange of air heated by the components for cooler ambient air. In some cases, soft cooling is the method of choice. Computer components can be throttled down to decrease heat generation.

Heat sinks consist of a metal structure with one or more flat surfaces, such as a base, to ensure good thermal contact with the components to be cooled, and an array of comb or fin like protrusions. Fins increase the amount of surface area that is in contact with the air and thus increase the rate of heat dissipation, as Figure 3.1 illustrates. Heat sinks are frequently used in conjunction with a fan to accelerate airflow over the heat sink. Fans provide a larger temperature gradient by replacing the warmed air with cool air faster than convection alone can accomplish. Fans are used to make forced air systems, where the amount of air moved to cool components is far greater than the flow due to convection.

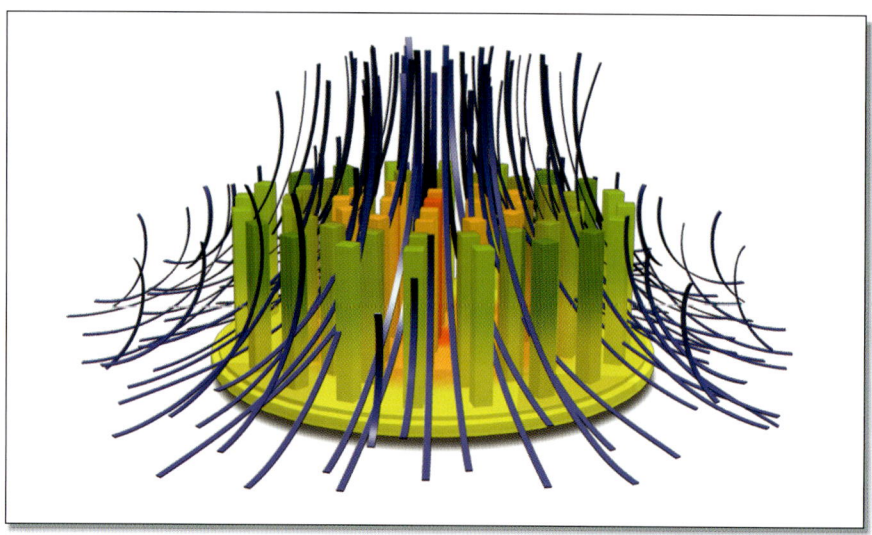

Figure 3.1 Natural Convection Heat Sink
Source: Wikipedia, 2008

Heat sink performance is defined as the thermal resistance from junction to case of the component. The units are °C/W. A heat sink rated at 10 °C/W will get 10 °C hotter than the surrounding air when it dissipates 1 watt of heat. Thus, a heat sink with a low °C/W value is more efficient than a heat sink with a high °C/W value.

A quality heat sink can dissipate thermal energy to an extent that additional cooling components need only be minimal. Heat sink thermal performance is determined by:

Convection or fin area.   More fins can provide more convection area, but care must be taken if a fan is used with a finned heat sink. In some cases, the pressure drop increases for forced air systems.

- A shortcoming of the conventional fan-top CPU coolers is the reduction of airflow due to pressure drop resulting from the airflow obstruction of the chassis cover and the fins of the heat sink itself.
- Fan performance is rated in cubic feet per minute (CFM) with zero pressure drop, and performance is severely compromised with only minimal air flow obstructions from either the intake or exhaust side of the fan.

Conduction area per fin. The thicker the fin, the better the conduction heat versus thinner fins.

- The most energy efficient heat sink designs will balance between multitudes thin fins and fewer thick fins.

Heat sink base spreading. Heat must be spread out as evenly as possible in the base for fins to work effectively. A thicker base is good for heat spreading.

- However since server form factors are limited to a specific height to fit in racks, the thicker base leads to reduced fin height and hence reduced fin area and increased pressure drop.

Table 3.1 shows a sampling of power increase by server form factor over time. The three classes of server are defined by IDC.

- Volume servers cost less than USD 25,000 and most commonly have one or two processor sockets in 1-2U rack mount form factor.
- Mid-range servers cost between USD 25,000 and USD 499,999 and are typically contain two to four processor socket or more.
- High-end server cost USD 500,000 or more and are typically contain eight processor sockets or more.

Table 3.1 Estimated Average Power Use (W) per Server, by Server Class, 2000 to 2006

Source: Koomey, 2007

Server class	2000	2001	2002	2003	2004	2005	2006
Volume	186	193	200	207	213	219	225
Mid-range	424	457	491	524	574	625	675
High-end	5,534	5,832	6,130	6,428	6,973	7,651	8,163

A pedestal server varies in width and is designed to optimize the performance and cooling of the server. Because these systems are not space constrained, they have large heat sinks, multiple fans, and great air cooling.

Rack and blade servers are designed to fit within a standardized 19" mounting rack. The rack server architecture and the limited height for air vents and fans cause them run hotter, and thus require more power in the data center for cooling infrastructure. 2U servers run hotter than a pedestal server, but cooler than 1U servers or blades.

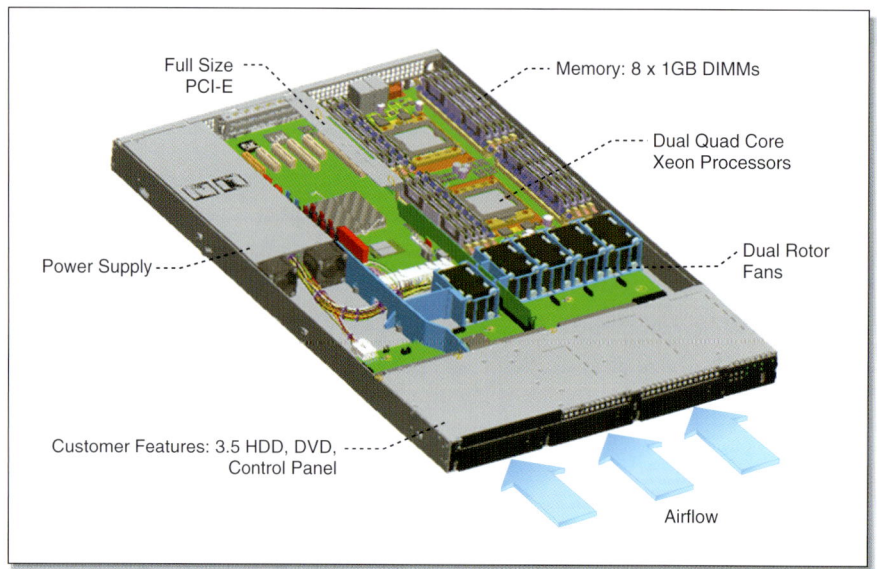

Figure 3.2 1U Server Architecture
Source: Intel Labs, 2006

A 2U server, at 3.5" high can use more and larger fans in addition to bigger heat sinks resulting in improved cooling capability and thus less power consumption than a 1U server. Most servers are designed to bring cool, fresh air in from the bottom front of the case and exhaust warm air from the top rear.

Rack server architecture typically locates customer-desirable features up front, such as disk drives forcing the hot components, such as the server processor and memory, in the back. With rack servers, manufacturers try to achieve a balanced or neutral airflow. This is the most efficient, and many servers end up with a slightly positive airflow that provides the additional benefit of producing less dust build up if dust filters are used.

The 1U form factor, shown in Figure 3.2, and blade server are the most difficult to cool because of density of components and lack of space for airflow cooling. Blade servers have the benefit of putting more processing power in less rack space and simplified cabling. As many as 60 blade servers can be placed in a standard height 42U rack. However this condensed computing comes with a power price. The typical power demand (power and cooling) for this configuration is more than 4,000 Watts, compared to a full rack of 1U servers at 2,500 Watts. Data centers address this demand by either increasing power consumption or using

Server Power Breakdown by Components 31

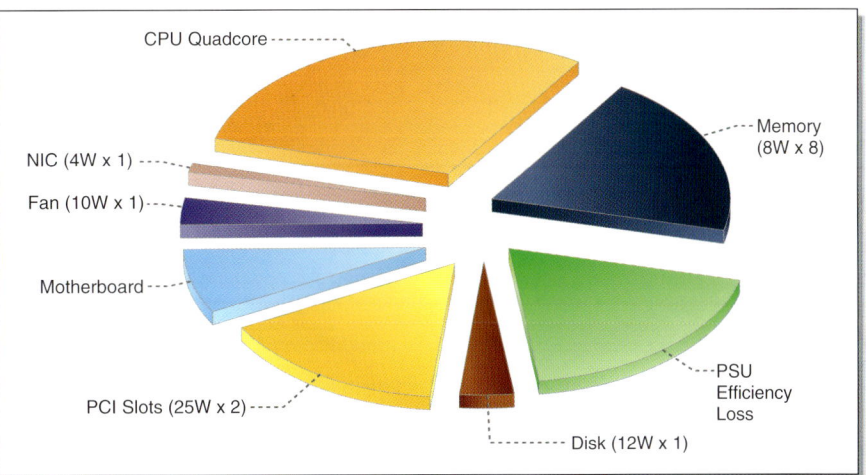

Figure 3.3 Server Power Consumption
Source: Intel Labs, 2008

more exotic ways of computer cooling, such as liquid cooling, Peltier effect heat pumps, heat pipes, or phase change cooling. These more sophisticated cooling techniques all use more power.

Server Power Breakdown by Components

Figure 3.3 highlights how power is consumed on average within an individual server. Processors and memory consume the greatest amount of power, followed by the power supply efficiency loss. Disk drive power only becomes significant in servers with several disk drives.

Processor power consumption varies greatly by the type of server processor used. Power consumption can vary from 45W to 200W per multi-core CPU. Newer Intel processors include power saving technologies, such as Demand Based Switching and Enhanced Speed Step technology. These newer processors also support power saving states such as C1E and CC3. Multi-core processors are much more power efficient than previous generations. Servers using the recent quad-core Intel® Xeon® processors can deliver 1.8 teraflops at peak performance using less than 10,000 Watts of power. Pentium® processors in 1998 would have consumed about 800,000 Watts to achieve the same performance. Processor power consumption will also vary with the workload.

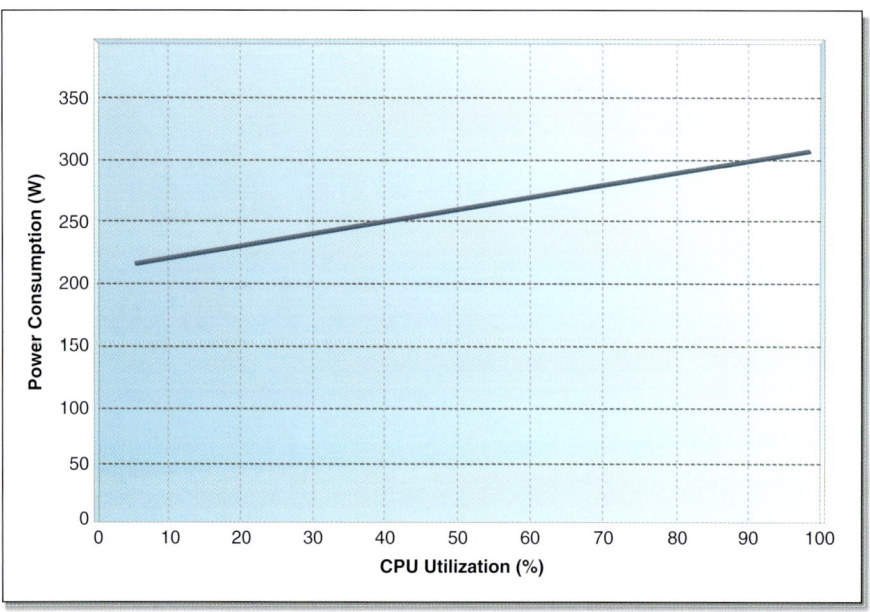

Figure 3.4 CPU Utilization and Power Consumption
Source: Blackburn, 2008

Figure 3.4 illustrates how processor energy efficiency, such as performance per Watt, increases as server utilization increases for a typical workload. Tuning workloads with optimized processor utilization can greatly affect power consumption and energy efficiency.

By taking average processor utilization over a defined period of time, it is possible to calculate an estimate of the power consumed for that period. Many server workloads scale linearly from idle to maximum power. When you know the power consumption of a server both at peak and idle usage, it becomes a simple arithmetic operation to estimate power usage at any utilization rate.

Estimating Power Consumption

An estimate of power consumption (P) at any specific processor utilization (n%) can be calculated if power consumption at maximum performance (P_{max}) and at idle (P_{idle}) are known. Use the following formula:

$$P_n = (P_{max} - P_{idle}) \times \frac{n}{100} + P_{idle}$$

For example, if a server has a maximum power draw of 400 Watts (W) and an idle power draw of 200W, then at 25 percent utilization the power draw would approximate to:

$$P_{25} = (400 - 200) \times \frac{25}{100} + 200$$

$$= 200 \times 0.25 + 200$$

$$= 250\,W$$

In this example, if the server were running at that average utilization for a 24-hour period, then the energy usage would equate to the following:

$$250\,W \times 24h = 6000\,Wh$$

$$= 6kWh$$

Through empirical measurement of various servers using a power meter this approximation has proven to be accurate to within ±5 percent across all processor utilization rates.

Power and Memory

The next largest consumer of power in a server is memory. Intel processor power levels are well controlled and capped in the latest generations. However, power consumption by memory chips is growing and shows no signs of slowing down in the future. Furthermore, applications continually seek more memory. Here are some of the reasons why demand for memory is growing in servers:

- Increases in processor core counts in latest servers to increase the memory that can be utilized in a server
- Virtualization, which is increasingly being adopted in today's data centers
- Memory-intensive search applications in new usages by Internet Protocol Data Centers, such as Google and Facebook

Memory is packaged in dual in-line memory modules (DIMMs) and these modules can vary in power from 5W up to 21W per DIMM, for DDR3 and FB-DIMM (fully buffered DIMM) memory technologies. The memory in a server with eight 1GB DIMMs can easily consume 80W. Many large servers now use 32 and 64 DIMMs, resulting in more power being consumed by memory than by processors.

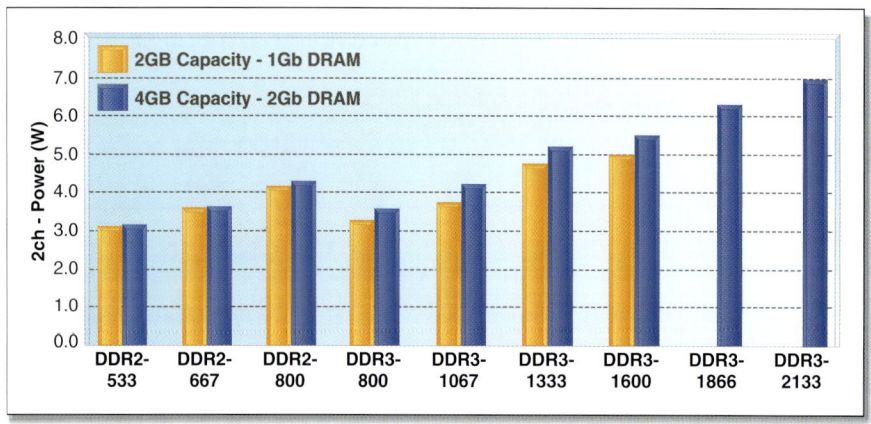

Figure 3.5 RDIMM Memory Power Conparison
Source: Intel Platform Memory Operation, 2007

For each generation of memory technology, there are key physical and electrical attributes of the DIMM that contribute to its power consumption and bandwidth. The dynamic random access memory (DRAM) packaging type and die count, number DRAM ranks on a DIMM, data transfer speed and data width define the DIMM capacity and power requirements. DIMMs can have registers, known as RDIMMs or be without registers, known as UDIMMs (unregistered DIMMs). RDIMMs consume slightly more power than UDIMMs.

Figure 3.5 shows how power consumption differs among RDIMMs using DDR2 and DDR3 technology. For power consumption of the latest DIMMs, check the websites of the leading memory manufacturers.

Power consumed by DIMMs is typically measured in active and idle standby states. *Active Power* is defined as: L0 state, 50 percent DRAM bandwidth, 67 percent read, 33 percent write, with primary and secondary channels enabled. The DRAM clock is active, and CKE is high. *Idle Power* is defined as: L0 state, Idle (0 percent bandwidth), primary channel enabled, secondary channel disabled, CKE high, command and address lines stable, and the SDRAM clock active.

On average, DDR3 DIMMs use 5W-12W when active. DIMMs from different vendors will vary based on their manufacturing process for the DRAM components and the components/configuration they use to make the memory module. Memory power consumed will also vary depending upon the application and workload running.

Table 3.2 shows sample RDIMM power consumptions in 2008, for DDR2 technology running at speeds of 667MHz. Table 3.2 highlights that power consumption by memory products varies widely among suppliers and configurations. For power consumption of the latest UDIMMs or RDIMMs, check the websites of these vendors.

Table 3.2 RDIMM Power Consumption by Vendor and Configuration

Sources: Publicly-available datasheets from each vendor, 2008

Vendor	Active Power	Idle Power	Configuration
2 GB Capacity			
Micron	5W	1.9W	2 ranks, 128Mb x 8
Elpida	6W	2.2W	1 rank, 18 1Gb parts
Qimonda	6.2W	4.0W	2 ranks
Samsung	6.8W	2.4W	2 ranks, 128Mb x 8
Hynix	7W	2.4W	2 ranks
Samsung	10.6W	2.4W	1 rank, 256Mb x 4
4 GB Capacity			
Hynix	8.6W	3.8W	2 ranks, 256Mb x 4
Qimonda	8.9W	5.3W	2 ranks
Micron	9.3W	2.6W	2 ranks, 256Mb x 4
Samsung	13.1W	4.2W	2 ranks, 256Mb x 4

As DIMMs increase in capacity, going from 4GB in 2008 to 16GB or 32GB in the near future, their power consumption will increase. DIMMs will also increase in speed over time, which increases the power consumption of the DIMM. Table 3.3 shows DDR3 RDIMM raw cards, DRAM density, capacity and the forecasted power use based on different speed targets of 1066MHz, 1333MHz and 1600MHz. Power is forecasted to trend higher with the memory speeds of 1866MHz and 2133 MHz. As Table 3.3 shows, memory power can vary significantly depending upon the memory technology used, the memory configuration, and the vendor.

Table 3.3 Future DIMM Power Consumption by Frequency, Configuration, and Capacity

Source: Intel Platform Memory Operation, 2008

Sample Card	Freq (MHz)	DIMM Configuration	DIMM Tech/Capacity	Power/ DIMM	64GB System Power
Card A	1066	QRx4	2Gb/8GB	15.5W	124W
Card B	1333	QRx8	2Gb/8GB	10.6W	84.8W
Card C	1333	DRx4	1Gb/4GB	10.6W	169.6W
Card D	1333	QRx4	2Gb/16GB	20.5W	82W
Card E	1600	QRx8	2Gb/8GB	10.1W	80.8W
Card F	1600	QRx4	2Gb/8GB	19.1W	152.8W

Cooling of memory is increasingly challenging and requires additional power in most server systems. In the past, memory bandwidth requirements were sufficiently low that memory was relatively simple to cool and required no thermal enhancements on the DIMM, no thermal sensors, nor throttling. The opposite is now true. The thermal analysis of the memory module includes the power of each component, the spacing between the memory modules, air flow velocity and temperature, as well as the presence of any thermal solution, such as a heat spreader.

DIMM memory is typically downstream from the processor, hard disks and fans, and therefore has a local higher ambient temperature. In typical server system layouts, cool air will flow from one end of the DIMM to the other, with the hottest DRAM component usually being the last one on the same side as the Register. However this conclusion is not consistent across all DIMM formats. For example, the fully buffered DIMM's hottest DRAM is near the center of the DIMM card, next to the Advanced Memory Buffer.

Memory thermals are important because good memory thermals improve system performance in addition to requiring less power. The thermal characteristics of memory subsystems are important because when memory subsystems operate at lower temperature, system performance improves and overall system power consumption is less. The memory thermals are characterized as a function of fan speed and preheat to the DIMMs. The required cooling capability in Watts per DIMM varies, depending upon whether or not the DIMM has a full DIMM heat spreader (FDHS) and whether or not the DIMM is in double refresh.

A DIMM under double refresh has a case temperature specification of 95°C rather than 85°C, thereby enabling a higher overall safe system temperature at the expense of a small power loss and slightly increased power consumption. The impact of double refresh (85°C versus 95°C) is a substantial improvement in cooling capability (by approximately two to three Watts) resulting in a significant improvement in memory bandwidth capability.

Throttling Memory to Reduce Power Consumption

Intel processor based servers include automatic memory throttling features to prevent memory from overheating without the processor or memory using additional power. There are two different memory throttling mechanisms that are supported by Intel chipsets: closed loop thermal throttling (CLTT), and open loop throughput throttling (OLTT).

Closed loop thermal throttling is a temperature-based throttling feature. If the temperature of the installed FB-DIMMs approaches their thermal limit, the system BIOS will initiate memory throttling to manage memory performance by limiting bandwidth to the FB-DIMMs, therefore capping the power consumption and preventing the FB-DIMMs from overheating. By default, the BIOS will configure the system to support CLTT if it detects that there are functional advanced memory buffer (AMB) thermal sensors present on all installed FB-DIMMs. In CLTT mode, the system fans run slower to meet the acoustic limits for the given platform but will also allow the fans to ramp up as needed to maintain the parts within temperature specifications under high stress levels.

Open loop throughput throttling (OLTT) is based on a hardware bandwidth count and works by preventing the bandwidth from exceeding the throttling settings programmed into the MCH registers. The system BIOS will automatically select OLTT as the memory throttling mechanism if it detects that one or more installed DIMMs does not have a functional AMB thermal sensor. Once the system BIOS enables OLTT, it utilizes a memory reference code (MRC) throttling algorithm to maximize memory bandwidth for a given configuration. The MRC code relies on serial presence detect (SPD) data read from the installed DIMMs as well as system level data as set through the FRUSDR Utility.

While memory throttling is good in that it prevents memory failures without consuming additional power, it has limitations in that it can negatively impact system performance. Program execution can be affected when the memory is shut down or when the memory bandwidth is limited by CLTT or OLTT. Chapter 7 explains how to improve system performance and power efficiency.

Power Supplies

Power supplies transform AC power into DC for use by server circuitry and power transformation loses some energy. The efficiency of a power supply depends on its load. The most efficient loads are within the range of 50–75 percent utilization. Power supply efficiency drops dramatically below a 50 percent load, and it does not improve significantly with loads higher than 75 percent.

Power supplies are typically profiled for efficiency at a very high load factor, typically 80 to 90 percent. However, most data centers have a typical loads of 10 to 15 percent. Thus power supply efficiency is often poor. Since most servers today run with 20-40 percent efficient power supplies, they waste the majority of the electricity that passes through them. As a result, today's power supplies consume at least 2 percent of all U.S. electricity production. More efficient power supply designs could cut that usage in half, saving nearly USD 3 billion.

A high efficiency power supply can significantly reduce overall system power consumption. For example for a 400W system load, a 60 percent efficient supply consumes 560W at the wall versus 460W with an 85 percent efficient power supply. Potential power savings from the change to a more efficient power supply is 100W.

In addition to the main power supply, servers utilize secondary power supplies that also can waste some power. These secondary smaller power supplies are distributed across the motherboard and are located close to the circuits they power. Secondary power supplies used in servers include point-of-load (POL) converters, voltage regulator modules (VRM) and voltage regulator down (VRD).

The output voltage from a VRM or VRD is programmed by the server processor using a voltage identification code (VID). Other secondary power supplies, such as POL converters, do not have this feature. VRM and VRD voltage and power requirements will vary according to the needs of different server systems. In many servers, approximately 85 percent of the motherboard power is consumed by the VRM/VRD exclusively for the server's processor.

To minimize power consumption with power supplies and the secondary voltage regulators, a server should run workloads to optimize the power supply efficiency. Intel® multi-core processors work with the VRM/VRDs so each core can operate in the most efficient way.

Power and Storage

A basic server with two or four hard disk drives (HDDs) will consume between 24W and 48W for storage. By themselves, a few disks do not consume that much power. But external storage systems in large enterprises have thousands of disks that consume significant amounts of power in the data center. Small businesses typically purchase servers with direct-attached storage, where the server contains many HDDs. Increasingly, small businesses also purchase networked storage systems shared by client and server systems.

Fewer storage devices consume less energy. Better utilization is the key. Poor storage management practices can consume significant amounts of power. The most common wasteful storage practice is operating disks that manage low-activity data spinning 24 hours per day. Underutilization of data access (and thus the data's value) increases power and cooling expenses when compared to better managed storage solutions that use energy only when data is accessed or written.

Storage utilization figures differ by operating system and type of storage device. On typical server systems, the average usage level for a hard disk is about 40 percent. New disk drive capacity is increasing much faster than drive performance. As a result of this imbalance, storage administrators typically use the redundant array of inexpensive disks (RAID) architecture and striping techniques to increase performance and reliability, but at the price of increasing the number of rotating drives. As utilization levels drop, more devices are needed, increasing total disk costs and energy expense.

Rotating drives consume energy and generate heat. Hard disk drives, like other computer components, are sensitive to overheating. Manufacturers measure off a minimal range of operating temperatures from +5 to +55°C as a rule (occasionally from 0 to +60°C), which is a smaller range than for processors, video cards, or chipsets. The reliability and durability of HDDs depend on operating temperatures. Increasing HDD temperature by 5°C has the same effect on reliability as switching from 10 percent to 100 percent HDD workload. Each Centigrade degree drop of HDD temperature is equivalent to a 10 percent increase of HDD service life.

The heat rate dissipated by a HDD is the product of its current and voltage in various states. The efficiency of HDD small motors can be less than 50 percent. Power consumption of hard drives is usually measured in states of Idle, SATA or SCSI Bus Transfer, Read, Write, Seek, Quiet Seek (additionally, if supported), and Start. Average power consumption of a

HDD can be calculated by measuring the power consumption of a HDD both during typical user operations and during intensive (constant) operations.

For every usage model, the percentage idle versus active of a HDD depends on disk capacity, applications in use, and related workloads. Average power consumption is estimated with the formula noted below, but it should be noted that power consumption will vary for actual power use.

Average hard disk power consumption for average operations, such as office work, $P_{Average}$ can be estimated by the following formula:

$$P_{Average} = \frac{P_{Idle} \times 75\% + P_{Write} \times 5\% + P_{Read} \times 20\%}{100\%}$$

where the states represent the power consumption of a drive from the voltage sources and the percentages represent the common percentage of the HDD state duration. This formula is based on the assumption that read/write HDD operations make up 10 percent of the total time for the average office usage.

Average power consumption during intensive hard disk operations such as defragmenting disks, scanning the surface, copying files ($P_{Constant}$) can be calculated by the following formula:

$$P_{Constant} = \frac{(P_{Write} + P_{Seek} + P_{Read}) \times 4}{5}$$

This formula is based on the assumption that read/write HDD operations in intensive operations is over 50 percent of the time.

The most efficient hard drives will consume on average 5 - 6W in idle state. Average SATA interface hard drives consume between 7 and 10W in idle. Today's SATA hard drives typically consume between 10 and 15W during active modes. And, as with other computer components, the efficiency of the latest generations is much better than those of previous generations.

Heat dissipation requirements have relaxed because power usage of hard disks has been steadily going down in recent years. Newer serial interfaces, such as SATA II and SAS, do increase power usage and heat dissipation a bit, but overall the heat dissipation trend is moving down. And, Quiet Seek mode (that is, slowing down the drive so the noise of rotating platters is equal or less than 128 decibels) can sometimes reduce heat dissipation of a hard disk much lower than it is increased by using a newer serial interface.

Summary

Electricity used by servers has doubled between 2000 and 2005 due to the increase in the number of servers installed and the required cooling equipment and infrastructure. Power use varies by server type, the configuration within each server, and the workload being run. All server components generate heat as they function. An increase of the local ambient temperature inside a server can cause reliability problems with the circuitry. Additional power is needed to keep systems and their components within a safe operating temperature range. As data centers move towards increased server density, the power and heat generated by servers will increase.

On a basic server system today, server processors consume the most power, followed by memory, then disks or PCI slots, the motherboard, and lastly the fan and networking interconnects. The recent shift to multi-core processors helps address energy consumption by the CPU and adds power management features that throttle processor power.

But today's applications are far more processor-intensive, which has triggered a trend toward high-density packaging and increased memory. This trend leads to memory as the largest power consumer in servers in the years to come. Memory cooling thus emerges as the primary thermal challenge.

Power supplies waste energy by converting AC power into DC. Most servers run today with 20 - 40 percent efficient power supplies that waste over half the electrical power passed through to them. At the typical server level, potential power savings from the change to a 15 percent more efficient power supply can be as great as 100W or more.

Storage power is minimal for an individual hard disk drive, but when servers utilize several disks and interoperate with RAID arrays and networked storage systems, storage power consumption is significant. Greater and cheaper disk drive capacity without performance improvements is leading to the trend of redundant disks and striping for performance and reliability. Good storage management techniques can offset this trend.

Power demands are trending upward, but newer server components are being manufactured to run more efficiently. The latest Intel Xeon processors, power supplies, memory and even hard disk drives all use less power, include power management features, and create less heat. With newer servers, data centers can evaluate servers by their performance per Watt and focus on business optimization instead of TCO costs.

Chapter 4

Data Center Power Consumption

Nothing in life is certain except death, taxes, and the second law of thermodynamics.
—Seth Lloyd

Data centers, which were designed for specific mainframes, are now becoming constrained by power delivery system limitations and an inability to remove waste heat. Overall power consumption is growing in the data center's house loads at a rate faster than the power consumption of individual servers. Electricity use for the house load can vary significantly depending on the efficiency of a data center cooling and power systems. In an average legacy data center, as much as 50 to 70 percent of the electricity could power equipment other than compute and storage servers.

There are many factors and variables that can affect power consumption in data centers. Understanding the tradeoffs and impacts of various power system design elements is imperative to building a highly efficient data center. Higher efficiency facility cooling and power systems can dramatically improve overall data center energy use. In addition to optimizing systems, controlling power loss in power conversions and transformation can also have a significant effect on the power bill.

There are tradeoffs between availability and power consumption. To make a data center resilient and eliminate single points of failure, much of the IT infrastructure has replicated components. Uptime Institute's data center tiers have become a major standard for availability. The system includes four tiers, where Tier 1 is the least available and Tier 4 the most robust. The higher the availability, the greater the amount of replicated equipment, and the greater power consumption.

Changing the Tier functionality your data center by moving from Tier II to IV can effectively double power consumption and costs. Moreover, research has shown that between 10 and 30 percent of the power consumption in a data center can be for servers, storage, and other equipment no longer in use. All these factors play key roles in increasing or reducing the power consumption in a data center. Therefore, to operate a highly efficient data center, you first need to understand how power is consumed in a data center.

Growth of Power Use in Data Centers

Data center facilities have been in use to house computing infrastructure for over 30 years. Mainframe computers require high levels of security and rigorous environmental controls, especially with respect to acceptable operating temperature and humidity envelopes. Computer rooms were originally designed and built to meet these relatively static requirements.

Designing a computer room for a specific mainframe's power and environmental requirements was straight forward. Once the mainframe was selected, power and environmental specifications were provided and the computer room fit up accordingly. Few if any power, cooling or humidification systems changes were required until that model mainframe was upgraded or replaced. Anticipated data center facilities design life was 20 years or more. In the event that additional mainframes were required, new rooms were designed and built to support each new computer.

Beginning in the 1990s when client/server computing became prevalent, IT organizations used existing computer rooms to house their populations of servers. These computer rooms were poorly equipped to sustain this transition to concentrations of distributed compute equipment. Increasingly, capacity for expanding compute infrastructure in the data center was constrained by the limits of power supply and power distribution systems and the ability to remove waste heat.

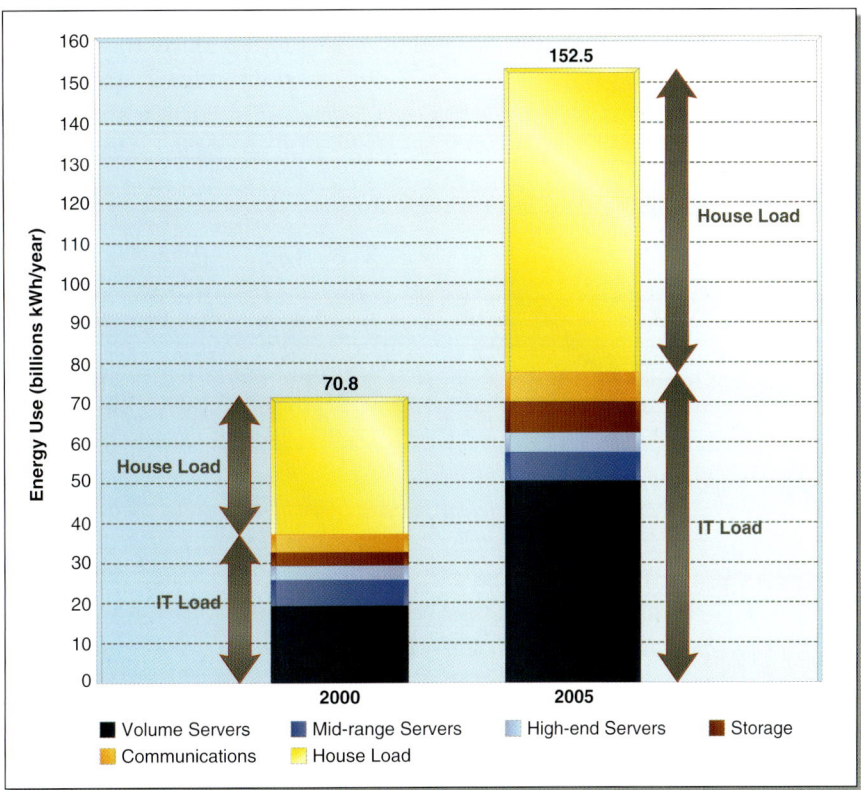

Figure 4.1 Worldwide Data Center Electricity Use
Source: Koomey, 2008

Data centers are recognized as significant consumers of electrical power. As Figure 4.1 shows, in 2005 U.S. electricity consumption by servers was approximately 0.6 percent of overall production (Koomey 2008). When the additional load of data center support infrastructure—UPS, cooling systems, lighting—is added, the total consumption jumps to an estimated 1.2 percent of electrical power generated in the US and 0.8 percent of power generated globally. Producing this power would take the equivalent of five 1000MW power plants and fourteen 1000MW power plants, respectively.

The power bill is USD 4.5 billion or about as much as is spent by 5.8 million average households. It is expected that if current trends do not change, data center power consumption will double again by 2011. The predominant cause of this growing consumption is directly attributed to the increased business demand for computing, the resulting growth in the installed base of servers and their required cooling. A substantially smaller amount of this growing demand is tied to the increased power consumption per server.

As power consumption continues to increase, many data centers find their growth plans by the available amount of power for compute systems and for associated facilities and cooling. Due to this critical limitation, it is important to understand how power is consumed in data centers and to look beyond just what servers consume.

Data Center House Load

The Koomey/LBNL study (2008) highlights how overall power consumption in data centers is growing as house load keeps pace with IT load, which is the power drawn by individual servers. House load is defined as the energy expended to distribute reliable power and remove waste heat from servers. Smaller components of house load includes the IT component support infrastructure, such as racks and power strips used to support the compute and storage servers, as shown in Figure 4.2. For every Watt consumed by servers—the IT load—a legacy data center typically requires an additional Watt of house load.

The major contributors to house load include facilities infrastructure such as HVAC systems, cable management systems, bypass airflow directors, fan motors, fluid pumps and compressors. Minor contributors to house load include items such as room lighting and environmental

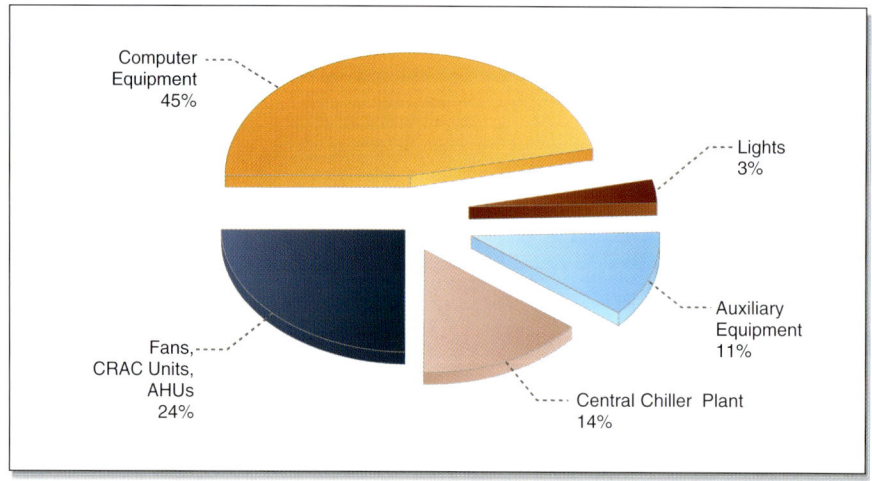

Figure 4.2 Components Consuming Data Center Power
Source: Mitchell-Jackson, 2001

health and safety systems and security systems required to meet the needs of people servicing the facility and the IT systems. All the house load components require energy to operate. Any component in the power supply chain, such as rack backplanes, AC/DC convertors, uninterruptable power supplies, and power distribution units, also produce some heat as a by-product of their operation. All of these systems introduce power loss between source and destination.

Proportionally, the largest component of house load within a data center is the energy expended for removing waste heat generated by IT systems and to a lesser degree, heat produced by various house systems. Approximately 38 percent of the total power consumed by a typical data center can be attributed to internal and external cooling system equipment. Fan motors, coolant pumps, and compressors all require energy to operate. The age and configuration of the equipment often has a significant impact on efficient power utilization.

The second largest component of house load is losses in the combined power distribution systems, consisting of PDUs and UPSs. These auxiliary systems represent approximately 11 percent of the total data center power consumption. Inefficient transformers, alternators and rectifiers, low power system loading, and redundant systems designed to improve compute availability all contribute in varying degrees to power losses and to house load.

Electricity use for house load can vary significantly depending on the efficiency of a data center's cooling and power systems. In an average data center, as much as 50 to 70 percent of the electricity could power equipment other than compute and storage servers.

Table 4.1 Estimated Average House and IT Loads in a 1MW Data Center
Source: Sawyer, American Power Conversion (APC), 2004

IT Load: 30%	House Load: 70%
Servers: 11%	Air-cooled chillers: 33%
Storage: 8%	Uninterruptible power supplies: 18%
Other IT devices: 11%	Computer room air conditioners: 9%
	Power distribution units: 5%
	Humidifiers: 3%
	Power transfer switches: 1%
	Lighting: 1%

Table 4.1 shows American Power Conversion's estimate of average house and IT load energy use for a typical 1MW data center. American Power Conversion (APC) is a vendor of backup products and services.

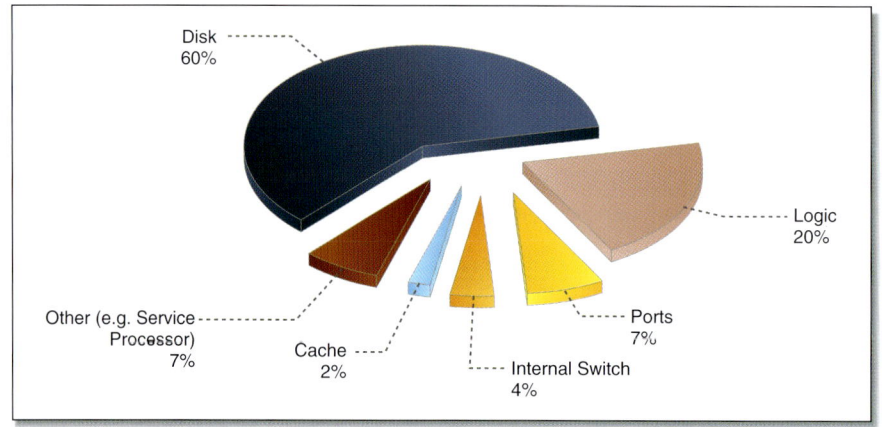

Figure 4.3 Technology Power Usage in High-End Storage, 2006
Source: Wikibon, 2006

Figure 4.3 shows the current relative power consumption of high-end storage solutions like SANs comprising site infrastructure, network equipment, storage, and servers. Just as processors draw the most power in servers, keeping disks spinning accounts for 60 percent of the total power usage in high end storage and disk arrays.

Most storage systems use redundant arrays of inexpensive disks (RAID) as a policy against disk failure, but, as shown in Figure 4.4, the

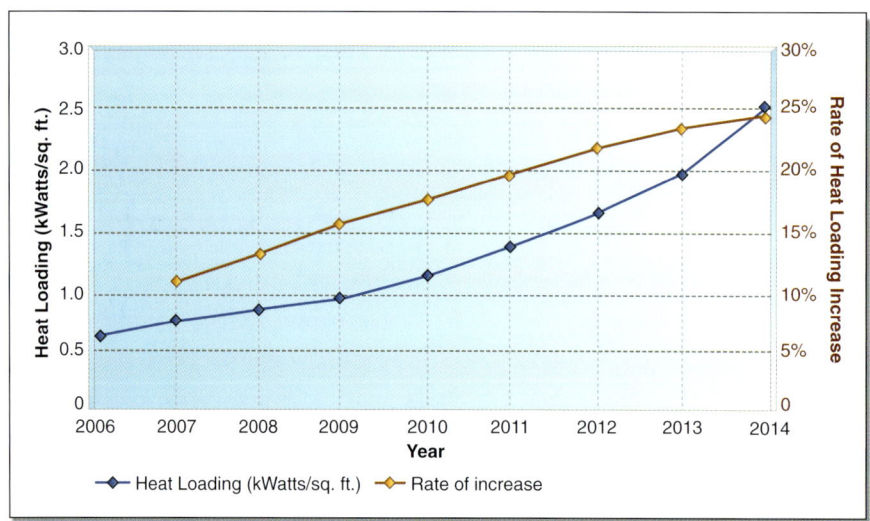

Figure 4.4 High end Storage Heat Loading, 2006-2014
Source: Wikibon.org, 2006

growth of data retention will also be mirrored by a growth of heat from the constantly spinning disks, and thus require more power to keep the data center cool.

Table 4.2 shows the Energy Star's breakdown of power consumption in Servers and Data Centers from 2000 – 2006 from a report submitted to Congress in August of 2007. The report was aimed at defining a vision for achieving energy efficiency in U.S. data centers. Energy Star presented the challenges related to the trend of the increasing energy consumption in servers and data centers and the opportunities for savings that could be realized with collaboration between the government, the IT industry, data center managers, and utility companies.

Table 4.2 Electricity Use by End-Use Component, 2000 to 2006

Source: www.energystar.gov, 2008

End Use Component	2000 Electricity Use (billion kWh)	% of Total	2006 Electricity Use (billion kWh)	% of Total	% of CAGR
Site infrastructure	14.1	50%	30.7	50%	14%
Network equipment	1,4	5%	3.0	5%	14%
Storage	1.1	4%	3.2	5%	20%
High-end servers	1.1	4%	1.5	2%	5%
Mid-range servers	2.5	9%	2.2	4%	-2%
Volume servers	8.0	29%	20.9	34%	17%
Total	28.2		61.4		14%

ASHRAE has studied the effect of heating and cooling of data center house equipment over many years. ASHRAE made its original projection of power density of data centers in 2003. Due to the rapid increase in per-unit power consumption, the organization had to revise these projections significantly upward in 2005 as shown in Figure 4.6. By 2008, high-end blade servers have already reached 1000 Watts per square foot in power density and power consumption is increasing at a rate of 30 percent per year for servers and telecommunication equipment.

50 ■ Chapter 4: Data Center Power Consumption

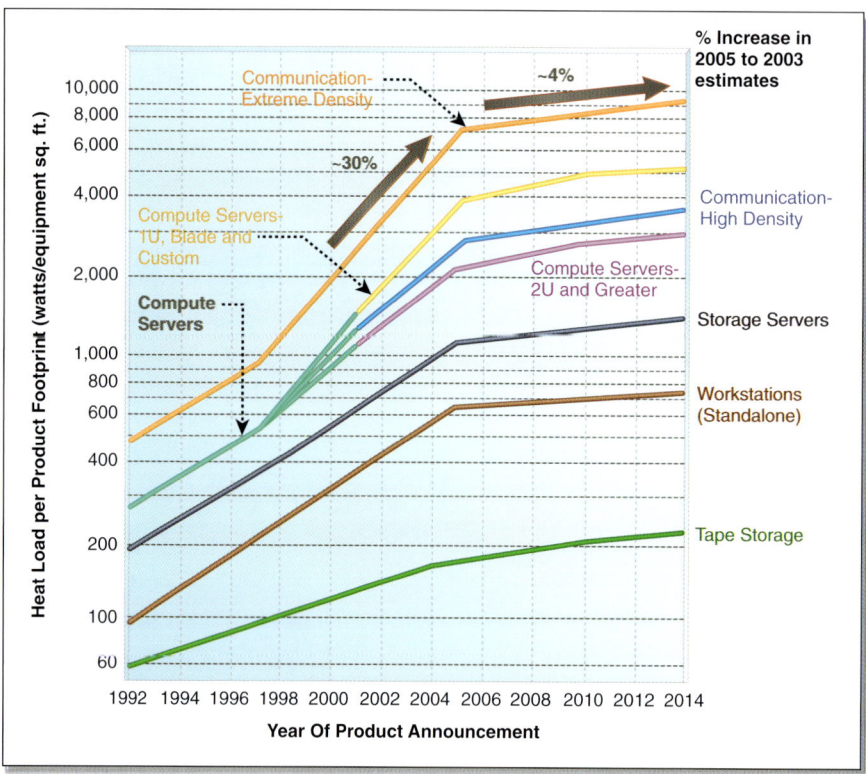

Figure 4.5 Data Center Power Trends
Source: ASHRAE, 2005

Data Center Efficiency and Power Use

Higher efficiency facility cooling and power systems can dramatically improve overall data center energy use. Understanding the tradeoffs and impacts of various subsystem design elements is essential to understanding data center energy consumption. Efficiency is typically quantified by two different measurements: power utilization effectiveness (PUE) and data center infrastructure efficiency (DCiE). These metrics are supported by the Green Grid initiative (Green Grid 2007).

First, here are the building blocks:

- IT equipment power, similiar in definition to IT load defined earlier, is the power consumed by equipment that is used to manage, process, store, or route data within the raised floor space.

- Total facility power is the power measured at a utility meter used solely to power the data center facility, including the IT equipment.

If the facility is a mixed-use building that contains both a data center and other functions, then power supporting other functions must be deducted from total facility power. Also, readers should notice that in prior discussions using other nomenclatures, we described power consumption as IT load and house load. To join these two terminologies, note that total facility load is the sum of IT load and house load.

PUC and DCiE Defined

The stage is now set to define PUE and DCiE.

- PUE is the ratio of total facility power consumption to IT system power consumption.

$$PUE = \frac{Total\ Facility\ Power}{IT\ Equipment\ Power}$$

A PUE of 2 means that for every 2 Watts of total facility load, there is 1 Watt of IT load. The lower the PUE, the more power efficient the data center power, cooling, and ancillary facilities systems.

- DCiE is the inverse of PUE stated as a percent In other words, DCiE is the ratio of IT equipment power divided by total facility power and multiplied by 100.

$$DCiE = \frac{IT\ Equipment\ Power}{Total\ Facility\ Power} \times 100$$

DCiE is useful for tracking the relative amount of power passing through to the IT equipment. The higher the DCiE, the more efficient the cooling and power delivery subsystems are.

Improvements in PUE and DCiE indicate either reductions in the total amount of power consumed by the data center (conservation) or higher available power capacity for computing (supply elasticity) within a given physical space. PUE and DCiE are metrics developed by The Green Grid in 2007.

Jonathan Koomey (2008) assumed a PUE of 2, meaning 50 percent for IT systems and 50 percent house load, as an underlying assumption for his estimates of total power consumption by data centers shown in Figure 4.1. This is a fair representation for the majority of data centers in 2008. However, PUEs in the 1.2 range are being achieved through use of innovative approaches such as direct current power distribution and wet and dry side economizers. In 2009, these data centers are early adopters and are not the norm.

Variables that Affect Power Consumption

There are many factors and variables that can affect power consumption in data centers. Some of the factors can be difficult to control, such as the distribution and conversion of DC power to the IT equipment and data center infrastructure. Other variables, such as older data center designs, density and age of compute/storage servers, or inefficient air cooling systems, can be easier to update or change to reduce power consumption.

House load can consume as much as 50 percent of the incoming DC power before it ever reaches any of the servers. Figure 4.6 identifies the major elements of house load. Power is consumed by power distribution units (PDUs) for the servers in racks, uninterruptible power supplies (UPSs) and automatic transfer switches (ATSs). While these devices provide redundant power circuits for power reliability, they do so at a cost.

The data center shown in Figure 4.6 has an air cooling system where air handing units (AHU) pull air across chiller coils and then distribute the cold air under the floor throughout the data center. This type of

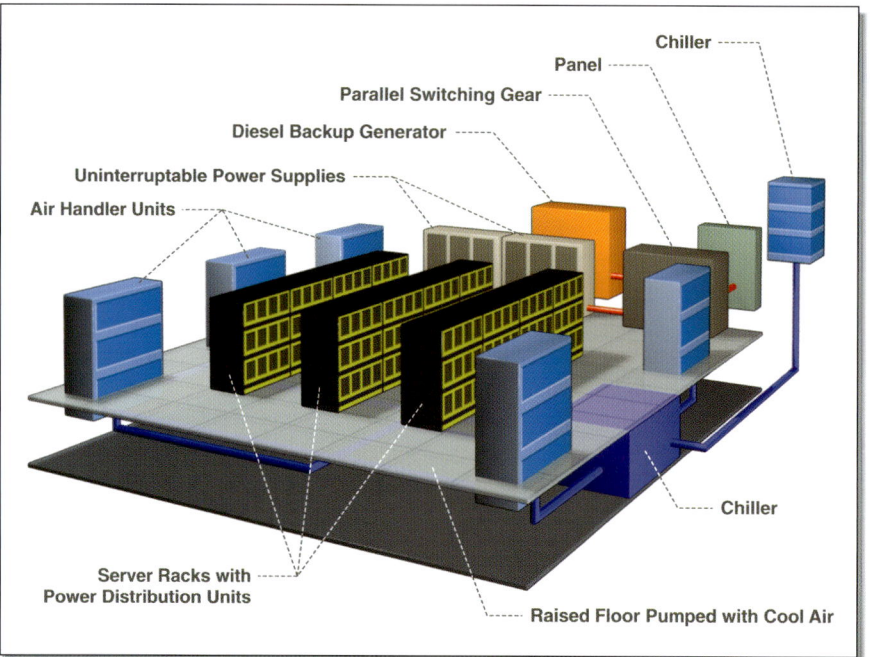

Figure 4.6 Facilities View of Power Usage
Source: Intel IT, 2005

facility layout can be scaled for efficient air cooling for very large rooms. For smaller buildings, computer refrigerated air conditioning units (CRACs) can efficiently replace the AHU.

The placement of servers in relation to the placement of chillers, air conditioners and humidifiers can either waste or save power. Chillers and air management systems are the largest portion of house load. Choice of microprocessors and system thermal management tools are directly linked to facility cooling and power use. While different physics and economics are in operation, the size of one directly affects the size of the other. Installing air conditioners at the room's perimeters may provide sufficient cooling capacity, for example, but using fans to push that cold air close to racks of blade servers in the center of a large room will require extra power and cost extra money.

For example, a 4kW rack of servers generally requires one ton of refrigeration and ~500 cfm of airflow at 20°F delta in temperature change. Generating one ton of refrigeration consumes from ¾kW to 1¼kW of input power.

Air handler coordination can also significantly affect power consumption. In some older designs that provide cooling and humidity control to large rooms or zones, air handling units can fall into competition with each other. One AHU may be supplying heat and humidification while an adjacent unit is attempting to cool and dehumidify. This can waste a significant amount of power.

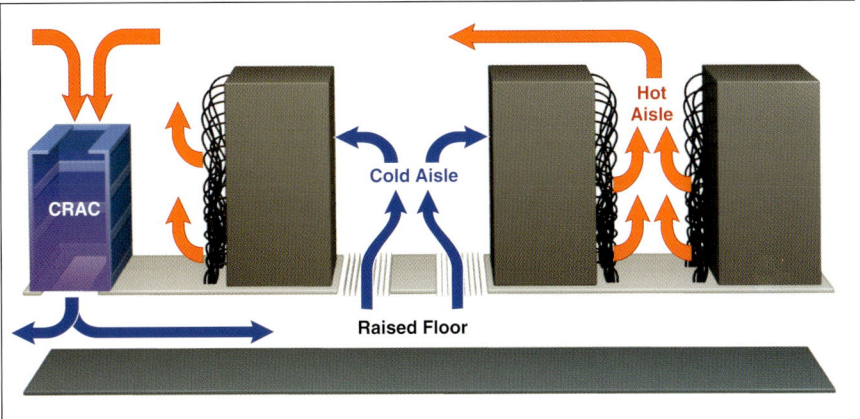

Figure 4.7 Server Rack Thermal Example

Source: Intel IT, 2007

Power loss can also occur on floors where the IT load and air flow are not configured in an optimal manner. If the data center has grown haphazardly, racks of servers may feed outgoing warm air into the air intake of adjacent server racks leading to compensatory overcooling of the entire room to avoid overheating some racks. Existence of bypass airflow in the computer room also wastes power. Bypass airflow occurs when cool air does not directly cool computer equipment, or in other words, the cool air leaks. The wasted cold airflow is typically caused by unsealed cabling holes in the raised floor, which allows cold air to circulate directly into the hot aisle. Sometimes the cold air supply escapes through perforated tiles incorrectly installed in the hot aisle, or installed randomly around the room. Intermixing of warm and cold air due to poor air management before it returns to the AHUs will increase the power consumption of the chillers for the data center.

An example of poor air management is shown in Figure 4.8. It illustrates within a legacy data center how bypass air flow—in other words, leakage—allows cold and hot air to mix. Heated air is permitted to flow from the rear of the cabinet into the front and mix with cooled air. This reduces the effective cooling capacity of the cooling system and

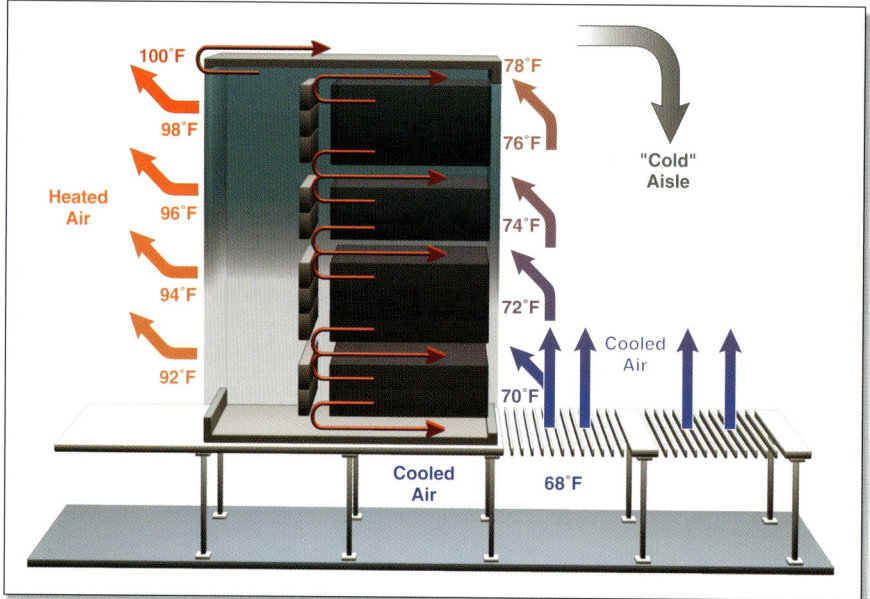

Figure 4.8 Bypass Airflow Leakage
Source: Intel IT, 2008

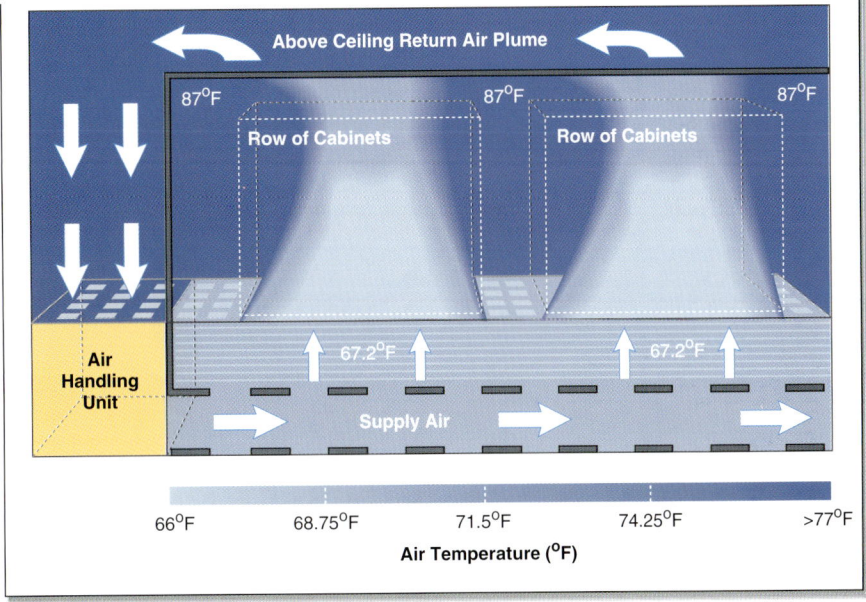

Figure 4.9 Thermal Image of Vena Contracta
Source: Intel IT, 2008

increases the entering air temperature for the servers at the top of the cabinet. When this situation happens, it creates a *vena contracta* effect. A vena contracta is created when the relatively high velocity air in the cold aisle creates a low pressure region that draws in heated air from the server exhaust. A thermal image of the vena contracta effect is shown in Figure 4.9.

The uniform placement of cooling units around the perimeter of the computer room can lead to inefficient cooling. This configuration produces uniformly distributed cooling capacity in what is often a highly non-uniform distribution of heat load. This creates both cold and hot spots in the room depending on the local power dissipation zones. Many times data center managers respond by installing and utilizing overcapacity in CRAC units.

Overcapacity in CRAC units is very common. With proper planning, the ambient temperature of the data center can be as high as 25.5°C (78°F). ASHRAE has recently updated its recommendations for data center operating temperatures of up to 28°C (82°F) (ASHRAE 2008c). Most data centers run at ambient temperatures of well below 21°C (70°F). You can recognize these data centers by noticing that employees are wearing coats and sweaters. It is important to remember that every degree of increased ambient temperature can reduce power consumption by a few percentage points for the cooling systems.

Air cooling efficiency can be improved with the use of variable frequency motors in CRACs or AHUs. Older systems designed for mainframe data centers can be power inefficient because they typically do not take advantage of technical improvements in electronic motors such as variable frequency (motor speed) capability and integrated programmable logic controllers (PLCs). For example newer designs utilizing variable frequency motors can be connected via PLC to temperature sensors and programmed so that motor speed is adjusted dynamically in response to thermal demands.

Increasing compute density does not substantially affect the size of the computer room, but it can double the size and cost of the underlying mechanical and electrical infrastructure. As a rule of thumb, the average data center air-cooling can handle up to 7kW of IT load in a rack. If adjoining racks have low to no load installed, that number can be increased to 10kW. Above these figures, supplemental cooling is required.

Most partially filled computer racks in existing data centers consume 2.1kW per rack. By comparison, a fully populated rack of blade servers can consume as much as 30kW or more of power or fifteen times what legacy computer rooms were designed to cool. Traditional air-cooled designs will work for 3.5kW/racks with large floor space. Many data centers have a difficult time maintaining stable and predictable cooling for racks beyond the 1-2kW range.

Major process improvements—additional power and cooling systems—are required for rack densities above 2kW. In a 2006 survey by The Strategy Group, 38 percent of data center managers reported that their server consolidation initiatives or blade server deployments created hot spots that were not being managed with ambient (room level) cooling strategies (Ziff-Davis Media, 2006). These companies had to invest in additional cooling to keep their servers in a reliable thermal range.

The overall computer room's heat density will be reduced by the white space for aisles and site infrastructure equipment. Uptime Institute recently completed a study of 19 computer rooms with more than 200,000 square feet of combined floor space. The study found data centers typically had 2.6 times the cooling capacity required, but wasted more than 60 percent of capacity because of poorly designed layouts and airflow bypass. As a result, more than 10 percent of the server racks ran above recommended high temperature limits. The average power consumption in those data centers was only 2.1 kW per rack. These hot spots affect power consumption and the bottom line.

A Georgia Institute of Technology study found that the university would save USD 160,000 annually in utility bills by using new technology that moves cooling systems closer to the sources of the heat (Dunn, 2006).

Power Distribution Systems

Power distribution systems are the second largest component of house load. In a typical data center, a minimum of four different voltage reduction steps take place prior to power being delivered to a server motherboard. Figure 4.10 shows a common four-stage flow of power conversion and reduction for an AC data center power distribution system (top) and an alternative design for high voltage DC distribution (bottom).

Every component of the power supply chain that alters current type (AC-to-DC or DC-to-AC conversion) or changes supply voltage also imparts a power loss. This is due to inherent conversion losses that take place in each piece of equipment involved in the process—the transformers, inverters, rectifiers, and so on. Understanding the tradeoffs and impacts of various power system design elements is imperative to

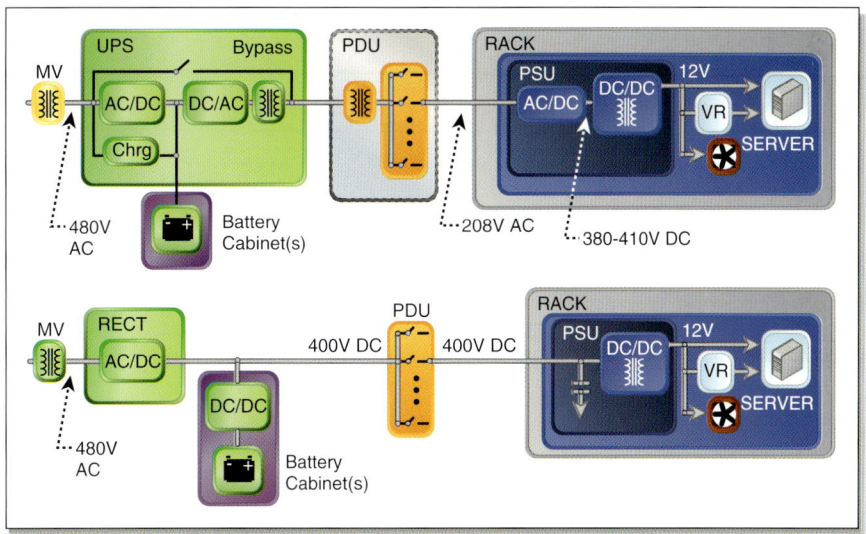

Figure 4.10 AC-DC Power Distribution
Source: Intel, 2008

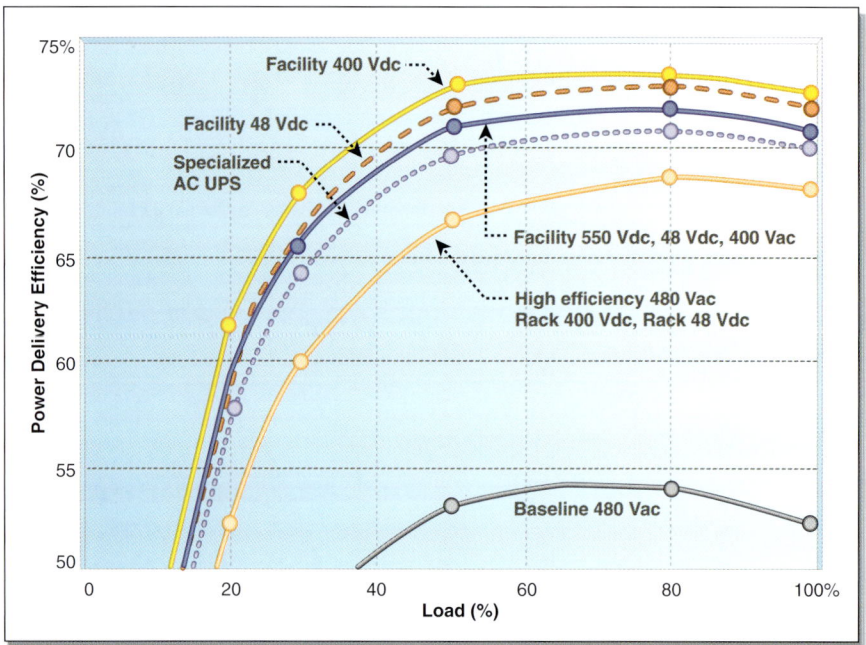

Figure 4.11 Power Efficiency of 48Vdc versus 480Vac
Source: Intel, 2008

building a highly efficient data center. Because power distribution systems are such a large factor in house load, they are a key subsystem to design, monitor, and manage for efficient power use. In other words, distribution system design is a major element of improving PUE in a data center.

DC power use minimizes any conversion losses in data center power distribution systems. As Figure 4.11 shows, a facility using 48Vdc is within one percent of the efficiency of a facility using 400Vdc, and far more efficient than 480Vac. Beyond efficiency, there are many other benefits of 48Vdc, such as equipment availability, better safety, and better reliability. This will be covered more in Chapter 8.

Uninterruptable Power Systems

Uninterruptable power systems also vary greatly in their power consumption and efficiency. Most online UPS units use a double conversion method of accepting AC input, converting it to DC for passing through the battery, then inverting back to AC for powering the IT equipment. There are two additional major contributors to UPS inefficiencies: the inherent losses of the UPS modules themselves, and how the system is implemented (right-sizing or redundancy). Often, when specifying UPS systems, the only efficiency value considered is the best case value published by manufacturers, which does not necessarily reflect the actual power usage or efficiency in a specific data center.

UPS system power efficiencies vary based on their load levels and between their manufacturers. Different UPS systems at the same load typically will not consume the same amount of power. The most efficient operating level for a UPS is at a 100 percent load level. But, except for emergency or maintenance scenarios, UPSs are never operated at 100 percent load levels. In reality, most data centers operate their UPS systems at 20 to 40 percent so the UPS can support the full IT equipment load in the event one of the redundant UPS units fail.

The range of efficiencies for typical UPS systems is shown in Figure 4.12 and Figure 4.13. Figure 4.12 shows the UPS performance curve highlighting the proportion of loss to the actual load. Note that until the UPS reaches about 20 percent of design load, inefficiency is significant. Figure 4.13 provides details to explain the efficiency curve. The blue bars represent all the power going to the IT loads while the red bars represent internal UPS losses that define the efficiency curve. For example, a 10mW UPS system at zero load will consume the same amount from conversion loss as it would at 100 percent.

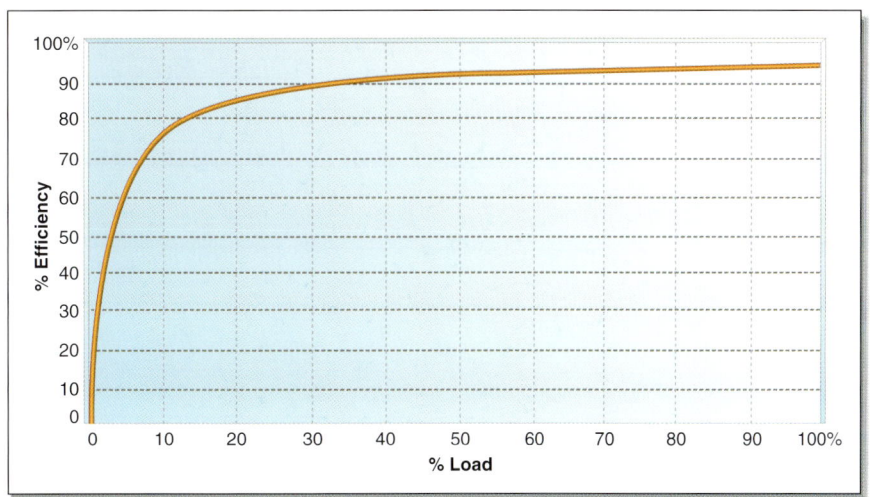

Figure 4.12 UPS Efficiency Curve by Load

Source: Sawyer, American Power Conversion (APC), 2006

Chapter 4: Data Center Power Consumption

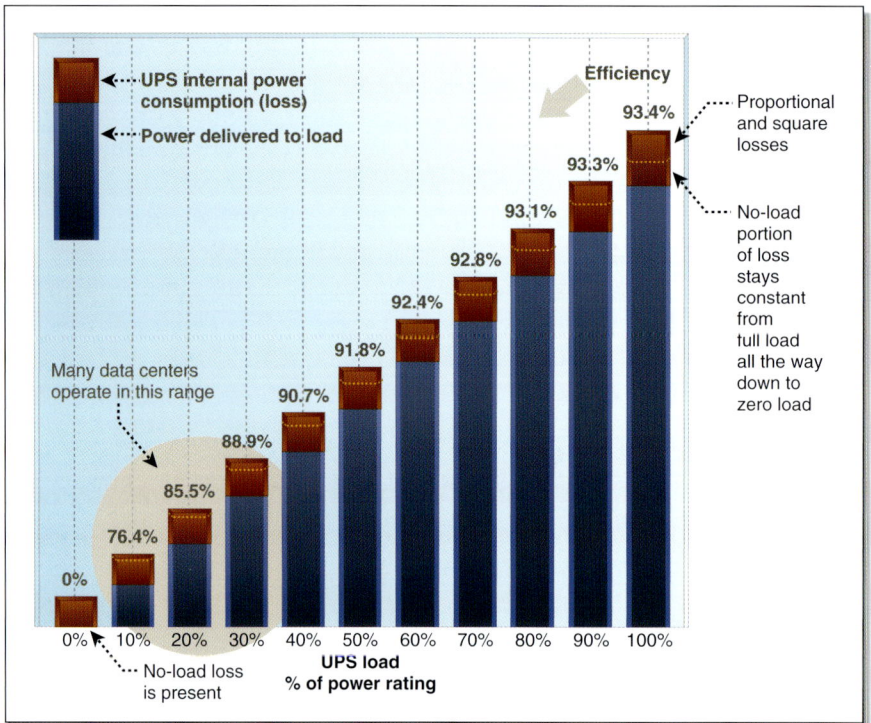

Figure 4.13 UPS Efficiency by Load

Source: V. Avelar, American Power Conversion (APC), 2006

Figure 4.13 shows that while we cannot reduce the power conversion loss to zero, it is possible to achieve greater efficiency by optimizing the use of UPS systems.

Table 4.3 shows the difference in power usage and costs between systems which are configured with two redundant UPSs. Both systems are utilizing a 30 percent load, and each UPS is supporting 150 kW. Each UPS in System #1 incurs an annual electrical cost of USD 10,470 in power losses versus USD 28,322 for each UPS in System #2, which is nearly a factor of three.

Table 4.3 UPS Cost Variance by Manufacturer

Source: Sawyer, American Power Conversion (APC), 2006

UPS System	UPS Loss Cost	Cooling Cost	Annual Cost of Inefficiency	10-year Cost of Inefficiency
UPS System #1	USD 20,940	USD 8,376	USD 29,317	USD 293,165
UPS System #2	USD 56,644	USD 22,651	USD 79,302	USD 793,021

Because there are two UPSs in each system, the electrical losses are doubled to USD 20,940 and USD 56,644 per year, respectively. These UPS losses create heat that must be removed by the cooling system. Assuming each kW of heat requires 400 Watts for the cooling system to remove it, cooling costs are an additional USD 8,376 versus USD 22,651 per year. If we assume a typical data center lifespan of 10 years, then the total cost of UPS system losses would be USD 293,165 versus USD 793,021 as shown in Table 4.4. This example shows how the power losses between two seemingly identical UPS systems can differ by almost a factor of three.

Transformer Losses

Another source of energy efficiency and power loss is data center transformer size. In general, many data center operators assume that energy efficiency improves as the voltage of the transformer increases. This generalization holds true if the workload matches the scale of the transformer. If the data center room is only two-thirds filled, a 25 kVA transformer could actually be more efficient than a much larger transformer, such as a 50 kVA or 500 kVA. Transformer efficiency depends on the data center fill rate as well as the overall data center modularity strategy. The following table highlights the power and cost differences between medium voltage and low voltage transformer units.

Table 4.4 shows annual energy loss based on 50 percent of nameplate load in the medium voltage example (top), and 35 percent of nameplate load in the low voltage example (bottom). Lifetime Energy Cost Savings is the sum of the discounted value of annual energy cost savings, based on average usage and an assumed transformer life of 25 years. The calculations in Table 4.4 assume an electricity price is USD 0.06/kWh, the federal average electricity price in the U.S.

Table 4.4 Transformer Cost-Effectiveness Examples

Source: U.S. Department of Energy

Performance	Base Model	Recommended Level
1500 kVA, Three Phase, Medium Voltage Dry-Type		
Efficiency	98.6%	99.0%
Annual Energy Loss	91,380 kWh	66,360 kWh
Annual Energy Loss Cost	USD 5,480	USD 3,980
Lifetime Energy Loss Cost	USD 81,300	USD 59,000
Lifetime Energy Cost Savings	–	USD 22,300
25 kVA, Single Phase, Low Voltage		
Efficiency	96.7%	98.0%
Annual Energy Loss	2,600 kWh	1,570 kWh
Annual Energy Loss Cost	USD 156	USD 94
Lifetime Energy Loss Cost	USD 2,300	USD 1,400
Lifetime Energy Cost Savings	–	USD 900

Power is consumed by idle or underutilized equipment. Between 10 and 30 percent of the power consumption in a data center can be for servers, storage and other equipment that are no longer in use but not powered off. By turning off these systems, a data center could save as much as USD 700 per year in utility bills. In three years this wasted power consumption can equal the cost of the hardware. Turning off idle equipment also frees up power and cooling capacity for the IT equipment doing productive work.

Virtualization can address underutilization of servers. Research by Uptime Institute has shows that systematic uses of virtualization can result in savings as much as 92 percent in kW consumed versus underutilized servers.

It is not just idle servers that can consume power; idle data centers themselves can consume large amounts of power. Power is constantly being consumed by house load, lights and cooling re-circulation in addition to the idling racks of servers and storage. The facilities load is consuming power whether the data center is in use or not.

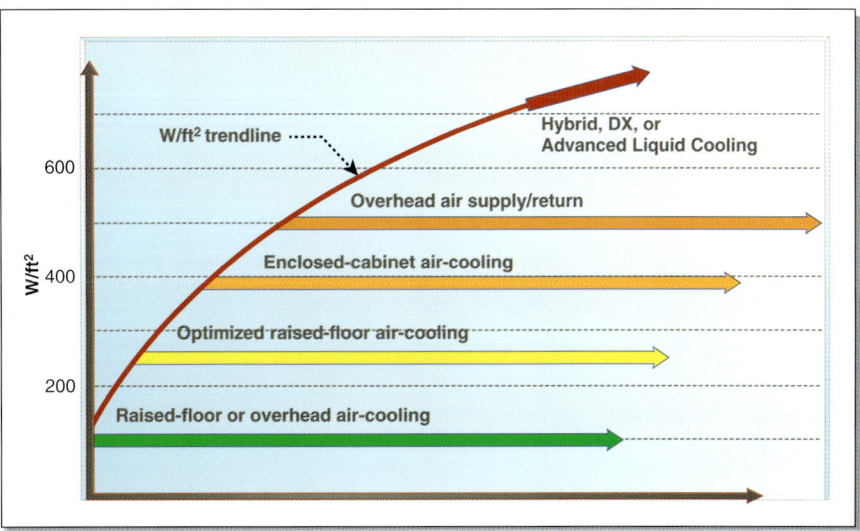

Figure 4.14 Thermal Management Technology versus W/ft^2
Source: Intel Labs, 2007

As Figure 4.14 illustrates, there are many components and facility layouts within the data center that can affect the cooling and power distribution system design and thus power usage. Depending on the equipment manufacturer's design, equipment age, facility design and implementation, power consumption can vary substantially. Some innovative designs that are in use today, but not covered in this chapter in detail include: wet side economizers, dry side (free air) economizers, heat wheels, liquid cooling cabinets, physical air separation, and containment systems between hot and cold aisles, variable speed drives on cooling unit fans and mechanical system pumps. Finally, implementing new servers with lower powered processors and direct current (DC) distribution designs and equipment will also reduce a data center's power use. These topics are covered in detail in Chapter 8.

Power Usage Varies with Data Center Tiers

The Uptime Institute tier classification of data center designs are aimed at improving availability. Ensuring high availability, however, will have a significant impact on a data center's power consumption. The duplication of equipment necessary to achieve higher tier availability standards will increase power consumption, and, by definition, Tier II, III and IV designs have redundant components. In addition, Tier III and IV data centers generally have all IT equipment plugged in to separate redundant power circuits. A Tier IV data center will have additional, multiple, independent and physically isolated systems that each have redundant capacity components and multiple, independent, active distribution paths simultaneously serving the computer equipment. As a result, more highly available data center facilities have inherently higher degrees of power inefficiency.

> **The Uptime Institute's Classification Tiers**
>
> The Uptime Institute is a consortium of companies that have a stake in the energy efficiency and availability of data centers. In studying data center designs, William Pitt Turner and John H. Seader created a four-tier classification system.
>
> - Tier I designs lack redundancy of components in a single power and cooling path. Availability is 99.671 percent.
>
> - Tier II designs have redundancy of components in a single power and cooling path. Availability is 99.741 percent.
>
> - Tier III designs have redundancy of components in multiple power and cooling paths, but with just one path active. Availability is 99.982 percent.
>
> - Tier IV designs have redundancy of components in multiple active power and cooling paths. Availability is 99.995 percent.
>
> Finer-grained definitions of these four tiers allow Uptime engineers to evaluate data center designs and construct both energy efficiency and availability estimates. Higher tiers achieve greater availability by replacing single points of failure with redundant components. In turn, redundant components consume more power.

Changing a tier, for example, upgrading from Tier II to Tier III, can effectively double power consumption and costs without adding any data center capacity or increasing the usable kW available for the IT equipment. Uptime Institute estimates the capital cost increase, measured in U.S. dollars per usable kW to be a factor of four between

Tier III and Tier IV due to the need for duplicate cooling and power delivery systems.

Additional systems installed to create data center availability create additional power loss. For example, two AC-to-DC-to-AC UPSs sized to independently carry a full facilities load (2N configuration) require twice the number of current and voltage conversions. This can result in a 2X drop in power distribution efficiency. If a data center had one UPS system, it would lose 7 percent power supplied to the distribution system circuits; if it had two UPS systems, then it would be expected to experience 14 percent power loss. If these UPSs are supporting an A and a B circuit that is feeding to a server connected to an A and B power circuit, total electrical loss might be as high as 40 percent as a result of under-loading server power supplies downstream from the UPS.

While redundancy does increase availability, companies can save significant energy costs by matching tiers to the business's true needs. It will take a powerful business case to say that a company can only afford 15 minutes of downtime over a five-year period (which is what Tier IV aims to provide).

Data Center and Power Use Examples

Table 4.5 shows calculations based on Intel's modeling for a high performance computing data center. This modeling was designed to support Intel's unique requirements for high performance computing in the most cost effective manner possible. Other companies with different use cases may arrive at different calculations based on requirements for their specific businesses.

Table 4.5 Intel IT Model High Performance Compute Data Center

Source: Intel IT Global Services, 2008

Usable power	2200KW-3740KW
Power target per server rack	10-17kW/rack. Includes required cooling
Facilities space	5,400 sq ft on 2 story design
Number of racks	220 rack locations
Server rack layout design	Contained hot/cold aisles with flow through design
Power distribution	UPS room at ground level
Security	Turnstile, interlocked material entry, cameras, card readers, digital recording
Utility capabilities	Clean room type air handlers (N+1)
	UPS modules (N – ability to go N+1)
	Emergency generators, with above ground tank 12 hour capacity (facilities and critical file storage load only)
	Chillers and pumps (N)
Total Power /sq ft Used	325 W/sq ft – 693W/sq ft (525 W/sq ft, nominal)

As a final example, Table 4.6 from Uptime Institute shows various attributes associated with data center Tiers. These attributes are not requirements of the tier definitions, but recommended parameters to achieve the performance goals of each Tier. These definitions illustrate the typical power consumptions for these styles of data centers.

Table 4.6 Attributes Associated with Data Center Tiers

Source: The Uptime Institute, 2008

	Tier I	Tier II	Tier III	Tier iV
Building Type	Tenant	Tenant	Stand-alone	Stand-alone
Staffing shifts	None	1 Shift	1+ Shifts	"24 by Forever"
Staff/shift	None	1/Shift	1-2/Shift	2+/Shift
Usable for Critical Load	100% N	100% N	90% N	90% N
Initial Build-out kW per Cabinet (typical)	<1 kW	1-2 kW	1-2 kW	1-3 kW
Ultimate kW per Cabinet (typical)	<1 kW	1-2 kW	>3 kW	>4 kW
Support Space to Raised-Floor Ratio	20%	30%	80-90+%	100+%
Raised-Floor Height (typical)	12"	18"	30-36"	30-42"
Floor Loading lbs/ft (typical)	85	100	150	150+
Utility Voltage (typical)	208, 480	208, 480	12-15 kV	12-15 kV
Single Points-of-Failure	Many + Human Error	Many + Human Error	Some + Human Error	Fire, EPO + Some Human Error
Representative Planned Maintenance Shut Downs	2 Annual Events at 12 Hours Each	3 Events Over 2 Years at 12 Hours Each	None Required	None Required
Representative Site Failures	6 Failures Over 5 Years	1 Failure Every Year	1 Failure Every 2.5 Years	1 Failure Every 5 Years
Annual Site-Caused, End-User Downtime (based on field data)	28.8 hours	22.0 hours	1.6 hours	.0.8 hours
Resulting End-User Availability Based on Site-Caused Downtime	99.67%	99.75%	99.98%	99.99%
Typical Months to Plan and Construct	3	3-6	15-20	15-30
First Deployed	1965	1970	1985	1995

Summary

Data center power consumption is a growing concern. Proportionally, data center house loads are growing at a faster rate than the power consumption of individual servers. The major contributors to house load include facilities infrastructure such as HVAC systems and power distribution systems, fan motors, fluid pumps, and compressors. Loads grow steeply when redundant designs are used to increase availability. In an average data center, as much as 50 to 70 percent of the electricity powers just the house load with the remainder going to IT equipment.

Electricity use for the house load can vary significantly depending on the efficiency of a data center cooling and power systems. Higher efficiency cooling and power systems and design can dramatically improve overall data center energy efficiency. There are many factors and variables that can affect power consumption in data centers. The most significant expenditure of a facilities power budget is usually spent addressing waste heat removal. Overcapacity in CRAC units is a very common means of compensating for improper center design. Other key variables include efficiency of power distribution systems and UPSs, density of compute equipment, and the physical layout of the data center.

Power is consumed by underutilized or idling equipment, as well. Between 10 and 30 percent of the power consumption in a data center can be for servers, storage and other equipment that are no longer in use but not turned off. Data center tier classifications, which trade redundancy for reliability, come with significant impacts to power consumption. Changing your data center's tier functionality from Tier II to IV can effectively double its power consumption and costs without adding any computer room capacity or increasing the usable kW available for the computers. Understanding the tradeoffs and impacts of various power system design elements is imperative to building highly efficient data centers.

Chapter 5

Power Metrics for Servers

If you can't measure IT, you can't manage IT.
—Modified from Andy Grove, Chairman Emeritus, Intel Corporation

In this chapter we cover methods and metrics for determining power consumption and energy efficiency in servers. The quantification of power consumption assists in setting plans and priorities for operational improvements. Measurements help in setting benchmarks, which are the basis for power tracking, reports, and continual improvements. Knowing the power consumption baseline helps data center operations teams understand the impact of implementing new practices and opportunities for improvement.

Just as with data center metrics, when measuring server power consumption it is important to directly associate performance/power measurements with business-oriented metrics. This helps identify "low hanging fruit" opportunities and prevents decisions that would reduce productivity along with power consumption. For example, if via measurements, idle resources are found they can potentially be rapidly re-provisioned in lieu of incremental resource acquisition.

To measure and establish a power consumption baseline:

1. Identify and document all running servers within the data center.
2. Determine each server's business purpose.
3. Measure their power consumption.

There are several methods and metrics to measure server power usage. Ranging from CPU utilization to derating nameplate values to system performance per Watt, facility managers should utilize the method or metric that fits their resources and organizational goals. While this may sound like a large amount of work, it is possible to generate estimates without too much difficulty.

Maintaining data center energy efficiency is an ongoing process. As additional energy efficient IT assets are added or used to replace older lower efficiency models, measured server power consumption should continue to show improvements in overall energy efficiency. Reductions in server power correlate to improved data center efficiency, which affects the power bill and the organization's bottom line.

Server Power Benchmarks and Metrics

Server power usage varies based on the server's configuration and usage model. Because of this, designing power benchmarks is not straightforward. The issue faced in designing benchmarks is how to create a realistic suite that generates numbers to accurately reflect the quantity being measured. For example, what do we consider a typical server or how do we characterize power consumption of the typical use model for a server?

Actual power consumption for each server should be measurable at any point in time. This real-time measurement allows a power-monitoring module to collect power consumption data for each server and aggregate power-usage values at the rack and data center levels.

Real-time power monitoring and historical aggregation allows data center managers to see the trend of power usage over time. This allows key values such as minimum, typical, and peak usage to be identified. This information is very useful in planning for future expansions, in identifying where there might be power and cooling constraints, and in locating areas where new servers can be deployed without violating power and cooling limits. In addition, the minimum, typical, and peak values can be used to determine an appropriate power policy for each rack and hence each server in the rack. System power can be monitored by communicating with power supplies that support the Power Management Bus (PMBus) interface inside servers.

A good benchmark or metric provides a toolset to test and improve server power efficiency. It offers a framework that is extensible and adaptable to many server topologies. Measured system power consumption, in conjunction with system performance, is needed to provide a complete picture of server power consumption. A key area to delineate is power consumed under load, and, more importantly, performance per Watt under load. By focusing on performance per Watt under load, the data center can be optimized by deploying fewer servers to meet the desired performance target. This method provides the most efficient power reduction program and may also lower the capital investment costs.

Published computer performance benchmarks are produced using specific computer systems, components and workload algorithms and measure the approximate performance of each server using the defined conditions. Any difference in system hardware, software or configuration may affect actual results. All organizations have different workloads that stress server resources in different ways, experts recommend using benchmarks or internal tests that reflect specific workload applicable to business requirements. Also, it is important to weigh idle and peak power consumption based on typical utilization rates in the target environment. There is no single benchmark or metric that will work for all businesses. The benchmarks and metrics that are selected should be the ones that best align with the organization's environment and business goals.

There are two essential benchmarks for measuring server power consumption: SPECpower_ssj2008 and System Performance per Watt. Additional generally accepted benchmarks include: Energy Star v.4 Specification for Computer Requirements and Thermal Design Power (TDP). For power supplies, the key metric is the 80 Plus Specification. In addition to these benchmarks, there are several performance benchmark workloads that are used to determine the System Performance per Watt, such as SPECint*2006, SPECjbb2005, and Black-Scholes.

SPECpower_ssj2008 is a new benchmark that uses a graduated workload to measure systems from idle up to maximum CPU utilization. The Standard Performance Evaluation Corporation (SPEC) released SPECpower_ssj2008 on December 11, 2007. It was created by a consortium of companies including AMD, Dell, Fujitsu Siemens, HP, IBM, Intel, Sun plus UC Berkeley, Virginia Tech and Lawrence Berkeley Labs.

SPECpower_ssj2008 benchmark suite uses a Java[†] application running on the server with a load generator that allows choices of load intensities, durations and utilization patterns. The benchmark can be used across several versions of UNIX, Windows[†], Linux[†] and other operating systems. The power and performance measurements are taken at 11 different load points, such as active idle (zero load), 10 percent, 20 percent, up to 90 percent and 100 percent. The percentages reflect a server workload throughput from a server side Java application. They are not CPU utilization rates. This benchmark measures total platform power consumption; essentially the AC watts used at the wall. The benchmark score is the sum of the 11 performance points divided by sum of the 11 power points, where a higher score is better.

Performance		Power	Performance to Power Ratio
Target Load	Actual Load	ssj_ops	Average Power (W)	
100%	99.7%	305,413	276	1,105
90%	90.3%	276,648	270	1,025
80%	80.1%	245,357	272	937
70%	70.3%	215,440	253	851
60%	60.1%	184,267	243	758
50%	49.7%	152,157	230	660
40%	40.1%	122,745	217	565
30%	30.2%	92,575	204	454
20%	20.0%	61,277	189	324
10%	10.2%	31,319	173	182
Active Idle		0	157	0
		Σ ssj_ops / Σ power =		682

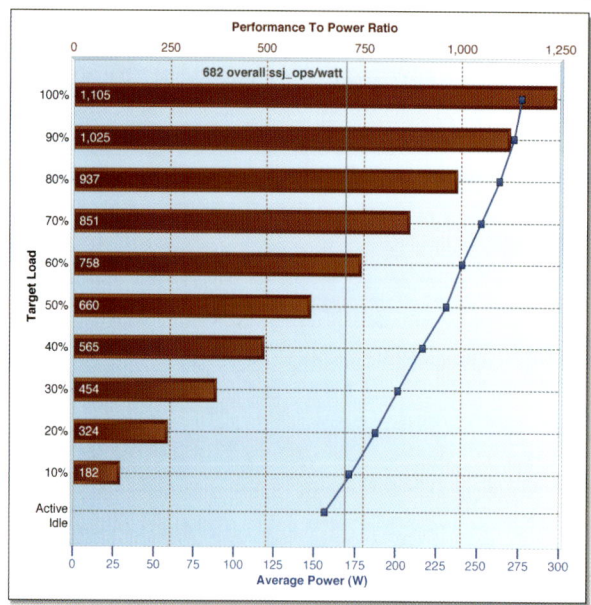

Figure 5.1 Example of SPECpower_ssj2008 Results
Source: Intel Labs, 2008

As shown in Figure 5.1, this benchmark identifies a server's energy efficiency across the entire load range and allows side by side power/performance comparison of systems.

SPECpower_ssj2008, in addition to side by side performance/power comparisons, is very useful in analyzing a server's power management capabilities. Upcoming plans for this tool include extending it to workstations, blades and virtualized environments.

The Standard Performance Evaluation Corporation hosts a website, *www.spec.org*, with additional information for various platforms. Organizations without the resources to perform internal tests might want to consider using the published SPECpower benchmark data. SPECpower_ssj2008 results for a variety of servers are available on the SPEC Web site at *www.spec.org/power_ssj2008*. This data can help organizations compare server energy efficiency using consistent and reliable metrics.

A second key metric is system performance per Watt. This metric identifies the system power consumed while running real workloads and calculates power needed for cabinets and racks. Performance per Watt is a measure of the energy efficiency of a server; it identifies the amount of computation that can be delivered for every watt of power consumed.

The more energy efficient a system is, the more workload it can process with a specified power input, or conversely, the less power it needs for processing a specified workload.

As the workload changes in the data center, the operating point of the servers on the respective efficiency curves will change. Measured system power consumption, in conjunction with system performance, is needed to provide a complete picture of server power consumption. A server's performance per Watt enables comparisons of server efficiencies and assists in determining best capital investment plans.

Performance per Watt is measured using a performance benchmark workload and simultaneously measuring the power used while running that workload. The performance metrics used should match the organization's business profile. If the typical workload of an organization varies during the day, week or month, it is recommended to include other measures of power usage such as peak power and idle power.

A Watt meter that reports *true* power, via the simultaneous measurement of the input voltage, current, and power factor is required to accurately measure the power use of a server (note that kVa, the product of voltage and current alone is not an accurate representation of the power used). Many watt meters also have the capability of reporting energy usage, which is the measurement of power over time (kWatt hours or Joules). Power consumption is needed for the performance per Watt metric, not the energy usage.

Some sample performance benchmarks used to determine Performance per Watt are TPC-C, SPECjbb2005 and Black-Scholes. These benchmarks, used with a watt metering system for a server, provide Performance per Watt measurements. This list is not comprehensive, but rather is a sampling of some commonly referenced benchmarks.

TPC-C is a performance benchmark for database and transactional computations. TPC-C has been developed by the Transaction Processing Performance Council, which is a non-profit corporation that defines and disseminates transaction processing and database benchmarks for the industry. The current version of the TPC-C benchmark is Version 5.10.1. The TPC-C benchmark continues to be a popular yardstick for comparing on line transaction processing (OLTP) performance on various hardware and software configurations. TPC-C measures transaction processing and database performance in terms of how many transactions a given system and database can perform per unit of time, such as transactions per second or transactions per minute.

SPECjbb2005 was developed by SPEC's Java subcommittee. The benchmark's workload represents an order processing application for a wholesale supplier. Performance is assessed by two metrics: *bops* (business operations per second), which measures overall throughput for all of the Java Virtual Machines[†] (JVMs) in a benchmark run, and *bops/JVM*, which measures the performance and scaling of a single JVM.

The Black-Scholes workload is a 64-bit financial modeling algorithm for the pricing of European-style options. The Black-Scholes workload is multi-threaded and allows users to specify the number of threads the program runs. Multi-threading is an important mechanism used to test the effective use of multi-core processors to improve computational performance. The test produces the time, in seconds, the server took to complete the workload. Lower completion times are better.

Released in November of 2008, the Energy Star v. 5 Specification of Requirements For Computers is currently defined for power consumption of PCs and workstations (*www.energystar.gov*). To qualify for the EnergyStar certification, a computer's average power draw must be less than or equal to $0.35(P_{max} + (HDD \times 5W))$ where P_{max} is the maximum power the workstation can consume and *HDD* is the number of hard disk drives. The P_{max} figure can be generated by running the SPEC ViewPerf benchmark with a Linpack benchmark (http://www.netlib.org/linpack/). Linpack is a FORTRAN benchmark; a Java version can be found at *www.netlib.org/benchmark/linpackjava*.

The EPA is currently expanding the specification to include servers. Plans are for the rating to measure server energy use at peak and idle demands. The EPA will is first releasing a Tier 1 standard that takes effect January 1, 2009. The Tier 1 standard will measure just two factors of energy use: the efficiency of the server's power supply and its energy consumption while idle. Server power supply efficiency must meet the following requirements:

Table 5.1 Energy Star Efficiency Requirements for Server Power Supplies
Source: www.energystar.gov

Power Supply Type	Rated Output Power	10% Load	20% Load	50% Load	100% Load
AC-DC Single Voltage	≤ 1000 watts	75%	85%	89%	85%
	> 1000 watts	80%	88%	92%	88%
AC-DC Multi-Voltage	All Output Levels	N/A	82%	85%	82%

Table 5.2 Energy Star Power Factor Requirements for Server Power Supplies
Source: www.energystar.gov.

Power Supply Type	Rated Output Power	10% Load	20% Load	50% Load	100% Load
Single Voltage	≤ 1000 watts	.65	.80	.90	.90
	> 1000 watts	.80	.90	.90	.90
Multi-Voltage	All Output Levels	N/A	.80	.90	.90

Thermal design power (TDP) is a lead design metric for server manufacturers. Also known as thermal design point, the TDP represents the maximum amount of heat the cooling system in a server is required to dissipate. The TDP is not the most power the CPU could ever draw, but rather the maximum power that it would draw when running real applications. The TDP of a server provides information for sufficient cooling within a server without the risk of reliability issues. Knowing this number can assist in determining how much power needs to be delivered to a rack, or the maximum number of servers for a rack with a given ambient room temperature while ensuring that the overall rack (hence room) power consumption does not exceed the limit.

A final power metric for servers is the 80 PLUS specification for the power supplies. The 80 PLUS performance specification requires power supplies in servers to be 80 percent or greater energy efficiency at 20 percent, 50 percent and 100 percent of rated load with a true power

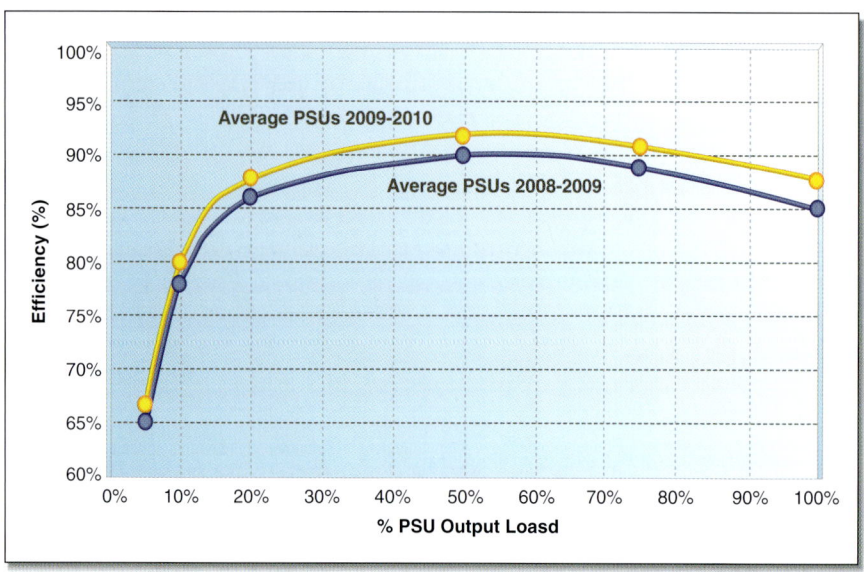

Figure 5.2 Power Supply Efficiency versus Load
Source: Intel IT, 2007

factor of 0.9 or greater. This is for both single and multiple voltage power supplies. Power supplies that qualify for this rating are substantially more efficient than a typical power supply. Figure 5.2 illustrates how power supply efficiency can vary with load. Figure 5.3 shows how an 80 PLUS compliant power supply can save between 20 and 35 watts in a server.

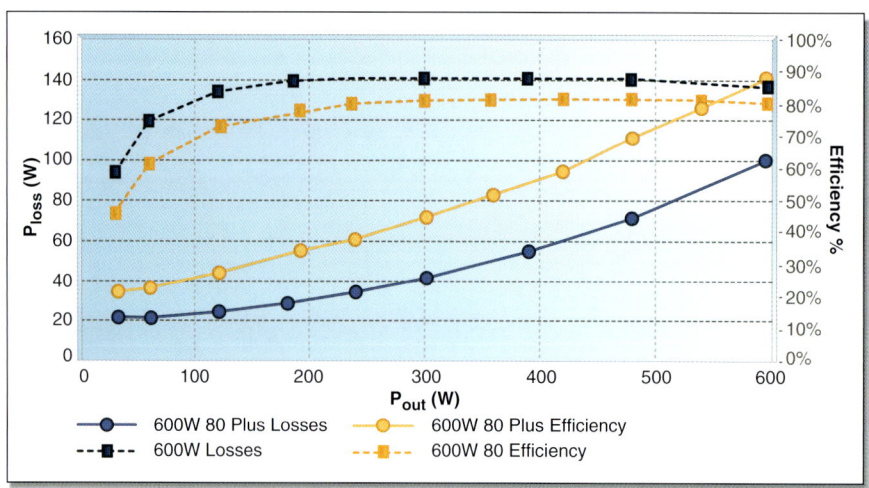

Figure 5.3 Efficient PSU savings
Source: Intel IT, 2007

For more information on this specification and benchmark, go to *www.80plus.org*.

Server Power Monitoring Methods

This section covers different methods and tools that are useful for measuring power at different levels of server architecture. Covered are nameplate values and derating to project server power consumption, CPU utilization for power estimates, subsystem power measurements and system instrumentation, power monitoring tools, and, finally, Intel processor power management technologies and tools.

Server Nameplate Values and Derating

For most data centers, there are two ways of projecting server power consumption: (1) using server nameplate power value, and (2) using a derated nameplate value. Historically, typical server power consumption never reaches the nameplate value. This is why many data center operators calculate a percentage to derate the nameplate power for density planning.

Servers are given nameplate ratings to indicate the maximum power draw of each machine. The main purpose of this label is to inform the user of the power infrastructure required to safely supply power to the server. Actual power consumption is typically much less than the nameplate power. As such, it is a conservative number that is guaranteed not to be reached. It is typically estimated by the server manufacturer simply by adding up the worst case power draw of all components in a fully configured system.

To illustrate the difference between nameplate power rating and actual power usage, consider the following configuration for a basic application server. The table below shows the power draw breakdown for a server built with two Intel® Xeon® 5100 series dual-core processors, a SATA disk drive, four DDR3 800 MHz DRAM DIMMs, and two PCI-e expansion slots. Using the maximum power draw taken from the component datasheets the total DC draw equals 213W. Assuming a power supply efficiency of 85 percent the total nameplate power is calculated to be 251W.

As previously mentioned, actual power consumption is generally much less than the nameplate power. The measured power consumption of this server using a power intensive benchmark reaches a maximum of 145W, which is 60 percent less than the nameplate value.

Table 5.3 Server Power Table
Source: Intel Labs, 2008

Server Component	Component Peak Power	System Peak Power (watts)
Dual CPUs	40	80
Memory, 4x DDR3 DRAMs	9	36
120GB SATA HDD	12	12
2 PCIe slots	25	50
Motherboard	25	25
Fan	10	10
PSU losses	38	38
Total	n/a	251

This measured rating is the actual peak power. As this example illustrates, actual peak power is a much more accurate estimate of a system's peak consumption.

Since many data center facility managers are aware of this discrepancy, a method used to safely increase server density is to derate the nameplate power by a certain percentage, depending on the workload that is deployed on the server, taking into consideration ambient temperature and the type of cooling system used. Determining the derating percentage for a server is as much of an art as a science. But the process can be simplified by use of an intelligent power distribution unit (iPDU) at each rack that meters each server's power consumption.

To determine an average power consumption of each server, measurements should be taken multiple times a day for several days. The time frame used should capture both peak activity and idle times for the workloads being processed. The captured measurements should then be analyzed and compared with the nameplate rating. The percentage reduction from the nameplate value that the servers actually use can then be used as the derating value. Since most data centers standardize on a limited number of servers, this derating value can be applied to all the same types of servers running similar workloads. As an example, if a specific server's measured power consumption typically ranged from 20 to 85 percent of its nameplate rating, averaging about 33 percent less, then a facilities manager could assign 30 percent as the derating value to this class of servers.

Using a nameplate value or derating the value is a simple method to project server power consumption. But, these methods have a fundamental problem in that they are not based on actual power consumption. The data center facility manager has no visibility into how much power each server (and, hence, the rack and the room) is consuming at any given time, neither do they have an understanding of the power consumption pattern over time. Without this visibility, the facility manager (or data center management software) is unable to decide how much power to allocate to servers/racks based on actual need.

In summary, using nameplate values or derating results in waste and can raise the total cost of ownership of the data center due to the following issues:

1. Underpopulation of rack space: Rack space waste is most severe when racks are populated using the nameplate power.

2. Underutilization of available power for computing: A static allocation of power based on worst-case scenario planning leads to inefficiencies and does not maximize the use of available power capacity.

3. Higher energy costs than actually necessary: This is primarily from the cost of over-cooling a room that is sparsely populated with servers.

4. Unnecessary power cooling capacity expansion: Although existing power capacity is not being utilized effectively (as described in 1, 2, and 3 above), if the data center needs to deploy new services, the operator might need to expand power/cooling capacity or even build a new (costly) data center.

CPU Utilization to Estimate Power Usage

A low cost, quick method to determine server power consumption is based on the server's CPU utilization. Many studies over the years with different servers and workloads have concluded that power consumption tracks very closely with CPU utilization. This single metric can be used as a relatively accurate estimate of power consumption.

Even though servers and workloads can be different, the CPU activity, as the manager of I/O subsystems and memory, is a good indicator of power usage. The CPU varies in its power draw, since the architecture has been optimized to enable large parts of the silicon to shut down when in idle states, and as such it can have a marked effect on system level power usage based on its utilization.

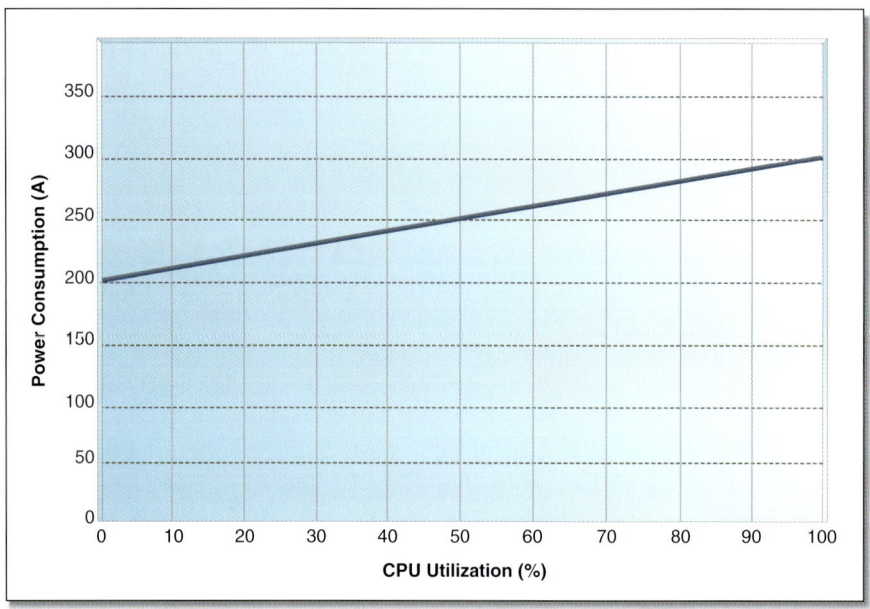

Figure 5.4 CPU Utilization to Power Consumption
Source: Blackburn, 2008

Figure 5.4 illustrates how systemic x86 server power consumption scales linearly with CPU utilization.

By finding the average CPU utilization over a defined period of time, it is possible to calculate an estimate of the power consumed for that period. By measuring the power draw of the server at peak and at idle usage and projecting a linear increase in power consumption between these measured points, it becomes a simple mathematical operation to estimate power usage at any CPU utilization rate.

Individual server power consumption measurements can be taken by many methods. Most servers already collect CPU utilization information via systems management software. In addition to this method, there are several easy-to-use commercial solutions that can provide these measurements including watt meters and intelligent PDUs.

Many organizations standardize on server specifications or models. Therefore, measuring the power consumption of a single server of each type should be relatively straightforward. This data can be extrapolated across the same types of servers. Data can then be aggregated to project annual consumption as an approximation of power consumption times 8,760 hours.

Once power measurements of peak power and idle consumption are taken, an estimate of power consumption (P) at any specific CPU utilization (n%) can be calculated using the following formula:

$$Pn = (P_{max} - P_{idle}) \times \frac{n}{100} + P_{idle}$$

Example: If a server has a maximum power draw of 300W and an idle power draw of 200W, then at 40 percent utilization the power draws would approximate to:

$$P_{40\%} = (300 - 200) \times \frac{40}{100} + 200$$
$$= 100 \times 0.4 + 200$$
$$= 240\,W$$

If the server was running at the 40 percent average utilization for a 24 hour period, then the energy usage would equate to the following:

$$240\,W \times 24 = 5760 \text{ Watt hours (Wh)} = 5.76 \text{ kilowatt hour (kWh)}$$

Google used this method of testing and determined that CPU utilization predicted power usage to within 1 percent of measured power use. In their modeling of CPU scaling under data center loads, Google found that data centers could see savings of 15 to 25 percent, depending on how aggressively they used the data (Harris, 2007).

Subsystem Power Measurements and System Instrumentation

The power consumed by various server hardware subsystems—CPU, memory, fans, disks, and so on—can also be monitored. Understanding the subsystem power consumption characterization for workloads can be valuable for power adaptations. Subsystem power monitored values can be used for intelligent fine-grained power control and optimization algorithms. With individual server subsystem level measurements, IT facility managers can accurately know what power their equipment is drawing and acquire precise numbers to aid their energy efficiency planning efforts.

The latest generations of servers feature built-in instrumentation and thermal sensors. Instrumentation in servers works by monitoring components within. This information is then captured or displayed in response to external queries via systems management console products. Most management consoles will automatically display a server's current power and temperature information from built-in instrumentation.

In addition to the hardware subsystems mentioned above, examples of subsystem components that can be managed using instrumentation include disks, peripheral devices, event logs, files, folders, file systems, networking components, operating system subsystems, performance counters, printers, processes, OS registry settings, OS security, OS services and device drivers. Management console products assess system resources or components (identified as data providers in instrumentation protocols) through scripts using the appropriate application programming interfaces (APIs). Management applications and scripts make requests to a server's instrumentation database to retrieve data, subscribe to events, run diagnostics or perform management related tasks.

As noted in Chapter 3, as much as 30 to 40 percent of a server's power consumption is spent on the disk, the network, the I/O and peripherals, the power supplies and the rest of the circuitry in the server. However, networking, disk and memory components rarely offer any low-power modes. The only low-power modes currently available in mainstream DRAM and disks are fully inactive. Memory is constantly being refreshed and drawing power regardless of whether it is being read or sending writes. Internal disks spin and draw power all the time, the only additional power they draw when being accessed is to move the read/write head. But with monitoring, via instrumentation, operators can build usage patterns that can be helpful in consolidation or virtualization planning, which in turn can reduce the power consumption of a data center.

Storage vendors are now moving toward power density and storage density as common metrics for disk product comparisons. Power density is the total capacity divided by the power consumption in kW; the higher the power density, the better. Storage density is the ratio of terabytes to square feet. With these metrics, higher storage density means less data center floor space which generally results in less cooling and less power usage.

If the system is not instrumented, memory and disk utilization can still be estimated. Since the CPU is used to manage and monitor the progress of the memory and I/O tasks, then disk and memory use can be correlated to CPU utilization. In addition, the power density and storage density metrics from vendor's data sheets can be used for planning storage.

Power Monitoring and Management Tools

Power management software is emerging as the next IT management tool bridging the gap between IT and facilities management. There are many commercially available solutions with a variety of features on the market. Many of the new energy management tools are Web-based to enable quick implementation. Some tools allow management and monitoring of uninterruptible power supplies (UPSs), some measure and report power consumption and air temperatures across servers while posting alerts in cases of variances from defined specifications. Some can identify which system is consuming the most power, percentage of power capacity consumed, quality of input power, related environmental data, cooling systems status and trend the data over time The selection of any of these solutions should be made in the context of what problem or opportunity a data center manager is pursuing.

Power monitoring and management eliminates the usage of nameplate or derated power value to determine the number of servers for each rack. To monitor power and dynamically allocate or reallocate power in a data center, a good power management tool will have a standard interface that supports the data center management software and the server being managed to do the following:

- Measure and display current power and temperature data from the managed systems
- Monitor actual power consumption over a planning period to understand historical usage patterns for capacity planning
- Provide trend data over the selected periods of time
- Provide current as well as peak power, minimum power, and average power use over an interval
- Set power capping for servers if their firmware supports it, respectively manage the Power Saver mode for servers
- Notify the higher-level management system if the power policy cannot be enforced
- Send alerts to higher-level management systems if a certain power threshold is reached

The American Society of Heating, Refrigerating, and Air-Conditioning Engineers (ASHRAE) publishes guidelines for data needed for designing and provisioning a data center. A power monitor's power usage reporting capability should support these requirements. In addition, a good power monitor should support the reporting requirements to calculate the PUE and DCiE of the data center.

The power manager can be deployed in various ways:

- As a firmware running on a dedicated microcontroller in the server
- As part of the baseboard management controller (BMC) that also performs other system management functions in the server
- As an in-band agent in the operating system
- As a combination of the above

While the power manager provides the capabilities described in the previous paragraphs, it depends on external management software to specify the policy parameters for it to operate effectively. The power manager exposes an interface to the management software for this purpose. The interface includes commands to read power consumption and thermal data. The interface also allows management software to specify commands to set and get power control policies (set power limit) and to receive alerts from the power manager.

For systems which do not have instrumentation on board, there are intelligent Power Distribution Units (iPDUs) available. Some iPDUs contain versatile sensors informing about not only the power consumption of the attached systems but also the environmental information such as temperature and humidity. The iPDU's serial and LAN interfaces allow for remote monitoring and management through a Web browser, any SNMP-based Network Management System, Telnet, or a console over a serial line. Events can be communicated by SNMP traps or email, and it is possible to send out daily history reports, also by email.

An example of how individual server power monitoring can help reduce data center power is by comparing power usage between a blade server system and a 2U rack mounted server. Power measurements were taken at the 20 percent and 90 percent CPU utilization levels using a benchmarking tool to generate a CPU load for each server. At 90 percent CPU utilization, the blade server system used 1248 watts while an equivalent system of rack-mounted servers used 3422 watts. This analysis showed significantly improved power utilization of blade servers compared to rack-mounted servers for the specific workload.

Some server platforms may consume more power than others for the same workload. This is very dependent on the server's configuration. A workload can be very different depending on the type of server and what it is doing. Examples of different types of work include: processing data, I/O or reading and writing data, or networking and routing packets. Such items as different spindle speeds of disk storage will consume different amounts of power per terabyte of storage provided. The impacts from different configurations or workloads need to be remembered when taking comparative measurements. Always make sure you are comparing apples to apples.

Intel Processor Power Management Technologies and Tools

Intel's current series of Xeon® server processors contains mechanisms that help control the power consumed by the processors. In addition, memory controllers provide methods of controlling power consumed by the Dual In-line Memory Modules (DIMMs). These can be used by the power manager as low-level effectors for power control.

The external interface of these effectors/power managers are exposed as extensions to industry-standard server management protocols such as Intelligent Platform Management Interface (IPMI) and Web Services Management (WS-Man). The data center management system communicates with the power manager using IPMI to continuously monitor actual power consumption of each server.

Intel® Dynamic Power Node Manager (Node Manager)

Node Manager is an out-of-band (OOB) power management policy engine that is embedded in newer Intel server chipsets. It works with BIOS and OS power management (OSPM) to dynamically adjust platform power to achieve maximum performance/power at node (server) level. Node Manager has the following features:

Dynamic Power Monitoring. Measures actual power consumption of a server platform within acceptable error margin of +/-10 percent. Node Manager can gather information from any PSMI instrumented power supply, provide real-time power consumption data (point in time, or average over an interval), and report through the IPMI interface.

Platform Power Capping. Sets platform power to a targeted power budget while maintaining maximum performance for the given power level. Node Manager receives power policy from an external management console through IPMI interface and maintains power at targeted level by dynamically adjusting CPU P-states.

Power Threshold Alerting. Node Manager monitors platform power against targeted power budget. When the target power budget cannot be maintained, Node Manager sends out alerts to the management console

Intel® Datacenter Manager (Datacenter Manager)

Intel® Datacenter Manager is a software add-on to Node Manager to monitor and control power for a group of servers. Intel Datacenter

Manager depends on Intel Dynamic Power Node Manager. It is a software development kit (SDK) designed to plug-in to software management console products. It also has a reference user interface which can be used as proxy for a management software product. Key Intel® Datacenter Manager features include:

- Group level monitoring of power
- Log and query for trend data
- Group power limiting
- Group level power alerts and notifications
- Support of distributed architectures (across multiple racks)

Summary

Benefits of measuring and monitoring the power usage of servers are numerous. With the knowledge gained from server monitoring, IT facility managers can make better power optimization decisions. Monitoring also provides insight into the idle, average and peak power utilization for a server or rack of servers. This knowledge can aid investment and efficiency decisions by:

- Identifying non-working processing assets
- Identifying low-efficiency processing assets (lots of power draw for little computational power)
- Providing data to assist capacity planning efforts to improve energy efficiency for all power protection, distribution and cooling infrastructure equipment

The steps for measuring server power consumption can be approached with several different methods and metrics. Two key metrics are SPECpower_ssj2008 and Performance per Watt. If resources are not available for individual server monitoring, CPU utilization is a simple method to determine overall power usage. Rack density and power distribution can be determined using a nameplate derating approach, but actual power measurements are recommended for better effectiveness. Last but not least, embedded in recent Intel server chipsets is the Intel® Dynamic Power Node Manager capability. This is an out-of-band power management policy engine that can work with the Intel® Datacenter Manager to monitor and control power for a single server or a group of servers.

Server power usage measurements have many uses. The data can be used to optimize power budgets and operations strategy based on the work load and business priorities. Load dependent power variations can be identified. Average and peak power draw of workloads can be determined. This information helps in two aspects; peak power draw is important for guiding the deployment and density of servers to a data center, and average power is the main factor of the power bill. As with data center metrics, you can only manage what you measure.

Chapter 6

Power Metrics for Data Centers

Control over computing belongs with users.
—Brandt Allen

This chapter defines methods for quantifying power consumption efficiency in data centers. These metrics enable energy and power consumption bench marking and provide a foundation for plans to reduce consumption and improve operations. The quantification of power consumption helps identify and set priorities for operational improvements.

Keeping a data center energy efficient is an ongoing process. Proper power measurements of the overall data center, including both IT equipment and infrastructure, determine power utilization effectiveness (PUE) and data center infrastructure efficiency (DCiE) ratios. Calculating a data center's energy efficiency rating enables IT managers to evaluate how efficient one facility is when compared with other data centers around the world.

In addition to PUE and DCiE, there are other metrics that can also help in profiling a data center for energy efficiency improvements. There is no perfect set of metrics for data centers because the science is continuing to evolve. Some of the most useful benchmarks and metrics are provided in this chapter along with descriptions to help IT managers identify the ones that best fit their organization.

After determining a facility's efficiency rating, the next steps in reducing power consumption are to implement power and cooling best practices and then monitor and recalculate to see how those changes improved the PUE and DCiE ratios. Power and cooling best practices will be covered in subsequent chapters. Improvements in DCiE and PUE ratios indicate improved efficiency, which in turn demonstrates a measurable reduction in your organization's power bill.

The Business of Metrics

Many corporate executives have limited understanding of the IT magic that connects their laptop to the network and of the technology that runs their company on a daily basis. Executives can make long lasting data center decisions based on data points, graphs and metrics. Given the impact of executive and budget decisions, it is wise and helpful to understand the best metrics for energy efficiency and power consumption management. The saying "you can't manage what you can't measure" definitely applies to power reduction analysis. However, care must be taken because some metrics and benchmarks can be misleading and thus lead to poor decisions that could actually hurt business. Appropriate metrics and benchmarks not only help to accurately profile power usage, but also to effectively communicate with executive management for key decisions.

The core function of most data centers is to provide sufficient power to the IT load and eliminate heat generated as a byproduct. With the wrong benchmarks, there is potential for underestimating or overestimating the power needs. Underestimating the required capacity may result in future power disruptions when forced to increase capacity, and over-estimating leads to excessive initial installation costs and higher ongoing maintenance and operations expenses.

As pointed out in previous chapters, energy is becoming expensive and will only increase in cost in the future. If a data center is located in a region where each kW of IT load costs USD 2,000/year, this equates to USD 20,000 over ten years. A 200 kW data center in this region would have a 10 year electricity cost of USD 4,000,000, which is a material expense for any organization. IT professionals should understand where the money—that is, the energy—is going and how various design and operational optimizations can significantly improve efficiency.

From a business perspective, not all optimizations will be cost effective. The cost generally must be less than or equal to the benefits of the energy saved and must be significant enough to meet materiality thresholds as set by the business. It is important to note that both monetary (pecuniary) and non-monetary (non-pecuniary) benefits can be used to determine value in accordance with standard benefit cost analysis methodologies to determine the viability of a proposed change.

Government is often concerned with the non-pecuniary aspects: air quality, carbon footprint, water quality and global climate change are a few examples. Law, policy, and taxes are the most common tools used to manage non-monetary impacts and benefits. Business, on the other hand, is generally focused on the monetary impacts of optimization opportunities as measured by marginal rate of return or more commonly, return on investment (ROI).

Not only do good metrics help in correctly designing capacity, they also help align the design with the organization's goals. For example, a good ROI metric of power usage should include criteria that are meaningful to the business, such as energy consumption or IOPS per kilowatt, or even revenue per Watt. The objective is not to compromise the organization's revenue purely for the sake of kilowatts. Reducing power consumption might save money on power costs, but if the total productive work output by the data center or server(s) is also reduced, loss in revenue due to reduced productivity (fewer IOPS) may actually cost more than the energy that was saved. This is why appropriate metrics will focus on power efficiency over the notion of simple power cost savings.

Valid measurements and metrics enable IT professionals to examine the correlation between performance/utilization against assets. They help IT managers understand not just that a given asset might be underutilized but if it has a significant role within the organization. By correlating utilization and business purpose, IT can make rapid, informed decisions and determine if additional analysis would have value.

There are many metrics that can be used to measure and evaluate thermal capacity, energy efficiency, power consumption and equipment utilization. Some, like PUE or DCiE are well known, others are newly being proposed or are in development. One of the key decisions IT managers need to make is to assess which metrics will work best for their organization and data center. While there currently are few published industry reports detailing PUE statistics for comparison between data centers, understanding a variety of metrics can help IT managers select the best ones to reduce power and improve their data center operations. A good set of consistently applied metrics will not only allow a data center operator to reduce and manage power consumption, but will also offer the following benefits:

- Identify opportunities to improve a data center's operational efficiency
- Provide statistics to compare one data center to other data centers (benchmarking)
- Determine if designs and processes are improving efficiency over time
- Reduce power consumption and provide energy to repurpose for capacity expansion without additional capital investment expenditures or in situations where no additional energy is available to the site

Amps, Watts, Power, and Energy

Distinguishing among the terms of amps, Watts, power, and energy is useful when considering measurements and metrics for a data center. Clarifying these terms not only helps in taking the appropriate measurements but also helps in decision making. For example, peak power demand affects how big the UPS, cooling system and utility feeders must be. In contrast, saving power tends to reduce the capital investment (CapEx) for new data centers and defers expensive physical capacity expansions to existing data centers.

Electric current is the flow (movement) of electric charge. The international system of units (SI) of electric current is the Ampere (amps), and electric current is measured using an ammeter. Amps are the amount of electric charge a piece of equipment uses per second. Power is defined as the rate at which electrical energy is transferred by a circuit. The SI unit of power is the Watt. Power measures a rate of energy use (or rate of energy generated). Work is done at a rate of one Watt when one Ampere flows through a potential difference of one volt. A kilowatt-hour (kWh) is the amount of energy equivalent to a steady power of 1 kilowatt (1000 Watts) running for 1 hour. Finally, with respect to cooling, one ton of cooling equals 12,000 British Thermal Units (BTU)/h cooling, which equates to 3.516 kW.

Power and energy are frequently confused in the general media. For this book, we define power as the spot measurement at a specific point in time. Energy is the consumption of power over a period of time.

Power is measured in kilowatts (kW), and energy is measured in kilowatt hours (kWh).

Understanding the difference between power and energy is important for data center planning and optimization. For example, if a data center turns off idle servers at night, it will save energy, but not reduce peak power demand. The data center still must be sized to accommodate times of peak compute demand (peak power consumption) when all servers are running. Power capacity costs are those associated with sizing the systems that deliver energy and increase with the design power level of the system. Examples of costs driven by power capacity are UPS costs, generator costs, air conditioner costs, and power distribution equipment costs. Energy costs, in contrast, are those associated with the electrical utility bill.

The power drawn by servers and storage is expressed in Watts or Volt-Amps (VA). The power in Watts is the real power drawn by the server. Volt-Amps are called the *apparent power* and are the product of the voltage applied to the server times the current drawn by the server. The Watt rating determines the actual power required from the utility company and the heat loading generated by the server. The VA rating is used for sizing wiring and circuit breakers. The VA and Watt ratings for some types of electrical loads, such as incandescent light bulbs, are identical. However, for servers and storage the Watt and VA ratings can differ significantly, with the VA rating always being equal to or larger than the Watt rating.

The difference between the steady state power and the peak power is important when calculating power capacity requirements. For installations where critical components like air conditioning, chillers, or standby generators are shared and used to supply other loads beyond the data center, the sizing of the system requires a more complete and complex analysis. Reducing non-productive energy consumption can reduce the power capacity related costs as well as the energy costs. In other words, an implementation that saves electricity in many cases can also save on the house load costs, which are primarily driven by the house load power demand.

There is a difference between reducing energy consumption temporarily and reducing energy consumption permanently. Temporary savings like load shedding or server power management reduce electricity costs but do not necessarily reduce the peak power rating of the house load systems and the related house load infrastructure costs. Permanent or structural changes like high efficiency servers or high efficiency UPS systems reduce both the electricity costs and the house load costs.

Energy Metrics: What to Measure and Where

Developing a thorough understanding of a data center's energy consumption is the first step on the road to reducing power consumption. Keeping your data center energy efficient should be an ongoing process. To get started, four major steps should be taken, starting at the bottom right and progressing upward to the right upon completion of that step, as shown in Figure 6.1.

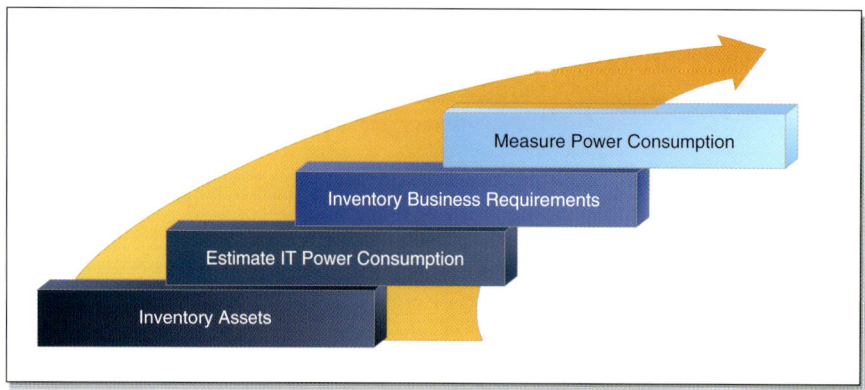

Figure 6.1 Four Steps to Initialize Power Management
Source: Intel Corporation, 2009

Inventory Assets

A complete inventory of IT assets includes software licenses, asset purchase dates, purchase and installation costs, owner, server identity, and so forth. The inventory should include a list of all such devices, with their nameplate power rating (the maximum power draw of a system), their voltage requirements, and whether they are single-phase or three-phase devices. The inventory should include security, fire, and monitoring systems.

Estimate IT Power Consumption

The next step is to size the IT load that must be served and protected. IT load includes the power consumed by all of the IT hardware components: servers, routers, computers, storage devices, telecommunications equipment, and so forth. IT load also includes power consumed by the security, fire, and monitoring systems that protect IT hardware.

The nameplate information should be adjusted to reflect the true projected or measured IT load. This is called *derating*. As Wikipedia explains it, "Derating is the technique employed in power electrical and electronic devices wherein the devices are operated at less than their rated maximum power dissipation taking into consideration the case/body temperature, ambient temperature, and the type of cooling mechanism used." Nameplate power is worst-case power consumption. The metric is required by Underwriter's Laboratory and, in almost all cases, nameplate power consumption is well above expected operating power levels.

Inventory Business Requirements

After the asset inventory and IT load information are complete, the next step is to inventory business requirements. It is important to understand the impact of the business cycle on the utilization of IT resources. Two examples of business cycle impact are as follows:

- Business workload variances: "Trade settlement applications require sufficient CPU and I/O resources to sustain a transaction rate of 1,000 tps."
- Business cycle variances: "Trade settlement transactions peak at 5 p.m. daily, and there are even larger business peaks both monthly and quarterly."

Understanding business cycle variances and other business requirements can ensure that a metric correlates with the organization's business goals. This assessment essentially establishes the availability needs of the business applications being processed by the IT equipment.

Measure Power Consumption

Initially, three measurement points of power consumption are needed to estimate power and energy consumption in a data center.

The first measure is total data center consumption at the utility meter, which determines the utility bill (both the energy portion and the power-based peak demand charge). It includes everything the data center uses, including house load, servers, lighting, and so on. Annual energy consumption at the utility meter will not simply be the peak power consumption times 8,760 hours, because it is possible for power load to vary throughout the day or week as servers adjust to different compute loads and the air conditioning system operates more or less efficiently in response to ambient conditions. The total data center consumption is important to know because it determines whether a utility can physically meet the demands of the site without having to increase the capacity of the power feed.

The second place to measure power and energy consumption is at the plug bringing conditioned AC input power to the input of the IT equipment. This power summed up over all the IT equipment in the data center's raised floor area identifies how much power must be delivered by the PDU and UPS systems. In most data centers, about 50 percent of the power consumed at the utility meter never makes it to the IT equipment; instead, it is consumed to run cooling equipment or dissipated in conversions within the UPS and PDU systems. Power not consumed by IT equipment is called house load, a concept defined and discussed earlier.

The third place to measure is the IT compute load inside servers and network equipment, to see how much of the power and energy at the plug actually makes it to the internal components that do the useful computational, storage and data transmission work. A significant portion of the power consumed inside a server is either wasted in power supply conversion losses or diverted to non-computing loads such as internal fans for ejecting heat.

To understand data center efficiency, it is important to understand the relationship between the power that is used and the workload that is processed.

Addressing Measurement Challenges

Many data centers are part of a larger building. For installations where critical components like air conditioning, chillers, or standby generators are shared and used to supply other loads beyond the data center, the sizing of the system requires a more complete and complex engineering analysis. Separating out data center power usage often isn't possible without retrofitting the room with sensors or installing a separate power meter.

Two approaches for determining and managing electrical capacity and power consumption in multi-use facilities are instrumentation and modularity.

Instrumentation provides the data necessary to understand and manage data center power consumption. While gross-level power consumption—such as the aggregation of all IT and facilities power for a data center—is useful, it is desirable to use a finer level of data resolution. This can be achieved by instrumenting at a subsystem level. The degree of data resolution will have a direct impact on an operator's ability to optimize, tune, and ultimately integrate facilities and IT subsystems into a dynamically self managing data center.

Modularity provides the means to more closely align electrical system design capacity with data center fill rate and availability requirements, shortening the time to optimal electrical load, right-sizing redundant systems, and thus reducing power loss from sub-optimization. Modularity permits electrical subsystems to run at their peak design efficiency, something that almost never happens in current large scale monolithic data center designs.

The art and science of designing self-optimizing data centers is in its infancy today. But just as computer controlled fuel injectors on internal combustion engines have improved mileage and reduced pollution, it represents a significant opportunity for improved data center efficiency going forward.

Make Measurement an Ongoing Process

While a snapshot of power consumption provides a starting place, the measuring process needs to be repeated and its precision improved. Improvements in power consumption in a mature IT organization follow the cycle described in Figure 6.2.

The number of measurement points increases, for example as consumption is tracked before and after AC/DC conversion in the power distribution design. The results of more precise measures fuel redesign efforts that pinpoint opportunities to make cost-effective improvements. Year-over-year measures validate cost avoidance and returns on investments. The cycle ends with plans for the next cycle of analysis and improvement.

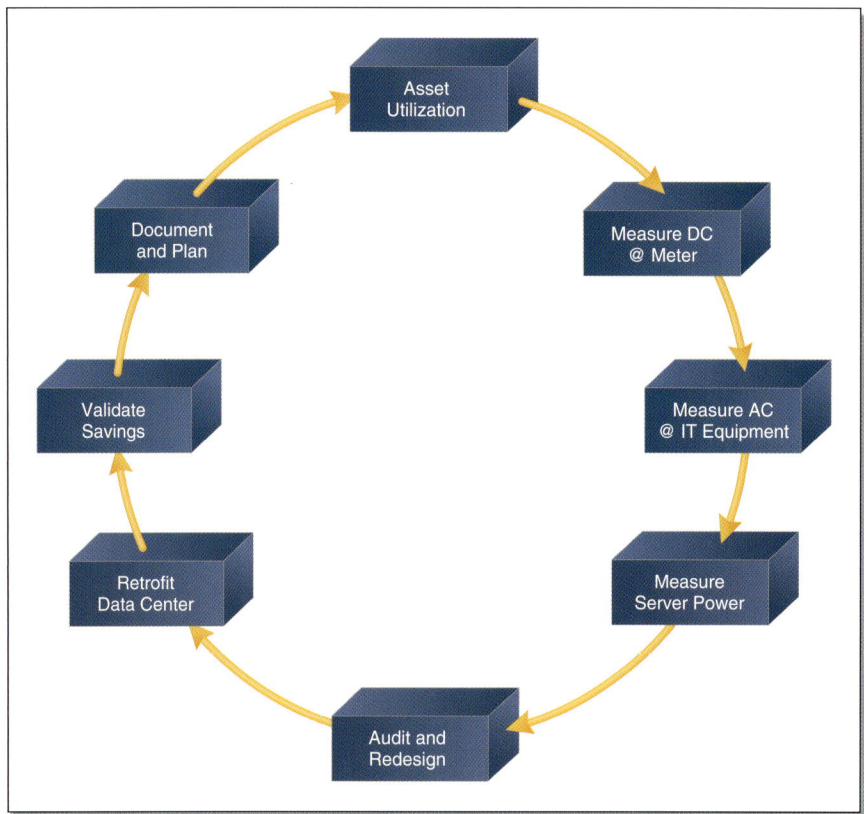

Figure 6.2 Cycle of Activities to Improve Energy Efficiency
Source: Intel Corporation, 2009

Metrics and Measures

There is no perfect set of metrics for all businesses. In this section, we provide formulas and descriptions for several basic metrics. Use the one that best fits your business. The metrics below are presented in order of general value.

Two Essential Metrics: DCiE and PUE

Power usage efficiency (PUE) and data center infrastructure efficiency (DCiE) provide information to help understand where a data center stands in terms of overall energy efficiency. The formulas are as follows:

$$DCiE = \frac{IT\ Equipment\ Power}{Total\ Facility\ Power} \times 100\%$$

$$PUE = \frac{Total\ Facility\ Power}{IT\ Equipment\ Power}$$

$$DCiE = \frac{1}{PUE} = \frac{IT\ Equipment\ Power}{Total\ Facility\ Power} \times 100\%$$

DCiE is a ratio, commonly reported as a percentage, that shows how much power is consumed by servers and other IT equipment as a proportion of total facility power—IT equipment plus consumption by power distribution, cooling, lighting, and so on. Driving this indicator up means fewer Watts are wasted as data center overhead. DCiE can be a good metric, but it does require usage and monitoring 24x7 to capture the details for peak and off-peak power consumption.

DCiE does not provide information about the energy efficiency of the IT equipment itself (servers, storage, and network equipment). DCiE does not indicate whether the return on investment (ROI) of this equipment is maximized, meaning that there are few idle resources. In the DCiE equation, *IT Equipment Power* includes the load that is associated with all IT equipment (servers, storage, and network equipment) along with supplemental equipment such as displays, workstations, mobile computers that are used to monitor or otherwise control the data center.

Total Facility Power includes power delivered to IT equipment as well as the power that supports the IT equipment load. Supporting equipment includes UPS, switch gear, generators, power distribution units (PDUs), batteries, cooling systems, compute, network, and storage nodes. The most likely measurement point would be at the output of the computer room power distribution units (PDUs). This measurement should represent the total power delivered to the compute equipment racks in the data center.

PUE is the reciprocal of DCiE, is expressed as a ratio, and has a minimum value of 1. Smaller values indicate greater efficiency. A PUE of 2, which is a typical value, indicates that for each unit of power consumed by IT equipment, a unit of power is consumed as overhead .

Estimating DCiE and PUE

Based on detailed analyses of the DCiE metric, Gary Verdun and a team of contributors from The Green Grid consortium offer a number of measurement recommendations. As Figure 6.3 illustrates, Total Facility Power should be measured at or near the facility's utility meters to accurately reflect all of the power entering the data center.

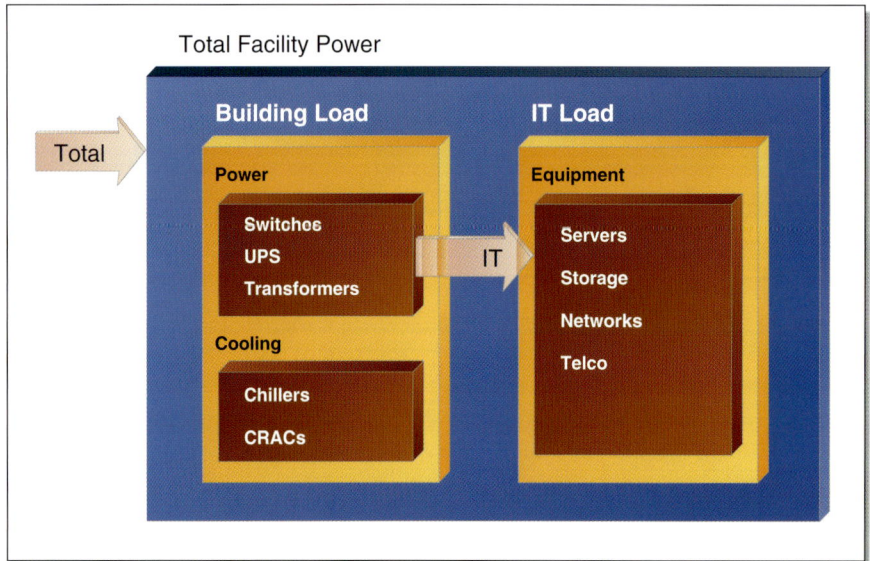

Figure 6.3 Total Facility Power
Source: Adapted from Verdun, 2008.

The *Total Facility Power* measure should represent the total power (that is, the power delivered by the electrical utility) consumed by the data center only, or faulty PUE and DCiE ratios will result. For example, if a data center resides in an office building, total power drawn from the utility will be the sum of the *Total Facility Power* for the data center, and the total power consumed by the offices. To calculate the power for the data center only, subtract an estimate or measurement of the amount of power being consumed by the non-data center offices.

According to Verdun and the Green Grid organization, *IT Equipment Power* should be measured after all power conversion, switching, and conditioning is completed and the power is distributed to the IT equipment itself. Measurements should not be taken if maintenance is being performed within the data center. This could negatively skew the DCiE measurement and provide unrealistic calculations.

DCiE should be monitored over a period of one year with ongoing systematic measurements to compensate for peak power usage and loading changes that occur within the data center. If it is not possible to monitor power consumption over a full year, select a period of time not less than one month and verify that the data center workloads are typical.

It is important to understand the difference between cumulative and instantaneous measurements and to identify the effect of variations in workload and environment on the overall infrastructure efficiency. An instantaneous reading of power for the IT equipment and the total facility power in kW will yield a point-in-time snapshot for DCiE. More frequent snapshot measurements will result in a better understanding of the sources of variation and an insight into the factors that influence the overall facility efficiency.

To get a useful single value for DCiE, calculate the metric using the cumulative energy consumed (kW/hr) for a period that is longer than the cyclic variation in workloads and environmental variances. For many facilities, this period of measurement may be a full year.

Remember that nameplate power ratings will not provide accurate DCiE measurements for any of the IT equipment or for any of the infrastructure components. Actual power measurements must be collected in order for DCiE to have any correlation to an operational data center. Organize the components from the largest power consumers to the smallest consumers. The rank order list will highlight the areas where improvement will most strongly affect the DCiE ratio (Verdun 2008).

Improving DCiE Measurement

Measurements to determine energy efficiency should be taken on an ongoing basis. Table 6.1 shows how measurement procedures can be improved to offer more comprehensive views of power consumption.

Table 6.1 Measurements and Intervals for the DCiE Metrics

Source: Verdun, 2008

	Level 1 (Basic)	Level 2 (Intermediate)	Level 3 (Advanced)
IT Equipment Power	UPS	PDU	Server
Total Facility Power	Data center input power	Data center input power less shared HVAC	Data center input power less shared HVAC and building lighting, security
Minimum Measurement Interval	1/month or 1/week	1/day	1/minute (continuous)

- Level 1 (Basic) calculations involve collecting power measurements on at least a monthly basis from the UPS equipment within the data center (the IT Load) and from the Main Distribution panel(s) feeding all of the mechanical equipment used to cool and condition the data center.

- Level 2 (Intermediate) calculations involve collecting data on at least a daily basis using measurements taken at the PDUs within the data center and from the distribution system used to power each of the pieces of equipment that make up the "Facility" equipment.

- Level 3 (Advanced) would involve collecting data from each individual piece of IT equipment and from each individual piece of facility equipment on a continuous basis. IT equipment is just starting to be equipped with instrumentation and sensors that will allow for continuous measurements, but it will be a few years before this becomes widespread.

For the Basic and Intermediate measurement processes, Verdun and his team recommend that the systematic measurements be taken at approximately the same time of day and same day of the week or month when the loadings in the data center is as consistent as possible with prior measurements. When making week to week comparisons, the day of the week should also be kept constant for comparable measurements.

The Advanced level of measurement is intended to be visionary. Continuous measures of each component would lead to the best estimates of consumption and, more importantly, would pinpoint specific loads where power consumption might improved.

A DCiE value of 33 percent (equivalent to a PUE of 3.0) suggests that the IT equipment consumes 33 percent of the power in the data center. Thus, for 100 dollars spent in energy, only 33 dollars are really used by IT equipment. Ideally, a PUE value approaching 1.0 would indicate 100 percent efficiency, meaning a DCiE value of 100 percent. Today, many data centers average a DCiE around 44 percent. An excellent DCiE would be more than 60 percent, thus many data centers have significant room for efficiency improvements. Tips to improve DCiE are discussed in Chapter 7, Chapter 8, and Chapter 9.

Currently, there are no comprehensive data that show the true distribution of PUE values for operating data centers. Some preliminary work indicates that many data centers may have a PUE of 3.0 or greater, but with proper design a PUE value of 1.6 to 1.2 should be achievable. This theory is supported by measurements completed by Lawrence Berkeley

National Labs which shows that the 22 data centers measured had PUE values in the 1.3 to 3.0 range.

Additional Key Metrics

Return on Investment (ROI). ROI measures how effectively a business uses its capital to generate profit; the higher the ROI, the better. ROI is a very common metric to use when comparing the value of one IT or facility investment to another. The return on investment equals the net present value of accumulated net benefits (gross benefits less ongoing costs) over a certain time period divided by the initial costs. ROI is usually stated as a percentage over a specific amount of time. In data centers, three years is the most common time frame since technology is often effectively obsolete after three years.

The equation for a 3-year ROI is:

$$ROI_{3years} = \frac{\frac{NetBenefit_{Year1}}{(1+DiscountRate)} + \frac{NetBenefit_{Year2}}{(1+DiscountRate)^2} + \frac{NetBenefit_{Year3}}{(1+DiscountRate)^3}}{InitialCost}$$

For example, if the initial cost for new software is USD 10,000, the annual benefits minus annual costs are constant at USD 5,000 for the next three years, and the discount rate is 10 percent, then the 3-year ROI would be:

$$ROI_{3years} = \frac{\frac{\$5,000}{1+.1} + \frac{\$5,000}{(1+.1)^2} + \frac{\$5,000}{(1+.1)^3}}{\$10,000} = 124\%$$

Marginal Rate of Return (MRR). Marginal analysis for a data center involves calculating marginal rates of return between technologies, proceeding in a stepwise manner from a lower-cost technology to the next higher-cost technology, and comparing the marginal rates of return to acceptable minimum rates of return. The procedure is useful for making recommendations for selecting alternative technologies. When IT managers have a choice of technology options, they should invest in the more costly technology as long as the marginal rate of return when switching from a lower cost technology to a higher cost technology is greater than the minimum acceptable rate of return and the net present value is increased.

Beginning with the lowest-cost technology and the next ascending technology, the marginal rate of return is computed by expressing the difference between the net benefit of the pair as a percentage of the difference of the total cost. The computed marginal rate of return gives an indication of what a data center can expect to receive, on average, by switching technologies. Hence, a 150 percent marginal rate of return in switching from old technology to new technology means that for each dollar invested in the new technology, the data center can expect to recover the USD 1 invested plus an additional return of USD 1.50.

Total Cost of Ownership (TCO). TCO represents the cost to build, as well as the cost over time to operate and maintain a data center. These costs are all brought back to a net present value (NPV) using appropriate engineering economics. A good TCO metric is cost/server when the specifics and number of servers are known. Alternately, cost/kW can be a useful metric, particularly when the servers to be installed are not known. In this metric, kW is the usable power available to the servers, rather than the total power into the data center. The use of cost/sq. ft. would not be valid as the high-density data center will have a greater cost/sq. ft., but may have a lower cost per usable kW.

Site Infrastructure Energy Efficiency Ratio (SI-EER). SI-EER is the ratio of power that comes into the data center to what is delivered to the computer equipment. In many data centers, for every 3W that comes into the building, only 1W is going to the computer equipment. This metric was designed to help executives determine how well they are managing the efficiency of their data center's site infrastructure systems. This metric is very similar to the Green Grid's DCiE. SI-EER is defined by the Uptime Institute, which is currently working to re-cast this metric in more intuitive and technically accurate terms.

Site operating data from many of the 85 corporate members of the Institute's Site Uptime Network indicates an actual SI-EER of 2.5. This means that for every 2.5 Watts passing through the data center service meter, only 1 Watt is delivered to the IT critical load. The very best ratio possible is 1.6 assuming the use of the most energy efficient components, no over provisioning of capacity, and no free cooling at any time during the year; in other words, for every 1.6 Watts delivered to the data center, 1 Watt is delivered to the IT critical load. This means sites could achieve a 40 percent energy reduction if they completed an energy efficiency tune-up and reduce their SI-EER score from 2.5 to 1.6. (Uptime 2007b)

Site Infrastructure Power Overhead Multiplier (SI-POM). SSI-POM is another ratio defined by the Uptime Institute. SI-POM is the ratio of data center power consumption at the utility meter divided by the total hardware power consumption at the plug for all IT equipment. It provides facilities engineers and IT managers with a good idea of the energy efficiency maintained by the facilities components such as transformers, UPS systems, PDUs, cooling systems, and lights. This metric is essentially the same metric as the Green Grid's PUE that we previously discussed. The formula for calculating it is:

$$SI\text{-}POM = \frac{\text{Data center power consumption at the meter}}{\text{Total power consumption at the plug for IT equipment}}$$

Deployed Hardware–Utilization Ratio (DH-UR). DH-UR measures the power drained by idle systems, or the amount of power wasted. DH-UR is calculated by dividing the number of servers running live applications by the total number of servers deployed. The equation for calculating it is:

$$DH\text{-}UR = \frac{\#\ of\ servers\ running\ live\ applications}{Total\ \#\ of\ servers\ actually\ deployed}$$

DH-UR can also be calculated for storage efficiency. To calculate storage power efficiency, use the number of terabytes of storage containing frequently accessed data divided by the total terabytes of storage deployed to get the view of power wasted by inactive or standby storage systems. Efficient data centers are those with a DH-UR rating as close to 1 as possible without disrupting availability.

This metric focuses on the real-time utilization of hardware, and is one of the best metrics for a dynamic data center. It points to how many deployed servers or storage servers are actually doing work, versus those that are sitting under-utilized or "comatose." This will be a very promising metric if it is used in conjunction with equipment that constantly optimizes how many servers are *on* and shuts down idled servers.

Deployed Hardware–Utilization Efficiency (DH-UE). DH-UE is used to indicate the power efficiency of operating servers and storage systems. It represents the minimum number of systems necessary to handle peak compute load divided by the total number of systems deployed. The equation for calculating DH-UE is:

$$DH\text{-}UE = \frac{Minimum \text{ \# of servers needed to handle peak load}}{Total \text{ \# of servers deployed}}$$

Because the amount of power it takes to run systems with low compute loads is very close to the amount of power to run systems with high loads, it makes sense to maximize the load on each running system. Unfortunately, many data centers run systems with low utilization in order to maximize uptime, improve stability, or reduce complexity.

DH-UE is another valuable metric that speaks to the capital efficiency of hardware. This metric quantifies how many servers need to be provisioned and on the floor, relative to how many servers are being used actively. It can help illuminate the efficiency of applications relative to hardware required.

Layout Efficiency. Layout efficiency measures data center square footage utilization. The units of measurement for layout efficiency are defined as racks per thousand square feet. This value is a measure of the efficiency of the data center layout. The typical range is 20 to 30, higher numbers representing better efficiency. This metric is independent of the size of the rack itself. This metric can be particularly useful when physical space constraints are limiting installation of additional IT equipment.

Even though some studies indicate that many of today's data centers underutilize their floor space, this metric has limitations on its value. Floor space can be the wrong metric for assessing data center capacity. As the density (as measured by power consumption per rack per unit of space) of IT systems increases, power and sometimes cooling capacity are exhausted far more quickly than space. These reasons illustrate how this metric has questionable value.

Watts per rack. Watts per rack is a useful metric in sizing power distribution to a rack and for determining the density limits for a full rack. Watts per rack should not be used by itself to define a data center unless the square footage of the work area is known and there is abundance of physical space in the data center.

Watts per square foot. This metric is typically used when analyzing data center density. However the metric is often misused because it lacks specificity in the denominator. It is typically assumed that the square footage refers to a raised floor area, but it could refer to a data center and support area, or even an entire campus. Consider also that 60-75 percent of the costs in a new data center are the power and cooling infrastructure which are largely independent of square footage.

Watts per square foot is well suited in the evaluation of cooling load in relation to the ability to move the required cooling air though the raised floor and the exhaust air through the hot aisle in relation to the physical space of the work area. However, a far better metric is PUE or DCiE. These metrics allow better comparisons, both design-to-design and data center-to-data center because it normalizes the capital costs for facilities infrastructure against the fundamental ingredients in computing power.

Computational Power Efficiency. This metric is measured in cycles per kilowatt-hour, comparing compute activity to the energy required to enable it. For a true reflection of energy input, data center managers should measure actual inputs of electricity consumed rather than make calculations based on component ratings. It is also important to measure all inputs, including power going to HVAC and lighting. This metric uses the SI units of 1 kWh = 3.6 mega joules.

ASHRAE Data and Temperature Measurements

Cooling consumes a significant portion of a data center power. Kilowatt power consumption and corresponding heat output are growing for all types of servers. Designing a data center to be scalable while keeping pace with changing technologies is a challenging task. To address this challenging task, this section is specific to cooling measurements and metrics. It is important to remember that any Watts saved on power efficient servers and storage systems will have a significant cascading impact on the overall power and cooling needed for the data center. A solid energy efficiency strategy requires continuous cooling measurement, power measurement, and benchmarking.

Data centers with multiple rows of racks require extensive cooling measures. For a smaller business with fewer servers, proper ventilation is the main requirement for the servers. A small number of tower-style servers dispersed throughout an open office will not need a separate air conditioning system or separate thermostat. The IT equipment shares the ventilation and the comfort level of employees, which usually exceeds the requirements of the servers.

Temperature can be measured and controlled at several levels. The best thermal management solutions control the flow of cool air from the computer room air conditioners (CRACs) down to the individual server level (server-by-server control) and down to the electronic component level within the servers, that is, CPU and memory thermal control of fan speeds.

The next best level of control is limited to the cabinet level (that is, cabinet-by-cabinet control), followed by the room partition level control (room-section-by-room-section control). The lowest level of control is no control at all, with the random placement of cabinets. Fine-grained multi-level control more effective management cooling, greater power savings, and improved energy efficiency.

ASHRAE, which is the American Society of Heating, Refrigerating, and Air-Conditioning Engineers, is an organization that seeks to advance the arts and sciences of heating, ventilating, air conditioning and refrigerating while promoting a sustainable world. ASHRAE's Technical Committee 9.9 (ASHRAE TC 9.9) has recommended that air entering the servers in the cold aisle to be between 68°F (20°C) and 77°F (25°C). Recently, ASHRAE extended the top end to 80°F (26.7°C). While a walk down a row of server racks can identify obvious hot spots or blasts of cold air, sensors are needed to identify accurate air temperature or air pressure at the inlet side of the servers. Instrumentation and analysis are the only accurate methods to tell if servers are getting too much or too little air cooling.

Computational fluid dynamic (CFD) modeling at multiple heights in a row of racks in conjunction with air pressure measurement under floor tiles can not only help you insure that you are getting enough cool air to the inlet of your servers, it can also help you maintain airflow to the recommended ASHRAE level to all IT equipment. Figure 6.4 shows a CFD model for an overcooled spot in a data center. CFD models can also help identify and eliminate hot isle/cold isle containment issues, that is, hot air leaking into the cold aisles and vice versa. Without such sensors or monitors, risk is mitigated by over cooling IT equipment to minimize downtime and hence power is wasted.

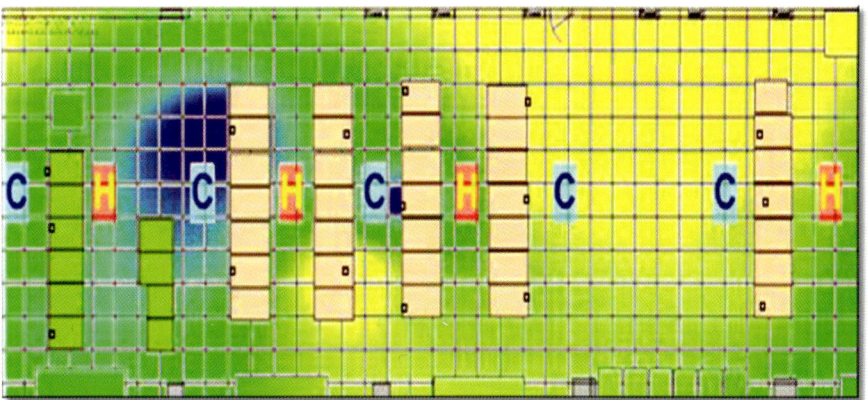

Figure 6.4 Computational Fluid Dynamic Example of Cold Spot in a Data Center

Metrics Measuring Cooling and Air Conditioning Efficiency

There are a number of metrics that help IT organizations measure and improve cooling systems. As with other metrics, no single metric is perfect for all businesses. Choose the ones that best fit your organization and equipment. We begin with the ratios that provide the best overall value, then follow with several cooling metrics.

Air Conditioning Airflow Efficiency (ACAE). ACAE is defined as the amount of heat that can be removed per standard cubic foot per minute (SCFM) of cooling air (Watts $_{cooling}$/SCFM). A higher value represents a more efficient power use for cooling. Intel data center engineers have studied various methods to increase ACAE. By measuring and optimizing the ACAE ratio, Intel has been able to reduce energy costs and also noise levels by using less air conditioning equipment. A higher ACAE value also reduced Intel's operating costs and facility support area per kW.

Figure 6.5 shows an example of the ACAE calculation for a traditional low density data center. This tool was developed by Intel data center engineers and is available through Intel's IT@Intel program office.

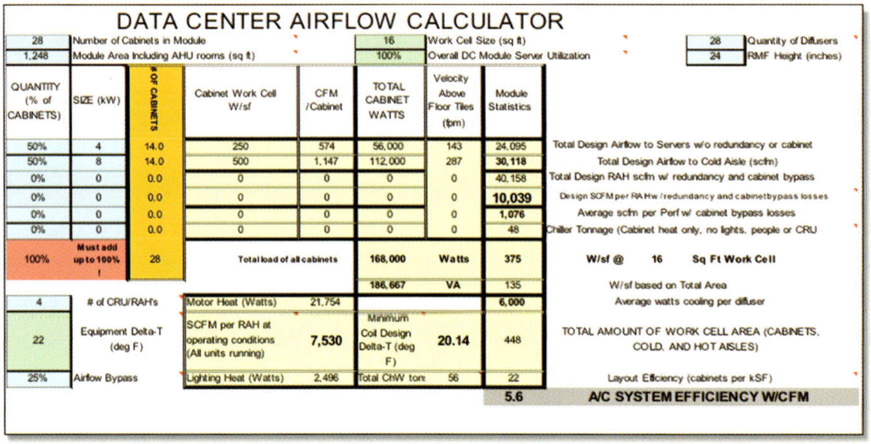

DATA CENTER AIRFLOW CALCULATOR

28	Number of Cabinets in Module	16	Work Cell Size (sq ft)	28	Quantity of Diffusers
1,248	Module Area Including AHU rooms (sq ft)	100%	Overall DC Module Server Utilization	24	RMF Height (inches)

QUANTITY (% of CABINETS)	SIZE (kW)	# OF CABINETS	Cabinet Work Cell W/sf	CFM /Cabinet	TOTAL CABINET WATTS	Velocity Above Floor Tiles (fpm)	Module Statistics	
50%	4	14.0	250	574	56,000	143	24,095	Total Design Airflow to Servers w/o redundancy or cabinet
50%	8	14.0	500	1,147	112,000	287	30,118	Total Design Airflow to Cold Aisle (scfm)
0%	0	0.0	0	0	0	0	40,158	Total Design RAH scfm w/ redundancy and cabinet bypass
0%	0	0.0	0	0	0	0	10,039	Design SCFM per RAH w/redundancy and cabinetbypass losses
0%	0	0.0	0	0	0	0	1,076	Average scfm per Perf w/ cabinet bypass losses
0%	0	0.0	0	0	0	0	48	Chiller Tonnage (Cabinet heat only, no lights, people or CRU
100%	Must add up to 100%!	28	Total load of all cabinets		168,000	Watts	375	W/sf @ 16 Sq Ft Work Cell
					186,667	VA	135	W/sf based on Total Area
4	# of CRU/RAH's		Motor Heat (Watts)	21,754			6,000	Average watts cooling per diffuser
22	Equipment Delta-T (deg F)		SCFM per RAH at operating conditions (All units running)	7,530	Minimum Coil Design Delta-T (deg F)	20.14	448	TOTAL AMOUNT OF WORK CELL AREA (CABINETS, COLD, AND HOT AISLES)
25%	Airflow Bypass		Lighting Heat (Watts)	2,496	Total ChW tons	56	22	Layout Efficiency (cabinets per kSF)
							5.6	A/C SYSTEM EFFICIENCY W/CFM

Figure 6.5 Data Center Airflow Calculator

Source: Intel IT, 2007

Computational Heat Efficiency. This metric is measured in cycles per BTU of heat produced. This compares computation to its main waste product, heat. Computational heat efficiency in some ways overlaps the measurement of energy efficiency, since the energy required to cool the data center must be included in the energy draw of the data center. However, it is a useful direct measurement of computational impact on the environment, especially in colder climates, where cooling for several months in a year can be a matter of circulating outside air rather than chilling hot inside air. The fact that cooling is achieved mainly by dumping heat directly out of the data center doesn't obviate the fact that the heat is being produced. This metric can also be defined in joules (1 BTU = 1055 J), but remember that this is joules out, not joules in.

Cooling tonnage to BTU. The cooling capacity (also referred to as size) of an air conditioner is measured in Tons or British thermal units (BTU's), both which are used interchangeably. Ton, although it sounds like a reference to weight, is not referring the how heavy the air conditioner is but the air conditioner's cooling capacity. Some sample sizes of air conditioners and their corresponding BTUs are:

- 1.5 ton (18,000 BTU)
- 2 ton (24,000 BTU)
- 3 ton (36,000 BTU)
- 5 ton (60,000 BTU

The correct size of air conditioning units is very important. A unit that is too large will turn on and off too frequently, work inefficiently, waste power, and most likely improperly dehumidify the data center. A unit that is too small will run continuously and may not be able to cool the data center sufficiently.

One approach to sizing a cooling system begins with an understanding of the amount of heat produced by the equipment contained in the enclosed space, along with the heat produced by the other heat sources typically encountered. In principle, it is easy to calculate the size of air conditioning unit needed for the data center. Simply add together all the sources of heat and install an air conditioning unit that can remove that much heat. In practice sizing is rather more complicated.

The amount of heat generated is known as the heat gain or heat load. Heat is measured in either British thermal units (BTU) or kilowatts (kW). As noted earlier, 1kW is equivalent to 3412BTUs.

The heat load depends on a number of factors. Taking into account those that apply in a data center and adding the factors together results in a reasonably accurate measure of the total heat. Factors to calculate include:

- Floor area of the room
- Size and position of windows, and whether they have blinds or shades
- Number of room occupants
- Heat generated by equipment
- Heat generated by lighting

Floor Area of Room. The amount of cooling required depends on the area of the room. To calculate the area in square meters or in square feet:

Room area BTU = length (m) × width (m) × 337

Room area BTU = length (ft) × width (ft) × 31.31

Window Size and Position. If the server room has no windows, this part of the calculation can be ignored. If, however there are windows then the size and orientation need to be included in the calculations.

South window BTU
    = South facing window length (m) × width (m) × 870
North Window BTU
    = North facing windows length (m) × width (m) × 165

If there are no blinds on the windows multiply the result(s) by 1.5.

For data centers in the southern hemisphere, swap the conversion factors because the heat on the north-facing windows will be greatest.

Add together all the BTUs for the windows.

Windows BTU = South window(s) BTU + North window(s) BTU

Number of Occupants. Purpose-built server rooms don't normally have people working in them, but if people do regularly work in the server rooms you will have to take that into account. The heat output is around 400 BTU per person.

Total occupant BTU = Number of occupants × 400

Data Center Equipment. The most heat in a data center is generated by the equipment, which includes both the house load and IT workload equipment. The wattage on equipment for cooling calculations is the maximum power consumption rating or nameplate rating; the actual power consumed would be less. For cooling, it is safer to overestimate the wattage than underestimate it. Add together all the nameplate values (wattages) for the servers, switches, routers and multiply by 3.5, then multiply by the utilization factor (, 30 percent utilization of all equipment is typical).

Equipment BTU = Total wattage for all equipment × 3.5 × utilization %

Lighting. Take the total wattage of the lighting and multiply by 4.25.

Lighting BTU = Total wattage for all lighting × 4.25

Total Cooling Required.   Add all the BTUs together.

Total heat load
= Room Area BTU + Windows BTU + Total occupant BTU
*   + Equipment BTU + Lighting BTU*

This is the amount of cooling required to handle that amount of heat generated in the data center.

Size of CRAC unit required.   Large CRAC units may be rated in tons of cooling. 1 ton of cooling is equivalent to 12 thousand BTUs (Laverty, 2007).

Table 6.2 summarizes the factors affecting overall heat in a worksheet and provides an example: a data center with no windows, 1,200 m^2 of floor space with 80 racks of 1U servers, and a staff of 10 people.

The data center is loaded to 40 percent of capacity. The total nameplate rating of all the equipment in the data center is 300kW. As

Table 6.2 shows, the room area generates 404,400 BTUs, staff members contribute 4000 BTUs, and the lighting generates 4,250 BTUs. The total equipment wattage at 40 percent utilization (and times BTU factor of 3.5) is 420,000 BTUs. The total cooling required would calculate out as 832,650 BTUs and would require CRAC units delivering a total of 70 tons of cooling.

There are several other metrics that are useful in determining the correct size of air-conditioning system for a data center independent of the approach used. These additional metrics associated with cooling and thermal management are listed below. These metrics and the above calculation are intended as a rough guide only. Complete accuracy cannot be guaranteed. Before deciding on an air conditioning unit, consider commissioning an audit from a suitably qualified air conditioning equipment specialist or installer.

Table 6.2 CRAC Calculation Worksheet

Item	Measurement	BTU Calculation	Total BTUs
Room area	Floor area in square feet or square meters	Sq. m x 337 (sq. ft. x 3,627)	404,400 BTUs
Windows, size and position	Windows BTU = South Window(s) BTU + North Window(s) BTU	South Window BTU = South facing window length (m) x width (m) x 870 (sq ft x 9,364) North Window BTU = North facing window length (m) x width (m) x 165 (sq. ft. x 1,776) If there are no blinds on the windows multiply the result(s) by 1.5.	0 BTUs
Occupants	Max number of personnel in data center	Number of personnel x 400	4,000 BTUs
Equipment	Total nameplate ratings in BTU x utilization %	Total equipment wattage ratings x 3.5 x utilization %	420,000 BTUs
Lighting	Total wattage for lighting	Total wattage x 4.25	4,250 BTUs
Total Cooling Required	Subtotals from above items	Room area BTU + Windows BTU + Occupant BTU + Equipment BTU + Lighting BTU	832,650 BTUs
Size of CRAC units	Tons of cooling required to dissipate heat	Total Cooling Required BTUs/12,000	70 Tons

Tons of Cooling

Chiller Refrigeration Tons

A chiller refrigeration ton is defined as:

1 *refrigeration ton* = 12,000 Btu/h = 3,025.9 k Calories/h

A ton is the amount of heat removed by an air conditioning system that would melt 1 ton of ice in 24 hours.

Cooling Tower Tons. A cooling tower ton is defined as:

1 *cooling tower ton* = 15,000 Btu/h = 3,782 k Calories/h

Water Chiller Cooling

Water flows with 1 gal/min and 10°F temperature difference. The ton of cooling load can be calculated as:

Cooling load = 500 (1 gal/min) (10°F) / 12,000 = 0.42 ton

Total Heat Removed

In a chilled water system the air conditioner cools water to between 40 and 45°F (4 and 7°C). The chilled water is distributed throughout the building in a piping system and connected to air condition cooling units wherever needed. The total heat removed by air condition chilled-water installation can be expressed as

$$h = 500 \, q \, dt$$

where
h = *total heat removed* (Btu/h)
q = water flow rate (gal/min)
dt = temperature difference (°F)

The efficiency of chillers depends on the energy consumed. Absorption chillers are rated in fuel consumption per ton of cooling. Electric motor driven chillers are rated in kilowatts per ton of cooling.

Cooling Load in kW/ton

The term kW/ton is commonly used for large data centers and industrial CRAC systems. This metric is defined as the ratio of the rate of energy consumption in kW to the rate of heat removal in tons at the rated condition. For example, if a chiller's efficiency is rated at 1 KW/ton, then the

COP=3.5 and the EER=12. The lower the kW/tons required, the more efficient the system. Note that cooling loads have startup peak loads that exceed the steady state values which are accounted for in this calculation. This will help establish the size of the electrical distribution system required to support the entire data center.

$kW/ton = P_c / E_r$
where
P_c = energy consumption (kW)
E_r = heat removed (ton)

Coefficient of Performance (COP)

The Coefficient of Performance is the ratio between useful energy acquired and the rate of energy input to the compressor of refrigerant based systems. The term may or may not include the energy consumption of auxiliary systems such as indoor or outdoor fans, chilled water pumps, or cooling tower systems.

KW/ton	=	12 / EER
KW/ton	=	12 / (COP x 3.412)
COP	=	EER / 3.412
COP	=	12 / (KW/ton) / 3.412
EER	=	12 / KW/ton
EER	=	COP x 3.412

For purposes of comparison, the higher the COP the more efficient the system. COP can be treated as an efficiency where COP of 2.00 = 200 percent efficient. It can be expressed as:

$COP = E_u / E_a$
where
E_u = useful energy acquired (btu in imperial units)
E_a = energy applied (btu in imperial units)

Energy Efficiency Ratio (EER)

The Energy Efficiency Ratio is a term generally used to define the cooling efficiency of a single CRAC system. The efficiency is determined as the ratio of net cooling capacity —or heat removed in Btu/h—to the total input rate of electric energy applied - in watt hour. The units of EER are Btu/Wh. The higher the EER the more efficient is the system.

$EER = E_c / P_a$
where
E_c = net cooling capacity (Btu/h)
P_a = applied energy (Watts)

Data Center Power Management Tools

Power sizing and efficiency calculators

There are many sizing and efficiency calculators on the market. These tools show how various design decisions and operating conditions affect the efficiency and electrical costs of a typical data center. Most of them function with a pre-set list of equipment and their standard power ratings. These can offer quick snapshot data points for managing a data center.

The interactive nature of these tools allows the user to experiment with what-if scenarios by modifying the characteristics of a load. A sample of a DCiE calculator from APC is shown in Figure 6.6.

To obtain actual efficiency values for a specific data center, you need to compile actual installation details and generate the specific values for the house load and IT equipment of that center.

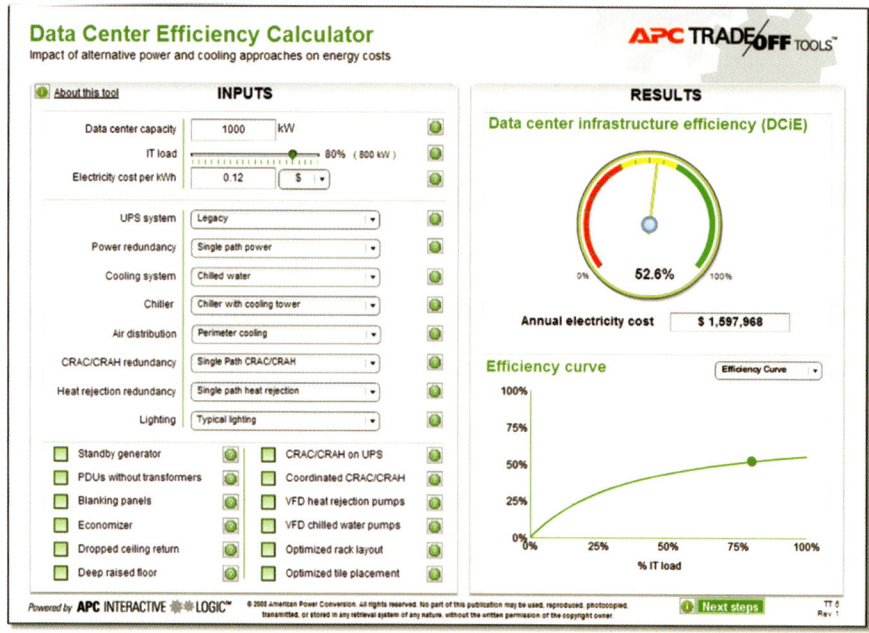

Figure 6.6 APC by Schneider Electric Efficiency Calculator

Source: www.APC.com

For IT equipment not listed in calculators as well as the power requirements for fire, security and monitoring systems, the following process should be used:

1. Add up the nameplate power of the anticipated loads. If the wattage is not listed on the device, it can be determined by multiplying the current (amps) by the voltage of the device to get the VA, which approximates the amount of Watts the device will consume.

2. Multiply the anticipated VA number by 0.67 to estimate the actual power, in Watts, that the critical load will represent.

Divide the number by 1000 to establish the kilowatt load level of the anticipated critical load.

Power Metering and Sizing Tools

Selecting a Good Power Meter

Key to measuring power use of equipment is to use a Watt meter that reports the "true" power, via the simultaneous measurement of the input voltage and current. Power meters operate in terms of accuracy, resolution, crest factor and bandwidth. Many Watt meters also have the capability to report energy usage which is the measurement of power over time (kilowatt hours or Joules).

Accuracy is specified in terms of percent error in the measurement. While a low error is desirable and often needed, one must note the specified range over which the accuracy is stated and whether or not it is specified as the accuracy of full scale. Having a uniform percentage error over the full range of operation is most important. Measurements with a maximum of ±5 percent error can be useful in determining overall power usage trends for level 1 measurement, but it is recommended that meters used have at least a ±2 percent accuracy.

Resolution is the term used for number of significant digits that carry meaning contributing to the accuracy and often will vary with the measurement range. A 0.1 Watt resolution is recommended for the measurement of a single piece of IT equipment. This level is not obtainable for the meter of a multi-megawatt data center utility feed. An acceptable meter resolution for level one measurement is 0.05 percent of full scale.

Crest factor of an AC current waveform is equal to the ratio of the peak current to the Root Mean Square (RMS) current. The meter selected must be able to handle the equipment's crest factor without introducing distortion in the measurement due to the top of waveforms being "clipped." Normally a full range rating of 3 is sufficient, though lighter loading of single equipment meters may require crest factors in the range of 6 to 8.

Bandwidth is a measure of the meters' capability to handle measurements that contain high frequency harmonics created by the power converters in the data center equipment (both IT and infrastructure). A minimum bandwidth of 3kHz is recommended.

Other considerations for power meters include choices impacting the ease of installation and data collection. Power measurement systems generally implement contactless current sensors rather than shunts (i.e. a device allowing electrical current to pass around a point in a circuit), because the latter cause power losses as well as installation and safety issues. The current transducers are normally transformers through which the electrical feed passes. Two common designs are solid and split-core transducers. A solid core sensor is the best choice (more accurate) for new permanent installations, while the split-core design is a better choice for retro fitting existing installations (less disruptive).

Split-core transformers are designed for the ability to be retrofitted into a live installation without disturbance (as opposed to a solid core transformer which would require the power cabling to be disconnected for a meter to be installed). Automatic meter reading (AMR) or remote meter reading (RMR) allow users to have the equipment communicate the measurements and not have someone physically read a display or download a data file. AMR or RMR may be "smart" meters, incorporating additional functions to report data in greater detail, such as power quality, outages and the ability to communicate data and alerts over a network. Smart meters will be needed to automate the measurement and calculation of DCiE.

Sizing of Utility Electrical Service

Sizing the electrical service for a data center requires an understanding of the amount of electricity required by the cooling system, the UPS system, and the critical IT loads. The power requirements of these elements may vary substantially from each other, but can be accurately estimated using simple rules once the power requirements of the planned IT load are determined. When calculating required electrical service it is important to distinguish between rated (peak) power and steady state power by comparing the electrical service requirements for both. In addition to estimating the size of the electrical service, these elements can be used to estimate the power output capacity of a standby generator system, if one is required for the data center loads.

It must be noted that the calculations below provide only an estimate, and that the final determination of the service size is highly dependent on accurate site specific information. It is strongly recommended that the services of a qualified professional consulting engineer be retained to verify the initial estimate and develop the final data center electrical supply design.

The electrical service required for a data center can be calculated as follows:

1. Take the total electrical capacity required in kilowatts and multiply by 125 percent to meet the requirements of the National Electrical Code and similar regulatory bodies.
2. Determine the three-phase AC voltage of the service entrance to be supplied by the utility company. Typically this is 480 Volts AC in the United States and 230 Volts AC in most other parts of the world.
3. Use the following formula to determine the electrical service size required to supply the data center, in Amps:

$$Amps = \frac{kWatts \times 1000}{Volts \times 1.73}$$

Sizing of Generator Standby Power Systems

Once the size of the electrical service has been determined, it is relatively straightforward to calculate the size of a standby power generator. Standby power generators provide power in the event of a utility failure and increase the availability of the data center.

Table 6.1 Data Center Power Requirement Estimate Calculation Worksheet
Source: Torell, American Power Conversion (APC), 2004

Item	Data Required	Calculation	Subtotal kW
Power Requirement — Electrical			
Critical load-sizing calculator value from APC website	Rating of each IT device	$\frac{Calculator\ Total\ in\ VA \times 0.67}{1000}$	#1_____kW
For equipment not listed in the sizing calculator, critical load – nameplate	Subtotal VA (include fire, security & monitoring systems)	$\frac{Subtotal\ VA \times 0.67}{1000}$	#2_____kW

Table 6.1 Data Center Power Requirement Estimate Calculation Worksheet *(Continued)*
Source: Torell, American Power Conversion (APC), 2004

Item	Data Required	Calculation	Subtotal kW
Future loads	VA of nameplate of each anticipated IT device	$\frac{\text{Total nameplate VA} \times 0.67}{1000}$	#3 _____ kW
Peak power draw due to variation in critical loads	Total steady state critical load power draw	(#1 + #2 + #3) x 1.05	#4 _____ kW
UPS inefficiency and battery charging	Actual Load + Future Loads (in kW)	(#1 + #2 + #3) x .32	#5 _____ kW
Lighting	Total floor area associated with the data center	0.002 X floor area (sq. ft.) or 0.0215 X floor area (sq. m.)	#6 _____ kW
Total power to support electrical demands	Total from #4, #5, and #6 above	#4 + #5 + #6	#7 _____ kW
Power Requirement — Cooling			
Total power to support cooling demands	Total from #7 above	For Chiller systems #7 x 0.7 For DX systems #7 x 1.0	#8 _____ kW
Total Power Requirement			
Total power to support electrical & cooling demands	Total from #7 and #8 above	#7 + #8	#9 _____ kW
Size of Electrcial Service Estimate			
Requirements to meet NEC and other regulators	Total from #9 above	#9 x 1.25	#10 _____ kW
Three phase AC voltage provided at service entrance	AC voltage		#11 _____ kW
Electrical service required from utility company in Amps	Total from #10 and AC voltage in #11	$\frac{\text{\#10} \times 1000}{\text{\#11} \times 1.73}$	_____ Amps
Size of Standby Generator Estimate (if applicable)			
Critical loads requiring generator backup	Total from #7 above	#7 X 1.3*	#12 _____
Cooling loads requiring generator backup	Total from #8 above	#8 x 1.5	#13 _____
Size of generator needed	Total from #12 and #13 above	#12 + #13	_____ kW

*WARNING: The 1.3 variable applies to fully power factor corrected UPS. A 3.0 multiplier must be used when using traditional double conversion UPS with input harmonic filters

When calculating sizing for the power generator, remember to include the electrical characteristics of the loads to be attached to the generator through the transfer switch. Mechanical loads, for example, require high starting currents and create harmonic currents that pose problems to a generator's ability to supply the power needed. The UPS itself may contribute to this problem if it does not operate at a high input power factor, and may cause generator failure if it imposes a leading power factor on the generator.

To estimate the size of the generator required for the critical loads, use the following calculation. Note the 1.3 multiplier applies to a fully power factor corrected UPS. A 3.0 multiplier should be used when using a traditional double conversion UPS with input harmonic filters.

$$\text{Size of standby generator} = P_e \times 1.3 + P_c \times 1.5$$

where

P_e = Total power to support full data center (kW)

P_c = Total power to support cooling demands (kW)

Facility Management Systems and Sensors

In modern buildings, many automated systems already exist: HVAC, lighting, fire or life safety, security, energy distribution, and any other type of equipment that operates on its own. And yet, these devices typically work independently, despite the fact that significant benefits can be achieved by coordinating control among them to achieve a so-called smart building or data center. There are systems that can coordinate and integrate these automated subsystems and manage them for energy efficiency. Two of the main categories of these systems are building management systems and supervisory control and data acquisition systems.

Building management system (BMS) is a computer based control system installed in large buildings (>50K sq ft) that centrally manages, controls and monitors the building's mechanical and electrical equipment. These systems, also known as building automation systems, enable the optimization a building's energy consumption through automation of the facility infrastructure. BMSs typically manage infrastructure components such as air handling and cooling plant systems, lighting, power systems, fire systems, and security systems. A BMS consists of software and hardware. The latest BMSs operate using Internet protocols and open standards (for example, SOAP, XML) with browser control, e-mail reporting and XML data exchange being integrated into intelligent controllers.

The core function of a BMS is to manage the environment temperature, CO_2 level, and humidity within a building. This means that the BMS controls the production of heating and cooling to achieve the desired room temperature and then manage the systems that distribute air throughout the building. A key secondary function is to monitor the level of human-generated CO_2, mixing in outside air with waste air to increase the amount of O_2 while also minimizing heat and cooling losses.

The challenge of a BMS is to make facilities subsystems work in conjunction with IT systems as if they were part of a single managed environment. In order for BMS to work, it requires a central software system to acquire facilities system status data, , field controllers to sense and transfer data from each subsystem to the central software system, and a user interface (computer monitor) that allows the user to interact with the system. As most buildings are fit with multi-vendor facilities equipment, issues can arise if the BMS cannot be configured to receive signals from the different field sensors—temperature, humidity, kilowatt hour, tank level, and so on—as well as flow switches and water and gas meters of the various building components and services.

BMS systems are delivered as fully integrated systems and services by companies like Siemens, Honeywell, Johnson Controls, TAC and others. New more flexible and open solutions that link BMS systems to enterprise management software and IT infrastructure management tools include Cimplicity[†], Tridium[†], and Gridlogix[†].

Supervisory control and data acquisition systems (SCADA)

These are another type of building management systems. These systems are process control applications that collect data from sensors and machines throughout a building or in remote locations and send them to a central computer for management and control. SCADA is used in very large data centers as well as in power plants, oil and gas refining, telecommunications, transportation, and water and waste control.

SCADA programs are used in industrial process control applications for centralized monitoring and recording of pumps, tank levels, switches, temperatures etc. A SCADA program normally runs on a PC and communicates with external instrumentation and control devices. Communication methods can be via direct serial link, radio, modem, fieldbus or Ethernet links. If a mixture of instruments with differing communication interfaces and protocols need to be interconnected, then converters or middleware can be used. SCADA is often used on remote data acquisition systems where the data is viewed and recorded centrally.

The SCADA program has a user configured database that tells the software about the connected instrumentation and which parameters within the instruments are to be accessed. The database may also hold information on how often the parameters of the instruments are accessed and if a parameter is a read-only value, such as a measured value, or read-write, allowing the operator to change a value—for example, an alarm setpoint. More sophisticated SCADA software can provide messaging modules for SMS or E-mail.

At the highest level of integration and optimization, BMS, SCADA and IT infrastructure monitoring tools can be integrated in a fashion that provides interdependent system's data to a policy based control engine via a series of feedback loops. When this level of sensory and control sophistication is achieved, power utilization can be dynamically and automatically adjusted based on workload (IT demand), ambient conditions (operating temperatures, weather conditions, etc.) and power availability. IT systems may be shut down or started up, for example, as required or work load can be logically moved in response to regional or time of day differentiated electricity costs supplied by the local utility company. Facilities subsystems may also by ramped up or dialed back in response to IT work load and external temperature and humidity.

Summary

There are several steps to reducing power consumption in a data center. But before a data center can be optimized, it first must be measured and profiled. There are many metrics and benchmarks available to support this activity. To be the most effective, the metrics used should support business goals and align best with the specific data center structure and IT equipment.

Understanding the difference between the terms of power, Watts, amps and energy is important for accurate measurements and data comprehension. Regardless of which metrics are used to profile energy efficiency, the basic knowledge of assets and purpose of the assets are required. With this data, the key metrics of PUE and DCiE can be calculated. These generally accepted ratios highlight how much power gets to servers, storage and network versus how much is consumed by power distribution, cooling and other house load items.

Beyond these main overall efficiency metrics, there are several other metrics in the areas of utilization, cooling, capacity, or finances. These additional metrics can assist IT managers in optimizing operations, making new technology selection decisions, or developing capital investment plans. Understanding the different metrics is important so that operators chose the best metrics to support sound decision making.

To aid the process of measuring and calculating efficiency, several vendors produce metering tools and calculators. These tools can provide quick snapshots of how various design decisions and operating conditions affect the efficiency and electrical costs of a data center. And, last but not least, vendors of Building Management Systems and SCADA systems are integrating with enterprise management software to provide solutions for on-going monitoring and control and to help implement energy efficiency improvements.

Energy Efficiency Templates

Appendix B contains templates from the Department of Energy that can assist in profiling a data center and developing benchmark measurements.

Chapter 7

Configuring Energy Efficient Servers

The attention span of a computer is only as long as its power cord.
—Anonymous

This chapter explains how to build or specify a server with reduced power consumption. The focus is on energy efficient designs for x86 servers. This information may or may not provide the same results with other types of servers. Improving the energy efficiency of a server can involve simple steps such as updating to the latest processors and newest BIOS, to much more complex changes like virtualization of the applications and storage. New generations of servers and subsystem components are making significant improvements in reducing power consumption. With electricity costs rising, it may provide a better ROI for new purchases to focus on energy efficiency coupled with increasing the refresh rate of servers from three to five years to two years.

We explore topics such as power supply efficiencies, fan size and fan speed control, power state management with operating systems and C-states with processors. These and many other features can all be optimized to reduce the power consumption of a server. By sizing the subsystem components correctly and increasing server utilization, not only will the server be energy efficient, but beneficial impacts spread to data center space usage, power distribution, and cooling systems efficiencies—in other words, data center capacity.

Impacts of a Low Power Server

The average server wastes from a third to over half of the power delivered to it. This wasted electricity unnecessarily increases the cost to power computers. Improving the energy efficiency of installed computers is one of the most cost-effective ways to reduce electricity consumption in a data center.

Efficient server technologies and configuration practices can reduce data center power consumption by 20 to 55 percent. On average, a current energy-efficient x86 server will consume approximately 25 percent less energy than similar x86 server models. This is true at all levels of utilization. For a given data center, the optimal energy efficient configuration will depend on the details of workload requirements, specific application types, the configuration of the server itself and usage profiles, among other important factors. However, the methods and tactics recommended in this chapter will reduce power consumption in general on any x86 server.

An energy efficient server consumes less energy (kWh) than non-energy-efficient servers. In general, an energy efficient server reduces energy usage by:

- Achieving aggregate power delivery efficiency of greater than 75 percent at workload and over 62 percent at idle (combined efficiency of VR and PSU)
- Reducing processor and chipset current leakage through technologies such as high-k gate dielectric materials
- Managing energy used for compute functions for lowest energy consumption per transaction
- Providing fine-grained component power management, such as memory power management and demand-based switching, along the load line
- Minimizing power consumption at system idle
- Providing monitoring and policy based-control of platform power consumption
- Controlling peak server power consumption during periods of high demand
- Providing feedback to the support infrastructure in the data center to throttle back the speed of fans, shut down surplus air conditioning units, and other similar dynamic adjustments

Power management features, such as policy and power capping, are key elements of an energy efficient server. A study of power usage at one of Google's data centers found that power management saved 40W per server without performance loss when the CPU was not fully loaded (Fan et al. 2007). Additional benefits power capping offered included being a safety valve by protecting the power distribution hierarchy against overdraw and enabling effective usage of the available power, thereby increasing rack population.

The recent generations of servers are being optimized for power consumption alongside speed, capacity and cost; increasing their computing capabilities and business value. A study conducted with CERN replaced 126 Intel Xeon® processor-based servers (6 racks) purchased in 2004 with 17 servers using 45nm Intel Xeon multi-core processors. These processors use the 45nm Hi-k next generation Intel® Core™ microarchitecture. The new servers delivered the same performance with:

- An 83 percent reduction in floor space
- An 87 percent reduction in energy cost over a four-year lifecycle (approximately USD 53,000 in savings, depending on utility rates)
- Full payback on the new servers in less than two years

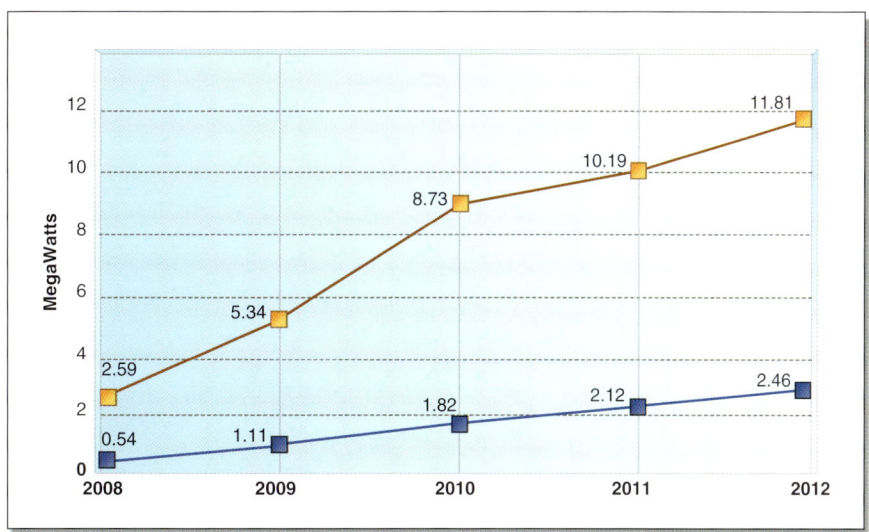

Figure 7.1 Projected Data Center Power Consumption (for CPU nodes)

Source: Intel, 2008

Finally, energy efficient servers will meet the new Energy Star specification for servers, which went into effect on February 1, 2009. To qualify for Energy Star, a server's idle power consumption must not exceed the maximum idle power levels for its category, as shown in Table 7.1 and Table 7.2. Blade systems (blade servers, blade chassis, blade storage) are excluded from the specification. Qualifications are met if the server's idle measurements are within the requirements in Table 7.1 plus the fully configured server being within guidelines for the components listed in Table 7.2. The latest on server requirements for Energy Star, can be found in the Partner Resources section on the Energy Star web site at *www.energystar.gov.*

Table 7.1 Base Idle Power Requirements

System Type	Idle Power Limit
Single Installed Processor (1P - All systems)	60 Watts
Two or Three Installed Processors (2P & 3P)	
Standard Availability Systems	151 Watts
High Availability, Low Installed memory (<16GB) Systems	169 Watts
High Availability, High Installed Memory (>16GB) Systems	221 Watts
Four Installed Processors (4P)	271 Watts

Table 7.2 Component Power Allowances

System Characteristic	Additional Idle Power Allowance
Second Hard Drive	15 Watts
Additional Hard Drives Over Two	8 Watts per Drive
Additional Memory over 32 Gigabytes	2 Watts/ GB

Components of Energy Efficient Servers

An energy efficient server requires the lowest power and the highest performance at every level of system and subsystem components. For many x86 servers, focusing on just the microprocessor, cooling fan(s), and power supply losses can significantly reduce power. These three subsystem components combined can account for up to 50 to 70 percent of total server energy use. However, for optimal power reduction, all subsystem components should be energy efficient.

In recent years, x86 servers have begun to incorporate the power saving architectures that have been common in both desktop and laptop computers. Features such as multiple core microprocessors with power management (dynamic frequency and voltage scaling) and the use of internal variable speed fans coupled with temperature sensors for on-demand cooling can result in overall system power savings without decreasing performance.

To build an energy efficient server, first start with the biggest power consuming subsystem component, the microprocessor.

Energy Efficient CPUs

Advancements in the design and manufacturing of integrated circuits have led to dramatic improvements in microprocessor speed, performance, and power efficiency. When selecting a processor for an energy efficient server, make sure it has the following power saving technologies: multiple cores, Demand Based Switching (DBS) or Enhanced Intel SpeedStep Technology, dynamic frequency and voltage scaling (P-states), and processor C-states.

Multi-core microprocessors contain two or more processing cores on a single die. The cores run at slower clock speeds and lower voltages than the cores in single-core chips. Multi-core designs handle more work in parallel (with proper software support) at the same or lower frequency than single-core designs. Moreover, because the cores share architectural components such as memory elements and memory management, signaling can be faster and consume less energy when compared to single-core systems. This combination of increased performance and reduced energy consumption has significantly improved performance per Watt. Measurements on multi-core processor-level energy savings range from roughly 40 to 60 percent over prior processor generations.

In addition to the core power savings, multi-core processors save power on the "uncore" or "edge" components. The edge components of a processor—drivers, voltage regulators, bus interfaces, and the like—use a substantial amount of power. Sharing these components between two cores uses less power than if they were duplicated in two separate processors. Newer processors also integrate the memory controller. An integrated memory controller cuts significant amounts of power while at the same time providing increased I/O throughput at lower power levels.

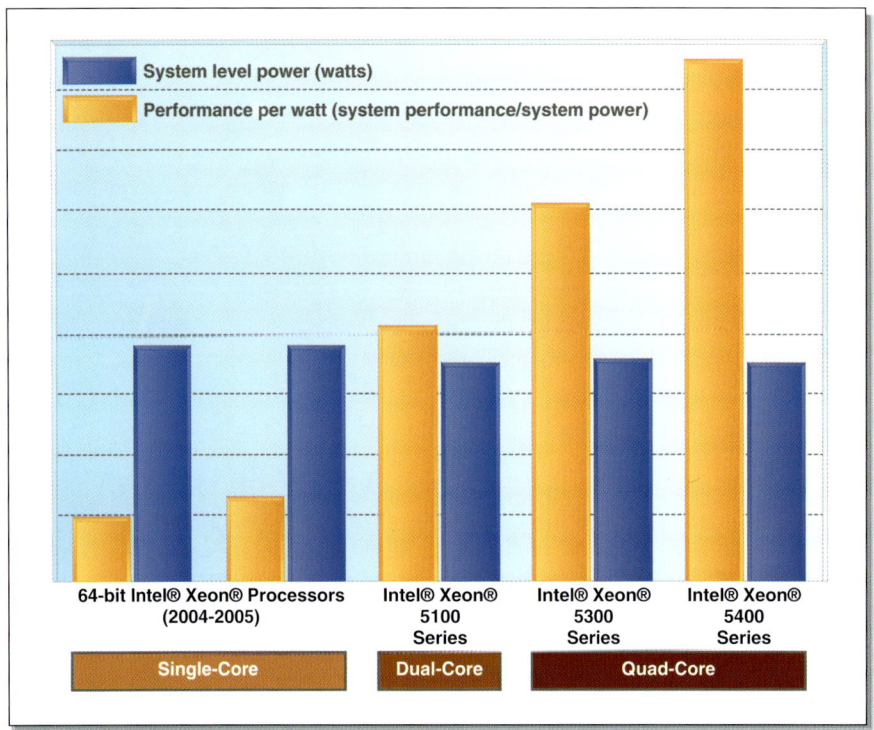

Figure 7.2 Boosting Server Energy Efficiency
Source: Intel Labs, 2008

New processors currently deliver a higher level of computing performance per Watt of power than ever before, as shown in Figure 7.2. In addition to active process or power efficiency, processor idle power has dramatically reduced over the last few years also. Intel has reduced the idle power of Xeon 5300 Series processors by 68 percent since their initial release. This reduction occurs while maintaining the same performance and same 80W Thermal Design Power (TDP) specification.

Intel is strongly focused on increasing performance per Watt in next-generation Intel processor-based servers. Future processors will include more execution cores as well as additional micro-architecture improvements. Multi-core processors based on the Intel® Core™ microarchitecture deliver about 5 times more compute power per Watt than single core processors based on the earlier Intel NetBurst® micro-architecture due to improved efficiency of the design. This means every processor core is delivering substantially more useful work per clock cycle. The latest Intel® Xeon processors also incorporate a number of advanced energy-saving technologies.

- Intel's industry-leading 45nm process technology improves energy efficiency at the most fundamental level, by reducing the amount of energy required per transistor.

- Intel® Intelligent Power Capability adds to these advantages, by powering up only those components of the processor that are needed to process a given workload.

- The recent 80W Intel Xeon E7340, E7330 and E7320 processors provide between 15 percent and 47 percent decreases in power. For ultra-dense deployments the 50 Watt Intel Xeon processor L7345 provides between 47 percent and 67 percent decrease in power from Intel 95- and 150-Watt processors.

Although the processors are just a fraction of a server's total power budget, the effect is still measurable at the power plug. The savings are most dramatic in the 20 to 60 percent utilization levels, which is where most server processors operate. When the difference is multiplied out across all servers in a data center, the savings can become substantial.

Demand Based Switching

The newer multi-core processors feature dynamic frequency and voltage scaling. This feature allows the microprocessor frequency or voltage to ramp up or down to better match the computational demands. Thus, when utilization is low, the microprocessor's clock speed can be reduced, which reduces energy consumption and heat dissipation. Frequency and voltage scaling are done automatically and constantly adjust to changes in computational demand, continuously minimizing processor energy consumption.

The power saving is achieved by reducing the frequency multiplier (frequency identifier or FID) and the voltage (voltage identifier or VID) of the CPU. Intel's version of this technology is known as either Enhanced Intel SpeedStep Technology (EIST) or Demand Based Switching (DBS). The combination of a specific CPU frequency and voltage is known as a performance state (P-state).

At its highest P-state, the processor runs at full clock speed and voltage, but during off-peak conditions it can be stepped down to *idle*, consuming as little as 25 percent of the full-speed power level. Processors today feature multiple P-states and can be throttled up or down in stages, quickly meeting performance needs while preventing unnecessary power use.

With DBS, power consumption and processor utilization are directly related. Traditionally, a microprocessor operates only at a single frequency and voltage. It is always on and always consuming full power. Processors with Enhanced Intel SpeedStep Technology can run at multiple frequency and voltage settings. A DBS-enabled operating system monitors processor utilization multiple times per second and downshifts to a lower frequency and voltage as appropriate. DBS-enabled operating systems can set policies based on P-states. Power usage is automatically tailored to match server workloads. This reduces waste, while allowing the system to deliver full performance when needed for peak workloads.

Better control and management of power consumption at the platform level can enable IT organizations to reduce their utility costs and optimize rack densities, while more effectively managing downtime risks. Demand-based switching, supported in the latest Intel Xeon processor-based servers, can help reduce data center power and cooling costs today.

How much can DBS affect the electric bill? Actual power savings from DBS will depend on utility rates, application workloads, the number and definition of power states and the policies that determine when and how these power states are changed. The data center advantages of DBS are most pronounced for low to medium utilization and halt states, which account for a very large percentage of server time in most environments. Intel tests have demonstrated power savings up to about 25 percent on systems operating within typical CPU utilization ranges, for annual savings of USD 75K to USD 100K per 500 servers. Savings would be even greater in regions where utility costs are particularly high.

Table 7.3 indicates that DBS can reduce power and thermal costs by up to 25 percent in a typical data center environment, which translates to about USD 100K annual savings per 500 servers. Benchmark details can be found on page 323.

C-States

An energy efficient server should support CPU C-states. C-states are part of the industry standard ACPI (advanced configuration and power interface), which is shown in Figure 7.3. The original ACPI power specification defined S-states for System states; in S0, the system is functional, in S1, S3 and S4, the system is sleeping or non-working. Currently servers do not use the S3 state. With recent updates to the specification, when the processor is working (S0 state), the processor can be assigned to any of the C-states.

Table 7.3 System Power Benefits with Demand-Based Switching (DBS)
Source: Intel, 2008

WebBench Power Measurements	Typical CPU Utilization		
Approximate CPU Utilization (DBS Off)	15%	30%	45%
System Power with DBS Off	258W	201W	316W
System Power with DBS On	201W	220W	240W
DBS Power Savings Per System	57W	71W	76W
Energy Cost Savings Per System* (Annual)	USD 148	USD 186	USD 200
Energy Cost Savings Per 500 Systems* (Annual)	USD 74,000	USD 93,000	USD 100,000

* Assumes USD 0, 10KWh and cooling costs that are roughly double the cost of platform power.

In C0, the processor is executing instructions. In C1, C2 or C3, the processor is halted. C1 and C2 are called coherent states because they must maintain up-to-date cache contents, versus C3 which is not cache coherent. While executing instructions in C0, the processor can be operating at different frequency/voltage operating points. These are the P-states mentioned previously.

When a processor supports C-states, the OS typically has a C-state policy in the kernel. This C-state policy controls when the processor uses which C-states. At boot time, the OS reads the ACPI table in BIOS and the table tells the OS which C-states are supported, how the C-states are currently defined for that system, and the associated latencies for those C-states.

The OS uses this information intelligently to put processors or logical processors (from use with Virtual Managers or threads) into different C-states. For each logical processor, there is a work queue of software threads. At the bottom of each queue is a thread called the Idle Thread. When a processor gets to the bottom of the queue, the OS puts that processor into a particular C-state using an MWAIT instruction.

Once the processor transitions into the specific C-state, the only way it can exit is via a break event, such as an interrupt (I/O timer, IPI) or monitor. When a monitor happens, the processor is trying to see if other hardware threads are trying to schedule work for other processors. All exits from non-working states are directly to the C0 state.

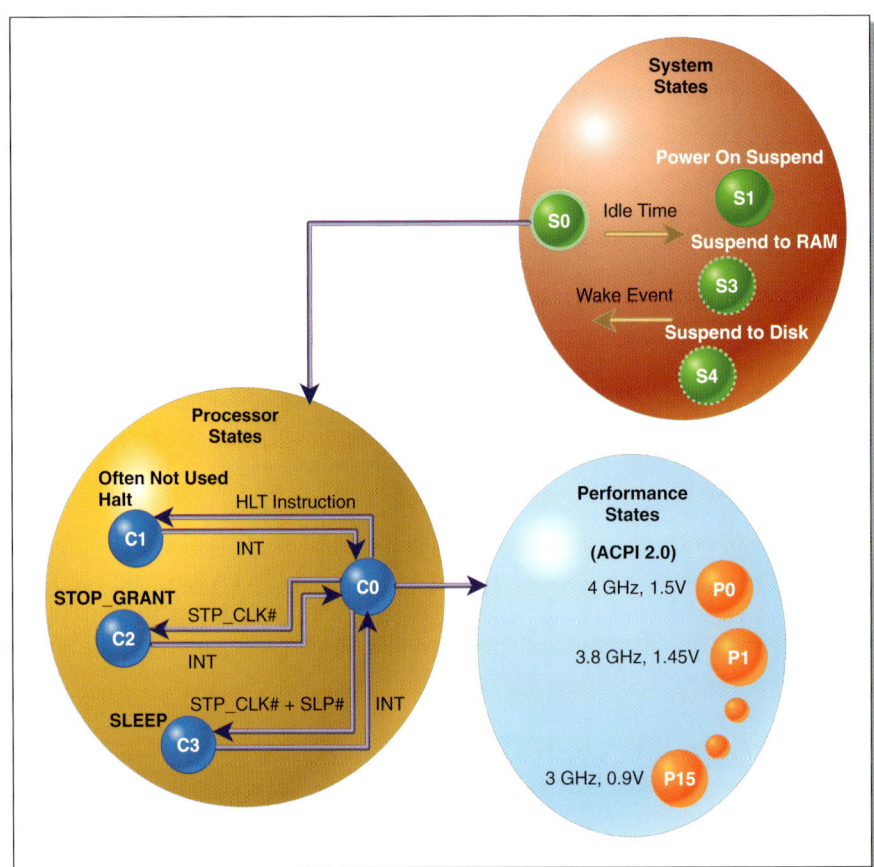

Figure 7.3 ACPI Power States
Source: Intel Labs, 2008

While in C-states, the processors utilize low power on key links. Intel® Quick Path Interconnect (Intel® QPI) technology, which provides extremely high server bandwidth, uses the L0S state when the link is idle, saving about 1W per x20 link. When all the cores in a system are idle, the QPI link will use the C3 and C6 states, saving about 3W per x20 link.

Intel processors enter C-states when all the cores in a package are idle. The C1E state reduces voltage and frequency. The C3 state reduces voltages, frequency, puts memory in self refresh, and the QPI link into its L1 state. The last C-state, C6, reduces voltages, frequency, puts memory in self refresh and the QPI link in L1 state.

The operating system can set the triggers for a C-state. Coordinating the C-state to the average CPU utilization of the servers provides the most power reductions. Examples of different C-state policies aligned to utilization for energy efficiency are:

- Use C1 when utilization is over 60%
- Use C2 when utilization is between 40% and 60%
- Use C3 when utilization is below 40%

A final note on C-states: the BIOS needs to be modified to support the different C-states. The BIOS should be enabled to support defined power domains. The ACPI C-state table should have the following values:

- Declare core-c3, core-c6 as C2 or C3 type
- If using legacy OS, use the I/O address in the table
- Otherwise, provide MWAIT in code for Microsoft Vista[†] and Linux 2.6.19 and onwards.

Intel's 45nm design enables processors to operate at an equal or lower total dissipated power (TDP) compared to 65nm, even though the performance continues to increase. The new quad-core 45 nm Intel Xeon series low voltage processors are rated at a power budget of 50W TDP while the dual-core 45nm Intel Xeon 5200 series low voltage are rated even lower at 40W. To meet industry specifications such as Energy Star that focus on system idle, most of Intel's CPUs operate under a low 8W idle power. If a user requires more compute power, some of Intel's new high performance quad-core processors based on the 45nm design operate at 12W power at idle, which also meets the new Energy Star requirements.

Processor power management is usually handled by the operating system and third party software which automatically make decisions based on performance demands and existing thermal conditions. For energy efficient servers, IT managers can tailor the power and thermal management of their servers' processors to the needs of their data center, even down to the specific requirements of a single room, rack or aisle.

Intel processor-based servers offer Node Manager for power management capabilities. Node Manager enables power management of the memory subsystem and processor socket power and is platform vendor independent.

Node Manager 2.0 offers the following features and capabilities:

- Monitors the memory subsystem and processor socket power
- Maintains the core power off at boot time
- Allows for processor power limiting
- Controls/caps the memory subsystem power via bandwidth management
- Provides platform power capping dynamically which during OS failure can prevent circuit breaker tripping

Node Manager 2.0 connects to IPMI (Intelligent Platform Management Interface) exposing monitoring, control and alerts to the user.

To implement Node Manager for energy management in a controlled fashion, it should be tested with a single server first. The purpose of single server testing is to make sure that Node Manager is well integrated with the server platform, and that the features of Node Manager are functioning properly. Single server testing also provides a baseline to calibrate that Node Manager against readings from the PDU. In addition, this process allows the user to characterize the application and the platform under test and identify the sweet spot for power management; optimizing power reduction in balance with performance loss.

After Node Manager is calibrated, it can then be set to limit power consumption in production. For optimum energy efficiency, the power should be limited to the system's maximum observed level during peak demand. Power capping sets the limit to a level that should not occur under normal operational circumstances. This is because of the significant performance impact that can occur if imposed consumption limits power during normal peak operating conditions. By establishing power limits for each server, the allocated power for the rack as a whole and the power actually consumed can be managed.

Power previously allocated for each single system but not required for their reliable operation can now be managed at a rack level. The surplus power harvested with this approach can thus be effectively used to add more systems to the rack. Maximum impact of this approach can be achieved by refreshing older lower performance per Watt systems with new, more efficient systems.

A final note on reducing power in microprocessors: underclocking, a process of running the CPU at voltages below the device specification draws less power. Underclocking reduces the performance of the CPU and server. A more efficient method that still supports business goals is to choose a processor that best fits the performance, power and price needs of the organization and use the tools designed to work with it to manage system power consumption.

Intel is also developing more energy-efficient chipset and memory technologies that will further increase server energy efficiency. To view the latest energy-efficiency benchmarks for Intel Xeon® processor-based servers, visit the Intel Web site at *www.intel.com*.

Reduced Power Memory Configurations

Memory can significantly affect the cost of a server and its power consumption. Server memory requirements are growing with multiple core processors, applications demanding higher bandwidth, increasing use of virtualization software and increasing growth of new Internet social applications such as Facebook and YouTube. As demand for memory grows for servers, this subsystem's power consumption will also grow. To build an energy efficient server, the memory should be chosen to:

- Be right-sized for the workload
- Utilize the latest memory technology
- Leverage the largest capacity and ranking per DIMM
- Support power reduction features

Given the cost and power impacts of memory choices, it should be chosen carefully.

To begin, memory for a server should be chosen to meet the workload designated for that server. The size and frequency of the memory modules should match the needs of the workload and the capabilities of the chipset. Anything larger or faster is a waste of budget and power.

The latest memory technology will generally be the most energy efficient. Recent advancements in memory technology are helping to improve the energy efficiency of servers. DDR3 (Double Data Rate 3) operates at 1.5V, compared with DDR2 which operates at 1.8V. DDR4 is forecasted to operate at 1.2V. According to manufacturer data, next-generation memory modules (DDR4) may reduce server memory energy consumption by up to 24 percent. Newer generations of memory technology take advantage of the latest manufacturing process technologies and improve power efficiency by reducing the amount of energy required per memory cell.

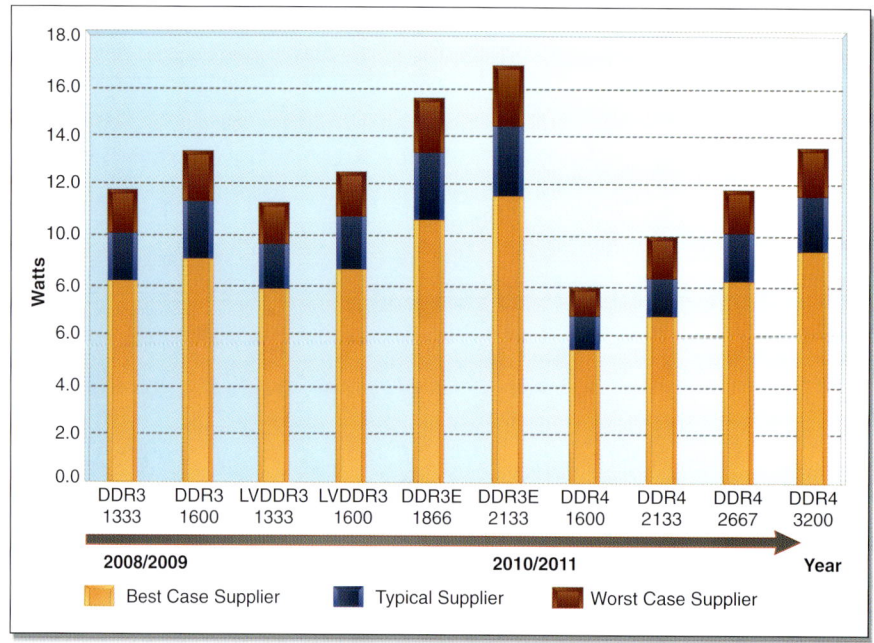

Figure 7.4 Server DRAM Power Per DIMM

Source: Intel Labs, 2008 (Power measurements were taken with 1 DIMM/channel, dual rank x4 ECC UDIMM, 2Gb, TDP workload 70% bandwith, 67% Read, Page close.)

Figure 7.4 illustrates how average and forecasted power consumption can vary between DDR3 and DDR4 memory modules.

Memory power consumption is heavily dependent upon the quantity, type, vendor and part number of DIMMs installed. A good memory rule of thumb for energy efficient servers is "the smaller the number of DIMMs, the less power consumed." A 1GB x4 DDR3-800 RDIMM consumes approximately 8W; a 2GB x4 DDR3-800 RDIMM consumes approximately 10W. If the workload requires 8 GB of memory capacity, eight times 8W (1GB RDIMMs) will consume 64W. However, four times 10W (2GB RDIMMs) only consumes 40W, a savings of 24W. Fewer DIMMs installed with larger GB capacity per DIMM is always better, if the performance allows.

Memory width is similar to smaller capacity DIMMs. A x4 DIMM takes more power than x8 DIMM. For the least power consumption, always install x8 DIMMs, if possible.

Selection of DIMMs with memory power management features can significantly impact power. Newer memory modules have two power reduction features. The first is dynamic CKE. The second state is Self Refresh.

Dynamic CKE is a technique which involves reducing the clock and clock buffering when the DRAMs on the DIMM are not being utilized. Dynamic CKE is only used when a full rank is idle. The penalty for idling the memory clock is minimal and this procedure does not affect performance. Dynamic CKE is active during normal memory operations, and the memory controller automatically activates dynamic CKE when it detects an idle rank. This feature will save about 1.9W per DIMM.

> **Definition of a Rank**
>
> The term *rank* was created by the memory industry standards group, JEDEC. A memory rank is an addressable 64-bit data area of a DIMM. Each rank must be 64-bits wide except on DIMMs that support Error Correction Code (ECC). ECC DIMMS use an extra 8-bit wide area for the ECC making the total width equal to 72-bits.
>
> DIMMs could support 1, 2, or 4 ranks making them either a single, dual, or quad rank module. A single rank DIMM or dual rank DIMM are not the same as a single-sided or double-sided DIMM.
>
> A rank can apply to:
>
> - The whole module (either single or double sided) This is known as a single rank module
>
> - Each side of a double-sided module This is known as a dual rank module
>
> - Multiple ranks within a double-sided module This is known as a quad rank module. This is known as a quad rank module
>
> In general, single-sided DIMMs are usually single-ranked. Doubled-sided unbuffered UDIMMs are usually dual-ranked. Last but not least, RDIMMs, can vary from single to four ranks, as illustrated in Figure 7.5.

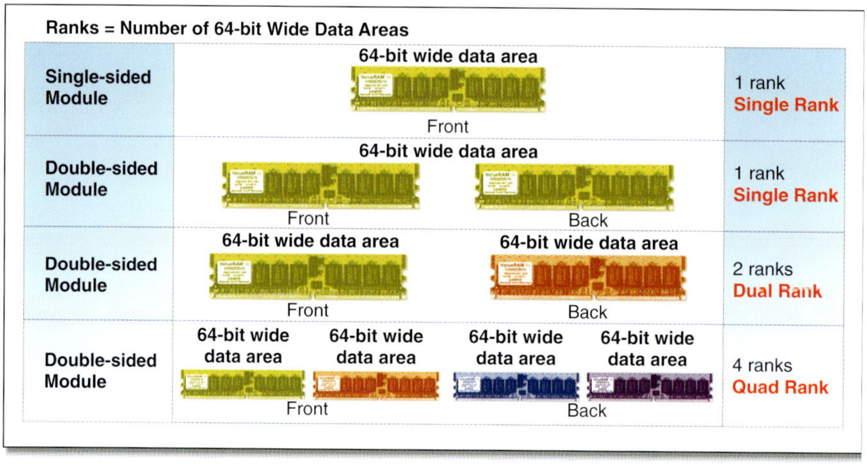

Figure 7.5 Ranks for DIMMs
Source: Kingston Technologies, 2005

Self refresh is a power savings technique used when all the cores in the CPU are idle or are in a deeper idle state, such as C3 or C6. When the processor is in this deeper idle or sleep state, there are no transactions going to memory so the memory can be detached and put into self-refresh mode. This results in a notable power savings from powering down IOs and interface logic. This feature saves about 2.4W per DIMM. The exit latency from this state is larger in this mode than dynamic CKE. The transition in-and-out of self refresh is also more disruptive since the server needs to bring the CPU cores out of idle at the same time.

While both dynamic CKE and self-refresh will reduce memory power, these features require long idle periods between memory accesses to be used successfully. For example, greater than 100 nanoseconds for dynamic CKE usage and greater than 100 microseconds are needed for channel memory self-refresh. Further, channels and ranks must be de-interleaved to enable alignment of the OS memory view with the physical memory view.

The OS typically interleaves blocks of contiguous memory over multiple memory channels, DIMMs, and ranks. This is a different view of memory than the memory controller view. Interleaving is typically used to avoid memory hotspots. It spreads an OS page (4K) across every DRAM chip. In addition to enabling the power management features, another power saving trick is to forgo the last few levels of interleaving. To do this, let the channel or rank map to large (GB) sequential memory blocks. The OS/VMM will then coalesce the memory by these large blocks. If there is low memory capacity demand; then one or more large blocks will be unused, and dynamic CKE can power down the corresponding channel/rank. By doing this, rank de-interleave accelerates the dynamic CKE usage.

Table 7.4 summarizes the options and considerations that should be used for reduced power consumption within the memory subsystem of an energy efficient server. Remember to always choose DIMMs wisely to reduce power consumption.

Table 7.4 Memory Summary

Item	Lowest Power Option	Power Savings (Per DIMM)
Number of DIMMs	Use less DIMMs. Use the least number of DIMMs to get the memory capacity needed (use quantity four 2GB instead of quantity of eight 1GB DIMMs	~5 - 21 W for each DIMM not installed
Component Density	Use higher density DIMMs. Use 2 or 4Gb DRAM components instead of 1Gb. This may impact DIMM price since higher density DRAMs usually command a price premium.	Up to ~ 8W. Power savings will vary by vendor and DRAM process technology.
Memory Configuration/ Memory Rank	Use higher memory configurations and ranks. Choose x8 in preference to x4. Choose the highest number of ranks for a given capacity. The number of memory controller chip selects available may limit the number of memory ranks supported. Also check that the RAS features required are supported with the x8 DIMM.	Up to ~ 8W. Power savings will vary by vendor and DRAM process technology.
DIMM Speed	Use lower speed DIMMs. For example, use DDR3-1067 MHz, instead of DDR3-1333. Note this will reduce memory performance.	~1.5 - 2.5W
Latency Timing	Use DIMMs with higher latency DDR timings. Use '5-5-5' instead of '4-4-4'. Higher latency may reduce memory performance.	~0.3 - 0.5W
Memory Power Management	Enable memory power management. Enable CKE and memory self refresh if these options are available in the BIOS.	Idle power reduction varies

Options for Reduced Power Storage

Green storage is a combination of technologies, practices and policies that lead to lower and more efficient energy use. As systems administrators consolidate applications onto larger and cooler servers, the emphasis on saving energy also requires consideration of disk storage systems. The optimal energy efficient storage solution, similar to servers, will depend on the details of an organization's workload requirements, specific application types and usage profiles, including reliability requirements. Reducing power consumption in storage is not as simple as shutting everything off and putting it on tape. Businesses have multiple types of data, and some of that data is most likely time and performance sensitive. Options for energy efficient storage include:

- Establishing tiered storage, with archival storage on tape
- Consolidating and virtualizing storage
- Using small form factor drives
- Using slower drives or solid state drives (SSDs) where possible
- Reducing data footprint
- Using variable speed disks or massive arrays of idle disks (MAIDs)

Data Tiers

One of the first methods of reducing power consumption associated with storage is to break the storage into tiers. Not all data needs to be immediately available; some data is rarely used at all but must be retained for legal or compliance reasons. The idea behind using tiers is to reduce performance in alignment with business requirements, and hence optimize power use.

Tiered storage is the assignment of different categories of data to different types of storage media; from magnetic tape at the low power end of the spectrum, through optical, to magnetic disk. Categories may be based on levels of protection needed, performance requirements, frequency of use, or other business considerations. Establishing tiered storage and constantly managing data to a specific tier is an ongoing process as is the need to de-duplicate data sets. Many software vendors provide solutions to automatically manage the process based on defined policies.

Here is an example of how tiered storage can reduce power consumption. Mission-critical, recently accessed, or confidential files are Tier 1 data that need to be stored on expensive and high-quality media such as double-parity redundant arrays of independent disks (RAIDs). Seldom used files, such as financial or HR classified files, are Tier 2 data and can be stored on less expensive, slower media which consume less power, perhaps in a conventional storage area network (SAN). Event-driven, rarely used, or unclassified files are Tier 3 data and can be stored on tape, which is the lowest power consumer. Additional power saving options to consider with Tier 2 or Tier 3 data storage include co-location of data and use of slower drives.

Storage consolidation and virtualization is another method to reducing power consumption. Storage consolidation is different than server consolidation. Server consolidation reduces the number of distributed servers in an organization to fewer, more powerful servers. Storage consolidation, in contrast, uncouples storage from servers, placing storage on a separate network where it can be shared. Doing so reduces capital investment and improves power efficiency. For consolidated storage, data files are shared on a network using network attached storage (NAS) devices or raw block data can be shared on a storage area network (SAN). Both of these storage technologies can reduce the number of rotating drive spindles and improve energy efficiency per GB.

Within storage networks, there are options for additional energy efficiencies. For large organizations that have a SAN, curtailing the proliferation of NAS devices for file storage can be accomplished by deploying a NAS gateway (that is, a head) to the SAN. Consolidating backup storage and SAN islands will also reduce storage power consumption. And as with implementing tiered storage, consolidating the storage networks to larger capacity disk drives will yield fewer storage systems and thus reduce the collective energy and cooling requirements. As with any efficiency programs, you should check that consolidation or virtualization changes do not put application service and performance objectives at risk. The best storage solution balances the business needs with the power needs and efficiency.

Storage Form Factor

Smaller form factor hard disk drives (HDDs) require less power. Compared to a standard 3.5 inch HDD, a 2.5 inch HDD can save considerable space, reduce generated heat, and improve cooling in a 1U server. For example, three 3.5 inch HDD will use 13.1 square inches of frontal server area. Four 2.5 inch HDD would use only 7.2 square inches of frontal area, providing a potential additional 5.9 square inches for airflow venting. If employed, the additional vent area would reduce air flow constraints and increase the volume of air that system fans can move through the server per unit of power required by their motors.

Smaller form factor (SFF) disk drives require less power for rotating their magnetic platters. 2.5 inch HDDs use about 5 volts versus 12 volts required for a standard 3.5 inch form factor. In general, 2.5 inch drives

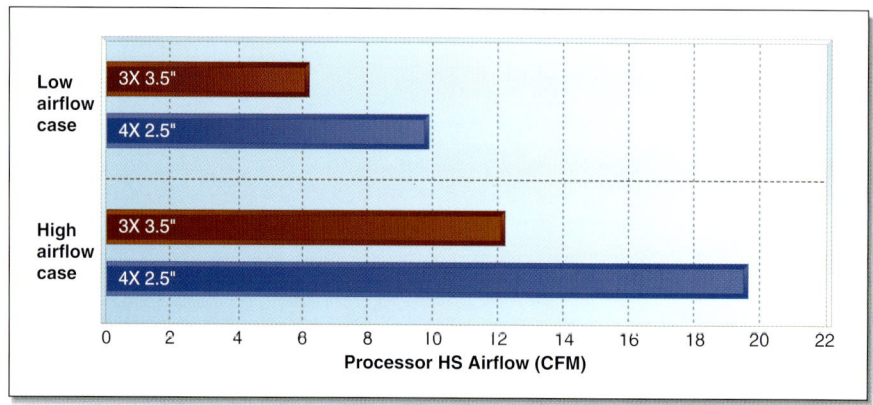

Figure 7.6 Storage Form Factor and CPU Cooling
Source: Intel Labs, 2007

use 40 percent less power and enable greater storage density. SFF 2.5 inch drives are 70 percent smaller than 3.5 inch drives, enabling them to deliver 130 to 150 percent greater system performance in the same footprint. When a SFF 2.5 inch drive is complemented with a Serial Attached SCSI (SAS) interface, it provides superior throughput (that is, 6 Gbits/sec) with more compact cabling and connectors that use less enclosure space, thus significantly enhancing airflow/cooling in high-density computing environments (Raffo 2007).

Figure 7.6 shows how 2.5 inch HDDs improve airflow by 56-58 percent versus 3.5 inch HDDs in a 1U server. Figure 7.7 shows how 2.5 inch HDDs improve airflow over memory even when the DIMMs are behind the HDDs.

Within any storage system or array, power is driven by drive size (number of platters and their diameter) and rotational speed of the component drives (RPM). A simple method to reduce power usage is to minimize the drive count, size, and rotational speed.

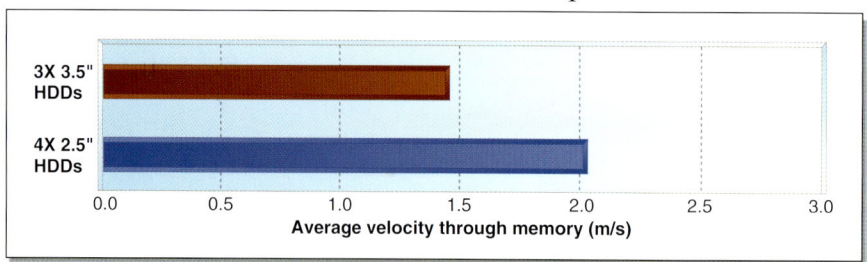

Figure 7.7 Storage Form Factor and RAM Cooling
Source: Intel Labs, 2007

Components of Energy Efficient Servers   **145**

Hard drives continue to grow in capacity and improve power-efficiency. For example, replacing a series of existing 250 GB hard drives with 750 GB or larger models will be more energy efficient. Capacity is dramatically expanded, but the actual number of drive platters stays the same. Power demands remain roughly equivalent.

Generally, to reduce power, use slower drives where possible. Using 7,200 RPM or 10,000 RPM disks versus 15,000 RPM drives will reduce power because the slower spin rates use less energy.

Newer drive designs are also changing to reduce power demands. Some drives support variable spindle speeds, allowing drives to slow down when they're not accessed. Hybrid drives include significant amounts of memory on the drive itself. This reduces regular platter access and allows the spindles to spin down more frequently and save power.

Solid-state Memory

The use of solid-state memory devices (SSDs) are emerging as an energy-efficient storage option in data centers. Most SSDs are composed of non-volatile (FLASH-NAND) memory as the storage media. SSDs are cost effective in terms of energy and space. As Figure 7.8 illustrates, they

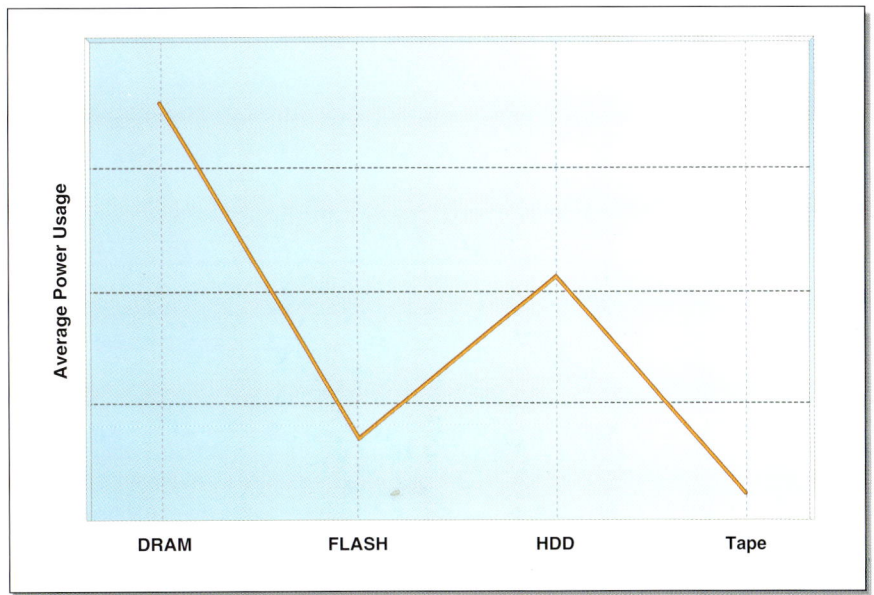

Figure 7.8   Relative Power Usage of Storage Media
Source: Intel Labs, 2008

require less space (than HDDs) and have lower overall power consumption (lower heat production per unit of storage and reduction of power due to elimination of moving parts). In addition, they offer performance benefits; each SSD can support hundreds to thousands of IOPS as compared to 100-300 IOPS per HDD.

Today, SSDs are more expensive per unit of storage than HDDs, but they can be cost effective in some environments. SSDs are a good fit for I/O intensive and time-sensitive applications or applications where short-stroking the HDD is used to improve performance. Environments in which there are low drive write demands are also ideal for SSDs.

SSD technology yields significant idle power savings per drive. The savings can be anywhere between 5W to 9W depending on the workload. SSDs can also reduce power consumption by as much as 18 Watts for blades. For workloads requiring many drives per server (for example, web or database servers), total power savings may be amplified by the reduction in number hard disk drives required and the supporting storage network/infrastructure that would be required for a large number of HDDs. This is due to the high bandwidth capabilities provided by SSDs.

For example, Intel Labs has tested a high IOPS application that required 450 80GB disk drives to meet performance targets. This same application reached the same level of IOPS using only 15 120GB SSDs. The cost for 450 hard drives, using industry average pricing, would be USD 175,000. The cost of 15 SSD drives would be USD 187,500. But the 450 HDDs also require multiple enclosures, racks, cables, transceivers, controllers and SAN switches necessary to house and connect all of the hard drives. This infrastructure brings the total HDD cost up to USD 413,000. The total SSD cost, which required one enclosure, rack, cable, transceiver, controller and switch, comes to a bit more than USD 201,000. This example demonstrates where a SSD solution would be much more cost effective than that of a HDD solution from a capital purchase perspective and drive significant power efficiency improvements throughout the data center ecosystem.

Reducing the Amount of Data

Reducing the number of disks is one method for reducing the amount of data center power that storage consumes. A direct approach to reducing the number of disks is to reduce the amount of data stored. Techniques that reduce the amount of data include data de-duplication and lossless compression.

Data growth is common across all businesses. Consider a typical email with a 1 MB sales presentation attached that is sent out to 20 colleagues. A typical business would keep copies of all emails on a central email server, which, in order to keep the email system reliable, includes a redundant server. The original file and the file at each recipient would be backed up daily to a server. The servers are then backed up to tape or archival disk. The original 1 MB email now has a footprint 100 times larger than itself. This typical example shows how storage data, and the number of disks (also power) quickly grow within a data center.

Data De-duplication

Data de-duplication is a technique for reducing storage volume by eliminating redundant data. Only one unique instance of the data is retained on the storage media, such as disk or tape. Redundant data is replaced with a pointer to the unique data copy. Data de-duplication can vastly reduce data storage demands by ratios of 20:1 or even 50:1. While de-duplication has mainly appeared in archive and virtual tape library (VTL) systems, the technique is appearing more frequently in primary storage. De-duplication is often coupled with tiered storage so that the online data is moved from high performance (power hungry) storage to slower, high capacity near-line storage as soon as possible.

Data de-duplication is really just traditional compression, except that it operates on much larger datasets, eliminating all duplicate chunks of data under management. Data de-duplication can generally operate at the file, block, and even the bit level. The de-duped data is compressed using more traditional pattern-based compression techniques. The amount of space required to store de-duped data is dependent upon the amount of redundancy in the data. It should be noted that there may be performance penalties when decompressing the data when it is needed.

In the example above, with data de-duplication, only one instance of the 1MB sales presentation attachment is actually stored. All other repeated instances are referenced back to one saved copy. In this example, a 100 MB storage demand is reduced to only one MB.

De-duplication is ultimately a post-processing activity that requires investment in net additional storage capacity to achieve. The technique provides cost avoidance by way of minimizing or slowing down the rate of future storage capacity investments. With file de-duplication, there is always a tradeoff relative to reliability and a single copy of data.

Lossless Compression

Lossless compression, on the other hand, requires a minimal footprint and typically works with existing storage to improve capacity and power efficiency. Lossless data compression is a class of data compression algorithms that reconstruct the exact original data from the compressed data. The term lossless is in contrast to lossy data compression algorithms that reconstruct an approximation of the original data in exchange for better compression ratios.

Lossless compression is used when it is important that the original and the decompressed data be identical, or when no assumption can be made on whether certain deviation is acceptable. Typical examples include executable programs and source code.

As with data de-duplication, lossless compression affects performance. With any data compression methods, latency is increased and there may be a significant unpack/inflate penalty. Also, these methods can develop hotspots. It is always a good idea to spread data across multiple disks.

Massive Array of Idle Disks

A final strategy is to power off selected drives. This last option is known as massive array of idle disks (MAID), which reduces energy use without compromising application performance. With a MAID, no more than 25 percent of all drives are powered up at any given time, significantly lowering power consumption while prolonging the life and MTBF of the disk drives. The acquisition cost of MAID subsystems is lowered because the MAID controller has to support only 25 percent of the memory, I/O connections, and total devices at any one time. While MAID technology is not recommended for high performance Tier 1 workloads, it is well suited for nearline and archival storage systems, or *write once read seldom if ever* (WORSE) applications.

A note of caution with implementing MAIDs: powering disks up and down may become a problem if they are fibre channel (FC), SAS or SCSI-based. These disks are designed to be powered up and run 7x24 for several years without spinning down. There is currently no clear agreement on whether these disks pose a problem in MAID systems. Some studies have shown that the reliability gain from not running equipment continuously can more than offset the reliability reduction from on/off cycles. Meanwhile, SATA drives are designed to be powered up and down. Manufacturer's ratings confirm approximately 30,000 power up/down operations can be expected from SATA devices.

In summary, options to reduce power consumption from storage include:

- Establishing tiered storage to move data from power hungry high performance disks to slower, more energy efficient storage media as business requirements allow
- Consolidating to higher-capacity storage devices and storage systems to reduce spindle count
- Taking advantage of new drive technologies that vary spindle RPM and reduce seek activity
- Switching to small form factor 2.5" drives for 40 percent less operating power than standard 3.5-inch HDD
- Using slower drives where possible
- Leveraging SSD with idle power savings for high performance workloads that have low write demands
- Reducing storage demand (data size and multiple copies) with data de-duplication and lossless compression tools
- Powering off drives with MAID systems

Fans: Keeping It Cool with Less Power

Efficient cooling inside servers has become more complex and challenging as server form factors have shrunk. Voltage regulator FETs are requiring higher airflow and HDD density continue to increase. On average a 1U server now holds six to eight SATA/SAS drives, spinning and generating heat. Energy efficient fans do more than reduce overall server power consumption, they can also increase reliability and provide lower TCO over the life of the system.

What constitutes an energy efficient fan and cooling system? While any method used to move air around or to computer enclosures would count as air cooling, fans are by far the most commonly used implement for accomplishing this task. In general, larger fans are more energy efficient. That is one reason that blade servers tend to deliver better performance per Watt than comparable tower or rack-mount servers. They typically have just a few large fans and power supplies to support multiple servers.

Ideal airflow for cooling a server is cool air coming in at the bottom and, following the natural convective pattern of heat, hot air coming out at the top. An efficient fan will provide cross-flow air across the components inside, normally with the cooler air being drawn in from the front and sides and hot air being exhausted out at the top and back. Any server airflow design also needs to take the power supply's airflow into consideration so that two airflows do not conflict with each other.

In older servers, fan power consumption may be greater than the power consumed by memory. This can be addressed by providing internal variable speed fans for on-demand cooling. Energy efficient servers should support closed loop thermal throttling (CLTT) on the fan speed control. Thermal sensors should be placed at the inlet and at as many key components as possible. The power to the fan will scale up and down with the load.

Many factors can affect fan power consumption. Larger fans generally will move the same amount of air using less power than a small fan. Fewer fans strategically placed will improve the internal airflow and thus lower the overall internal case temperature in relation to ambient conditions. The use of larger fans also lowers the amount of waste heat along with the amount of noise generated by the fans while in operation.

Figure 7.9 Four-wire Blower Style Fan
Source: CoolerMaster, 2008

Four-wire blower style fans, as shown in Figure 7.9, are the most energy efficient. For optimal power reduction, fan speed should be set to the minimum or the lowest percentage while still supporting the required thermal limits for the server as recommended by the manufacturer. If the server has low utilization, it is possible to even consider using *off* as the lowest setting for the fans.

Other components within a server can affect the thermals and airflow and cause the fans to work less or more frequently. Many cards generate a lot of heat, such as RAID on board, or graphics. Some graphics cards have independent cooling fans to control the temperature of the graphics processing unit (GPU). Try to either leave the slot next to these cards open, or use a shorter card in these slots to allow airflow around the cards that are heat producers. Heat producers are typically those cards with many electrical components.

High-speed hard drives (especially 10,000 RPM SCSI hard drives) produce a great deal of heat. One way to minimize the heat with these drives is to use smaller form factor drives (2.5 inch) and mount them in larger full size (3.5 inch or 5.25 inch) drive bays, which allows a greater airflow around them, and more effective cooling without excessive fan utilization. In larger chassis, the drives may be staggered through the drive bay to provide open space in between for airflow.

Use of rounded cables within a server reduces surface area and increases airflow. Older systems use flat ribbon cables to connect storage drives (IDE or SCSI). These large flat cables greatly impede airflow by causing drag and turbulence. Rounded cables, with the conductive wires bunched together tightly will not hinder any airflow through the case and if the cables are short, the effect of crosstalk is negligible.

Finally, there are some exotic methods of cooling servers which, while they are not inexpensive, also do not consume significant power. Two of these methods are heat pipes with heat sinks and liquid submersion cooling. Heat pipes are sealed hollow tubes made of a thermo-conductive metal such as copper or aluminum that are used in conjunction with a standard heat sink and fin style blades.

Figure 7.10 Heat Pipes and Heat Sink
Photo source: Wikipedia.org, 2008

An example of heat pipes is shown in Figure 7.10. These systems are very efficient at transporting large quantities of heat within small spaces. The heat pipe is a tube or pipe that contains fluid or coolant (such as water, ethanol, or mercury) that passively transports heat away from the source to be dissipated at another point. In this case the heat pipe wicks heat away from the base to the fin area which usually sits strategically positioned in the airflow to maximize dissipation. The advantage of heat pipes is their great efficiency in transferring heat and thus relieving the fans from the cooling work. The heat from the source powers the process; no additional electricity is required.

Liquid submersion cooling is an uncommon practice that submerses the computer's components in a thermally conductive liquid. Computers that are cooled in this manner do not generally require any fans or pumps, and may be cooled exclusively by passive heat exchange between the computer's parts, the cooling fluid, and the ambient air.

The liquid used must have sufficiently low electrical conductivity in order for it not to interfere with the normal operation of the computer's components. If the liquid is somewhat electrically conductive, it may be necessary to insulate certain parts of components susceptible to electromagnetic interference, such as the CPU. For these reasons, it is preferred that the liquid be dielectric.

Efficient Power Supplies

Choosing a high efficiency power supply can have the single greatest effect on overall system power. By using energy efficient power supplies, the potential power savings can be 100W or greater per system. To illustrate this point, a 400W system load using a 60 percent efficient power supply consumes 560W at the wall. This same load using an 85 percent efficient power supply will only consume 460W. Furthermore, the 60 percent efficient server produces heat with the additional 100W that it consumes!

Power consumption from power supplies is heavily dependent upon the power supply sizing and its efficiency. Greater efficiency means less power consumption because more of the AC power is converted into DC for the computer, rather than wasted as heat. The savings can really add up over time.

Choosing a Highly Efficient Power Supply

How should you choose a high efficiency power supply? First, always choose supplies that meet or exceed the 80 PLUS Specification standard. Power supply efficiency and performance can vary even within a vendor's product line. The 80 PLUS performance specification requires power supplies in computers and servers to be 80 percent or greater energy efficient at 20 percent, 50 percent and 100 percent of rated load with a true power factor of 0.9 or greater. This makes an 80 PLUS certified power supply substantially more efficient than average power supplies. Information on this standard can be found at *www.80plus.org*.

It is important to note that with power supplies, similar to the server systems, the manufacturer's rated power does not equal the actual measured power. The rated power is the summation of the system component TDPs for a fully loaded system. The measured power is the actual power (that is, Watts) drawn from the wall. Power supplies for servers are sized for the maximum loads expected when the server is fully configured, so the actual measured loads observed in typical installations are much lower than the rated power of the power supply. To

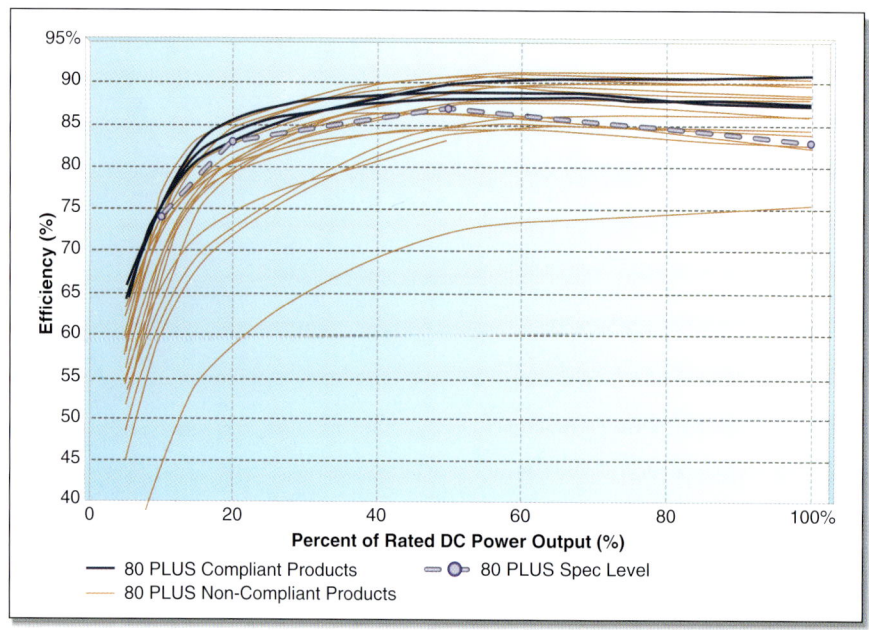

Figure 7.11 Efficiency of Single Output PSUs versus 80 PLUS PSUs
Source: Ecos and EPRI, Server Research Report, February 2008

obtain the actual measured power consumption of any power supply, use a power meter inserted between the system under test and the wall outlet.

To properly compare power supplies, wattage claims must state the maximum ambient temperature for continuous, full-load operation. Unfortunately manufacturers usually do not publish this information and tend to exaggerate their wattage claims. They do so by assuming an unrealistic ambient temperature of only 25°C (77°F), even though the actual internal power supply temperature is at least 40°C (104°F). Since the proper full-load rating is 25°C higher for data center use, these power supplies produce 33 percent to 50 percent less power than their advertised ratings.

There are additional items which can reduce power consumption in power supplies. Things to keep in mind when selecting power supplies include:

Avoid power supplies with modular plugs. Modular plugs limit power by adding to electrical resistance and the voltage drop can be as much as would occur in two feet of standard wire. Best choice is uninterrupted wire.

Favor DC power supplies over AC/DC conversion power supplies. Removing the AC/DC conversion and directly feeding DC could improve both reliability and efficiency. With DC power, there are fewer potential points of failure and fewer conversion losses.

Use a power supply with venting in the processor region. This means that the primary air-intake is on the bottom of the power supply, not the front of the power supply. Some power supplies have *NLX-style* venting where the primary air intake is at the front of the power supply. NLX-style power supplies do not pull air from the processor area. By pulling air from the processor region, the power supply can help with system cooling.

Choose single fan units over dual fan power supplies. A power supply with two fans doesn't exhaust any more air from the case than a power supply with one. This is because, due to space limitations, only one fan can be used for exhaust while the other is limited to spot cooling.

Avoid multiple 12 volt rails in favor of a single 12 volt rail that will waste less power. A single 12-volt rail (without a 240VA limit) can transfer 100 percent of the 12-volt output from the power supply to the server. A multi-rail 12-volt design has distribution losses of up to 30 percent of the power supply's rating. Those losses occur because power literally gets trapped on under-utilized rails. For example, if the 12-volt rail that powers the CPU is rated for 17 amps and the CPU only uses 7A, the remaining 10A is unusable because it is isolated from the rest of the system.

Avoid oversized power supplies and avoid using redundant supplies if possible. Aim to keep the load in the efficient portion of the power supply efficiency curve.

Newer power supplies offer feature improvements such as fan speed control and over-current protection. Recent motherboard and chipset improvements permit monitoring the revolutions per minute (RPM) of the power supply fan via BIOS and a Windows[†] application supplied by the motherboard manufacturer. These new designs offer fan control so that the fan only runs the speed needed to keep the system board and various components within operating temperature limits.

Power supplies now also have a circuit called over-current protection (OCP). If a component in the server malfunctions intermittently, perhaps due to an improperly seated card, the component will draw excessive current, trip the OCP circuit, and shut off the computer.

Energy Star Standards for Power Supplies

Last but not least, the EPA has set standards for power supply efficiency in computers. The new Energy Star standard, which took effect in July 2007, requires power supplies to be at least 80 percent efficient for most of their load range. In addition, it puts limits on the energy used by devices when inactive and requires systems to be shipped with power management features enabled. As shown in Table 7.5, the Energy Star standard started with requirements for desktops, laptops, and workstations but now includes the following high-efficiency targets for x86 servers (1U/2U single- and dual-socket servers) and gradually increases the efficiency requirements over the next four years, as follows:

1. From July 2008 through June 2009, the standard increases to 89 percent minimum efficiency for the PSU at 50 percent of rated output (and 85 percent minimum efficiency at 20 percent and 100 percent of rated output).

2. From July 2009 through June 2010, the standard increases to 92 percent minimum efficiency for the PSU at 50 percent of rated output (and 88 percent minimum efficiency at 20 percent and 100 percent of rated output).

Table 7.5 EPA Power Supply Unit Requirements

Source: www.energystar.gov

	Volume server minimum efficiency targets			
	July '07 – June '08	July '08 – June '09	July '09 – June '10	July '10 – June '11
85% PSU	≥ 20%	≥ 80%	≥ 80%	100%
89% PSU		≥ 20%	≥ 40%	100%
92% PSU				≥ 20%

Effective February 1, 2009, all power supplies in servers must meet the minimum efficiency and power factor requirements contained in Table 7.6 and Table 7.7.

Table 7.6 Efficiency Requirements for Server Power Supplies

Source: www.energystar.gov

Power Supply Type	Rated Output Power	10% Load	20% Load	50% Load	100% Load
Multi-Output (AC-DC & DC-DC)	All Output Levels	N/A	82%	85%	82%
Single-Output (AC-DC & DC-DC)	≤ 1,000 Watts	75%	85%	89%	85%
	> 1,000 Watts	80%	88%	92%	88%

Table 7.7 Power Factor Requirements for Server Power Supplies

Source: www.energystar.gov

Power Supply Type	Rated Output Power	10% Load	20% Load	50% Load	100% Load
DC-DC (All)	All Output Levels	N/A	N/A	N/A	N/A
AD-DC Single-Output	≤ 1,000 Watts	0.65	0.80	0.90	0.90
	> 1,000 Watts	0.80	0.90	0.90	0.90
AC-DC Multi-Output	All Output Levels	N/A	0.80	0.90	0.90

Configuring OS and Applications for Low Power

Altering the CPU's P-state can reduce a server's power consumption at low utilization without limiting any of the performance needed at peak demand levels. The switch between P-states is dynamically controlled by the operating system and occurs in micro-seconds, causing no perceptible performance degradation.

There are six P-states, ranging from P0 at full CPU utilization to P5 in which the CPU is at idle. The highest P-state runs the processor at full clock speed and full voltage. But during off-peak conditions, the clock can reduce clock speed back to a 1GHz idle, saving as much as 75 percent of the full-speed CPU power.

Although a processor may be P-state capable, both the system Basic Input-Output System (BIOS) and the operating system must be capable of enabling the feature to make use of it. P-states can be defined and managed in the BIOS, but most multiprocessor-based servers will implement them in the operating system's kernel. Servers respond very quickly to P-state changes so the processor power and speed closely follow the workload. As a result, heat does not build up unnecessarily, which also provides for greater power savings from reduced cooling loads.

Operating System Capabilities

Microsoft Windows[†], Linux[†], and Sun[†] OpenSolaris[†] are the top three operating systems for x86 servers and each has power management capabilities. We shall explain the tools and methods for managing power consumption and the P-states on a server.

The Microsoft Windows[†] Operating System

Microsoft Windows XP[†] has several power-down states, including global-level states, sleep states, device-level states, and four dedicated C-states for the processor. Within its highest-power C-state, C0, the processor driver can impose several subdivided performance states. CPU power management technologies can operate independently of Windows XP as long as the OS has invoked the C0 state. Although it is somewhat unusual for server operating systems to invoke sleep states, if the OS were to go into standby, it would instruct the processor to go into its C3 state, which uses the lowest amount of power of the C-states.

Windows XP organizes its power management into policy and non-policy groups. These groups communicate with the processors through the Advanced Configuration and Power Interface (ACPI). The adaptive policy, for example, reduces processor performance to the lowest voltage and frequency state available whenever processor demand does not justify a higher state. This policy does not utilize linear stop-clock throttle states, except in response to thermal events.

Non-policy states, in contrast, are designed to conserve power in emergencies or prevent thermal damage. If the temperature exceeds a passive thermal point stored as a registry value, the OS uses successively lower performance levels to reduce the temperature below this point. If reduced performance levels do not alleviate the problem, the kernel uses stop clock throttling to help prevent damage.

Microsoft operating systems from Windows Server[†] 2003 onwards automatically include Intel P-state support. Add-in drivers are available from server manufacturers that enable support in Windows 2000[†]. Although the relevant drivers may be installed, the correct Windows[†] power scheme must also be selected for P-state control to be put into effect.

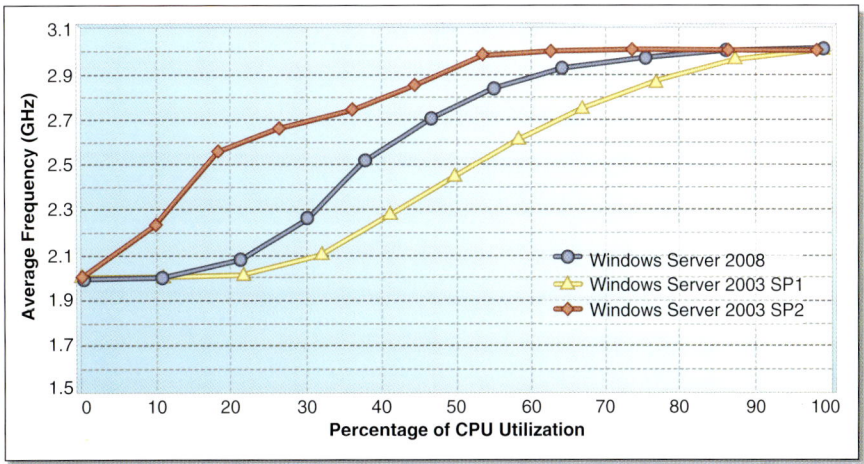

Figure 7.12 SPECpower_ssj2005 Results for Versions of Windows[†] Server
Source: Intel Labs, 2008

The power scheme to enable this function in Windows 2000[†] Server and Windows Server 2003 (up to Service Pack 1) is called Minimal Power Management. In Windows Server 2003 Service Pack 2, the scheme is called Server Balanced Power and Performance. Windows Server 2008 automatically enables P-state control for the system with no user interaction required. Figures 7.12 and 7.13 illustrate the power savings from Windows Server 2008 over Windows Server 2003 SP2.

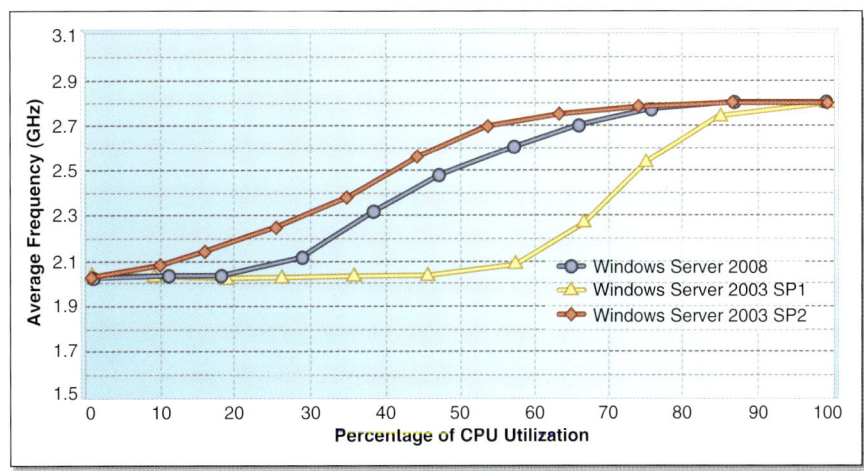

Figure 7.13 TPC-C Results for Versions of Windows Server[†]
Source: Intel Labs, 2008

Windows Server 2008 does a better job of power management than Windows Server 2003 SP2. Windows Server 2008 enables power management by default.

The power management features are automatic as long as they are enabled in the BIOS. With these features enabled, up to 20W savings can be seen in the SPECpower_ssj2005 benchmark and up to 10W savings can be seen with TPC-C benchmarks.

Linux[†] Operating System

Linux[†] has proactive OS-directed power management (OSPM) cooling policies and a comprehensive ACPI implementation with table-driven settings that map to the microprocessor P-states. OSPM provides both an active cooling model for performance and a passive cooling model for reduced power consumption. OSPM also provides critical points with multiple thermal thresholds which can be implemented for system protection and orderly idling or shutdown in case of thermal failure.

The energy-saving choices available with the Linux 2.6 kernels shipped with RHEL[†] 5.1 and SUSE[†] Enterprise Linux 10 focus on the ability to throttle back CPU clock speed through a kernel module called cpufreq. These power-saving modes are called *governors* and are officially referred to as *performance*, *on-demand*, *power save*, and *conservative*. There is a fifth, *user-space governor*, but it focuses only on specific, policy-defined root objects. The server's BIOS and firmware must be sufficiently upgraded to correctly support these features under Linux.

The Linux kernel, starting from version 2.6.18, supports multiple power saving settings. The following commands enable access to the settings:

/sys/devices/system/cpu/ controls the Multi-core related setting
sched_mc_power_savings
Setting - 0 (default, optimal performance; , no power saving)
Setting - 1 (power saving enabled)

/sys/devices/system/cpu/ controls the multi-threading setting
sched_smt_power_savings
Setting - 0 (default, optimal performance; , no power saving)
Setting - 1 (power saving enabled)

The latest information on updates to Linux power management can be found at *www.intel.com*.

Demand Base Switching (DBS) works with Linux operating systems out of the box. There are a few exceptions of specific distributions which are identified below.

- Distributions that do not support P-states
  - RHEL3 and earlier
  - SLES8 and earlier
- Distributions that support P-states with user-level governor:
  - RHEL4 and SLES9
- Distributions that support P-states with on-demand:
  - RHEL5 and SLES10 and later

Linux power management first started with APM, but now all current versions support ACPI. ACPI places the responsibility of power management away from the BIOS and into the hands of the operating system. ACPI Linux is newer than APM Linux, it is more flexible in responding to power management events, and has seen much more recent development.

There are two parts to ACPI under Linux: the ACPI driver built into the kernel itself, and the ACPI daemon (ACPID). The current version of ACPID is very straightforward: monitor /proc/acpi/event and respond with appropriate actions. Even if the daemon is not loaded, the ACPI features, such as processor thermal support, are built into the kernel and still function.

To determine which version of the ACPI driver you are using, along with supported suspend states, use the following:

```
bash $ cat /proc/acpi/info
version: 20030619
states:  S0 S1 S3 S4 S4 S5
```

If the ACPID daemon is not installed on your servers, you can download it from *http://sourceforge.net*. The server startup scripts should be configured to activate it on boot:

```
if [ -x /usr/sbin/acpid -a -d /proc/acpi ]; then
  echo "Starting ACPID Daemon: /user/sbin/acpid"
  /usr/sbin/acpid
```

There is a new tickless version of Linux that has power-saving benefits. System-interrupt ticks are time slices that the operating system uses to queue activities. Usually CPUs are set to 1,000 ticks per second, each of which serves as an interruption to the CPU. The tickless version of

Linux kernel interrupts the CPU far less than 1,000 ticks per second. If your servers do not run the tickleless version of Linux, the best method for reducing server power under Linux OS is to keep all systems updated to the most recent distributions.

Sun OpenSolaris[†]

The Sun Solaris[†] operating system provides a scripted, command-line interface control language that affords data center managers full command over the OS-independent ACPI and lower-level P-states. Thermal management can be tailored to individual servers and workloads.

The Solaris operating system supports P-states with tools to enable these states. One such tool is called Project Tesla: OpenSolaris Enhanced Power Management[†]. Information on this tool can be found by searching for tesla at *www.opensolaris.org*.

This tool features CPU frequency/voltage scaling support, CPU throttling and support for suspend to RAM on x86 servers. The Solaris operating system takes advantage of P-states by default, that is, no user configuration is required. The following command will list the available P-states for the CPU on a server:

$ kstat -m cpu_info -s supported_frequencies_Hz

If more than one supported frequency is listed for each of the CPU instances, this means that Solaris supports frequency scaling of those CPUs.

CPU power management can be enabled on Intel Xeon® servers. The CPU idle threshold can be set by adding the following two entries to the power configuration file:

cpupm enable and cpu-thresholds

After the desired idle threshold has been reached, verification that the CPU(s) are running at the lowest supported frequency can be validated via the following command:

$ kstat -m cpu_info -s current_clock_Hz

Optimizing Applications for Reduced Power Consumption

Multi-core processors deliver immediate performance and energy efficiency benefits for multi-threaded applications, which include all major OSs and database software, as well as many technical, financial and high-performance computing (HPC) applications. They can also improve total throughput for multiple applications running simultaneously in virtualized server environments.

Optimizing software for multi-threaded throughput can accelerate performance and improve utilization, which reduces the amount of energy required to accomplish the same work. Sixty-four bit migration can deliver similar benefits for data-intensive applications, enabling faster response times and better scalability within approximately the same power envelope.

Intel provides software development tools to simplify migrating applications for energy efficiency. Intel compilers, performance analyzers, threading tools, and libraries are now used by over 200,000 commercial, open source, and corporate developers. These tools are optimized for multi-threaded throughput and are compatible with popular development environments. They help to deliver leading performance and energy-efficiency of applications across all compatible server platforms, while delivering best results for Intel processor-based systems (because they are highly tuned to take advantage of Intel's unique architectural features).

A power management strategy should be set for each application when that application is in development. At a high level, the power management strategy should include capturing power consumption data of the application as it is executed on a target system. The next step is to make modifications to the application to improve the application's energy efficiency. Each application should incorporate a power scaling library. Finally, all applications should be modified to use the dynamic frequency and voltage scaling functionality provided by the power scaling library.

Some additional steps which can improve energy efficiency of applications are as follows:

- Design software to avoid excess code and inefficiencies. Treat the CPU cycles as a finite resource.
- Utilize developer tools designed to improve efficiency of software.
- Enable applications to shift the computational load among systems for maximizing energy efficiency.
- Upgrade applications no longer supported on the latest technology and/or operating systems, allowing removal of legacy servers.
- Implement virtualization to allow consolidation of server and storage hardware.

Finally, there are several methods to activate sleep settings across entire networks of servers. These solutions utilize free software tools and are relatively straight-forward to use.

- Microsoft's Windows Vista[†] operating system provides a way to centrally manage and monitor computer power management features.
- EZ GPO allows a network administrator to centrally control computer power management and monitor power management settings using Group Policy Objects.
- If your IT organization replicates hard drives from a template image when upgrading operating systems or rolling out new hardware, enabling sleep settings in the template image will ensure that all computers receive these settings.
- Powerconfig.exe can be used in a logon script to configure power management settings in Windows XP and Vista. This method requires enhancing registry rights, which can be configured through Group Policy.
- Windows Task Scheduler[†] can be used to put servers into standby or hibernate mode.
- EZ Wizard is a simple software tool that automatically activates sleep settings on individual servers. Because it can be launched from a website, EZ Wizard is an ideal solution for diverse computing environments.

For assistance with application migration or tools, Intel® Software Network offers extensive training and code development support for energy efficient applications. More information on the Software Network can be found at *www.software.intel.com/en*. Additionally, the Intel® Software College (*www.intel.com/software/college/*) offers training, information and resources that can help software developers optimize their software for power reduction more effectively and at less cost.

Power Impacts of Consolidation and Virtualization

Under-utilization of servers is one of the most common reasons for sub-optimal energy efficiency in data centers. Maximizing the utilization of existing servers therefore represents one of the greater opportunities for energy savings in many data centers.

Initially, many IT organizations deployed their infrastructure in a one application per server configuration. Some warm spare or clustered configurations designed to improve availability actually used more than one server per application. As an alternative, IT organizations can use virtualization technology to divide the resources of a single, powerful server among several applications. Combined with other virtual computing enablers, such as storage area networks (SANs), virtualization creates a pool of computing resources that can be used as necessary. Consolidation enables a data center to add applications without adding hardware, easing the load on cooling and heat management systems.

For data centers where primary workloads are designed with efficient distribution across multiple servers, virtualization can still provide benefits. Secondary workloads and infrequently used applications can be consolidated and virtualized, reducing the number of servers.

Virtualization will increase the processor utilization level and power usage of the host server. However, this incremental gain in host server energy use is more than offset by the savings from eliminating the capital cost of additional infrastructure and the significant energy load associated with running multiple servers at low utilization rates. Additional benefits from virtualization technology include:

- Facilitating easy movement of applications among servers to increase application availability
- Controlling hot spots and thus optimizing thermal loading of the data center
- Maximizing the utilization of compute resources by shifting workloads

The savings from virtualization offer both immediate and long term savings and good payback for investing in a consolidation project.

While virtualization can provide significant cost reductions from higher application density per server, data center operators need to remember that high-density solutions do require more power per rack. A good target for server virtualization is at 60-65 percent CPU utilization. This target equates to a consolidation ratio of around five to 10 legacy servers to one new blade server. The new blade server with increased efficiencies will likely require less power and cooling than a comparable rack server. However, when fully populating each blade server chassis with blades and fully populating each rack with chassis, the rack may now require 20 - 35kW of power.

For many organizations, the combination of energy-efficient servers and better utilization can provide energy efficiency gains of up to 25 percent and higher. How is this possible? Typical server utilization is about 5-15 percent for organizations that use a one-application-per-server deployment model. Server utilization with virtualization is typically 30-60 percent, for about a factor of five improvement. Intel Xeon® processors with four cores are ideal for virtualization. They include integrated support for Intel® Virtualization technology, which reduces the need for compute-intensive software translations between the guest and host operating systems. With their greater processing capacity and superior virtualization efficiency, they can increase virtualization performance by as much as 2.5 times compared with typical dual-core systems.

Application consolidation, virtualization and server refresh can also reduce data center footprint and provide a more flexible and manageable IT infrastructure. In the future, interaction of server manageability technologies and facilities building management systems will provide even larger opportunities for energy efficiency and operating cost reductions.

Summary

Energy-efficient servers mean more than reduced power and cooling costs. They also enable higher application to server ratios and higher compute density, which translates to fewer servers and fewer racks for a given workload. Identifying energy wasters, enabling power saving features, right sizing components, powering down underutilized servers, and decommissioning legacy servers all represent major energy savings opportunities for data center operators.

The most dramatic advances are evident in the new generation of high-performance, energy-efficient Quad-Core Intel Xeon processors. Replacing single-core servers with new 45nm Quad-Core Intel Xeon processors provides IT payback in two years. Managed Core 2 Duo processor-based platforms are four times more efficient than prior generation un-managed platforms. Intel Xeon 5400 processors have up to 68% lower power in idle than prior generation (C1E) state.

Below is a summary of key points for building an energy efficient server.

1. Take advantage of new energy-efficient Dual-Core and Quad-Core Intel Xeon processor-based systems. They can improve performance by up to 3 times, while reducing power consumption (and heat generation) by more than 3 times.

2. Procure and configure new servers with latest memory technology. Doing so can increase performance by up to 11 percent for memory-intensive workloads while decreasing memory power consumption by 30 to 40 percent. Configure memory for the least power consumption by using higher capacity DIMMs with high density DRAM components. Use the highest number of ranks for a given capacity, for example, x8 instead of x4. Enable memory power management.

3. Virtualize and tier storage, keeping only time-sensitive data on high performance, power hungry disks. Consider SSDs for high performance, low write applications. For other data, use smaller form factor disks spinning at fewer RPMs. Put archival data on tape or move to data center locations with low electricity costs. Reduce data growth with data de-duplication or lossless compression. And use variable spin or MAIDs to take advantage of idle power savings.

4. Select larger fans with closed loop thermal throttling capability to provide the most efficient cooling.

5. Choose power supplies that meet or exceed the 80 PLUS specification standard.

6. Explore the benefits of blade servers. Blade architectures may reduce total power consumption per unit of compute power and deliver substantial TCO improvement due to reduced cabling, easier provisioning, and improved modularity. However, they may increase power and cooling density. It is therefore important to look at feasibility, total costs, risks, and benefits within your particular physical and operational environment to guide IT architecture and data center strategy.

7. Move to newer OSs for all platforms. Microsoft Windows Server 2008[†] supports Demand Based Switching, which can substantially reduce average system power consumption for servers operating at typical data center utilization rates. Enable the OS and BIOS to use power management and P-states.

8. Consolidate workloads to boost utilization. Multiple OS and application stacks can be consolidated on fewer servers using virtualization software, such as VMware[†] ESX Server, Microsoft[†]

Virtual Server or Xen[†]. Optimize applications for multi-thread support and workload management. This can substantially reduce total power consumption by making better use of existing infrastructure. Aggressive workload management can also help to increase data center power efficiency.

Case Study Example

Host Europe

Host Europe is a leading European internet service provider (ISP) and a subsidiary of Pipex Communications. Host Europe provides a comprehensive range of services including managed hosting, dedicated servers, shared hosting, co-location and domain name registration. The company manages over 300,000 domain names, 120,000 virtual servers, and 6,000 high-end servers for more than 100,000 customers.

Challenge

Host Europe is one of Europe's leading premium internet hosting companies, supporting its customers' websites, on-line shops and mission-critical internet applications. The company has experienced incredible success in the small and medium sized enterprise market and, in 2003, was ranked as the sixth fastest-growing European technology company by Deloitte. In 2004, Host Europe was acquired by the Pipex Group for 26 million GBP (48 million USD). The company's success is now flourishing beyond the small and medium sized enterprise sector and Host Europe is increasingly serving large organizations with more sophisticated hosting requirements. To keep pace with this growth, it needs to significantly increase the capacity and power of its server infrastructure housed in its data centers in Cologne, Germany. However, as an ISP, Host Europe spends significant sums of money on energy supply and data center space. The real challenge for Host Europe as it grows is to achieve the highest possible density of processing capacity into its data centers while minimizing electricity costs.

Having worked closely with Intel and Dell for many years, Host Europe was keen to evaluate the promised performance and power efficiency increases of the new Dual-Core Intel Xeon processor 5100 series as part of its continuing search to make more efficient use of its data center space.

Deployment

Host Europe ran a series of benchmarking tests to evaluate the new processor. Dell supplied a Dell PowerEdge[†] 1950 server powered by two Dual-Core Intel Xeon processors 5100 series and performance was compared to Dell PowerEdge 1850 server powered by two single-core Intel Xeon processors. Using SpamAssassin[†] as the mail filter, Exim[†] as the message transfer agent and Debian[†] GNU/ Linux 3.1 operating system, Host Europe tested the speed with which the servers could perform spam and virus checking on incoming emails.

Results

As soon as the new Dell server was up and running, its advanced performance and efficiency astonished Host Europe. The Dual-Core Intel Xeon processors 5100 series led to an increase in performance of 299% while using 13% less energy than the earlier generation Intel Xeon processor. Over the two months of testing, the new hardware platform was 100% reliable with no loss of availability due to hardware failures.

Future

Host Europe expects to continue the incredible growth it has experienced in recent years. The ISP is currently adding, on average, 200 servers a month to its server infrastructure and expects to open a new data center later this year. The company is planning that Dell PowerEdge servers, powered by the new Dual-Core Intel Xeon processor 5100 series, will be the primary platform for future purchases. "The incredible performance per Watt of the new processor will allow us to increase the computing capacity of our existing data centers. This translates into bottom-line savings for us. And for the new data centers, it will help us build a powerful, flexible and robust infrastructure to support our customers' mission-critical applications," said Braun.

Impact

Host Europe expects the combination of improved power-consumption and performance gains provided by the latest Dual-Core Intel Xeon processor 5100 series-based Dell servers to radically improve the efficiency of its data centers. "With this new processor architecture from Intel, we're getting the best of both worlds. We can pack even more processing power into the same space while lowering our energy bills," said Uwe Braun, Managing Director, Host Europe. The ISP estimates that the improved energy use could reduce electricity costs in excess of 100

EUR (126 USD) per server each year. With more than six thousand servers currently located in Host Europe's data centers, the potential cost savings could quickly reach hundreds of thousands of dollars.

The unique reliability features built into the processors will allow Host Europe to deliver higher levels of data integrity, availability and capacity, all of which translate into higher uptime for its customers. Braun explained: "Our customers rely on us to make sure their business-critical internet applications are available around the clock, 365 days a year. Outages affecting their customers, partners or employees can have significant business impact. Dell servers powered by Dual-Core Intel Xeon processors 5100 series support our consistent course towards quality of service, reliability and scalability."

The company has also been impressed with the platform's comprehensive support for virtualization software. Host Europe currently manages 120,000 virtual servers and anticipates that virtualization will become increasingly important in the planning of its data center utilization. As the company continues to grow, virtualization will increasingly contribute to the efficiency and flexibility of its server infrastructure.

Chapter 8

Energy-Efficient Data Center Tuning

We can accomplish more by prudence than by force.
—Publius Cornelius Tacitus

There is no single solution to reducing power demands or increasing power efficiency in a data center. This chapter focuses on many interrelated items that should all be considered when considering how to reduce power consumption in an existing data center. Tactical information will be provided for the equipment selection and optimizing efficiency of the house and IT load. Some of the energy efficiency measures that will be covered include: server and storage efficiency, airflow management, tips to improve cooling efficiencies, rack layout, liquid cooling methods, economizers and optimization of power distribution systems.

This chapter will also discuss airflow distribution related to overhead and under-floor designs, ceiling height requirements to eliminate "heat traps" or hot air stratification, raised-floor height, and proper distribution of the computer equipment in the data center such that hot spots or high temperature issues are mitigated. Various air distribution configurations will be examined with respect to cooling effectiveness.

Finally, best practices and recommendations for building new data centers are discussed. Included for data center expansion options are discussions of new energy efficient strategies such as modularity and containers.

The reader should be aware that improvements in data center and data processing equipment designs, systems integration, operational optimization, and theory are occurring at an accelerated pace as a direct result of increasing energy costs and environmental concerns. This rapid change necessarily implies that specific assumptions, theories and known methods for data center design and operations, whether from this text or elsewhere, must continuously be reviewed and updated to reflect what is considered truly state of the art and to account for technical advancements. Therefore, while specific recommendations and approaches are described, it is important for the reader to understand the principles at work in order to apply them to specific situations that may be encountered in the future.

Tuning Existing Data Centers – Overview of the Opportunity

In Figure 8.1 the EPA has projected several different data center energy consumption scenarios. There are many options for improving data center energy efficiency ranging from tips and best known methods

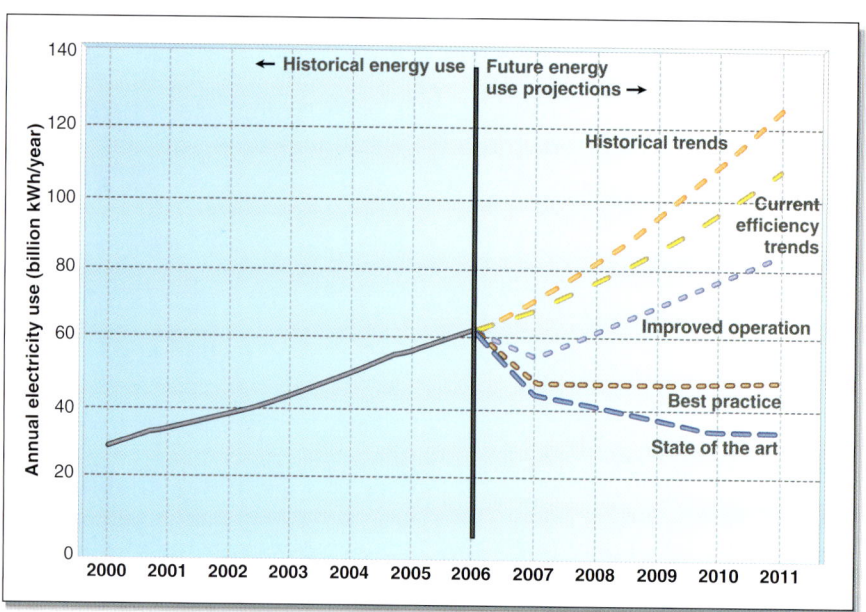

Figure 8.1 Value of Tuning a Data Center for Energy Efficiency
Source: EPA Energy Star Report to Congress, Aug 2007

(BKMs) in cooling infrastructure and power distribution systems management to the design and layout of racks. As the chart shows, utilizing a subset of these best practices can have a positive impact on the energy consumption of a data center. Implementing many or all of the recommendations and emerging technologies, in combination, may improve a data center's energy savings to the degree depicted toward the *State of the Art* scenario line.

The different scenarios in the chart depict U.S. annual savings by 2011 of between approximately 23 and 74 billion kWh compared to current levels. If the majority of data centers implemented the State of the art recommendations, the potential reduction in cumulative data center peak load savings is the equivalent of up to 15 new power plants and annual electricity costs reductions of USD 1.6 billion to USD 5.1 billion could be achieved. The *Best Practice* scenario shows that electricity use in servers and data centers can be reduced below 2006 levels during the next five years without significant change existing data center technology. Contrast this with projected near doubling of consumption for the same period if current practices continue.

Energy Efficiency Tuning of the IT Load

Each scenario in the graph describes levels of energy efficiency technology adoption and the expected savings. The scenario summaries are provided below to provide the reader with a quick snapshot of different levels of effort required for obtaining the projected energy efficiency improvements.

The simplest scenario is the *Improved Operation* scenario. This scenario incorporates energy-efficiency improvements that are essentially operational in nature and require little or no capital investment. This scenario represents the "low-hanging fruit" that can be harvested simply by operating the existing IT equipment more efficiently.

With the Improved Operation scenario, a data center can save up to 30 percent on power and cooling by migrating 25 percent of the servers to newer energy efficient designs and enabling power management on 100 percent of servers that support it. The expectation is that newer servers incorporate power supplies meeting EPA Energy Star requirements for efficiency. Software should be designed to avoid excess code and inefficiencies (treating CPU cycles as a finite resource). Improved operation facilities have software and hardware support for virtualization enabled providing the ability to shift computational loads among systems for maximizing energy efficiency. This scenario recommends x86 server virtualization to support a physical server reduction ratio of 1.04 to 1 for server closets and 1.08 to 1 for all other server space types. With this virtualization rate, it is assumed 5 percent of legacy servers could be eliminated.

The next scenario of energy efficiency is *Best Practice*. This scenario represents the efficiency gains that can be obtained through the more widespread adoption of the improved operational practices and recent technologies used in the most energy-efficient facilities in operation today. No significant technical barriers exist to achieving this level of savings, but they could require capital investments.

A data center implementing Best Practice recommendations can save up to 70 percent on infrastructure energy efficiency by migrating 60 percent of servers to newer energy efficient designs, implementing 100 percent power management and consolidating 40 percent of all servers. All applications that are no longer supported on latest technology and/or operating systems would be upgraded, allowing removal of legacy servers. All dead, obsolete, or excess equipment should be turned off or, ideally, removed. Equipment that isn't used for extended periods of time, such as development systems not in active use and systems for future expected increases in activity, are power managed and not on during inactive periods. Active servers are enabled with power-management features for frequency/voltage scaling. Best Practice facilities have updated all active servers to use efficient power supplies meeting EPA Energy Star requirements over the full operating range (including DC-DC conversions) or directly accept moderate DC voltage. Best Practice also recommends utilizing high-efficient variable speed fans within all active servers. Server virtualization would be moderately increased leading to a physical server reduction ratio of 1.33 to 1 for server closets and 2 to 1 for all other space types. And finally, centralized servers (large systems) are recommended where possible to improve sharing of computer resources.

The last scenario is State of the Art, which identifies the maximum energy-efficiency savings that could be achieved using available technologies. This scenario assumes that servers and data centers will be operated at maximum possible energy efficiency using only the most efficient technologies and best management practices available today.

In this final category, a data center can achieve up to 80 percent improvement in infrastructure energy efficiency, by migrating 100 percent of servers to newer energy efficient designs, 100 percent power managed, plus aggressively consolidating all servers, aggressively consolidating all storage and enabling power management at data center level of applications, servers, storage and networking. Systems (both individual and clusters) would include low utilization power management to reduce energy use (whether the resource is processing capacity, memory, communications or etc.) All new servers would include recent processors with lower current leakage designs and increased system integration. The State of the Art data centers utilize aggressive virtualization for both servers and storage. 100 percent of storage would be virtualized. Server virtualization (x86) would be extensive leading to a physical server reduction ratio of 1.66 to 1 for server closets and 5 to 1 for other space types.

Server Efficiency

There are many actions that an organization can take to reduce server inefficiency in the data center. Some actions are as simple as turning off unused servers. Existing servers can be managed with available power tools. These measures can cut data center energy drain by as much as 20 percent.

It is very common for data centers to have a significant number of installed servers that are not used at all. Anecdotal data cites the average enterprise utilizes somewhere between 5 percent and 25 percent of its server capacity. With underutilized data centers, most of the power consumed by the hardware is just heating the room during idle cycles. Typically, unutilized systems in a data center are older servers that have fallen out of use but have not been decommissioned. Finding and removing these systems is a key operational element of all data center efficiency improvement activities.

Certain types of servers will regularly go unused for random, lengthy periods of time. These should be targeted for powering down, or power management strategies that power down these systems for certain periods of the day. For example, servers executing backup software are normally only required at night and remote based servers are normally only used during the day. In test and development environments servers are only used until a test run has finished. Development build systems are used only when a build run is required. Both these types of servers could be powered down until needed.

To find unused servers, data center managers should perform analysis and profiling of server utilization data (CPU, disk and network) across all servers over a defined period of time. Average utilization for servers is likely to follow a daily, weekly and/or monthly pattern. These machines can be identified by analyzing their use (or lack thereof). Unused servers will stand out as only active when there is periodic maintenance, such as a virus scan or backup.

To increase energy efficiency, servers which are only periodically used could be scheduled to power down for the periods of time that they are idle and then powered up in time to perform desired work. For example, a server executing backup software that is only busy from 10PM until 6AM could be scheduled to power itself down at 8AM every day and then be powered up by operations management tools or a job scheduling system at 9PM ready to perform the next night's backups.

In addition to finding unused systems, utilization data can assist in making informed decisions on how many actual servers are required to support peak service levels. Systems that provide service resilience via warm or hot sparing strategies or clustering must be identified to exclude them from power management or removal activities that would compromise critical service availability. In many cases data centers are vastly over-provisioned. The number of servers actually needed is likely less than the actual number of servers in the data center, meaning that the surplus capacity can be powered down to conserve energy and/or additional applications can be landed without adding hardware.

Once a machine has been identified as "unused" it is possible to confirm this status by analyzing network statistics and tagging any system for which network packets can be determined to be "house keeping" only. This exercise will ensure that all connections to the machine in question are from management systems and not from other business systems or from end users.

Keeping a legacy server around simply because it is available may be poor efficiency practice. New servers available today offer better performance with significantly reduced energy consumption. If the decision is made to retire legacy servers, they should be processed for recycling and/or repurposing.

Storage Efficiency

Many data center operators dismiss the notion of managing the power consumption of storage systems as impractical. In data-intensive industries, the power, cooling, and floor space consumed by storage systems is projected to grow 50 percent annually unless steps are taken to affect this trend.

There are several approaches to achieving storage efficiency. Saving energy can be as simple as migrating to larger capacity disk drives.

Others approaches are more complex, such as use of massive arrays of idle disk (MAID) systems, removable disk cartridges for backups, thin provisioning for On Line Transaction Processing (OLTP) or optimizing SAN and NAS topology.

Starting with simple approaches first, migrating data to larger capacity disk drives can reduce power consumption by 5 to 20 percent. For example, if backups today are written to 250GB SATA disks, write those backups to 500GB SATA disks, half the number of disks will be needed and energy and floor space will be conserved. If possible consider storage-system software and infrastructure architecture optimized for SATA drives, because they are more energy efficient than fibre channel.

As covered in previous chapters, there is a direct correlation between the number and speed of disk drives and the electricity these devices consume. The more disks there are spinning, the more energy is required to keep spindle motors turning and to remove waste heat byproduct. Reducing the energy requirements for disk systems is relatively straightforward: reduce the number of spinning disks or spin the disks at a slower rotational rate. These techniques work well to store infrequently accessed data such as archival or backup data, but the same techniques may not meet the business needs of OLTP applications.

Other techniques have been developed to make disk storage more energy efficient. Keeping disks powered off until they are needed via power management policies, implemented in the bios or with data center management suites. Some of the newer MAID storage systems detect when a disk drive hasn't been accessed for several minutes. Once the preset period of inactivity is reached, the drives are rotated at a slower speed which saves energy. When a request to access data on the disk is received, the drive increases to its normal speed. This is perfect for archival data, hierarchical storage implementations or backup systems which are seldom if ever accessed. Data centers using MAID storage systems report a 10 percent to 20 percent reduction in storage power consumption.

Some IT organizations use increased storage to make up for the lack in performance. A well architected IT infrastructure can side-step this pitfall by systematically eliminating performance bottlenecks.

As with servers, storage subsystems will be the most efficient if all associated infrastructure technologies, including hardware, software applications and networks are kept up to date with software and firmware revisions per the manufacturer's recommendations.

Storage consolidation can reduce the data access and system response time, keeping end users satisfied while simultaneously reducing power use. An additional benefit of storage consolidation is the ROI; shared data storage can maximize utilization of expensive storage arrays..

Storage growth (and hence power use) can be reduced using a thin provisioning architecture. Thin provisioning is a technique that allocates disk blocks to a given application only when the blocks are actually written rather than at initial provisioning and partitioning. By employing thin provisioning along with good storage management software, not only is disk consumption reduced, but the storage management system itself can accurately calculate and project how much storage will be needed based on use history, instead of relying on a database administrator or customer guestimate.

Instead of increasing storage for increased performance, consider optimizing the SAN or NAS topology. Maximize the use of high performance ports by aggregating multiple slower ports to create a faster (higher bandwidth) storage port and increasing the fan-in ratio. Large port count fibre channel and/or network switches and directors can be used to replace multiple smaller switches that are networked together using inter-switch links (ISLs) to improve on locality and improve performance. This works well for time sensitive applications such as OLTP.

Keeping local storage traffic local on the network or fiber mesh, as much as possible, can also improve SAN performance in some environments. Storage efficiency is best achieved by integrating the technology as close to the point of data creation as possible and by avoiding latency incurred from multiple switch or router traverses (hops) This is also known as SAN segmentation.

Another solution for storage energy efficiency is appropriate use of optical and tape systems. The power and cooling requirements for tape systems are much less than similar capacity disk systems. Tape cartridges and optical media, when stored on a shelf, require no electricity.

The most logical way, however, to save power is to store less data. Best Practice and State of the Art data centers use software that recognizes and eliminates duplication (sometimes referred to as de-duplication software). Storage growth almost always occurs because of stored redundant data. Enterprises should identify data that isn't accessed actively and move it to secondary or "near-line" storage such as optical or tape storage to maximize control of storage growth (and data quality). Data center managers report data-reduction rates as high as 10:1 or even 20:1. The results are clear: storing less data requires fewer disks and saves energy.

A final point: data de-duplication has significant benefit for heavily virtualized environments. Each virtual instance redeploys the operating system files repeatedly. Data de-duplication not only reduces the storage space required by virtualization, but it also increases the likelihood that when data is needed, it's already in filer's cache. Both go a long way toward improving the energy efficiency and performance of virtualized storage.

Server Virtualization, Consolidation, and Refresh Efficiency

If the most energy efficient data center is one that is not built, then the most energy efficient server is the one that never gets turned on. Server virtualization and consolidation are among the first steps in maximizing an existing data center's potential capacity and efficiency.

Many IT organizations historically employed a 1:1 application to server ratio as a holdover from limited processor power and legacy distributed architectures aimed to minimize business impacts of IT infrastructure outages. While this compartmentalization strategy was at least partially successful, it was accompanied by a rapid increase in associated costs for data center facility capacity investments and operational overhead, including rising power costs. This, in turn has driven analysis and redesign of IT architecture to satisfy business interests.

Processor power and operating system capability have far outstripped the demands of most any application that a server can run. In fact, most servers sitting in a data center will operate at or below 20 percent CPU utilization. The other 80 percent or so simply idles while it waits for more instructions or data.

Virtualization allows multiple applications to reside on one server and thus increases the utilization rate of that server asset. Most importantly, this also reduces power consumption per application as the inevitable power losses occurring at the server platform level, from initial power up, are effectively amortized across the number of co-resident applications. Certainly, platform power consumption increases as CPU, memory, storage and network activity increase but power supply efficiency for example, improves.

Virtualization and consolidation are among the most effective tools with a quick ROI for increased data center energy efficiency. One dual-socket quad-core server configured with ample memory can replace 30 or more older, lightly loaded single-processor systems. The power savings from unplugging these older servers will be in the range of 12 to 15 kilowatts. Depending upon the electric rate for the site, a consolidation program achieved via virtualization can pay for itself within a year.

Virtualization is necessary but insufficient by itself to maximize the productivity of the power consumed by a data center. Consolidation is enabled to a large degree by virtualization.

Leveraging the opportunities provided by server virtualization requires collaboration from multiple teams, such as data center operations teams, IT architects, and application developers to consolidate existing applications onto a smaller number of more powerful servers.

Virtualization and consolidation of the computing environment allows data centers to increase energy efficiency by:

- Using otherwise idle computer resources to accelerate business processes
- Increasing the resiliency and utilization of the IT environment
- Optimizing the infrastructure to balance workloads and provide extra capacity for high-demand applications
- Allowing physical server count and footprint to be significantly reduced or, conversely allowing existing IT inventory to support more business application
- Increasing capacity headroom thus giving a company room to grow while avoiding expensive investment in new data centers

Finally, while covered in more depth in Chapter 9, it is important to include equipment refresh strategy in the discussion on IT power efficiency optimization. Periodic refresh (replacement) of aging equipment has a dramatic multiplier impact on both business and energy efficiency.

Intel has conducted extensive internal analyses of alternative investments in data center facilities and IT infrastructure as a component of a multi-year data center efficiency program. The analysis looked at the total cost of ownership impacts, including energy consumption costs, between various compute capacity alternatives. Investment in server replacement on a four year cycle was found to be significantly more cost effective than building new data centers.

This finding is largely due to the improved computational power per watt and decreasing capital cost of new CPU and server designs. Every four years the processing capability of new processors offsets the cost of the new hardware and provides several times the processing horsepower while holding power consumption per server relatively flat. Intel's case study is provided below to support this point.

It is important to consider this data in the context of server virtualization and consolidation opportunities previously discussed. The multiplier effect of increased performance per watt (itself an opportunity for improved power efficiency), coupled with virtualization and consolidation programs can significantly improve data center energy efficiency, business productivity and value and can actually free up sufficient data center capacity to reduce or eliminate the need for new facility construction.

These inter-related practices improve power efficiency (application per server increase, server count decrease and performance per watt increase) but they also can provide significant space and cooling supply elasticity (headroom) for an existing facility. Consideration of this opportunity is a "must do" for any company desiring power and cost effective IT services.

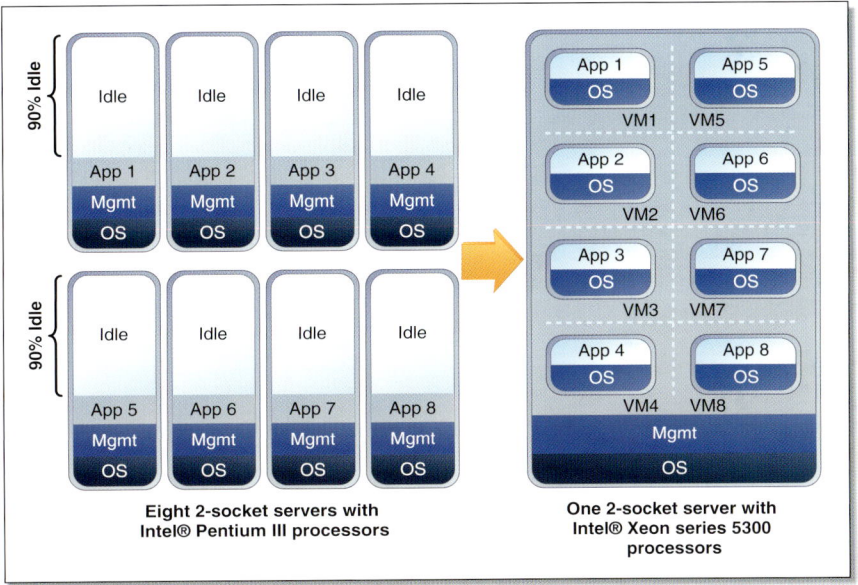

Figure 8.2 Server Upgrade Efficiency
Source: Intel IT, December 2007

> In August of 2007, Intel IT conducted a study of ROI with refreshing IT servers using new 45nm Quad-core Intel® Xeon® brand servers (code named Nehalem).
>
> The study used 126 two-socket Intel® Xeon® Processor 3.6GHz servers with 8x1GB DDR2-400 DIMMs.
>
> These systems had the following power measurements: idle power (225W × 16 hours/day), at full load (382W × 8 hours/day), for one year at 0.10 kWh = USD 30.69k × 2 (HVAC factor) = USD 61.4k electricity cost per year.
>
> Compared to 17 two-socket Intel® Xeon® Processor 3.0GHz servers, with 8 x2GB FB-DIMMs. These systems had the following power measurements: idle power (237W × 16 hours/day), at full load (353W × 8 hours/day), for one year at 0.10 kWH = USD 4.16 × w (HVAC factor) = USD 8.29k electricity cost per year.
>
> **ROI:**
>
> The cost of each server was USD 6,246. The cost of 17 servers = USD 106.5k divided by USD 53k/year energy savings. This resulted in a 2-year ROI on the servers alone.
>
> Additional savings in the data center were:
>
> - Floor space: 240 sq. ft. to 60 sq. ft (85 percent reduction)
> - Annual energy costs: 48kW to 6kW (87 percent reduction)
> - Yearly Energy Savings: USD 53k (USD 61.4K - USD 8.29k) = USD 53.11k

Cooling Efficiencies

There are numerous best practice cooling techniques for energy efficiency. Some of these cooling techniques can be achieved with a minimal amount of upfront costs. These include operational BKMs such as establishing effective hot and cold aisle arrangements, tactical rack airflow management and periodic computational fluid dynamics room cooling and airflow modeling. Others require sizable investments including such examples as central air handling unit retrofits, in-ceiling air return ducting installation and server cabinet replacement. But all methods will have a measurable impact on the data center energy costs.

As with the other sections of this chapter, before making any sizable investments in energy efficient technologies the reader should measure and benchmark the current environment to determine and document current cooling and airflow conditions. Benchmark the DCiE and PUE of your facility, to the extent possible, as a means of documenting your starting point, and measure or calculate the impact of each operational, organizational or systems change; this will provide the data to support additional recommendations and business impact analysis. It is also recommended that emerging technical and best practice innovations be surveyed to assist with defining and prioritizing activities and soliciting investment decisions from management.

Manage the Airflow

The first step in reducing power use for cooling requires managing the airflow to ensure that it is used effectively to remove waste heat from the data center. Air management is a key part of effective and efficient cooling and one of the largest opportunities for facilities operators to improve. According to statistics presented by The Uptime Institute, the average data center has bypass airflow (leakage) of approximately 30 percent. This means that 30 percent of the cold air does not reach the IT equipment and thus is wasted along with the corresponding energy consumed by cooling systems and fans used to produce and transport the air.

Improving air management or optimizing the delivery of cool air and the collection and removal of waste heat involves many design and operational considerations. Poor air management results from many things including:

- Openings in racks between installed server or network equipment allowing air to be pulled from hot aisle to cold aisle via Bernouli Principle affects of incoming cold air
- Hot air flowing over the tops of racks and being re-entrained with cold air
- Airflow constrictions on the back of racks; usually the result of cable management structures and network cable tie down location, which creates back pressure
- Cold air short-circuiting back to air conditioning units through openings in raised floors such as cable openings or open floor tiles
- Poor location of computer room air conditioning units or hot air returns
- Undersized hot air return plenum

- Large quantities of cabling under raised floors causing air blockages and constrictions. (cold airflow perpendicular to cable tray layout is particularly bad)
- Short circuiting of cold and hot aisles from server racks with side or top-air-discharge adjacent to front-to-rear discharge configurations

The general goals for achieving better air management should be to minimize or eliminate inadvertent mixing between cooling air supplied to the IT equipment and hot air exhausted from the IT equipment, minimization of the volume of air to be moved and the distance over which it must be moved, and finally to maximize the absorption of waste heat by the cold air. Air distribution in a well-designed system can reduce operating costs, reduce investment in HVAC equipment and allow for increased utilization.

Most system, rack and room-level cooling issues are created by inefficient or insufficient airflow. To quantify cooling efficiency, best practices recommend measuring the Air Conditioning Airflow Efficiency (ACAE) in the data center. ACAE is simply the amount of heat that can be removed per standard cubic foot per minute of cooling air. As bypass air is reduced, ACAE increases.

Insufficient airflow will often result in hotter systems with decreased cooling efficiency (heat rejection). This can result for a number of reasons but is most often the result of increasing server power density beyond room operational design limits. This will generate an imbalance between floor supply volume and rack-level air demand. In a raised floor environment, recirculation will then occur between hot-aisle and cold-aisle as the hot air is sucked back into the cold aisle by chassis fans. In this situation the upper systems in the rack draw heated and mixed air from the rear of the rack over the top and thus become hotter than systems at the mid levels. If not plugged, hot air may also be drawn back into the cold aisle through gaps in IT equipment and associated racks. Finally, if under-floor static pressure is increased in an attempt to offset the bypass leakage, increased cold air velocity, created as the air is pressed through vented tiles in the floor of the cold aisle, can actually starve lower position systems of cooling as it speeds past the equipment cooling inlet.

To address air management issues, the first step is to clearly define power and cooling requirements at the room, row, and cabinet level. These requirements should be based on system level inlet air temperature and airflow requirements. Computational Fluid Dynamics (CFD) tools can help model and design the initial cooling system as well as providing data useful for periodic rebalancing the room contents are rearranged of time.

There are some simple solutions to improve efficiency and reduce some of the air management issues. To address recirculation of air between hot and cold aisles, best practices include strict containment and segregation of air between the hot and cold aisles. This technique will reduce the power required by the fans to circulate air and reduce wasted cooling energy from dilution.

Central custom-designed air handler systems provide better performance than traditional multiple distributed unit or direct expansion (DX) cooling systems. Centralized systems use fewer, larger motors and fans, which are generally more efficient. They are also well-suited for adjustable volume operation through the use of variable frequency drives that can be dynamically adjusted to match cooling demand as the room is fills with equipment or to respond to periodic peaks and ebbs in server utilization. Since central units are controlled centrally, they are less likely to "fight" one another—for example, simultaneous humidification and dehumidification by adjacent air handlers—than distributed units with independent and uncoordinated controls. The coolant supply for central air handler systems is usually a central chiller plant that produces chilled water for circulation through a closed loop delivery system. This design is typically significantly more efficient than alternative water-cooled or air-cooled computer room designs. Central air handlers can also be readily adapted to use both wet-side and air-side economizers to improve energy efficiency—something that distributed computer room air condition system designs make more difficult.

There are best practice design tips for air handler units. For example, when a data center design couples AHUs (air handling units) with typical raised floor room designs, the most efficient design is to limit the air *throw* (the distance that the chilled air is pushed beneath the floor) to approximately 35 feet per AHU. Design for uniform static air pressure, using 0.8 – 1.0 m raised floors, adjustable vent tiles with no vent tiles next to AHU.

A design that places AHUs on opposite sides of the room in a directly opposing arrangement can span about 70 feet of floor width based on the above parameters.. When the unit sizing of currently available off-the-shelf chilled water plants are taken into account and floor width limit from the above calculation is applied, floor length is optimized at approximately 80 feet for a total square footage of 5600 square feet of data center per chiller plant module (assumes 525 watts per square foot power density and 24-inch raised floor).

Additional best practice tips in the area of operations efficiency:

- Ensure that all cooling units are functioning properly and that the set points and sensitivities are consistent.
- Check that the return air sensors are in calibration; and don't forget to calibrate the calibrator.
- Airflow volume should be at the specified level for the IT equipment and racks.
- The AHU should be functioning properly at return air conditions.
- Check that the AHU does not produce greater than 15°F delta temperature at 100 percent capacity.
- Adjust the chilled water temperature to eliminate any latent cooling.
- Finally, make sure the cooling unit's blower motor is turned off if the throttling valve sticks for chilled water type units or if a compressor fails for CRAC units.

The following sections provide solutions and best practice tips to common air distribution problems and offer improved energy efficiency.

Rack It Up

Selecting the right server rack will help to effectively power, cool and protect the IT equipment. A proper sized rack offers additional benefits of keeping servers in optimal thermal ranges for best reliability which will reduce any potential downtime. Proper racks make the management and organization of a data center more efficient. The type of rack chosen is best if it relates to the cooling methods and platform mix used in the data center environment.

Best practices for efficient cooling with racks start with understanding server requirements and then standardizing on the appropriate racks. First define and document the server and storage inventory (for existing data centers) or the server and storage technology roadmap projected for future deployment. System form factor and power density are key elements in defining physical requirements of racks and cabinets. Next, model the thermals and related airflow requirements for the servers within your data center. Understanding the requirements for specific equipment will enable an efficient rack-level design and cooling strategy.

Standardizing on an appropriate rack design and layout makes it much easier to establish and enforce effective power and thermal policies.

A rack strategy should specify use of either fully perforated racks or sealed racks and cabinets. The baseline kW of heat output per rack varies widely, depending on the type and density of equipment and the specific configurations (memory and storage) and can be anywhere from 4 kW to 12 kW or more per rack. Heat output and airflow management/cooling technology design, will provide the basis for selecting a fully perforated rack, a sealed rack or perhaps a direct liquid cooling type design.

Fully perforated server racks are best for maximum air flow if the primary method of cooling in the data center is ambient air cooling (fans, air handlers, blowers, and/or CRAC units and a raised floor). Avoid shallow racks to ensure that the rack cabling does not obstruct the airflows. Best practices recommend cabinet/rack door faces with a minimum of 50 percent open perforation with 65 percent or higher being the best.

Other ways to improve cooling with perforated server racks include selecting a rack with built-in channels for keeping cabling out of the intake and exhaust air flows and utilizing blanking panels to seal interstitial gaps between racked equipment and the racks themselves. Both these items improve air flow efficiency in perforated racks and eliminate a significant amount of bypass. It is also desirable to minimize obstructions to proper airflow by removing any obsolete or unnecessary equipment from the rack.

In addition, 3-phase power distribution will significantly increase available amperage into the server rack and reduce the overall number of PDUs and associated cabling needed to power equipment. This opens more space for airflow.

For high-density systems fully-sealed server racks or fully contained hot aisles may be the optimal choice. Full containment refers to the ability to completely segregate cold air from hot, constraining cold air to flow only through the systems being cooled. In effect, this eliminates the energy lost through bypass leakage and significantly improves the efficiency with which the entire cooling system works. Sealed cabinets offer the ability to supplement cooling for individual racks without compromising room-wide efficiency. This allows isolated hot spots or high density blade server deployments to be addressed incrementally. Fully-sealed racks are the best choice if a liquid cooling unit or rack air conditioner will be used in the data center.

Liquid cooling units are modular air/water heat exchangers, within or adjacent to the racks themselves. These units provide uniform, effective cooling for very dense compute racks. One of the benefits of modular liquid cooling units is that they result in little or no impact to the existing HVAC system. Liquid cooling units are mounted at the rack base or in a rack "side car" with three cooling modules possible per equipment rack, and can provide a total cooling capacity of 30kW or more. The positioning of the heat exchange coils in close proximity to the racked IT systems is referred to as close coupled cooling.

Rack air conditioners are generally not used in traditional data center environments with adequate CRAC systems. Rack air conditioners are intended for use in large spaces. They generate condensation and exhaust hot air into the room where the enclosure is located. For every kW consumed by rack air conditioners, there will be 3412.14 BTU generated and exhausted. In a large room, the heat will dissipate, but in a smaller room or confined space like a server closet, the exhausted hot air from the rack air conditioner unit can cause the room to overheat.

Tape Up, Baffle and Blank It

Best practices recommend the use of blanking panels and end baffles. By sealing the openings in and between racks/cabinets, blanking panels improve airflow through the racked equipment, minimize bypass air leakage, and help to prevent exhaust air recirculation. End baffles, perform a similar function, and provide similar benefits, at the ends of data center rows.

Blanking panels are recommended for all empty areas in the cabinet-mounting surface, between the mounting rails and the edges of the cabinets. In short, the objective is to force the chilled air in the cold aisle to pass only through the IT equipment air inlets, remove the maximum amount of heat, and then return as directly as possible to the heat exchangers without intermixing with and diluting the cold air.

Hot and Cold Don't Mix

Hot aisle/cold aisle layout is a relatively easy to implement and inexpensive cooling best practice. A hot aisle/cold aisle arrangement involves alternatively setting racks of servers such that the cold inlet sides of two rows face each other with the hot discharge sides facing toward the hot discharge of the next adjacent row. This establishes cool air supply areas for intake with alternate row areas that become hot (exhaust side) to optimize hot air collection and return for re-cooling

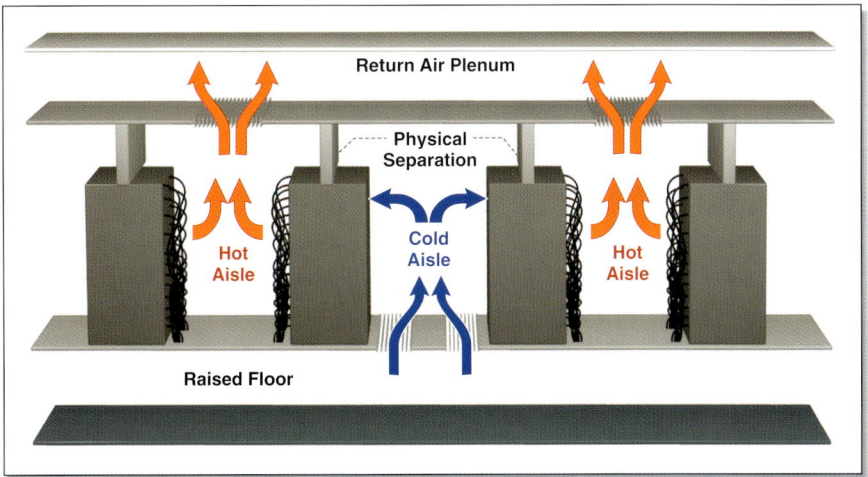

Figure 8.3 Hot Aisle – Cold Aisle Arrangement

Source: Greenberg et al., 2006

and thus avoid hot air/cold air intermixing. Figure 8.3 illustrates a typical arrangement.

For this strategy to be effective, the cold air must be delivered to cold aisles and hot air extracted from hot aisles. The racks should be aligned front-to-front along cold aisles, and back-to-back along hot aisles. Within each row, racks should be tightly abutted.

The best practice is for a 14 foot cold aisle to cold aisle separation with cabinets that are 42 inches or less deep, and a 16 foot cold aisle to cold aisle separation with cabinets that are between 42 and 48 inches deep. Always maintain proper spacing of the cold aisles. The spacing is best if it is 48 inches wide with two full rows of tiles which can be removed. In addition, it is important to have all the perforated tiles located only in the cold aisles with no perforated tiles located in the hot aisle side. Data center managers have been known to install perforated tiles in the hot aisle to provide cooling because they "feel hot". In effect, all this does is to provide a different path for bypass air. The result is a actually loss in cooling efficiency with corresponding reduction in overall cooling capacity and energy efficiency. Hot aisles are, by design, hot.

The proper spacing of hot aisles includes a minimum of 36" with at least one row of tiles able to be removed. Ensure cabinets are installed with the front face of the frame set on or just behind a tile seam in the cold aisle to allow under floor access right up to the front of the cabinet.

Care must be taken to eliminate hot-air remixing, which will cause short cycling or "short-circuiting" of the cooling system. In air-cooled racks with the air moving from front-to-back, the chilled-air supply, whether from a raised-floor tile or via diffusers from the ceiling, is typically only a fraction of the rack airflow rate. This is due to the limitation of the perforated tile or diffuser flow rate. The remaining air for the rack made up from ambient room air through recirculation or through make up air ducting that allows a controlled amount of air to be introduced from outside the room. Unmanaged ambient air intermixing patterns not only waste energy, they can also be detrimental to the performance and reliability of the servers

The effect of recirculation of hot exhaust air on server temperatures can be significant. Servers are typically designed to operate at air inlet temperatures in the 10°C to 35°C range. Because of the diluting effects of recirculation, a wide range of inlet air temperatures may occur across the rack. Inlet air temperature can range from 10°C to 15°C at the bottom of the rack close to the chilled air supply from the perforated tiles, to as much as 30°C to 40°C at the top end of the rack, where the hot air can form a self-heating recirculation loop. Since the rack heat load will be limited by the rack inlet air temperature at the hottest part of the rack, this temperature distribution can severely limit the total number of servers each rack can support and is reflected in a suboptimal data center power density capability and wasted energy.

There are many options to deal with the complex mixed air patterns. The first step would be to leverage sensors inside servers and in the racks. Build a visual with this data by utilizing computational fluid dynamic modeling to help ascertain areas of excessive cooling or heating. Implement physical barriers between the hot and cold aisles whenever possible to eliminate hot air flow over the tops of racks and intermixing with the cold air supply. Increase the temperature differential between the hot-aisles and cold-aisles (called Delta T). Optimally, hot aisles are operated as hot as possible since this is key to achieving the highest Delta T. The higher the Delta T, the more efficient the heat extraction process is.

Cooling Efficiencies 191

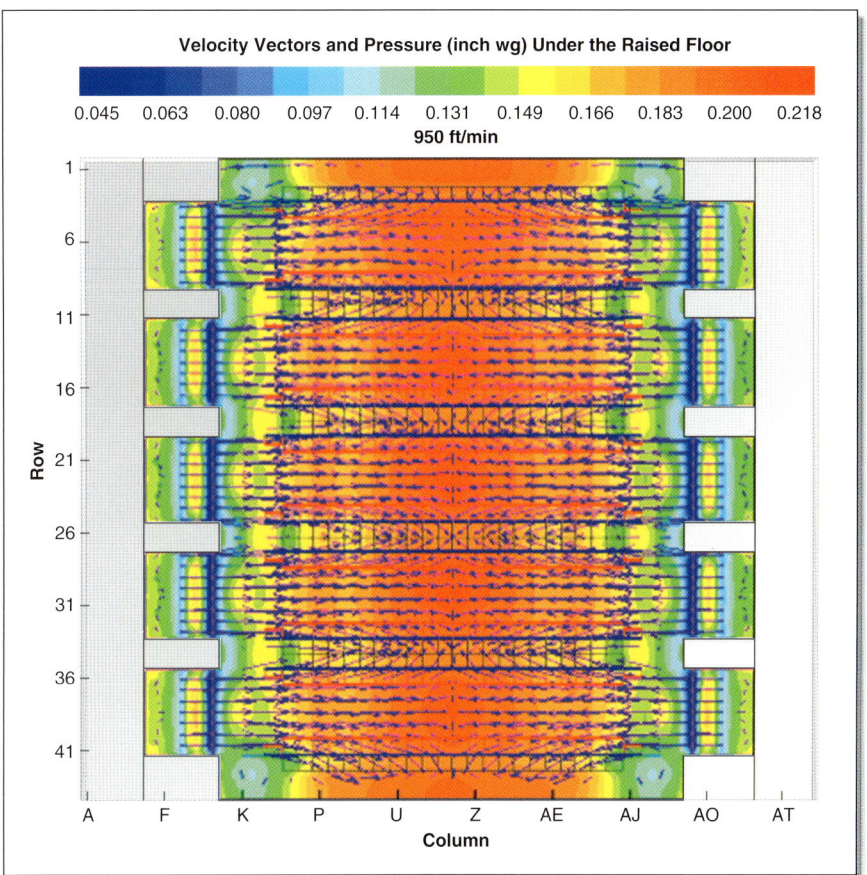

Figure 8.4 Pressure and Velocity CFD Model
Source: Intel IT, Data Center Analysis, February 2007

The CFD model in Figure 8.4 shows a pressure and velocity plot of a typical data center using opposing down flow RAHs to push air under a raised floor, through standard perforated tiles and into cold aisles for delivery to racked servers. Note that the static pressure is lowest and air velocity highest at the outside ends of each row. Conversely, static pressure is highest and air velocity lowest in the middle of each row.

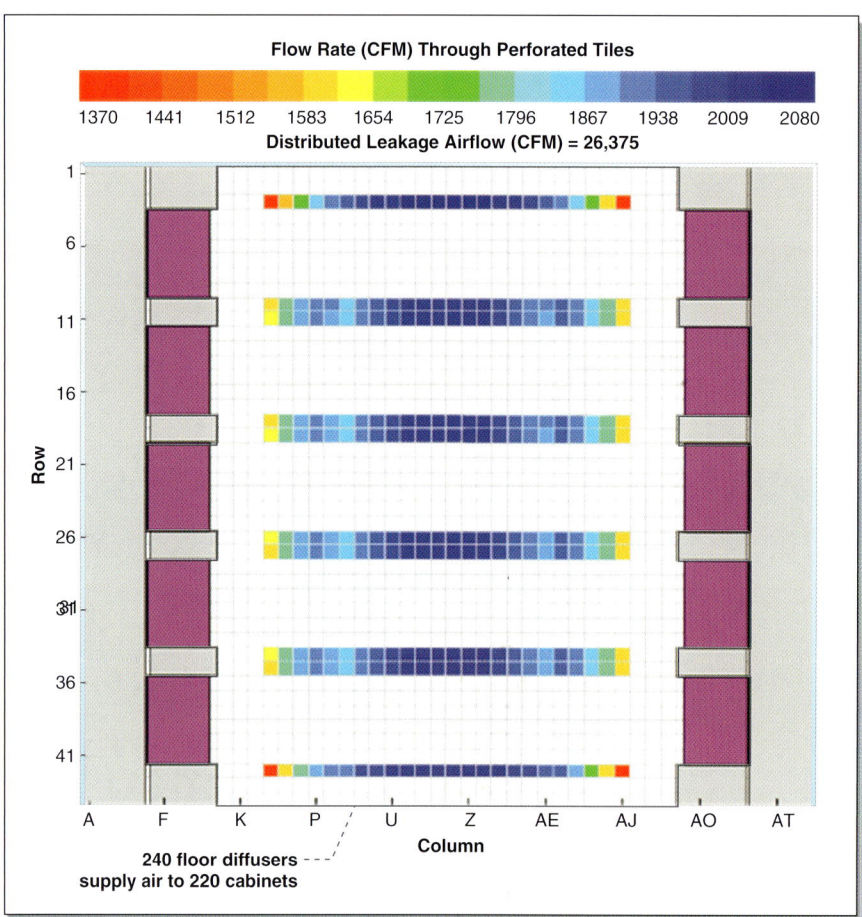

Figure 8.5 Flow Rate per Floor Diffuser
Source: Intel Data Center Analysis, February 2007

The CFD model in Figure 8.5 illustrates an air flow rate plot showing the calculated air flow from each standard perforated tile in the same data center model as previously shown. Note the significant drop in airflow from the end tiles in each cold aisle.

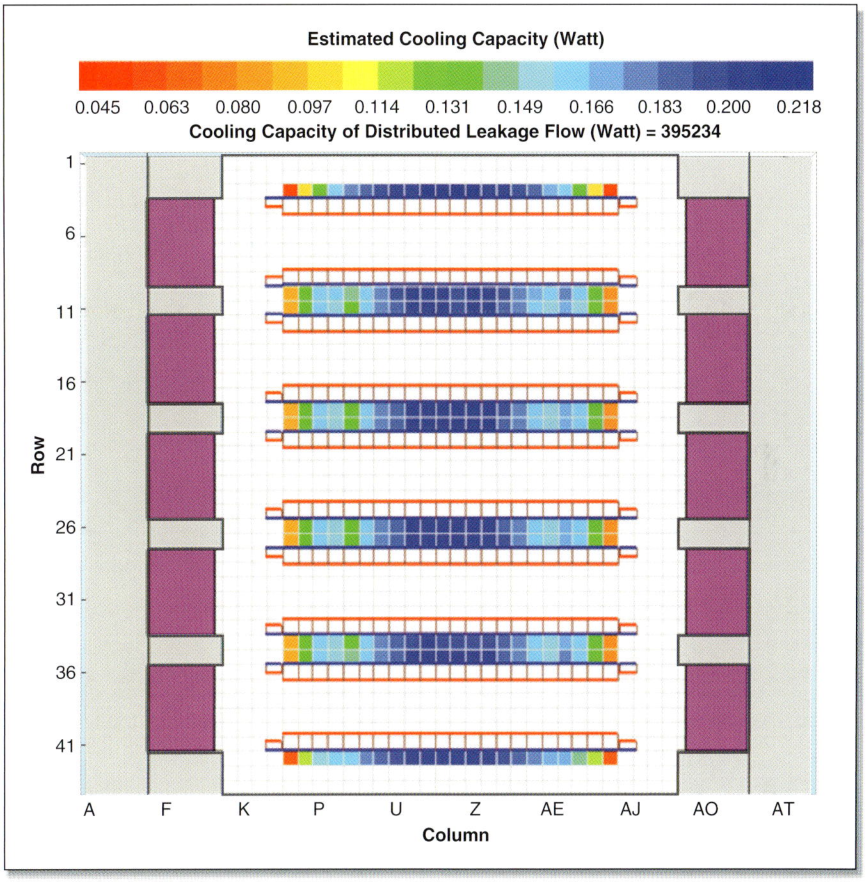

Figure 8.6 A kW per Floor Diffuser
Source: Intel Data Center Analysis, February 2007

Figure 8.6 shows a CFD calculation of kW per cold aisle perforated tile cooling capacity (roughly equivalent to capacity per rack) using the same data as the previous two plots. Highest cooling, and thus rack power density capability, occurs in the middle third of this room (assumes equal air flow through each rack of equipment). This type of modeling is essential to optimizing and managing room layout for maximum capacity and efficiency throughout the life of a data center.

Using air flow barriers such as walls or plastic curtains above the server racks to eliminate hot and cold air recirculation is sometimes not a viable alternative because of fire code restrictions. In these instances, best practice techniques are to focus on using cabinet blanking panels to

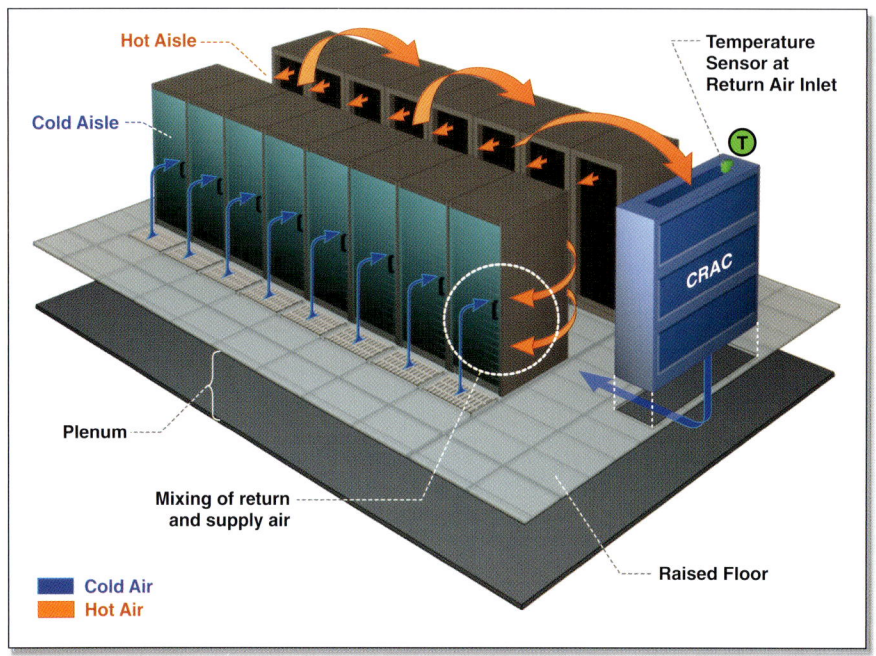

Figure 8.7 Visual Model of Air Recirculation in a Data Center
Source: www.microsoft.com, 2008

help keep the hot and cold air contained to their aisles. Eliminate any gaps in rows; seal any cable cutouts. Also, work to balance server air flow consumption with both cold air inlet pressure and hot aisle air extraction, using ducting to return hot air directly to air handlers to prevent intermixing. Finally, use long rows and place high-power density systems dual or quad-processor server racks near the middle of the rows.

Look Underfoot

Another source of energy loss is experienced on floors where the IT load and air flow are not configured in an optimal manner. The space under the raised floor is often used as an air-supply plenum, with perforated tiles distributing chilled air. With raised floor data center designs, typically the space above the false ceiling is used as the air supply return plenum to the AHU. To provide an energy efficient cooled environment of controlled temperature and humidity, you need good uniformity of the air distribution via the raised floor and false ceiling return air plenums.

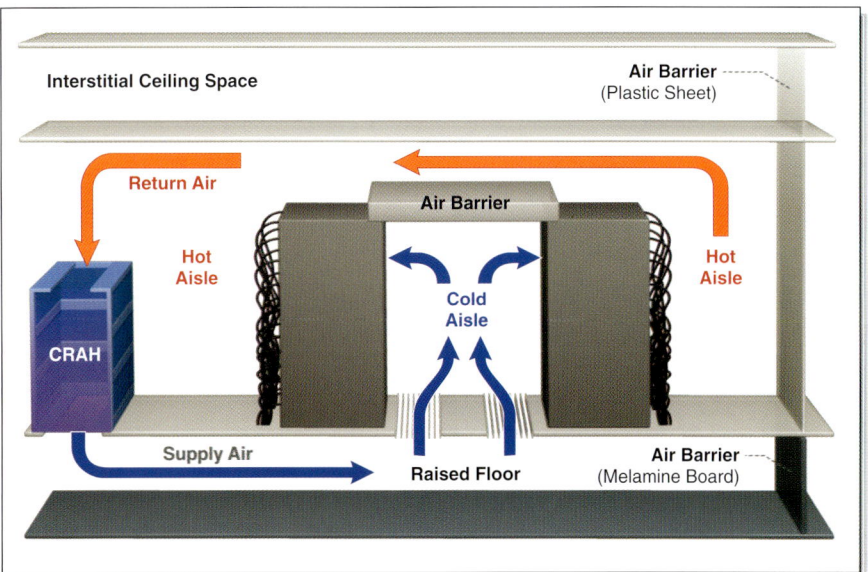

Figure 8.8 Data Center Raised Floor Airflows
Source: Silicon Valley Leadership Group, 2008

For raised-floor designs, sufficient static pressure is necessary underfloor to drive uniform air to all floor tiles. To achieve good static pressure, a minimum raised-floor height of at least 18 inches is recommended. Best practices call for 24 inches if the cabling is overhead, with no chilled water, condenser water pipes or any other constrictions under the floor blocking the airflow. If there are airflow blockages, then 30 to 36 inches is recommended.

Install only the number of perforated tiles necessary to cool the load being dissipated in the cabinet/rack in the area immediately adjacent to the perforated tile. The optimum number of perforated tiles can be calculated by taking the total cooling unit airflow divided by 750 cfm to determine the maximum number of perforated tiles to be installed. Do not use perforated tile air flow dampers and remove all existing dampers from the bottoms of perforated tiles. Air flow dampers can reduce maximum air flow by 1/3, as they often close without reason. Best practices also recommend increasing volume flow rate of air supply as high as possible, but not to the point of blowing floor tiles. In addition to the tile damage, high air velocity (LFM) could starve lower systems in racks of cold air, creating a wind tunnel in the data center.

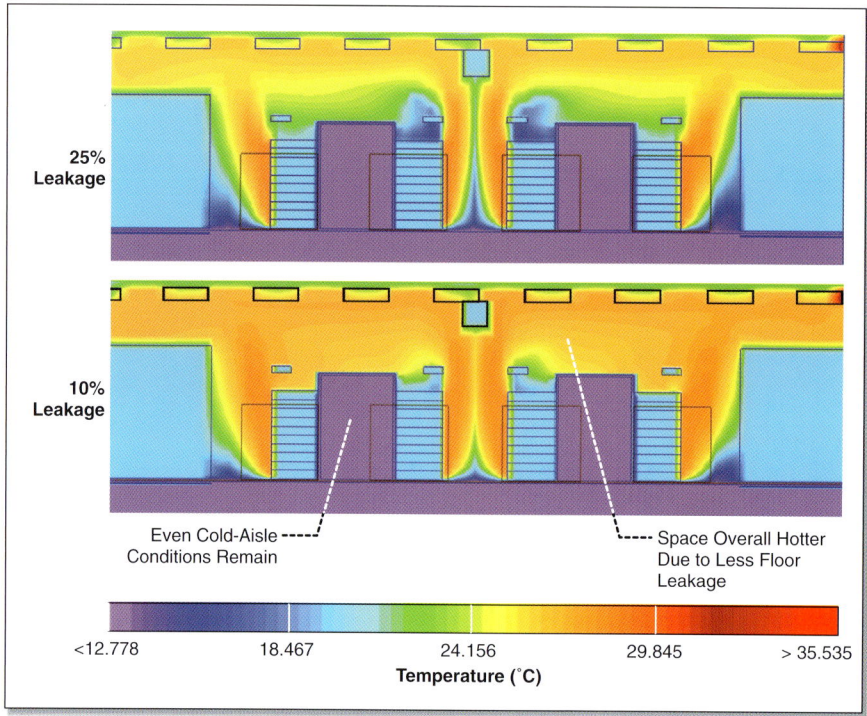

Figure 8.9 Energy Wastes with Floor Leakage
Source: Intel IT, 2008

Make sure perforated floor tiles are properly installed so they don't impede the flow of cool air from under the floor. Seal holes, unused floor openings and other openings to prevent cool air from escaping and hot air from circulating. The CFD illustration above reflects two end views of two server racks, one with 10 percent floor leaking and the other with 25 percent floor leakage, with all other factors held constant. The differences in the thermal contours for the heat being exhausted show that the cold aisle conditions remain more constant and the hot aisles are hotter (which is good) due to less floor leakage. Seal all cable cutouts and other openings in the raised floor with grommet closures. Best practices recommend the use of overhead bus bar power distribution systems or alternatively, spreading power cables out on the subfloor, preferably under the cold aisle to minimize airflow restrictions. Place data cables in trays at the stringer level in the hot aisle. Chilled or condenser water pipes should be placed in suppressed utility trenches if the computer room is built on grade.

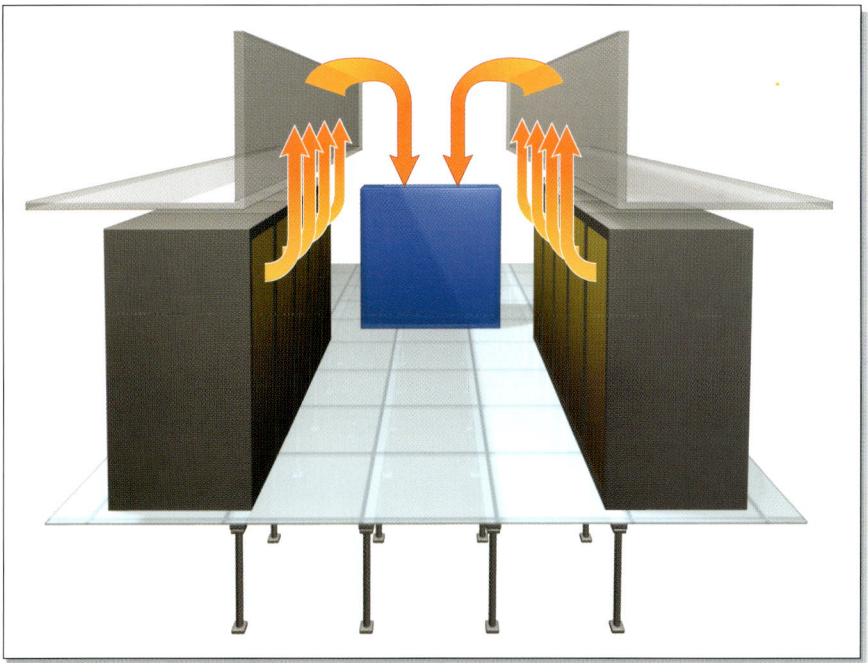

Figure 8.10 Data Center Ceiling Hot Air Return Plenum
Source: www.plenaform.com/PlenaFormDataCenter02.htm

Look Overhead

The purpose of false ceiling air plenums is to efficiently return heated air to the air handler(s). Use short partitions installed around the supply openings to minimize short-circuiting of supply air to returns (short-circuiting occurs when air takes the path of least resistance). Best practices include the use of baffles and completely enclosed hot air return ducts of sufficient size to not impede flow as the most efficient method of eliminating bypass leakage or cold air remixing. The use of baffles and right-sized hot air return ducts in ceiling plenums maximize the efficiency of heat return from the hot aisles to the CRAC unit intake heads.

Concentrate Cooling

Placement of CRAC systems is another key factor affecting energy efficient cooling. Depending upon the placement of the CRAC and AHUs, there can be a five-fold variation from worst to best on cooling power consumption. This is due a number of factors, including how the cooling is generated and distributed, but placement of the CRAC units or AHUs is a key part of effective and efficient cooling. Effective cooling allows more servers to be inserted into racks, which often have empty slots to avoid heat buildup.

Moving cooling systems closer to the servers helps ensure that cool air is concentrated in the right place and that the energy used to transport the cold air is minimized. In addition, there should be accurate placement of overhead fan/coils that pull hot air out of the hot aisle and blow cold air into the cold aisles. Use of computational fluid dynamics (CFD) modeling can help to determine the optimum placement of CRAC units and modular fans/coils during design or retrofit. Floor tile openings from day 1 through the full lifecycle of the facility can be modeled against installed load and relocated as required to optimize cold air delivery. Best practices recommend using only sensible cooling at 72°F with 45 percent Rh when calculating the capacity of cooling units to help determine their placement through CFD modeling.

There are many techniques that can help improve temperature control and airflow distribution. First, zone the computer rooms to a maximum of one to two building areas. Create appropriate cooling capacity, with redundancy, in each zone of the room. Match the sum of IT equipment airflow with CRAC airflow to limit recirculation over top of racks and provide cool air to all servers. Install a minimum of two cooling units even it only one is needed to provide for unit maintenance without impacting data center availability; install one-in-six to one-in-eight redundant cooling units in larger areas. Turn off cooling units that are not required by the heat load to reduce energy consumption. An exception to this is for redundant units.

Cooling units function best at the end of equipment rows. Align the cooling units with hot aisles where possible. Orient CRAC units perpendicular to hot aisles, so they draw hot air down the hot aisles. Face the cooling units the same direction to achieve uniformly distributed cooling and do not have units that compete with each other. If possible, limit the maximum cooling unit throw to a distance of 50 feet.

If overhead cable racks are used, the racks should run parallel to the rows of racks. Crossover points between rows of racks should be located as far from the cooling units serving the area as practical. Utilize heat exchangers located above the racks near the ceiling.

Finally, air handler coordination is important. In some older designs that provide cooling and humidity control to large rooms or zones, air handling units (AHUs) can fall into competition if not using synchronized settings or central controls. One AHU may be supplying heat and humidification while an adjacent unit is attempting to cool and dehumidify. This can waste a significant amount of electricity.

Liquid Cooling

The most effective way to minimize overheating of high power density servers is to implement supplemental cooling directly at the source of heat. Liquid cooling is a far more efficient method of transferring concentrated heat loads than air, due to much higher volumetric specific heats and higher heat transfer coefficients. However this practice is not yet seeing wide industry adoption with x86 servers due to concerns about potential leakage risks and implications to overall construction and operational complexities.

Best practice data centers make greater use of water to cool the air in the data center or directly cool the server racks. Currently the most common approach is to use a chilled water coil integrated in some manner into the rack itself. The power dissipated in each cabinet must be coordinated to the capacity of the supplemental cooling system installed. This approach is referred to as close-coupled cooling.

Capturing heat at a high temperature directly from the racks allows for much greater use of wet side economizer free cooling, which can reduce cooling energy use by 60 percent or more when operating. Water flow is a very efficient method of transporting heat. On a volume basis, it carries approximately 3,500 times as much heat as air, and moving the water requires an order of magnitude less energy. Water-cooled systems can thus save not just energy but space as well. Liquid cooling energy efficiencies are typically realized because such systems allow the use of a medium temperature chilled water loop (50 to 60°F rather than ~45°F) and by reducing the size and power consumption of fans serving the data center. With some systems and climates, there is the possibility of cooling without the use of mechanical refrigeration (cooling water circulated from a cooling tower would be enough).

Some of the energy efficient liquid cooling technology options include:

- Self-contained cabinets with chilled water fan/coil systems, which provide a closed loop cooling cycle
- Supplemental rear doors with chilled water fan/coil units, which pre-cool the hot exhaust air before it returns to the normal cooling units

- Incline chilled water fan/coil units replacing equipment cabinets, which pull hot exhaust air from the hot aisle and blows cold air into the cold aisle

In the future, servers may have built-in direct liquid cooling of components. Direct liquid component cooling offers the promise of ultra high cooling system efficiency by eliminating airflow needs entirely. These products might work via methods ranging from fluid passages in heat sinks to spray cooling with refrigerant to submersion in a dielectric fluid. While not currently widely available, such approaches hold promise and should be evaluated on a case-by-case basis.

Let It Get Hot

The inside ambient air temperature in data centers is generally set to meet the server and storage manufacturers' requirements. The equipment installed in most data centers is from many different manufacturers, each having a different environmental specification. With these varying requirements, data centers frequently overcool to meet the specifications of the equipment with the tightest requirements.

This overcooling has a huge impact on the data center power bill. The manufacturers really only require that the inlet temperature and humidity to the electronic equipment be maintained within their specifications. All manufacturers have a temperature range on their specifications. Best practices for data centers recommend exploring raising temperatures in facilities, while remaining within manufacturer's guidelines. ASHRAE has experimented with this and now recommends increasing average room temperatures from 25°C (77°F) up to 26.7°C (80°F). If the data center can be operated at a few degrees higher, it will cut power consumption and increase the energy efficiency and PUE for the data center.

Some voices in the industry today are arguing for an acceptable operational dry bulb temperature of 32.2°C (90°F) for all servers and disk drives. This is based on the desire to expand potential opportunities for free air cooling application as a means of completely eliminating requirements for chiller plant and the associated ongoing power consumption.

Note that the guidelines are different for higher elevations. Higher elevations require lowering of the maximum dry bulb temperature 1°C for every 218m (720 feet) above an elevation of 1,287m (4,250 feet) up to a maximum elevation of 3,028m (10,000 feet). These temperature requirements are to be maintained over the entire front of the two meter height of the rack where air is drawn into the system. At higher elevations, a data center may need to operate at lower temperatures (for example, 25°C, 77°F) to maintain reliable operating environments per equipment specifications.

Save with Economizers

Economizers can offer great energy efficiency as part of a data center cooling solution. There are two types of economizers in use today: water-side economizers which use outside air to cool chilled water and air-side economizers, which bring outside air directly into the data center. Data centers that are 65 percent economized for outside air using chilled water supply have the potential to achieve an annual PUE of 1.10. Airside economizer designs can theoretically achieve even higher PUEs, especially if operational temperature limits for IT systems are raised because of the elimination of chiller systems and associated pumps and fans. Several 100 percent free air designs are currently being developed and tested in preparation for operational deployment.

For data centers that can take advantage of cool, dry climates, air-side economizers can offer free cooling with great energy savings. Air-side economizers achieve the greatest efficiency when operated in regions with cool, dry climates. Many hours of cooling can be obtained at night and during mild conditions at a very low cost.

Air-side economizers and their data center benefits are currently somewhat controversial. Data center professionals are split in the perception of risk when using this strategy. It is standard practice, however, in the telecommunications industry to equip their facilities with air-side economizers. Some IT-based centers routinely use outside air without apparent complications, but others are concerned about contamination and environmental control for the IT equipment in the room. ASHRAE's data center technical committee, TC 9.9, is also concerned with this issue and plans to develop guidance in the future. Control strategies to deal with temperature and humidity fluctuations from air-side economizers must be considered along with contamination concerns over particulates or gaseous pollutants. Mitigation steps such as filtration work for many data centers. Even with the humidity controls and filtration systems, data centers that implement air-side economizers report significant improvements in energy efficiency.

Best practices for cooling efficiency recommend using a standard commercial building economizer with an engineering evaluation of the local climate and contamination conditions. Data center architectural design for air-side economizers requires that the configuration provide adequate access to the outside. Central air handling units with roof intakes or sidewall louvers are most commonly used, although some internally-located CRAC units offer economizer capabilities when provided with appropriate intake ducting. In many areas, use of outside air may be beneficial, however local risk factors should be understood before any capital investments are made.

In 2008 Intel completed a proof of concept using an air-side economizer on one half of a small partitioned high performance data center in New Mexico. Traditional chiller technology was run, in parallel, on the other half of the data center. The evaluation ran for over 10 months with no significant operational differences observed between the two halves of the data center. The servers from the free air cooled side of the data center have been returned to the manufacturer to be analyzed for degradation related to external air exchange but no conclusive data has yet been returned. Please see the case study at the end of this chapter for more details.

The second type of economizer is the water-side or wet side economizers that use outside air to cool chilled water, as shown in Figure 8.11. Free cooling can be provided through water-side economizers using evaporative cooling (usually provided by cooling towers) to indirectly

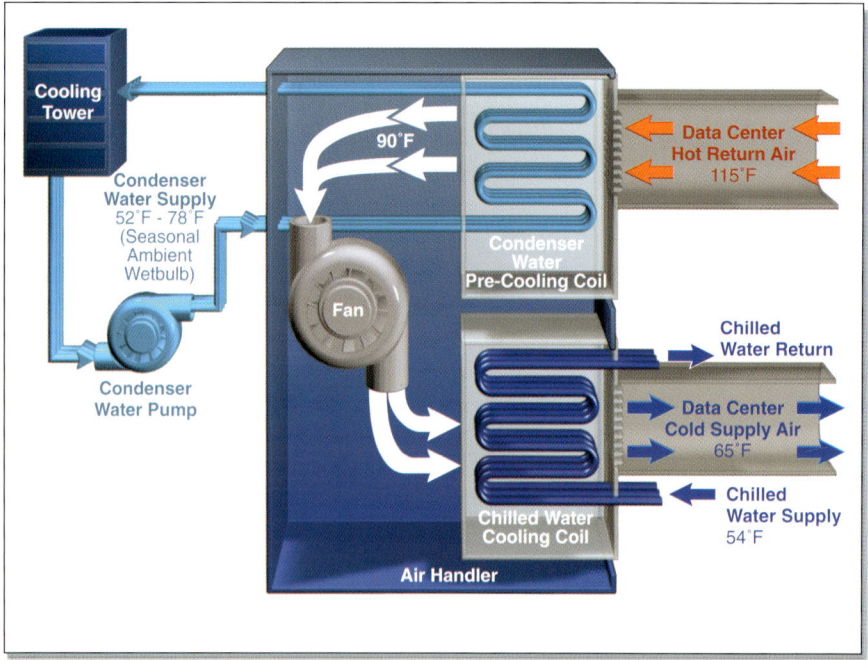

Figure 8.11 Decoupled Wet Side Economizer System
Source: Intel IT, 2007

produce chilled water to cool the data center during mild outdoor conditions or at night in many climates.

Water-side economizers are most efficient within climates that have wet bulb temperatures lower than 55°F for 3,000 or more hours per year. Water-side economizers can improve the efficiency of the chilled water plant by pre-cooling the chilled water before it enters the chiller(s). Water-side economizers can also offer the benefit of completely eliminating the need for compressor cooling when in operation. This potential benefit is dependent upon the outdoor conditions and overall system design.

Implementing a water-side economizer is a highly recommended best practices in areas conducive to their operation. Data centers utilizing wet-side economizers have realized power consumption reductions of up to 75 percent. In addition, these data centers found related improvements in reliability and maintenance through reductions in chiller operation and attendant maintenance. Since this solution doesn't raise concerns over contamination or humidity control for air passing through the IT equipment, it can be an economic approach for retrofitting existing chilled water cooled centers with free cooling.

Below are the EPA categories for cooling efficiency. Details of these can be found at *www.energystar.gov/ia/partners/prod_development/downloads/EPA_Datacenter_Report_Congress_Final1.pdf*.

Improved Operations. Data centers should utilize air cooled direct exchange system chillers with constant speed fans, humidification control and redundant air handling units.

Best Practice. Data centers of this level would have variable-speed drive chillers with economizer cooling or water-side free cooling in moderate to mild climate regions. Also recommended are variable-speed fans and pumps and redundant air-handling units.

State of the Art. Data centers of this classification utilize liquid cooling to the racks. Cooling systems should utilize both air-side and water-side economizers in moderate and mild climate regions. Central air conditioning units are implemented with variable-speed fans and pumps. The data center has redundant air handling units.

Cooling Efficiency Summary

There are many ways that air management and cooling can become inefficient in data centers. Facilities cooling is currently the most power consumptive function of data center facilities infrastructure. Most air management issues are the result of poorly designed airflow or hot air recirculation and bypass leakage. Just as there are many issues which can cause cooling inefficiencies, there are many best practices to improve the environments.

Energy efficient data center cooling is a balance of performance, availability, layout and capacity. Central cooling plants and ventilation systems should be right-sized to operate efficiently both at inception and as the data center load increases and moves around the data center over time. Central air-handling units with high fan efficiency are a more energy efficient solution than distributed units. Proper planning includes choosing appropriate racks for the types of servers in use. Fully perforated racks are best for rooms cooled primarily with ambient air and CRACs. Fully sealed racks or fully contained hot aisles are best for high density servers. Empty spaces in racks should be sealed with blanking panels and end baffles. Liquid cooling in fully sealed racks is a very efficient method to cool high power density servers. Hot and cold aisle room organization improves airflow efficiency. Raised floors and false ceilings provide good air distribution, but care must be taken to eliminate any blockages or leaks; sealing cable openings with raised floor grommets is a good example of this. Cooling systems, when concentrated close to the servers provide more tune-ability and efficiency. Significant power can be saved if the data center room ambient temperature is allowed to rise a few degrees. Finally, for data centers in cool, climate regions, air-side and water-side economizers can provide significant energy savings.

Power Distribution Efficiency

Data centers require special power handling to smooth out and transform the grid supplied power into something that the IT equipment can safely consume. This is referred to as power conditioning. Power conversion from AC to DC and back to AC occurs within double conversion bypass Uninterruptible Power Supply (UPS) systems resulting in large energy losses that occur with each conversion step. These losses are compounded by the energy for cooling needed to remove the heat generated by the conversion. The conditioned power travels through a Power Distribution Unit (PDU) that transforms the input power, with varying degrees of efficiency, to the correct phase and voltage for attached IT systems, and then delivers it to the IT equipment. Both UPS and PDU components of the power distribution system can have a signif-

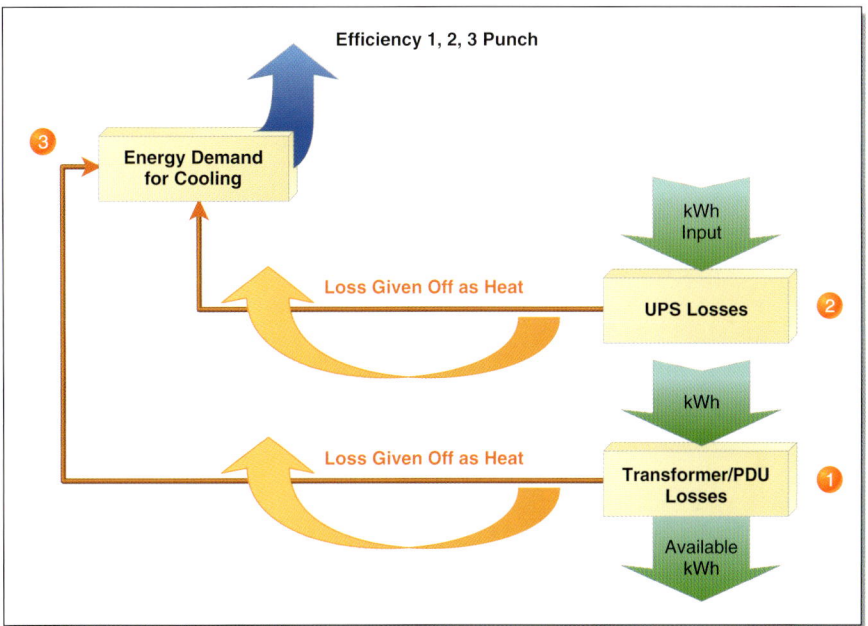

Figure 8.12 Energy Impacts from Inefficient UPS and PDUs
Source: PowerSmiths, 2008

icant effect on power efficiency. Figure 8.12 shows how the efficiency factors of the UPS and PDU conversion losses can impact the cooling efficiency of a data center.

These two components, UPSs and PDUs, have a sizable effect on data center house load energy efficiency. Additional factors which can affect power distribution efficiency include distribution system operating voltage, three-phase power transmission, alternating current (AC) versus direct current (DC) transmission system selection and data center sizing.

The relationship between older, inefficient UPS or PDU systems to energy efficiency is straight forward; increasing the efficiency of the power conversions results in reduced power loss and reduced heat generation. Understanding the tradeoffs and impacts of various power system design elements is important to designing a highly efficient data center. Because distribution systems are generally the third largest component of house load they are a key factor in determining Power Utilization Effectiveness (PUE) of a data center.

UPS

There are many different types of UPS systems. UPS systems vary significantly in both the technology and efficiency. The actual efficiency of a UPS varies as a function of the IT load running on the UPS. Replacing UPS systems that have been in service for 15 years or more can result in substantial savings. New best-in-class UPS systems can experience as much as 70 percent lower conversion loss than existing UPS equipment.

Types of UPS systems include double conversion, delta conversion, rotary and flywheel designs. UPS manufacturers provide efficiency data for their systems that is expressed as a percent of power input to full-power input. However, for data centers that are designed with fully redundant (2N) UPS, each UPS system is typically carrying only 40 percent of the IT load. In a (2N+1) scenario, each UPS is loaded to a maximum of only 33 percent of full load. For this reason the efficiency of the UPS system at partial load should be the focus for designing optimized energy efficiency.

Underloading a UPS—allowing lower draw than the full design rating—often increases inefficiency due to the inherent conversion efficiency curve of each transformer in the supply system. Therefore, data center fill and rate of fill also impact the overall efficiency of the power distribution system with higher degrees of efficiency typically occurring as the IT load approaches 80 percent of distribution system design rating. This is very similar to and caused by the same electrical properties as those identified in an earlier discussion of server power supply efficiency.

Most UPS systems operate from batteries which have a limited life span. If there are a frequent number of discharges of the UPS battery the operational duty cycle of a battery powered UPS can be reduced from 15 to 10 years or less.

Flywheel UPS systems are highly efficient; they involve fewer power conversions and pass power from the grid directly to IT equipment. The flywheel can operate in a greater temperature range than batteries and require much less floor space than battery based UPS systems. The EPA rates flywheel types of UPS as a best-in-class technology for low IT load utilization efficiency. This is because stored kinetic energy in a flywheel can be converted back to electricity of the right current and voltage with a minimal number of transformations across a broader range of loads.

Simply specifying a more efficient UPS system in a data center design can result in a 10 to 15 percent reduction in conversion losses associated with the powering IT equipment. This will provide a corresponding reduction in power consumed for cooling as the result of lower loss

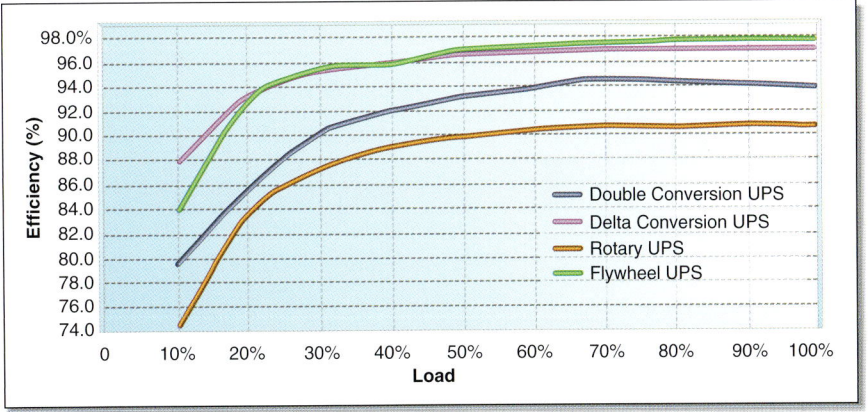

Figure 8.13 : UPS Efficiency Comparisons
Source: U.S. Department of Energy, 2008

related heat generation. Figure 8.13 is a chart reflecting the general efficiency curves of various types of UPS systems at various power loads.

Power Distributions Units (PDUs)

PDUs offer another layer of isolation from the anomalies in utility power. PDUs house transformers and circuit breakers that are used to create multiple branch circuits of varying voltage and amperage from a single feeder circuit. These branch circuits supply power directly to the IT equipment throughout the data center. PDUs provide metering and voltage transformation. That means the transformer within the PDU is an essential component in the data center power system and a key component of energy efficiency based on each design's inherent conversion curve.

An energy efficient PDU generates less heat. When an inefficient PDU is located on the computer room floor, it generates excessive heat that in turn increases data center cooling costs. Even a slight improvement in transformer efficiency can yield large savings in utility bills. PDUs that include transformers that meet or exceed the Department of Energy Candidate Standard Level 3 Efficiency, (CSL-3) had 60 to 70 percent lower operating cost than other PDUs measured.

Table 8.1 PDU Efficiency Analysis

Source: Eaton Powerware, 2006

	Pre-Regulation Transformer	Energy Efficient Transformer	Difference
Capital Cost	USD 2,000	USD 3,200	USD 1,200
Efficiency	96.7%	98.0%	1.1%
Annual cost of losses*	USD 1,113	USD 422	USD 691
Simple payback (yrs.)	–	4.09	4.09
Lifetime cost of losses*	USD 10,297	USD 3,985	USD 6,312
Present value of savings	–	USD 1,353	–

*Assumes an average 35-percent load, energy cost of USD .0994/kWh, and demand of USD 7/kWh month. Present value calculated at 30-year transformer life and a discount rate of 10 percent.

Three-Phase Alternating Current Power

Another design consideration for increased distribution system efficiency within the data center is use 208V three-phase power. Compared to single-phase power, three-phase power uses fewer circuits and provides a more balanced power load. In addition, three-phase power requires fewer PDUs, and thus transformers, to power equipment and significantly increases available amperage into the server racks. Finally incorporating three-phase power circuits into an IT infrastructure can provide energy to support future increased power demands of high density environments and also conserve floor space.

To illustrate how three-phase power can provide energy savings, consider a traditional data center environment which uses four 20-amp single phases circuits to provide the required power of 64 amps (assuming a maximum 80 percent design load) to each rack. A three-phase circuit can provide up to 51.6 amps per circuit, or more than 82 amps of available power, while only requiring two circuits (assuming a maximum 80 percent load). This reduces both energy lost through PDU conversion as well as the capital cost and energy required by copper production required by the single phase implementation.

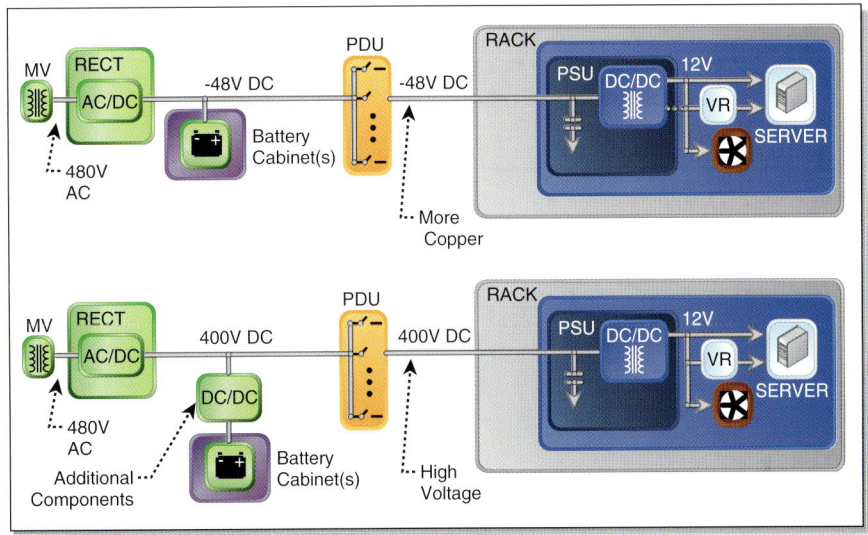

Figure 8.14 Facility-level DC Distribution Options
Source: Intel IT, 2007

Direct Current Distribution (-48V and 400V DC)

IT equipment incorporates power supply units to convert alternating current to direct current. Distributing direct current bypasses as much as 50 percent energy loss due to multiple steppings and AC to DC conversions in UPS, PDU, and power supply systems in the end-to-end power supply chain. DC distribution has been calculated to be between roughly 5 to 25 percent more efficient than AC distribution, depending on the specific designs being compared.

The highest efficiency for a data center facility is to operate at 400Vdc but the difference in efficiency compared to low voltage DC distribution is within a few percentage points, at best. High voltage DC has some additional drawbacks; it can potentially be very dangerous for untrained IT and facilities personnel and requires significant operational practice changes to reduce associated risks. In addition, as of this writing, some components of high voltage distribution systems such as breakers, high voltage inverters, and IT equipment interconnect plugs either do not exist and must be produced on a custom basis or are specialty items with very limited availability. In each case, the cost and difficulty of obtaining these specialty components coupled with the as yet unproven operational track record of HVdc distribution designs creates a significant barrier to adoption.

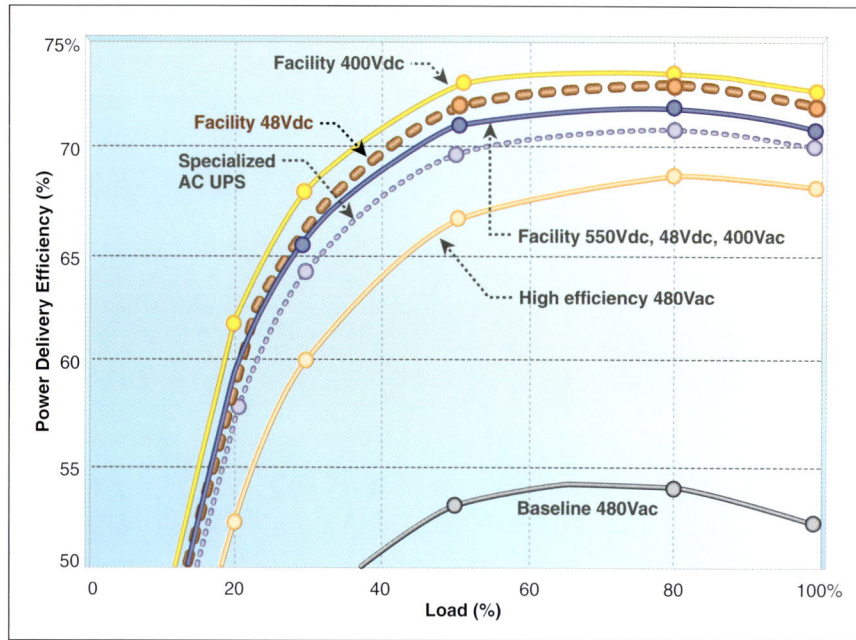

Figure 8.15 DC Efficiency Comparisons
Source: Intel IT, 2007

On the other hand, low voltage DC distribution (typically -48 volt) has been in use for decades in the telecommunications industry to support telephone switching systems in central offices and remotes switches. Designs are mature and operational experience well developed. Given this state of comparative maturity, low voltage dc distribution is very low risk. The energy efficiency of facilities using -48Vdc distribution is within 1 percent of the efficiency of a Facility 400Vdc design and offers other benefits. For these reasons, the authors recommend consideration of DC distribution system for any new or retrofit data center project.

Beyond efficiency, there are a number of other reasons to use -48Vdc in the data center. There are multiple vendors providing data center IT equipment today for -48Vdc. Equipment, both for infrastructure and IT equipment is very sparse for 400Vdc. -48Vdc eliminates the need for power factor correction. Additionally, 48Vdc provides better safety for the data center, provides better reliability than equivalent AC systems, and enables higher data center density than 400Vdc.

Right Sizing the Data Center Design

Given that projections of IT equipment electrical requirements is an inexact science and that business requirements can change dramatically, it is nearly impossible for planners and engineers to design and build a data center that will meet all future requirements for capacity and availability. It is nonetheless important to size electrical and mechanical systems to the data center workload, based on the best information available. Over-provisioning for resilience increases power consumption, sometimes for years until the IT infrastructure fills the space and draws power and cooling at efficient design levels. Ideal energy efficient designs, provide sufficient electrical systems such that they will operate efficiently while overall loading is well below ultimate capacity, yet be scalable to accommodate larger loads or changed availability requirements, should they develop. In other words, there is seldom, if ever, that a data center will operate under the ideal conditions to achieve maximizing energy efficiency. Therefore, it is essential that the facility and IT load be considered dynamic with appropriate ongoing monitoring, measurement, analysis and adjustment in order to balance the various components that contribute to energy consumption.

We close this section with the EPA categories of efficiency for power distribution components.

Improved operations. Data centers utilize 80 percent efficient UPS and 95 percent efficient transformers. These changes will reduce power consumption by 10 to15 percent.

Best practice. Data centers utilize 90 percent efficient UPS and 98 percent efficient transformers. These data centers retrofit UPS topologies for more efficient ones which provide energy efficiencies below 40 percent and then maximize the UPS load capacity. These changes can reduce power consumption by up to 20 percent.

State of the Art. Data centers utilize 95 percent efficient UPS and 98 percent efficient transformers. Data centers of this category include modular power distribution systems that scale with redundancy. These data centers have redundant configuration that do not exceed (N+1) or 2N. Higher efficiency may be achieved with UPS without input filters.

To summarize, basic steps to improve energy efficiency within the power distribution system include:

- Upgrade older UPS and PDUs to newer units with higher levels of efficiency for low load utilizations

- Convert from AC to low voltage (-48Vdc) distribution. This can be done in phases, such as starting with DC storage arrays
- Right size the power load to the data center
- Investigate recent power technology advancements such as three-phase power

Organization Culture Efficiency

A good way to help maintain and grow energy efficiency in the data center is to make it a part of the organization's goals and culture. Energy efficiency improvements trend faster when they are part of every team that works within the data center. This awareness and focus can be created by making energy efficient metrics a standard part of regular operational communications. What gets measured gets managed. Managers and organization decision makers should receive regular reports on the data center energy efficiency standings, savings and progress. Improvements and changes, with correlating ROI will not only keep management updated, they may also help garner more organizational support for energy efficiency programs.

Energy efficiency focus and goals can expand beyond the data center staff. Engineering, operations and purchasing could include performance per watt in purchasing criteria and goals. Energy efficiency could be tied to Total Cost of Ownership (TCO) targets and incentives. By including energy efficiency goals with purchasing guidelines, purchasing will note differences between manufacturers which will actually result in increased savings for the organization.

Measure and Improve

To increase efficiency, requires knowledge of the current data center environment and the impact of any changes. Monitoring and control of energy efficiency performance requires deploying monitoring tools to capture equipment performance (both IT and facility), temperature, and power usage throughout the data center. Close monitoring of server inlet temperatures in real time helps in determining how well the cooling system is working and can help eliminate wasteful overcooling.

In addition to measuring and monitoring energy efficiency, best practices include documenting all changes, problems and solutions. This historical archive can become a goldmine of information for devel-

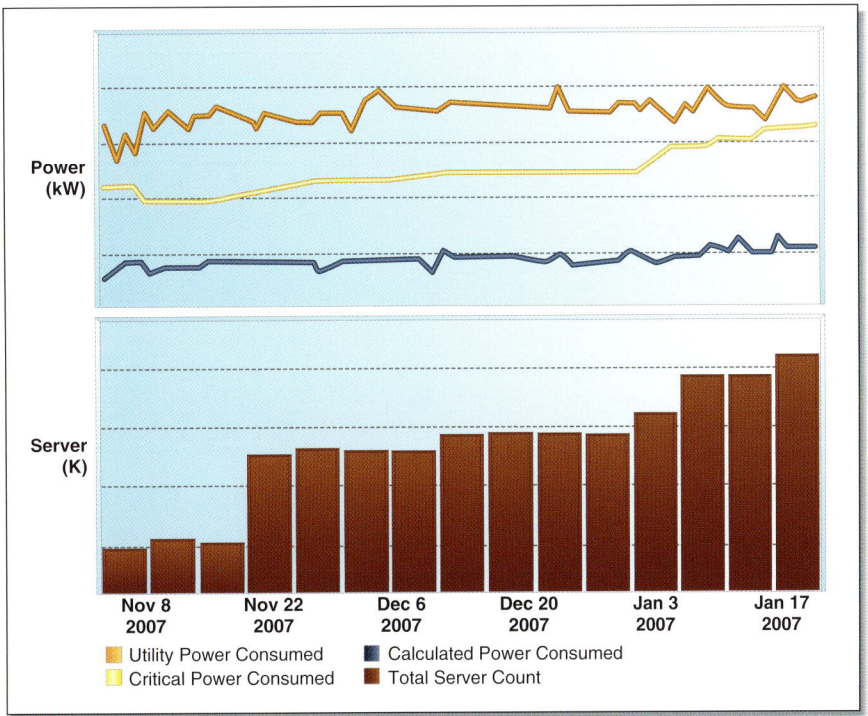

Figure 8.16 Data Center Best Practices
Source: Microsoft, 2008

oping a comprehensive understanding of how to improve operations or quickly troubleshoot an issue. As an example, Figure 8.16 highlights how many servers are in a data center and how much power is being consumed over time. This information helps educate the data center operator on historical capacity and corresponding power consumption, which can be leveraged in future data center planning.

The Power Usage Effectiveness (PUE) is a metric that is recommended to track and monitor progress towards energy efficiency of a data center. PUE is a standard promoted by The Green Grid and others in the data center industry to provide a consistent way to measure the ratio of power delivered to IT equipment versus the total amount of power used by the facility. PUE puts a focus on maximizing the power devoted to the equipment running applications and minimizing the power consumed by support functions like cooling and power distribution. As an example, a PUE of 2.0 indicates that for every watt of IT power, an additional watt is consumed to cool and distribute power to the IT equipment.

The ideal PUE value is 1.0, corresponding to a data center where all of the electrical grid power supplied to a data center is devoted to IT equipment and no power is used for cooling and power distribution. A PUE <1 would be possible with for a data center with on-site generation from waste heat, but in most cases this is currently commercially unfeasible.

The EPA report to Congress on Data Center Efficiency estimates that in 2006, the typical enterprise data center had a PUE of 2.0 or higher. The PUE ratings expected from implementation of their three scenarios are as follows:

Improved operations: data centers that implement equipment efficiency improvements alone, with current practices will result in a PUE ratio declining to 1.7 for all space types.

Best Practices: Data centers combining these efficiency gains with better operational practices are expected to reach a PUE ratio of 1.7, with the ratio declining to 1.5 for server closets and server rooms.

State-of-the-Art: Data centers with advanced efficiency solutions are projected to reach a PUE ratio of 1.4 declining to 1.3 for enterprise class data centers. And data centers, employing exotic energy-efficient power and cooling technologies such as liquid cooling and combined heat-and-power energy generation solutions, could reach a PUE of 1.2.

Google has stated it is averaging a PUE rating of 1.21 across its six company-built data centers, and one of its facilities is operating with a PUE of 1.13 (Google 2008).

A consistent measurement methodology is necessary to have good data for PUE analysis. The PUE of any data center is a dynamic number and not a static value. It varies owing to a variety of factors, such as periodic peaks and valleys of server and storage utilization, the percentage of IT power actually in use relative to facility design, outside temperatures, equipment changes and other variables.

Constant, consistent monitoring and instrumentation helps to provide accurate and sufficient data to determine the cause and effect of PUE changes. Multiple meters permit detailed power and energy measurement of the cooling infrastructure and IT equipment separately, to ensure that all of the power-consuming elements are accounted for in the PUE calculations. For large data centers this may require dozens or even hundreds of power meters.

Some larger data centers only measure facilities with an actual IT load above 5MW to eliminate any inaccuracies that can occur from measuring small values below this threshold. Regardless of what is chosen as the data set, the important part is to take regular periodic measurements and be consistent in selecting data sets and measurement used to monitor the health, operating cost, and relative efficiency of the data center and its subsystems.

For example, one option could be to count only the servers, storage and networking equipment as IT equipment power. With this example, electrical losses in a server's power cord would be counted as overhead, not as IT power. Another option would be to include measurements of the power at the utility side of the substation so that losses in substation transformers are included in the PUE. Different approaches should be considered within the context of the data center operator's intended objectives. As long as the methodology is consistently applied, the measurements can provide meaningful comparative data are useful for supporting systematic energy conservation activities.

If all power measurements adhere to the Green Grid PUE standards, the data center power consumption and efficiency analysis can be

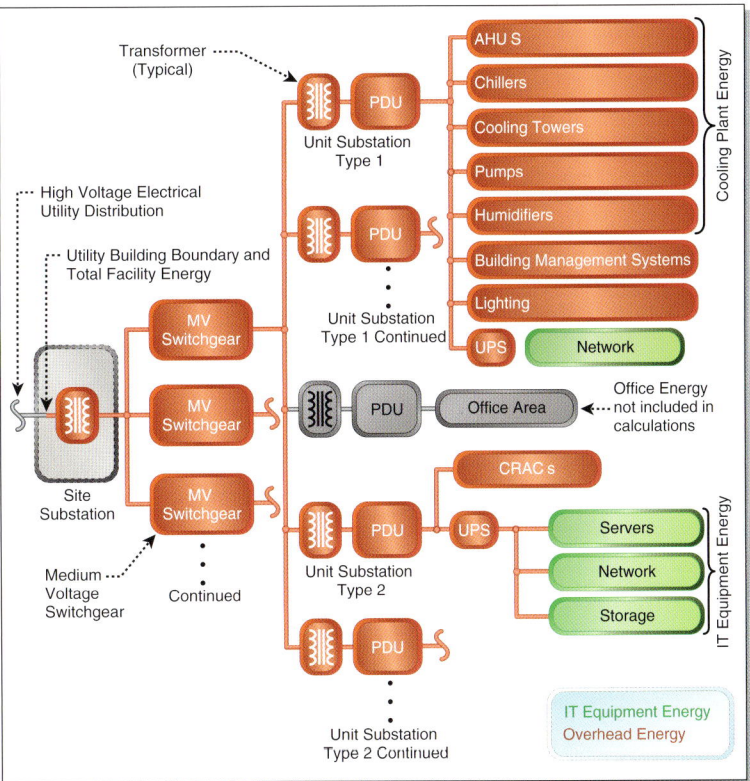

Figure 8.17 Google's Measurement Groups

Source: Google, 2008; http://www.google.com/corporate/datacenters/measuring.html

meaningfully compared with other data centers in the industry. Figures 8.17 and 8.18 show two simplified power distribution schematics and two different options for power metering in different data centers. Google measures at different levels of power distribution. Microsoft takes power measurements where shown as a circled "M" in Figure 8.18. Both of these options support the Green Grid PUE standards.

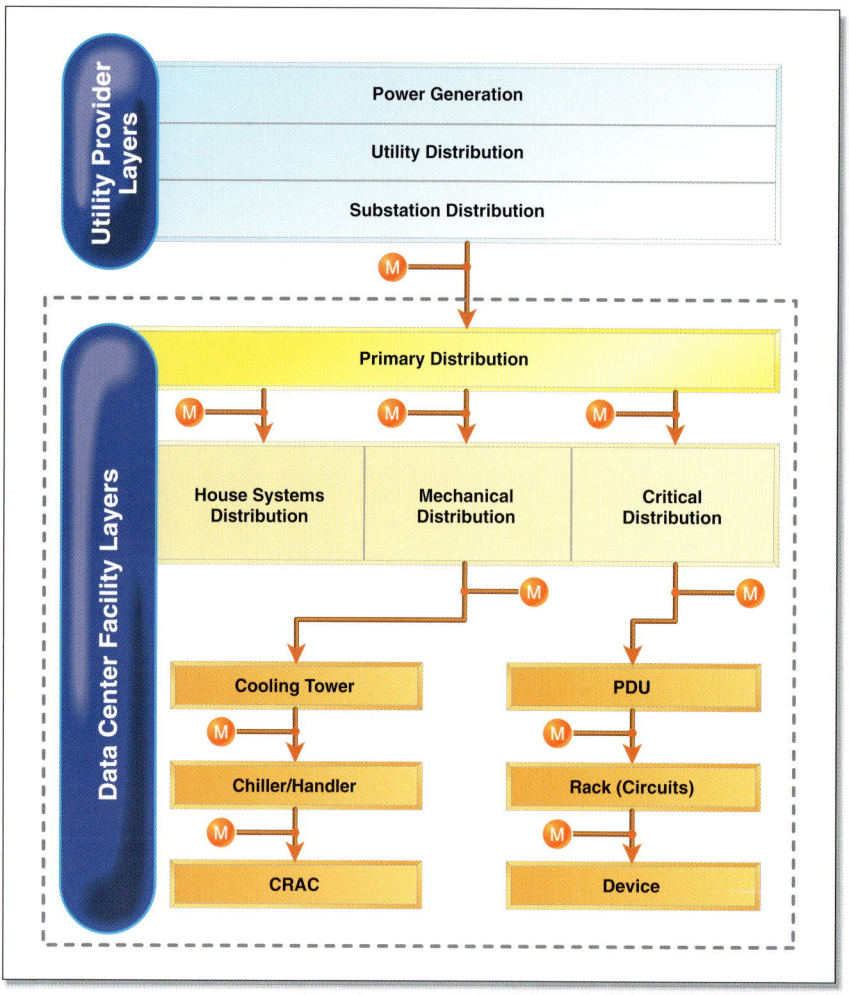

Figure 8.18 Microsoft's Measurement Points
Source: Microsoft 2008

Share and Learn From Industry Partners

Once a data center has been profiled and it's PUE tracked over a period of time, another best practice technique is to review this data with other data center managers. Best known methods, strategies, tips and techniques can be learned when comparing the energy efficiency of one data center to other data centers.

Membership in data center energy efficiency organizations and other operations focused forums promotes knowledge sharing across the industry and provides for information exchange on different data center best practices. Recommended organizations and sources of information include: The Green Grid, Climate Savers Computing, Environmental Protection Agency, Lawrence Berkeley National Labs, American Society of Heating, Refrigeration, and Air-Conditioning Engineers, The IEB Data Center Operations Council, Intellectual Capital Exchange Program and the Association for Computer Operations Management.

Summary

There are many challenges and issues around reducing power consumption in a data center, as well as a diverse number of solutions and approaches. The best one will be the one that meets all the organization's specific requirements. This may vary by location, application service level needs, as well as specific ratio of servers to storage, among other items.

There are many helpful tips and best known methods to improve the energy efficiency of a data center. Lower power consumption, from the servers, the facilities' cooling systems and higher utilization of computing resources translate into a better ROI for the data center and a big reduction on the data center power bill.

To begin with, increase utilization of all IT equipment. Turn off unused servers or power-manage servers that won't be used for extended periods of time, such as development or backup systems. Enable power management features, such as frequency/voltage scaling on equipment in use. Maximize the utilization of storage and reduce number of operating disks through optimized SANs, data compression and data de-duplication. Where possible, implement virtualization and consolidation for additional energy efficiency of IT equipment.

Air management is a key part of energy efficient data centers, and one of the largest opportunities to reduce power bills. Start with minimizing hot and cold air mixing and eliminating hot spots. Maximize the delta-temperatures between hot and cold aisles. Hot aisles are meant to be hot! Adjust the thermostat. Raising the cold aisle temperature will minimize chiller energy use. Overcooling has a huge effect on the power bill. Let the cold aisles run at 28°C (80F); virtually all equipment manufacturers allow this. Data centers in cool climate regions can realize tremendous energy savings by utilizing air-side and water-side economizers.

Raised floor designs affect efficient airflow. Care needs to be taken to insure sufficient static pressure to drive uniform air to all floor tiles. This includes no blockage in the under floor space with cables and sealing all the air leaks. Similar care should be taken to insure that the hot air return ducts in false ceilings are of sufficient size to not impede the flow of hot air.

CRAC and AHU units are most efficient if located close to IT equipment to insure that cold air is concentrated in the right pace and that the energy used to transport the cold air is minimized. To insure proper air flow through the server racks, choose the proper type of rack for the type of servers in use. Proper rack selection not only helps effectively power and cool servers, it can also improve reliability. And with racks, baffles and end panels can eliminate open holes in racks and on the ends.

With respect to power distribution, there are efficiency choices to optimize power distribution. Whenever possible use high-efficiency transformers and UPS systems. Power distribution efficiency can result in a 10 - 15 percent reduction in conversion losses. Flywheel UPS systems are considered the most efficient. The EPA recommends data centers should utilize at least 80 percent efficient UPS and 95 percent efficient transformers to achieve a Best Practice category savings.

Finally, provide incentives for purchasing to specify and buy high-efficiency servers and data storage systems. The Climate Savers Computing Initiative Web site *(www.climatesaverscomputing.org/tools/smarter-computing-catalog/)* offers resources to identify power-efficient servers, and governmental agencies around the world are working on efficiency standards and labeling for servers and other IT systems to support energy-conscious procurements. Table 8.2 on Page 221 is a summary of data center improvements by the EPA. Categorized as Improved Operations, Best Practice, and State of the Art, each recommendation scenario offers increased energy savings.

Table 8.2 Summary of EPA Efficiency Scenarios

	IT Equipment	Site Infrastructure Systems
Improved Operation	• Volume server virtualization leading to a physical server reduction ration of 1.04 to 1 (for server closets) and 1.08 to 1 (for all other space types) by 2011 • 5% of servers eliminated through virtualization efforts are not replaced (, legacy applications) • "Energy efficient" servers represent 5% of volume server shipments in 2008 and 15% of shipments in 2011 • Power management enabled on 100% of applicable servers • Average energy use per enterprise storage drive declining 7% by 2011;	• PUE ratio declining to 1.7 by 2011 for all space types assuming: • 95% efficient transformers • 80% efficient UPS • Air cooled direct exchange system chiller • Constant speed fans • Humidification control • Redundant air handling units;
Best Practice	• Moderate volume server virtualization leading to a physical server reduction ratio of 1.33 to 1) for server closets) and 2 to 1 (for all other space types) by 2011 • 5% of servers eliminated through virtualization efforts are not replaced (, legacy applications) • "Energy efficient" servers represent 100% of applicable servers • Power management enabled on 100% of applicable servers • Moderate reduction in applicable storage devices (1.5 to 1) by 2011; • Average energy use per enterprise storage drive declining 7% by 2011	• PUE ratio declining to 1.7 by 2011 for server closets and server rooms (Using previous assumptions) • PUE ratio declining to 1.5 by 2011 for data centers assuming: • 98% efficient transformers • 90% efficient UPS • Variable-speed drive chiller with economizer cooling or water-side free cooling (in moderate or mild climate region) • Variable-speed fans and pumps • Redundant air-handling units
State of the Art	• Aggressive volume server virtualization leading to a physical server reduction ratio of 1.66 to 1 (for server closets) and 5 to 1 (for all other space types) by 2011 • 5% of servers eliminated through virtualization efforts are not replaced (, legacy applications) • "Energy efficient" servers represent 100% of volume server shipments 2008 to 2011 • Power management enabled on 100% of applicable servers • Average energy use per enterprise storage drive declining 7% by 2011 • Aggressive reduction of applicable storage devices (~2.4 to 1) by 2011	• PUE ratio declining 10 1.7 by 2011 for server closets and server rooms (using previous assumptions) • PUE ratio declining to 1.5 by 2011 for localized and mid-tier data centers centers (using previous assumptions • PUE ratio declining to 1.4 by 2011 for enterprise data centers assuming • 98% efficient transformers • 95% efficient UPS • Liquid cooling to the racks • Cooling tower (in moderate or mild climate region) • Variable speed fans and pumps • CHP

Chapter 8: Energy-Efficient Data Center Tuning

Customer Examples

Reducing Data Center Cost with an Air Economizer

Profile: Air Economizer PoC

- 900 heavily utilized production servers in a high-density data center
- 100 percent air exchange at up to 90°F, with no humidity control and minimal air filtration
- 67 percent estimated power savings using economizer 91 percent of the time—an estimated annual savings of approximately USD 2.87 million in a 10-MW data center

To challenge established industry assumptions regarding data center cooling, Intel IT conducted a proof of concept (PoC) test that used an air economizer to cool production servers with 100 percent outside air at temperatures of up to 90°F. With this approach, we could use an economizer to provide nearly all data center cooling, substantially reducing power consumption. This could potentially reduce annual operating costs by up to USD 2.87 million for a 10-megawatt (MW) data center.

We ran the PoC in a dry, temperate climate over 10 months using about 900 production blade servers, divided equally between two side-by-side compartments, as shown in Figure 8.19. One used standard air conditioning, the other an air economizer.

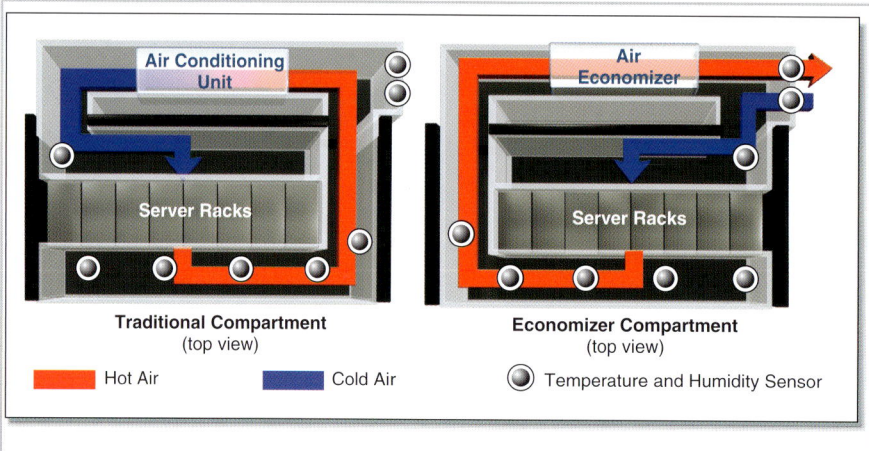

Figure 8.19 Proof of concept (PoC) data center environment.
Source: Intel IT, 2008

Servers in the economizer compartment were subjected to considerable variation in temperature and humidity as well as poor air quality; however, there was no significant increase in server failures. If subsequent investigation confirms these promising results, we anticipate using this approach in future high-density data centers.

Background

Data center power consumption is soaring, driven by increasing demand for computing capacity. In a typical data center, 60 to 70 percent of data center power may be used for facilities power and data center cooling.

At Intel, our data centers need to support the rapid growth in computing capacity required to design increasingly complex semiconductors. At the same time, we are trying to minimize data center power consumption and operating costs.

Our strategy is based on high-performance, high-density data centers containing thousands of blade servers. These blades deliver considerable computing capacity, but they also generate substantial heat. We supply cooling air to the blades at 68°F; as the air passes over the blades, the air temperature rises by 58°F, resulting in an exit temperature of 126°F. This means that we need to cool the air by 58°F before re-circulating it. The air conditioning units required to do this consume a considerable amount of electricity.

Air economizers represent one potential way to reduce data center power consumption and cooling cost. Instead of cooling and re-circulating the hot air from the servers, air economizers simply expel the hot air outdoors and draw in outside air to cool the IT equipment.

The current industry assumption is that the usefulness of air economizers is limited by the need to supply cooling air at a relatively low temperature. The implication is that air economizers can only be used at times when the outside air is relatively cool. There is also concern about variation in humidity, because the humidity of outside air can change rapidly. A third area of concern is particulate counts in outside air.

We decided to challenge these assumptions by employing an economizer to cool a high-density production environment using a much wider range of outside air temperatures—up to 90°F. We reasoned that this might be feasible because server manufacturers specify that their products can operate in temperatures as high as 98°F. We also wanted to push the accepted limits of humidity and air quality.

If we were successful, we would be able to use air economizers for most of the year in dry, temperate climates. This could drastically reduce power consumption and cooling costs while improving Intel's environmental footprint.

Proof of Concept

We conducted a large PoC test using approximately 900 production design servers at a data center located in a temperate desert climate with generally low relative humidity. We began the PoC in October 2007, and continued the test for 10 months until August 2008.

We set up the PoC in a 1,000-square-foot (SF) trailer that was originally installed to provide temporary additional computing capacity and divided the trailer into two compartments of approximately 500 SF each. To minimize the cost of the PoC, we used low-cost, warehouse-grade direct expansion (DX) air conditioning equipment. Temperature and humidity sensors were installed to monitor the conditions in each compartment.

We cooled one compartment with a traditional approach, using a DX unit to recirculate hot air and provide cooling at all times.

For the other compartment, we used essentially the same air-conditioning equipment, but with modifications that enabled it to operate as an economizer by expelling hot air to the outdoors and drawing in 100 percent outside air for cooling.

Because one of our goals was to test the acceptable limits of operating temperature, we configured the cooling equipment in the economizer compartment to supply air at temperatures ranging from 65°F to 90° F. We designed the system to use only the economizer until the supply air exceeded the 90°F maximum, at which point we began using the chiller to cool the air to 90°F. If the temperature dropped below 65°F, we warmed the supply air by mixing it with hot return air from the servers.

We made no attempt to control humidity. We also wanted to test the limits of air quality, so we applied minimal filtering to incoming air, using a standard household air filter that removed only large particles from the incoming air but permitted fine dust to pass through.

Each room contained eight racks. Each rack contained four blade servers with 14 blades each, for a total of 448 blades per compartment. This represented a power density of more than 200 watts per square foot (WPSF).

During the PoC, we used the servers to run large production batch silicon design workloads, resulting in very high server utilization rates of about 90 percent.

Customer Examples 223

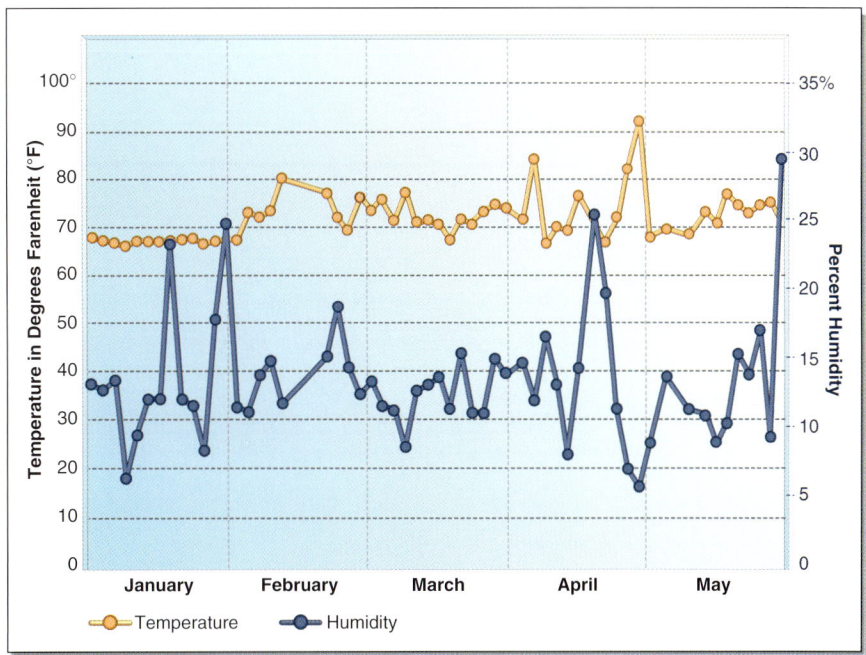

Figure 8.20 Temperature and Humidity Variation in the air economizer Compartment from January through May 2008.

Source: Intel IT

We measured server failure rates in each compartment and compared them with the failure rates that we experienced during the same period within our main data center at the same location.

Results

During the PoC, the servers in the economizer compartment were subjected to wide variation in environmental conditions, as shown in Figure 2.

- The temperature of the supply air varied from 64°F to more than 92°F. This variation slightly exceeded our set points partly due to the slow response of our low-cost air conditioning units.
- Humidity varied from 4 percent to more than 90 percent and changed rapidly at times.
- The servers and the interior of the compartment became covered in a layer of dust.

Power Consumption

Total power consumption of the trailer was approximately 500 kilowatts (KW) when using air conditioning in both compartments. When using the economizer, the DX cooling load in the economizer compartment was reduced from 111.78 KW to 28.6 KW, representing a 74 percent reduction in energy consumption.

Server Failure Rates

Despite the dust and variation in humidity and temperature, there was only a minimal difference between the 4.46 percent failure rate in the economizer compartment and the 3.83 percent failure rate in our main data center over the same period. The failure rate in the trailer compartment with DX cooling was 2.45 percent, actually lower than in the main data center.

Table 8.3 Average Annual Temperatures at the Proof of Concept (PoC) Test Location

Month	Average High	Average Low
January	48°F	24°F
February	55°F	28°F
March	62°F	33°F
April	70°F	41°F
May	80°F	49°F
June	90°F	59°F
July	92°F	65°F
August	88°F	63°F
September	83°F	56°F
October	71°F	44°F
November	57°F	32°F
December	48°F	24°F

Analysis

We estimated the average annual power savings we could achieve in a data center that uses an economizer. To do this, we used historical weather data for the data center location, summarized in Table 8.3. Analysis of the data indicated that during an average year, the temperature is below our 90°F maximum 91 percent of the time.

Based on our 74 percent measured decrease in power consumption when using the economizer during the PoC, and assuming that we could rely on the economizer 91 percent of the year, we could potentially save approximately 67 percent of the total power used annually for cooling compared with a traditional data center cooling approach. This translates into approximately 3,500 kilowatt hours (KWH) per KW of overall data center power consumption, based on an assumption that 60 percent of data center power typically is used for mechanical cooling systems.

This would result in an estimated annual cost reduction of approximately USD 143,000 for a small 500-KW data center, based on electricity costs of 0.08 per KWH. In a larger 10-MW data center, the estimated annual cost reduction would be approximately USD 2.87 million.

In addition, we could avoid certain capital expenditures in new data centers because we would require less cooling equipment. Even when the outside air temperature exceeded our maximum supply air temperature, we would only have to cool the air to our specified maximum rather than to the 68°F used in our traditional data center approach. Reducing the complexity and cost of the cooling system also reduces the number of failure modes, increasing overall resiliency.

Conclusion

We observed no consistent increase in server failure rates as a result of the greater variation in temperature and humidity, and the decrease in air quality, in the trailer. This suggests that existing assumptions about the need to closely regulate these factors bear further scrutiny.

Air economizers seem particularly suited to temperate climates with low humidity. A data center equipped with an air economizer could substantially reduce Intel's environmental footprint by reducing consumption of both power and water. In dry climates, traditional air-conditioned data centers typically include evaporative cooling using water towers as a pre-cooling stage. With an economizer, this would not typically be used, potentially saving up to 76 million gallons of water annually in a 10-MW data center.

We plan to further test for possible hardware degradation using a server aging analysis that compares systems used in the economizer compartment, in the air-conditioned compartment, and in our main data center.

If subsequent investigation confirms our promising PoC results, we expect to include air economizers in future data center designs. A possible next step would be a 1-MW demonstration data center using the equipment designed for the PoC.

Chapter 9

Designing New Energy Efficient Data Centers

*It's always good to take an orthogonal view of something.
It develops ideas.*
—Ken Thompson

This chapter focuses on recommendations for building new data centers. Given the difference in useful life spans of IT equipment relative to facility infrastructure, planning for long term energy efficiency is complex. Many factors need to be analyzed to achieve efficiency over the 15+ year life span of a physical building. Such factors as technology changes, future compute demands, power and cooling capacity needs and business environments must be balanced during design and planning. Options for floor space expansions are reviewed, including compute density and containers. Finally, this chapter covers options which can improve energy efficiency in data center designs and planning. The options range from geographic location impacts, to modularity and equipment placement.

Investment Considerations

Capital investments in data center facilities and support infrastructure (HVAC and power distribution systems) are typically subject to long term depreciation rules under current tax laws. Thus, most data centers are designed with 15 to 20-year plus life spans in scope. In addition the large cost associated with constructing a new facility, or even retrofitting an existing one, constitutes a significant financial justification barrier for most companies.

In contrast, IT systems are subject to a much shorter four-year depreciation schedule, arrive in much smaller server-sized increments, and consequently receive a significantly lower degree of financial review. This short lifecycle and low cost coupled with accelerating technical changes in IT equipment designs creates an unavoidable incongruity in the rate of change between supply and demand.

While IT infrastructure changes rapidly, the facilities infrastructure does not. In other words, the opportunity for implementing significant HVAC and electrical distribution system improvements in the stock of existing legacy data centers is financially and temporally constrained and thus limited relative to that of IT equipment. Addition or replacement of existing systems with new facilities technologies is difficult to justify based solely on technical merit. Such changes are made only at the end of systems' useful life as determined by financial, availability or capacity criteria.

The result is that once a facility is completed, it is difficult to modify the inherent power efficiency of the design or installed facility subsystem equipment. Uptime Institute cites a 15-year usable facilities infrastructure lifespan based on changes required to support new IT systems. This is because after every fifth generation of server technology a facility must be renovated or replaced in order to support the new IT requirements (Uptime, 2007). Proper evaluation of business requirements, technology roadmaps (both facility and IT) and the implications to total cost of ownership (TCO) are essential to support selection of the best design choice for the operator from the beginning of the design-build process.

Various TCO models have been developed by organizations such as Green Grid as well as by individual corporations. Therefore no attempt will be made to define a detailed model here. What is pertinent to this text is that the cost of energy, facilities systems efficiency and IT architecture requirements anticipated must be balanced in order to arrive at the optimal business solution. Energy cost is one of the most significant long term variables in virtually all models. Green Grid, IDC and other research indicate that energy costs over the life of a server have or will soon exceed the capital cost of purchasing a server, including the capital cost of the facilities infrastructure that supports it. At a high level, power efficiency must be balanced against required performance. This said, in many situations multiple combinations of IT systems and facilities systems can produce the same levels of ROI as is demonstrated by the graph below.

IT Load Planning and Capacity Factors

Fundamental to optimizing the design of a data center facility is an understanding of the characteristics of the demand; physical size, weight of systems, total planned power capacity and potential thermal load. Together these attributes will determine the overall capacity required (design capacity) over the life of the facility.

The design capacity must be projected into the future in order to support the business without significant disruption. In other words, sufficient spare capacity must be built in to the design to support both immediate (day one) needs as well as projected needs in the future. Figure 9.1 shows an example of how compute demand can be projected into the future to relate to capacity needs.

Supporting projected capacity poses a bit of a conundrum. Delivery of capacity *just in time* reduces non-productive sunk capital and operational costs (including power). However, the long construction lead times and useful life of facility, and the large commitment of capital

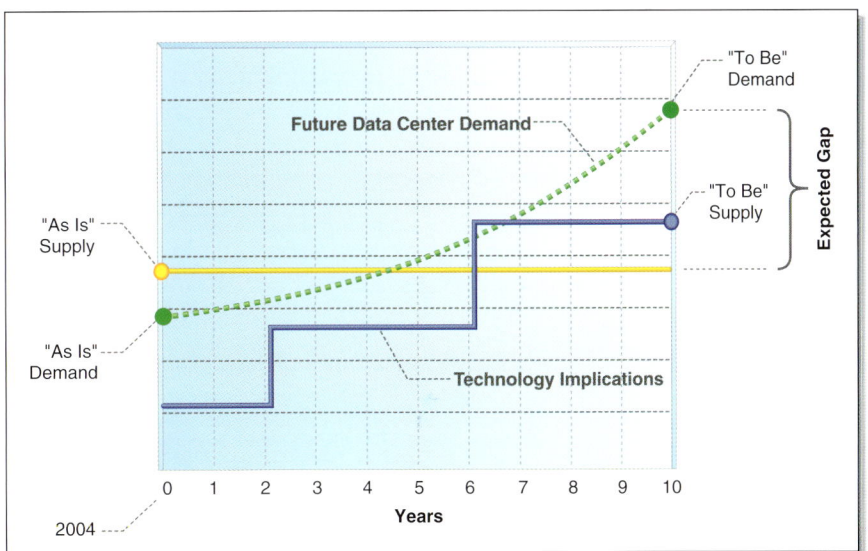

Figure 9.1 Capacity Planning Model
Source: C. Rego, Intel Solution Services, 2005

generally required tend to create a situation in which companies err on the side of building large increments of data center capacity. This is in part due to the need to mitigate the risk of under sizing the design. Construction is usually slow to start and requires a year or two to bring on line. In addition, because of the scale of investment, once committed to, an existing facility will be slow to adapt to new infrastructure technologies.

Many data centers end up with non-productive energy consumption due to under loaded power distribution and cooling systems. This is difficult to overcome, because of the long construction lead times, extended facilities life span and the uncertainty introduced by disruptive technologies and rapid business condition changes.

Service availability requirements must then be factored in. Depending on the required uptime, specific redundancies will need to be designed into new data center facilities.

In order to maximize the effectiveness of any specific design elements, the most impactful approach is to prioritize efforts based on proportion consumption within the data center starting with the largest area of consumption and working progressively downwards. As discussed in previous chapters, the balance of consumption between facilities load and IT load is relatively equal for the majority of data centers that exist today.

Customers must know how to plan for the power and cooling within these data centers. In newly built data centers, IT equipment must be deployed as rapidly as possible to quickly achieve maximize use of the large sunk capital cost and unavoidable operational costs, including power overhead consumed by infrastructure systems. Without sound planning, this may mean that minimal time can be spent on site preparation, which can result in thermal issues after the equipment is installed. The construction cost of a data center exceeds USD 15,000/m^2 in some metropolitan areas, with an annual operating cost of USD 500 to USD 1,500/m^2. For these reasons, the aim is to obtain the most from data center space and maximize the utilization of the infrastructure. Unfortunately, the current situation in many data centers does not allow for this optimization.

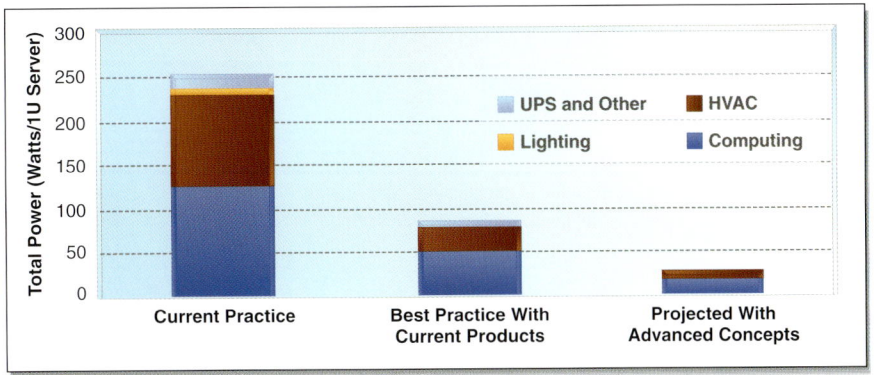

Figure 9.2 Efficiency Opportunities: RMI Charrette Results
Source: RMI

Considerations for Compute Density or Expanding Floor Space

Data center capacity growth is being driven by the increase in demand for compute resources to support business and scientific applications and projects and the explosion of Internet based content and services. The sheer volume of servers in data centers is driving a notable increase in overall power demand, as discussed in the earlier chapters. With this increasing demand, there are fundamental trade-offs between increasing IT Loads and the impacts to thermals to power. Besides the thermal issues, continuous upgrading of power and cooling is not viable as long-term strategies within operating data centers. Many data centers today reach a breakeven point at power densities of around 250 watts per square foot.

When considering new data center designs, consideration must be given to the question of whether to scale up or increase floor space. Each approach requires the same amount of power to run a given number of servers or amount of IT load. Spreading out requires longer copper network and power conductor runs. Increasing floor space also increases the volume to be cooled and the distances that air or other coolants must be transported. There is also the additional materials cost for a larger building shell and data center space. From a data center capacity supply perspective, higher power density reduces USD /kW costs and usually yields the best business cost efficiency.

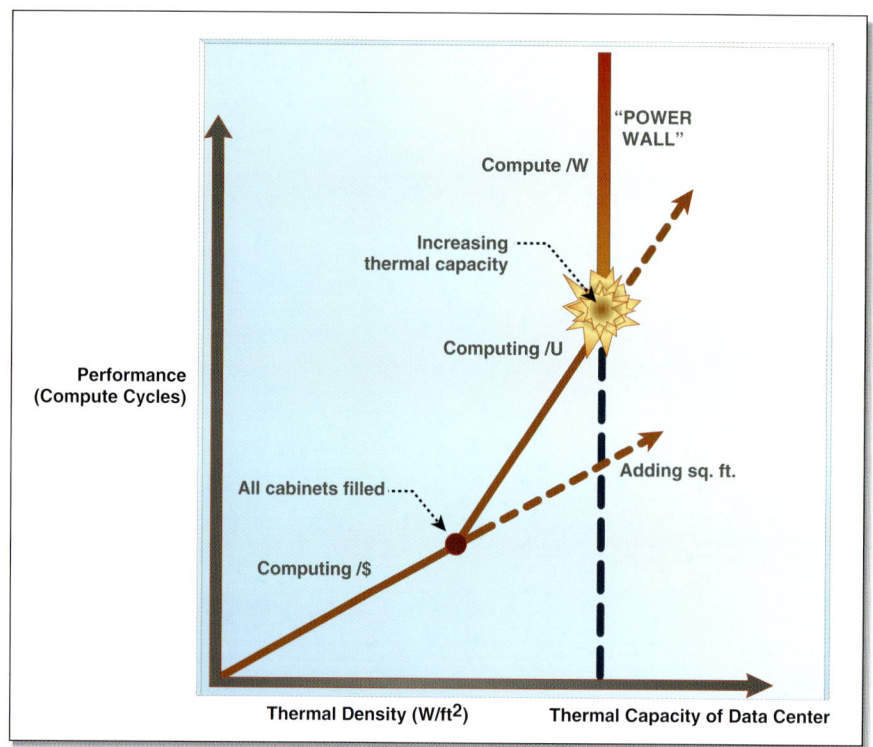

Figure 9.3 Data Center Constraints and Drivers
Source: Intel IT, 2007

Options available to address this challenge include expanding existing space with the same watts per square foot, retrofitting power and cooling systems to increase power density or construction of a new data center. New construction projects should consider building a new structure that can ultimately support a 300 to 500 watts per square foot power density, taking into consideration a facility's 10 to15 year life cycle. The optimal energy efficient choice would focus on expanding the overall compute resource without expanding space. Dense can be good.

With the low cost of high density x86 servers, it is often more cost effective to increase compute density instead of expanding data center capacity (that is, its floor space). Higher power density usually results in a reduced USD /kW capital cost, assuming the same level of facilities subsystem design availability.

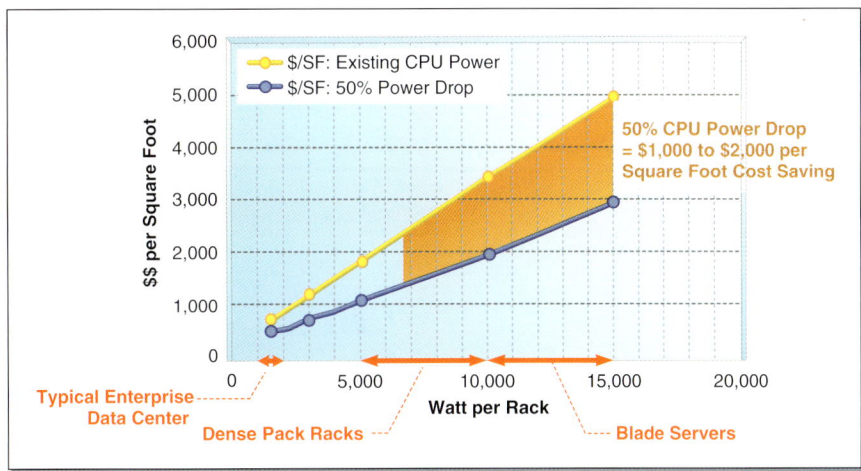

Figure 9.4 Data Center Cost versus W/Rack
Source: High Performance Data Center Task Force, Intel 2006

Another benefit of increased density lies in leveraging subsystem efficiencies. Facilities subsystems run at peak energy efficiency when they are operating at between ~65 and 85 percent of design power capacity. Lightly loaded data centers running below 50 percent utilization are extremely energy inefficient. Those running above 85 percent experience a slight drop in efficiency as well as potentially increasing the rate of cooling and power delivery systems failures due to limited head room for handling spikes in power demand. So, when at all possible, rapidly filling a data center to above 50 percent load reduces electrical inefficiencies and consequently the power cost per unit of compute. Conversely, this has a direct bearing on choosing the optimal size of data center increments to be constructed.

New Data Centers: Starting With a Plan

If the decision is to build a new facility, there is typically financial pressure to quickly deploy IT equipment to obtain maximum use of a large financial asset; this may mean that minimal time can be spent on site preparation. With construction cost of a data center exceeding USD USD 15,000/m^2 in some metropolitan areas and with annual operating costs of USD 500 to USD 1,500/m^2 (and growing), pressure to bring the data center online quickly must be balanced against the appropriate planning and design in order to manage operational risk exposure. Planning is critical given the 15 to 20 year life span of a data center. Data centers planners must know how to plan for energy efficient power and cooling in concert with capacity and availability requirements. For these reasons, the aim is to obtain the most from data center space and maximize the utilization of the infrastructure. Unfortunately, the current situation in many data centers does not allow for this optimization.

New data centers can be engineered for both cost and energy efficiency. The most resource-efficient designs meet the individual requirements of the data center's users and specific site conditions. All environmental data, organizational factors and latest technologies for IT equipment, power distribution and cooling system technologies and future road maps should be analyzed and understood when starting the planning for a new data center.

Plans for an energy efficient data center should include assessments of multiple factors. Designers need to consider all the costs: land, building, generators, power distribution equipment, cooling equipment, electricity, water, network and staff. Software tools are available that can help assess climates and geophysical data to help determine ideal locations. One factor to consider with regard to a site location is whether you can run an economizer to use free air to cool the data center.

After a location is selected, building design and equipment need to be evaluated to create efficient configurations with low TCO over the life of the data center. To optimize the data center power and thermal design, test different room configurations with Computational Fluid Dynamics modeling tools.

Power distribution and equipment costs exceed 40 percent of the cost of a typical data center, while the building itself costs just over 15 percent. As a result, a difficult trade-off must be made when selecting power density. If the data center is provisioned to support very high power densities (high power to floor space ratio) the risk is that some of the power will go unused if the actual racks that are installed consume less power/square foot than the data center design point. This could waste expensive power equipment. On the other hand, if the data center is provisioned with a lower power density, the risk is that floor space will be wasted due to inability to completely fill each rack. Wasted floor space is much less expensive in most cases than wasted power capacity.

This tradeoff is difficult to balance exactly, so most IT data center operators err toward provisioning to lower power densities because a mistake in this direction is much less costly than providing more power than can be used. As a consequence, most facilities are power bound with much wasted floor space. This is an unnecessary cost that also negatively impacts cooling and power distribution efficiency. For this reason (and others), best-practice data center designs today utilize modular design principles, as shown in Figure 9.5. In a modular design, the data center floor space can be adjusted to match the power supply and distribution capabilities of the center when changes in business requirements and IT system technology shifts occur.

Most data centers start with over-built capacity and then run for years with only partial loads. A modular design allows only parts of the data center's infrastructure to be built and operated when the data center is initially brought on line. As demand for capacity increases, additional rooms can be built and brought on line in response. When technology changes require, individual modules can be retrofitted to support or take advantage of the changes without impacting the other modules' ability to operate. Modularity also permits systems to reach and operate at peak efficiency very quickly—something that almost never happens in current data center design.

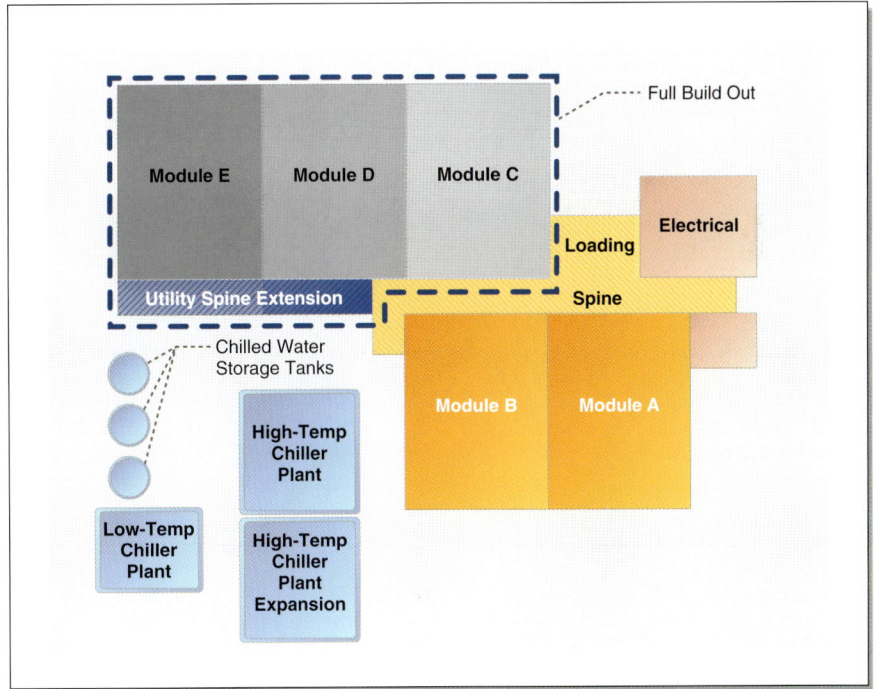

Figure 9.5 Sample Modular Building Plan
Source: Intel Global Data Center Services, 2005

Regardless of the technology deployed, all of these systems—from chillers to UPS systems to humidifiers to computer room air conditioning units—operate most efficiently when they're working at or very near their rated load. Modular data center designs that allow systems to either run at load or be turned off will be far more efficient than designs that load facilities systems at some fraction of capacity for an extended period.

Modularity of data centers is key to maintaining IT and facilities owner's agility and adaptability over the life of a data center investment. If designed into a new data center, a modular approach allows phased delivery of capacity in planned increments. As Figure 9.5 shows, the optimal size of each module is dependent on the planned fill rate, compute platform configurations and mix, design power density and time to deliver incremental data center capacity.

In order to maximize the effectiveness of any specific design elements, the most impactful approach is to prioritize efforts based on proportion of consumption within the data center starting with the largest area of consumption and working progressively downwards.

Power and cooling systems can be designed to divert power from areas where it is not needed. Best practices use flexible designs that allow power and cooling systems to be reconfigured for redundancy, capacity etc. If equipment or rooms are designed to receive a specific amount of power, but a work load is not run, the power becomes 'stranded'. Stranded power can result in millions of dollars of wasted electricity.

Finally, locate compute hardware where it is most efficient for power and cooling. In some situations, it's impossible to put a piece of equipment in the ideal location, but wherever possible remove physical barriers. The further power and cool air must travel to meet requirements of the IT Load, the more opportunities for waste and inefficiency. Additionally, greater distances of house load infrastructure require increased maintenance and costs. The closer the infrastructure equipment is to the IT equipment, the better.

Container Options

Data Center design and construction can be slow; a typical 10 to 15-megawatt facility takes over 24 months and tens of millions of dollars to build. One approach to significantly reduce time to data center capacity and leverage modularity advantages lies in the use of pre-fabricated containerized data centers. Container data centers provide an inflection point opportunity to drive data center affordability.

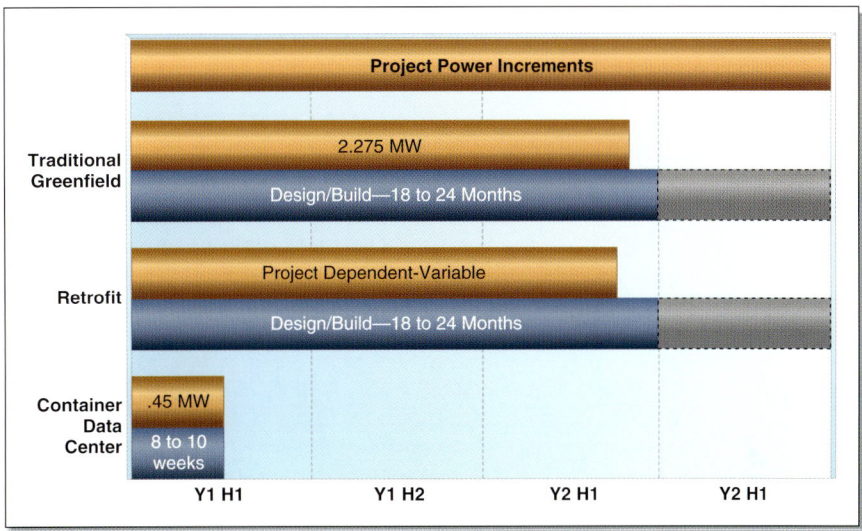

Figure 9.6 Data Center Capacity Delivery Comparisons
Source: Intel IT Data Center Services, 2008

As shown in Figure 9.6, containers can be planned, procured and provisioned in less than six months. They offer a 30 percent reduction in dollars spent for concrete and steel facilities. Intel IT Data Center Services found that containers offer an end-to-end TCO NPC cost avoidance of more than 9 percent per compute cycle from day one. They also offer just-in-time fully utilized data centers that immediately optimize asset use and reduce planning and investment uncertainty. The viability of this approach is highly dependent on the server procurement and governance model of each organization and the business being supported.

Many data centers' long range forecasts are only 40 percent accurate beyond any 12 month period while traditional capacity additions via retrofit or new construction take 18 to 24 months to complete. Container data centers allow a rapid response to changing business and technology shifts. Planning for data center containers can be done well within a 12 month horizon and thus align capacity investments very closely with emerging changes in demand.. Container data centers provide fast turn planning and provisioning capability which reduces the risk of over or under investing in data center capacity significantly.

Containers are very efficient with recycling. Container data center power and cooling systems can be recycled at the same rate as the server payload. This enables more energy efficient and sophisticated facilities

238 ■ Chapter 9: Designing New Energy Efficient Data Centers

systems to replace older ones in concert with servers and network equipment. An integrated self-contained data center unitized and integrated module offers significant power efficiency opportunities due to the ability to balance overall design parameters with payload requirements and recycle these together at the optimal replacement ROI rate.

A container data center is built in a 20 or 40 foot standard shipping container; ISO 668 shipping containers are a common choice.

Figure 9.7 shows a sample ISO 668 shipping container. The facilities and IT equipment are configured and burned in, and the container is then delivered as a fully operational module with full IT and in-room facilities systems installed in a ready to run no-service-required package. All that needs to be done upon delivery is provide power, networking, and chilled water supply connections.

A central building is still needed in most cases to house power, networking, and cooling equipment and provide some physical security,. But the containers can safely be stored outside. The only requirement is a secured, fenced, paved area to place the containers around the central facilities building. In some situations, the addition of skid mounted power generators, UPS and chiller systems can further reduce the type of interconnection required to that of network.

Figure 9.7 20 Foot ISO 668 Shipping Container
Source: Microsoft, 2007

Figure 9.8 Exterior and Interior of a Container-based Data Center
Source: Rackable Systems, 2008

Container data center units can also be used for capacity augmentation where floor space is not available. They can be deployed by placing them in parking lots or on roofs. The containers can be stacked 3 to 5 high allowing high-density data centers to be built out at low costs. The low cost container-based model helps make smaller data centers in remote locations more affordable.

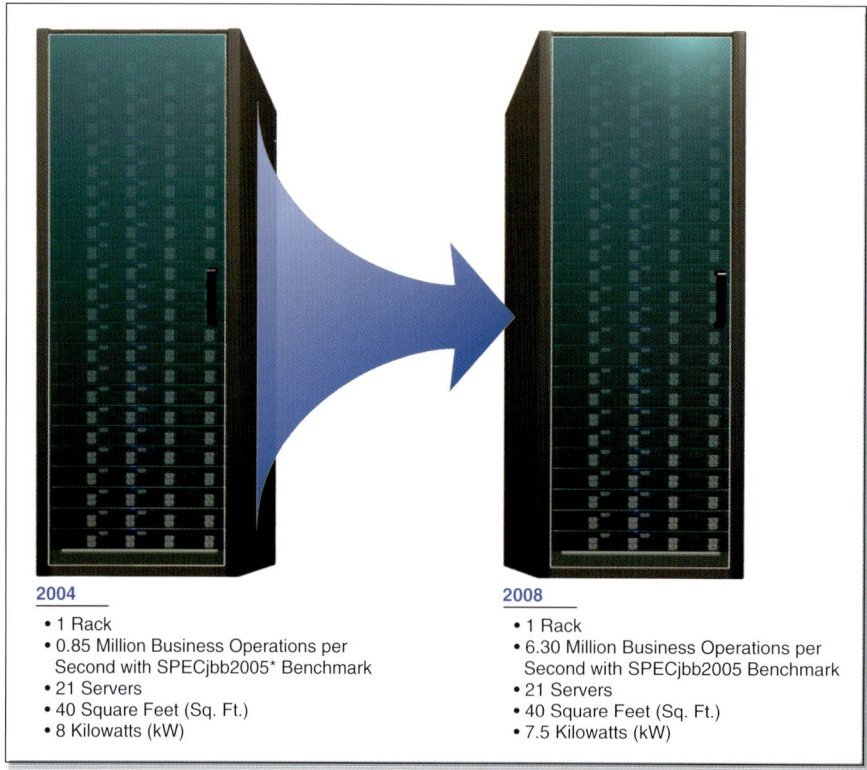

Figure 9.9 Seven Times the Compute Capacity in the Same Space Using Less Power

Source: Intel IT

Data centers built using containers are not only cheap to construct but they are also cheap to move. When capacity is no longer needed in a specific location, the entire data center can be moved to a different place where it can be utilized. The container can be cost-effectively shipped over highways, by rail, or across oceans. Containers can be placed in any secure location with network capacity, chilled water, and power and it will run minimal hardware maintenance for its service life (typically four years, based on tax accounting rules). The fixed assets are just a central services building and a fenced compound rather than an expensive facility that must be sold or dismantled at the end of its useful life.

More to the point of this book, container data centers are highly energy efficient. Typical container operation run rates via power and cooling efficiency shows 20 percent efficiency gain and almost 80

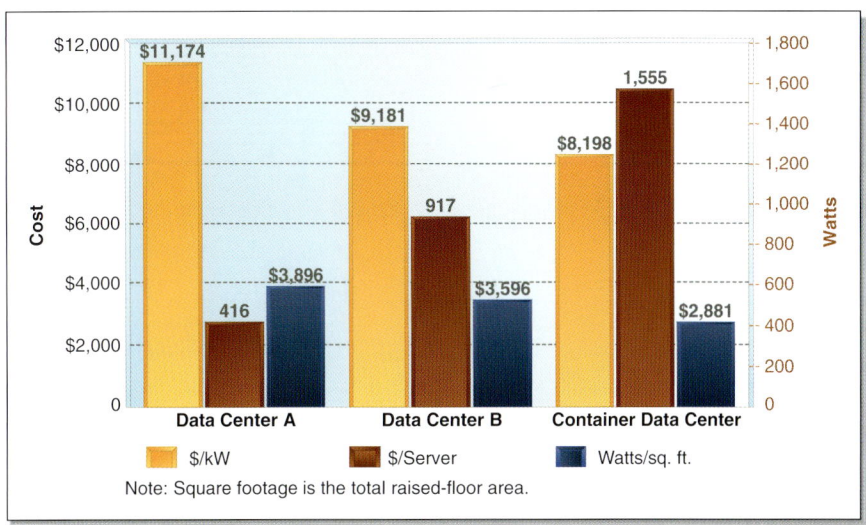

Figure 9.10 Data Center Module to Container Cost Comparisons
Source: Intel IT, 2007

percent improvement in air cooling efficiency over concrete and steel facilities.

Containers are more efficient than concrete and steel facilities because they utilize close coupled cooling and thus eliminate space requirements for CRAC units. Also, space is not required for human service or for high volume airflow. As a result, the system density can be much higher than is possible with conventional air-cooled racks.

Power distribution systems are also very efficient in containers. Some containers utilize a rectifier/transformer unit at the rack level rather than having an inefficient switching power supply with each server. With the rectifier/transformer unit AC current is converted to DC current just once and is then directly distributed to all systems within the racks. To minimize losses on the way to the container, high voltage AC is used, 480VAC is the common choice. Using efficient DC transformers on each server coupled with high efficiency rack or container level AC to DC rectifier/transformers yields significant power savings. This efficiency can be further enhanced by using in-rack DC powered UPS. This approach sidesteps the losses inherent to most AC to DC to AC (double conversion) UPS systems usually deployed in legacy data centers. In addition to being more efficient, this approach has proven to be more reliable in field usage as well.

One additional energy efficiency note: containerized data centers typically require far less total energy for construction, fit up and installation than do traditional brick and mortar data center designs. This is because of the assembly line manufacturing and fit-up techniques that are used.

Some companies that deploy containers implement a 'fail-in-place' strategy to also save on maintenance costs. The containers are configured with enough redundancy that, as servers fail surviving nodes continue to support the processing load at required levels. There is no service, repair or replacement of the individual failed systems. The entire container just slowly degrades over time as more and more systems suffer non-recoverable hardware errors. When the lowest threshold of acceptable performance is reached, the container is disconnected, a replacement is brought in and the old container returned to the manufacturer for refurbishment or recycling. To illustrate this, consider a container that is configured with 1,000 servers to support a workload that needs 900. For this discussion, say that over time, 50 servers fail, but the 1,000 system container is still operating with 95 percent of its original design capacity. The key architectural requirement for this container to meet business service levels is that software applications implement sufficient redundancy so that individual system failures don't negatively impact overall service availability.

Container data centers can be very green and efficient as a means of reducing material waste. At the end of a container's service life, the container is returned to the supplier for retrofit/recycling. During recycling, the container is refitted with current generation systems. Parts that can't be reused are recycled. Waste is minimized in two ways:

- Component level packaging waste is minimized because systems don't need to be packaged for shipping, unpacked, and racked.

- At end-of-service-life, the entire unit is shipped back to the manufacturer for rebuild and recycling without requiring repackaging for shipment. In essence, the container is the package.

A container data center strategy leveraging mobility aspects reduces site sunk cost exposure from typical concrete and steel data center facilities. This eliminates many of the problems associated with site divestures. Containers conserve both power and materials. They also allow companies to quickly respond to changing business needs or natural disasters like the Malaysian Tsunami or the Chengdu earthquake. In short, they provide a very energy efficient, low cost response to changing business geography requirements.

Summary

When considering data center expansion, given the low cost of x86 servers, it is more cost effective to increase density and optimize utilization of the house load than expand physical capacity. New data center designs that implement modular designs can be optimized for maximum efficiency and utilization and can be more readily adapted to changes in technology and/or business requirements over time. Finally, containers are an efficient means for expansion and remote located data centers. They provide efficient power distribution with transformer units at the rack level and cooling is efficient due to the close coupled cooling and elimination of CRAC space requirements.

Chapter 10

Energy-Efficient Server and PC Management

Computing is not about computers any more. It is about living.
—Nicholas Negroponte

Preventative maintenance allows servers to run cooler, quieter and maintain a top performance per watt. But ensuring servers and databases remain energy efficient requires IT labor. For large data centers, server maintenance labor can be more expensive than the server hardware. An average large data center houses over 1,000 servers; individual server maintenance is impractical.

Intel IT is now advocating a four year server refresh cycle as the most cost effective for maintaining server energy efficiency. The changes in performance per watt are significant enough to outweigh the capital investment for the refresh and the energy efficiency gain is huge. Intel IT has refreshed 25 percent of the servers in 2008 and has seen a ~6.6X improvement in performance per watt. This has resulted in significant capital spend avoidance, as well, since growth in compute demand, absent performance improvements from new servers, would have required investments in several new data centers.

This chapter will provide examples and case studies on server refresh strategies showing how large data centers operate and manage their servers for increased energy efficiency. The ROI for these case studies will reflect key strategies that not only are energy efficient, but have a strong financial return also.

For small businesses, with a few servers, preventative maintenance can save a lot of money, power and problems. Basic server maintenance procedures, upgrades and troubleshooting are provided in Appendix A of this book.

Server Life Cycle Costs: The Complete View

Server maintenance involves constant tuning, monitoring and periodic cleaning tasks. The sidebar on page 283 of Appendix A shows a basic maintenance schedule. Following a schedule like this would be problematic for a data center with hundreds of servers, but these steps are required to keep problems from occurring and to maintain peak energy efficiency. An alternate method to server maintenance is to upgrade/replace servers when the ROI starts to decrease instead of waiting a traditional five to seven year as many companies do today.

Intel IT conducted a detailed return on investment (ROI) study across its inventory of nearly 70,000 servers and found costs could be reduced by refreshing servers after four years. Previously, Intel kept servers in use for longer periods, to maximize their useful operational and financial life. The analysis conducted showed that by consolidating older servers onto newer, more powerful platforms, the compute capacity of the existing data centers could be increased. This allowed Intel IT to avoid capital expenditures for new expensive data center construction and avoid the associated increases in power costs.

Intel IT found that traditional server maintenance was not practical. This was partially because the energy efficiency improvement obtained offered a low return on labor. This is also partially because Intel avoids shutting down servers if at all possible. Shutdowns have been shown to be the main cause of server failures (primarily resulting from disk drive friction, but also due to solder joint thermal cracking).

A four-year server refresh strategy provided the best ROI for Intel. Some IT managers of Fortune 500 companies are even advocating a new concept of *fail in place* versus server maintenance. The fail-in-place concept relies on buying 10 to 20 percent more servers than needed for service level agreement baselines and application demand. With this methodology, IT managers simply let servers that fail (for whatever cause) sit powered off until the failure level reaches equilibrium with required compute capacity. IT managers then have the server vendor or outsourced maintenance team replace the dead systems. This concept clearly illustrates how a server's acquisition costs are a very low relative to IT labor for maintenance.

Why is three to four years the optimal timing for refresh? After a system's third operational year, maintenance costs (including patching, support, upgrade, and warranties) far surpass what an enterprise would otherwise pay to acquire and implement a new server. IT managers can better leverage their spending power by applying monies towards newer, more powerful servers every 30 to 40 months, instead of accommodating the increasing operational costs of older servers.

The reason many companies retain servers past four years is the false notion that hardware acquisition is the largest component of server TCO. In fact, acquisition costs only account for between 20 and 30 percent of a typical server deployment and lifecycle costs. Because of this belief, many businesses can negatively affect their cost structure, by allowing server life cycles extending to five years or beyond. IT management should optimize costs by focusing attention on the largest server cost components: related maintenance and support.

Traditional server life cycle financial models are not based on ongoing maintenance and energy costs, but instead are grounded on capital acquisition views. Buildings and machinery maintain their useful value over periods of five, ten and twenty years, matching the financial depreciation schedules and tax laws put in place to address these types of assets. But these same financial models depreciate computing hardware investments over four years. Companies often view continued use of compute assets beyond four years to be 'free' since there are no tax implications. As a result of the differences, these depreciation schedules encourage the enterprise to depreciate compute assets over five years or more.

IT managers must overcome this issue with a complete accounting of server costs. A complete financial model incorporating capital costs, maintenance, upgrades, power and labor costs should be used for evaluating server life extension versus new server acquisition strategies. Furthermore, the use of virtualization technologies can reduce enterprise hardware and power requirements by allowing a single high performance multi-core/multiprocessor x86 based server to replace multiple older low efficiency servers. A rationalized evaluation of these one-time and ongoing cost components will demonstrate that expenditure hikes begin after approximately the third production year.

A complete financial model should include the following cost categories:

Hardware. Server cost is an important element of TCO, but it is not the largest contributing factor to overall costs (and this continues to decline). Cost impacts of server consolidation and virtualization strategies should also be included to evaluate opportunities for reduced hardware costs and energy savings (including avoiding construction of new data centers) that can dramatically change a company's investment strategy.

Deployment. This category incorporates the cost of building system operating system and application images, installing new hardware, migrating system loads, and decommissioning old hardware. Companies should not keep older servers as a safeguard against failures from new installations. Older servers run the risk of getting "lost in the system" if proper asset management practices are not in place. Older low efficiency servers often end up in remote departments or labs continually drawing higher power than necessary and requiring increased labor for maintenance.

Power and Cooling. Power and cooling are becoming an increasing expense for enterprise data centers. Corporations may see power and cooling requirements drop by as much as 50 percent in the fourth year of operation, if they replace older equipment with newer, more efficient processors. Additionally, companies may also be able to further save energy in data centers by refreshing after three to four years, given that newer systems will produce proportionally less heat.

IT Labor. This category should include all IT labor costs associated with provisioning, administrator training, software upgrades, fault troubleshooting, installing patches and fixes and with disposal costs. Salaries are typically the largest component of any IT Operations TCO category. Estimates of administrative cost reductions using a three to four year refresh instead of a five-year cycle place this at approximately 30 percent or greater.

IT Labor can be especially high with servers running versions of Windows Server 2003[†] operating system or older. Microsoft has recently added a focus on power management technologies to Windows Server 2008[‡]. With the older versions, degradation of the operating system's performance occurs naturally over time. This happens for many reasons including poor Windows Registry management, and requirements for frequent system patching and updates.

Moreover, Windows uses dynamic link libraries (DLLs), which are shared software elements that may be required by the operating system or one or more applications. Software and security updates typically cause DLL incompatibilities that require operator attention to ensure proper system operation. Typically, this rate of degradation becomes significant enough to require a rebuild on or around the three to four year period.

Corporations should make server purchasing and refresh decisions based on a complete TCO model. The models below demonstrate that corporations can save at least 11 percent on x86 based server TCO by adopting a three to four year life cycle instead of a five-year refresh policy. IT managers should base refresh decisions on analyses using their own internal cost structures, projected cost-related improvements expected over a five-year period, and vendor pricing to determine the specific gains possible for their companies.

The five-year TCO model shown in Table 10.1 is based on typical hardware pricing for an x86-based server with two CPUs and internal storage. The model shows that the lowest TCO occurs at year 3 at an average cost of USD 6,055 per year. While this is not significantly less than the year 4 cost of USD 6,067, the salvage value difference between the two years is significant. A server traded into a vendor at the end of year 3 would have a value of USD 175 or 7 percent of initial cost, while a server surrendered at the end of the fourth year would have a value of USD 75 or 3 percent of initial cost. Thus, trading in a server at the third year's completion is approximately 4 percent more cost effective.

The ongoing costs for keeping an x86 server in operation increase by USD 12 per year or by USD 48 per server over the four-year cycle. Results deteriorate further in the fifth year of operation, where extending server use increases costs by USD 267 per year as compared with the third year numbers. This would result in an extra USD 1,355 cost per server over five years as compared with third year costs. Therefore, a corporation with 1,000 x86 servers would incur an additional cost of USD 48,000 more than necessary by keeping servers for four years and a staggering USD 1,355,000 if all the servers were kept in operation for five years. That number would increase by USD 213,000 to USD 1,568,000 when lost salvage value the cost of disk overwrite and proper disposal in year five are considered.

Table 10.1 Five-year TCO Model Without Refresh
Source: Robert Francis Group, 2006

	\multicolumn{5}{c}{Five-year Analysis With No Refresh}
	Year 1	Year 2	Year 3	Year 4	Year 5
One-Time Costs					
Server Hardware	USD 2,500	–	–	–	–
Deployment	USD 200	–	–	–	–
Provisioning	USD 110	–	–	–	–
Warranty Cost	USD 1,548	–	–	–	–
Ongoing Costs					
Administrator Training	USD 71	USD 75	USD 79	USD 96	USD 116
Administrator Salaries	USD 3,862	USD 4,093	USD 4,339	USD 5,366	USD 6,500
Software Upgrades	USD 60	USD 93	USD 110	USD 196	USD 215
Patch Deployment	USD 120	USD 120	USD 151	USD 192	USD 232
Power Consumption and Cooling	USD 191	USD 210	USD 231	USD 266	USD 280
Facilities Costs	USD 5	USD 5	USD 5	USD 5	USD 5
Annual Cost	USD 8,662	USD 4,592	USD 4,910	USD 6,105	USD 7,343
TOTAL ACCUMULATIVE COST	USD 8,662	USD 13,254	USD 18,164	USD 24,269	USD 31,612
AVGCOST Per Year	USD 8,662	USD 6,627	USD 6,055	USD 6,067	USD 6,322
NPV Calculation 5 Year No					
Cost of Capital	USD 0.06				
Outflows	USD (8,662)	USD (4,592)	USD (4,910)	USD (6,105)	USD (7,343)
NPV 5 year own	USD (26,764)				
Per year	USD (6,353)				
NPV Caculation 3 year Purchase					
Cost of Capital	USD 0.06				
Outflows	USD (7,660)	USD (4,592)	USD (4,777)		
NPV 3 year own	USD (15,324)				
Per Year	USD (5,100)				

In Table 10.2, the value of a 3 to 4 year refresh strategy is even more pronounced. It should come as little surprise that operational costs are greatly reduced between years 3 and 4 when refresh occurs at the end of year 3. This is because the erosion in operating system and application performance becomes especially noticeable around this time, potentially triggering a server rebuild.

Table 10.2 Five-year TCO Model With Refresh
Source: Robert Francis Group, 2006

	Five-year Analysis With Refresh				
	Year 1	Year 2	Year 3	Year 4	Year 5
One-Time Costs					
Server Hardware	USD 2,500	–	–	USD 2,500	–
Deployment	USD 200	–	–	USD 200	–
Provisioning	USD 110	–	–	USD 110	–
Warranty Cost	USD 540	–	–	USD 540	–
Ongoing Costs					
Administrator Training	USD 71	USD 75	USD 79	USD 72	USD 76
Administrator Salaries	USD 3,862	USD 4,093	USD 4,339	USD 4,024	USD 4,266
Software Upgrades	USD 60	USD 93	USD 110	USD 60	USD 93
Patch Deployment	USD 120	USD 120	USD 151	USD 120	USD 120
Power Consumption and Cooling	USD 191	USD 210	USD 231	USD 177	USD 128
Facilities Costs	USD 5	USD 5	USD 5	USD 3	USD 3
Annual Cost	USD 7,660	USD 4,592	USD 4,910	USD 7,747	USD 4,603
TOTAL ACCUMULATIVE COST	USD 7,660	USD 12,251	USD 17,162	USD 24,908	USD 29,591
AVGCOST Per Year	USD 7,660	USD 6,126	USD 5,721	USD 6,067	USD 6,322

NPV Calculation 5 Year No					
Cost of Capital	USD 0.06				
Outflows	USD (7,660)	USD (4,592)	USD (4,777)	USD (7,747)	USD (4,633)
NPV 5 year own	USD (24,959)				
Per year	USD (4,982)				

NPV Caculation 3 year Purchase					
Cost of Capital	USD 0.06				
Outflows	USD (7,660)	USD (4,692)	USD (4,777)		
NPV 3 year own	USD (24,959)				
Per Year	USD (4,982)				

Further examination demonstrates that ongoing costs for those two years are reduced by more than 7.5 percent—or USD 1,018 per server—by selecting a 3 to 4 year refresh strategy and purchasing a new server in year 4, versus keeping a server for 5 years. Therefore, an enterprise with 1,000 x86 servers would save a total of USD 1,018,000 in years 4 and 5 by choosing to refresh its servers in year 3 rather than keeping them in operation for 2 extra years.

Server life cycle decisions should be based on a complete life cycle methodology. The models provided here incorporate all the major components of a server life cycle and should serve as a conservative basis for IT executives to consider when creating their own models. These should be based on projected numbers extrapolated from past experience and should include improvements expected to be implemented over the next five years. Because IT administrator costs are the largest contributors to overall server TCO costs, IT managers should focus their efforts primarily on trying to reduce those costs by leveraging improvements in technology. In addition, they should work with trusted vendors to encourage limits to upgrade and patching costs while maximizing server availability.

Companywide Power Management Plan for PCs

This section covers energy efficiency with desktop PCs. While these are not located in data center facilities, this section is included as power management of PCs can result in significant power savings for companies. Technology is now available to make significant improvements in power conservation on desktop and laptop computers. These technologies enable IT departments to both conserve energy and cut costs.

Power management of company computers typically represents a huge opportunity for conservation efforts. In many offices, computers are left on overnight, wasting power for those approximately 100 hours per week that they are not being used. During the off-hours, those computers are creating heat and requiring buildings to use more cooling, which uses even more energy.

For a companywide PC power plan to be effective, there are a few provisions. First, PCs need to retain the ability to remotely install emergency patches. This protects against newly announced viruses with the ability to deploy security patches at night or over weekends. Also, employees should still be able to remotely access information as required and that information would not be lost when computers are shut down or put to sleep. This covers cases where someone may leave an application open with newly entered data.

There are many PC management software applications on the market which offer the features of saving files and data prior to shutting down or putting PCs into sleep mode. It also allows computers to be turned off from a central location, at a specified time, while providing extensive reports for management.

When a desktop PC is turned off, it consumes just three to five watts per hour, as opposed to the average 89 watts consumed when idle. Additional savings can be realized by utilizing a staggered schedule for powering up computers. A staggered wake schedule prevents straining the network and getting a spike in the energy bill because it may trigger peak energy demand rates.

While turning off PCs at night seems like a simple solution, it can reap huge energy savings for large enterprises. For example, a company with a base of 50,000 desktop computers can expect to realize up to a 40 percent reduction in computer-related energy costs, which could translate into USD 1.8 million in savings annually.

Case Study: Intel IT Four-Year Refresh

Synopsis

Intel IT is accelerating the rate at which the design computing servers are refreshed, driving expected savings of up to USD 250 million over eight years while substantially reducing energy consumption.

The Challenge

Like most IT organizations, in 2007 Intel IT was facing the challenge of accommodating ever-increasing compute requirements within current data center space, cooling, and power constraints.

Most of Intel's servers support semiconductor design, and as Intel® processors were becoming more complex, design computing requirements were rising sharply, driving a rapid increase in the number of design computing servers required from about 1,000 in 1996 to 68,000 in 2007. As compute requirements outstripped existing data center capacity, Intel IT would add or expand data center facilities. However, building data centers is extremely expensive.

It was also expensive to maintain and operate an increasing population of older, less-efficient, and lower performance servers. Intel IT had been

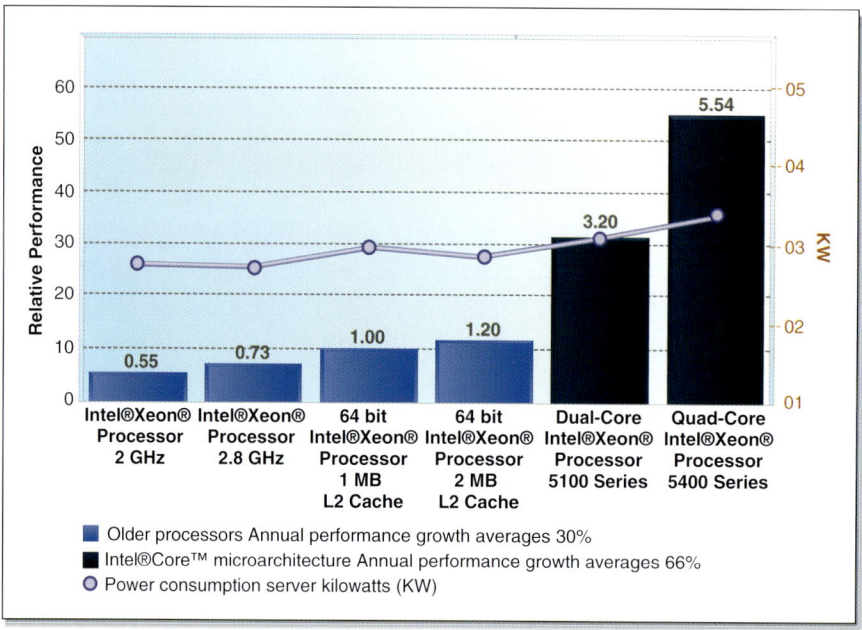

Figure 10.1 Performance Accelerates; Power Consumption Remains Flat
Source: Intel IT, 2008

keeping most servers beyond their 4-year warranty to maximize their useful life and reduce IT depreciation costs.

The Opportunity

The introduction of processors based on Intel® Core™ micro-architecture in 2006 enabled greatly improved performance. Moreover, despite providing tremendous performance improvements, the new processors proved to be much more energy-efficient. As Figure 10.1 shows, server power consumption was found to be remaining about the same.

As a result, in 2007, as part of an enterprisewide, eight-year data center efficiency program, Intel IT began considering an alternative server refresh strategy.

The ROI Analysis

To determine whether accelerating server refresh would deliver financial benefits due to reduced data center construction, Intel Finance performed an extensive analysis.

The following factors were examined because they can significantly affect ROI:

- Total server costs (acquisition, warranties, repairs, etc.)
- Construction cost avoidance
- Data center utilities cost
- Network costs
- Tax impacts (depreciation, operating expenses, etc.)

Intel's analysis compared each cadence with the existing approach, in which only about 20 percent of servers were replaced after four years. This baseline effectively resulted in an overall 100 percent refresh cycle cadence of more than seven years.

Differing refresh cycles were modeled in order to fully comprehend the business impact of each. Additional opportunities based on server virtualization and platform consolidation were factored into each of the alternative refresh cycles.

The financial models examined total costs over eight years. It was assumed that the cost of each new server would remain stable over this evaluation period, while computing requirements would continue to increase at 15 percent per year. The analysis took into account regional variation in construction and utilities costs.

Software costs were excluded because potential efficiencies in that area were included separately as part of a broader data center efficiency program.

Findings

The analysis showed that by by accelerating the rate at which servers were refreshed, Intel IT could take advantage of the newer server performance and energy efficiency increases to reduce costs.

Intel Finance found that a four-year refresh cycle delivered the greatest ROI. In general, faster refresh rates resulted in increased total cost for acquiring new servers because more servers were purchased over the eight-year evaluation period. The analysis assumed consolidation onto blade servers. Consolidation ratios are based on expectations of the performance of future Intel processors and vary depending on the refresh cadence and type of application. Higher refresh rates reduce network switch port costs because higher network consolidation ratios can be achieved.

The newest, most powerful servers support the highest consolidation ratios, reducing the need to expand facilities. Therefore, faster refresh rates result in the most construction cost avoidance. The most recent server models are also the most power-efficient. The more frequent the server refresh, the more that could be saved in power and cooling costs.

Eight year net benefit was calculated at nearly USD 250 million, due to optimized construction cost avoidance, server refresh costs, and utilities savings.

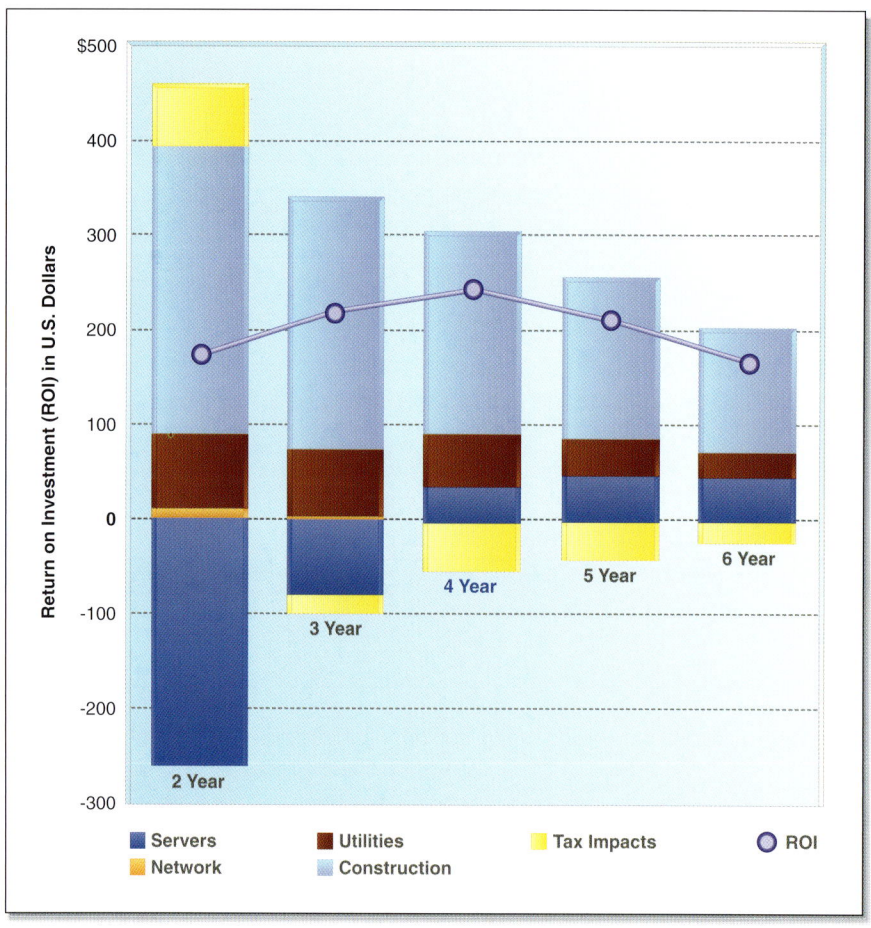

Figure 10.2 ROI Analysis of Refresh Cadence
Source: Intel IT, 2008

In 2008 Intel IT had already saved USD 10.4 million by consolidating 3,200 older servers onto platforms using Quad-Core Intel® Xeon® processor 5400 series, enabling them to avoid new construction at four locations. The new servers are also much more energy-efficient, sharply reducing energy consumption and cost. Furthermore, by consolidating multiple server workloads onto newer, more powerful platforms, they could increase the compute capacity of the existing data centers and accommodate growing compute demands without adding facilities.

The results of the analysis are summarized in Figure 10.2.

Other Benefits

An accelerated refresh cycle also delivers other benefits that were not included in the ROI analysis: the enablement of green computing and and increase in the productivity of design engineers.

With a four year refresh, Intel IT could significantly reduce power consumption thus reducing Intel's carbon footprint. Based on the high consolidation ratios obtained in design batch computing, it was estimated energy consumption could be reduced by up to 700 kilowatts (kW) for every 500 four year old servers consolidated using dual socket Quad Core equipped blade servers. Adopting more energy-efficient servers may also enable Intel to qualify for significant local government energy credits in some U.S. states.

Many of the older servers had 4 GB of memory or less. Increasing design complexity is driving a need for more memory. Current semiconductor design jobs require up to 8 GB per processor core, and validation jobs can require 12 GB. Newer servers can accommodate this need. For example, high-performance computing servers based on the Quad-Core Intel Xeon processor 5400 series can accommodate up to 128 GB of memory. Intel IT is currently configuring new servers with as much as 64 GB to accommodate these requirements. As the number of these newer servers is increased in Intel's environment, Intel IT is helping to accelerate chip design and improving compute efficiency by enabling the design engineers to become more productive and by reducing batch job failure rates.

Ongoing Server Refresh Strategy

Intel IT is moving forward with the accelerated server refresh strategy, implementing a four-year refresh cadence across the entire design environment, removing all servers that are more than four years old.

In early 2008, Intel IT began consolidating the workloads of older servers onto blade servers based on the Quad-Core Intel Xeon processor

5400 series. As a result, about 3,200 older servers were removed from the design environment and Intel was able to avoid data center construction at four sites. Intel achieved a net savings of USD 10.4 million, mostly due to construction avoidance.

The company is currently on track to replace over 20,000 servers at the end of the first year of the accelerated refresh program.

When consolidating four-year-old servers equipped with 32-bit Intel Xeon processors, Intel IT is currently achieving consolidation ratios of more than 7:1 for batch jobs, which fully exploit the increased computing power of the latest Intel processors. Interactive servers are seeing consolidation ratios of approximately 4:1.

One other impact of the large scale accelerated server refresh and consolidation strategy at Intel has been the closure of approximately 40 data centers around the world. This has dramatically reduced the carbon footprint of the corporation's IT operations and has resulted in lower operational costs due to elimination of maintenance and power consumption at the closed data centers.

Intel will continue to look for data center consolidation and closure opportunities throughout the future as part of its overall drive for efficiency.

Refining the Strategy

Server refresh evaluation is an iterative process. Each year Intel IT may adjust their strategy to deliver maximum savings, taking into account changes in server price and performance, construction costs, and other factors including energy costs. Because of this potential variation, projections for actual savings range between USD 200 million and USD 250 million over eight years.

Conclusion

Accelerated server refresh is part of Intel's broader data center efficiency program, which also includes initiatives such as data center consolidation and server virtualization and aims to generate overall savings of USD 1 billion or more.

As demonstrated, accelerated server refresh is a major contributor to the goals of this program and plays an essential role in helping achieve these savings.

Case Study: Intel IT Power Management to the Limit

Synopsis

A risk/benefits/cost analysis and detailed computational fluid dynamics (CFD) model helped identify the best solution for injecting new life into a 20-year old data center's inefficient cooling delivery system without an expensive infrastructure overhaul.

The Challenge

Intel's older enterprise data center was almost maxed out.

Even though it had just been through a USD 7 million power upgrade, it already contained just about as many servers as its aging infrastructure could support. Intel IT Global Facilities Services (GFS), which operates the company's data centers, needed to add 300 new servers to support an upcoming SAP† software re-platforming project—without exceeding the facility's cooling capacity.

Another wrinkle: Intel expected to decommission the facility within the next five years, so it was essential to find a way to free up capacity for the new servers without a major capital investment.

Analysis

To formulate a strategy for making best use of the data center's existing infrastructure, Intel GFS engineers and planners carried out a detailed analysis that predicted the effect of adding new servers and compared it to the data center's potential thermal limits.

Consultants also investigated ways to improve the data center's overall efficiency using the available electrical power under the current infrastructure.

In today's typical data center, several factors can contribute to inefficiency, higher-than-necessary power use, and spiraling costs-most notably, the ineffective use of the cooling infrastructure, poor management of cool airflow, and underutilized IT equipment.

Fortunately, there are some fairly simple—and inexpensive—ways to address these factors and immediately reduce energy consumption once the root cases are understood. Energy conservation can translate directly into increased data center compute capacity without the high cost of new construction or major retrofit of facilities infrastructure.

In the older enterprise data center, Intel IT identified four key problems that were preventing the facility from optimizing its power load and efficiency:

- Inefficient data center layout
- Poor management of cold air supply distribution and pressure
- Isolation of cold and hot air
- Ineffective removal of hot air

Because this data center's operational life was limited, it wasn't practical to evaluate the most expensive solutions to air mixing: installing isolation chambers in hot or cold aisles. Instead, Intel IT focused on quick and inexpensive fixes such as relocating perforated tiles, reducing tile leakage, and turning around server cabinets to form well defined hot and cold aisles.

Changing the location of perforated tiles is harder than it looks because of the counter-intuitive behaviors of fluids. Therefore, the team developed a computational fluid dynamics model (CFD) to optimize perforated tile placements using first principles of physics. A solution using tables or heuristics instead of physical simulation would not be able to maximize potential cost savings.

The consultants took a methodical approach to gathering data, modeling and analyzing problems, and identifying solutions. First, they collected data and modeled the data center using CFD tools. Then they validated the results to ensure the modeling output was accurate. The process measured many parts of the data center including:

- Temperature readings at the racks
- Cubic feet per minute measurements of all perforated tiles
- Survey of server cable blockages, under-floor obstructions, power distribution and cable distribution systems impact on airflow
- Percent fill of each cabinet
- Survey of blanking panels
- Under-floor obstructions
- Tile cutouts and their location in the room
- Server room layout validation at the time of measurements
- Raised floor height

The CFD tool also helped validate the size and location of every piece of equipment and perforated tile in the room. Consultants used the tool to capture physical measurements, build a model of the current environment, and then compare the results of the model to actual measurements.

The physical modeling enabled the consultants to consider a number of solution alternatives, ranging from "do nothing" (the status quo) to a sophisticated air management design that would allow expanding the thermal limits for landing servers within the constraints of the current infrastructure.

While the model for the older enterprise data center was not the largest ever built by Intel, it was one of most complex because of the characteristics of the data center:

- It used a common under-floor air supply plenum.
- The floor plan was divided into several small rooms sharing the plenum.
- It had several different kinds of rooms, including fully closed rooms surrounded by under-floor obstructions, closed rooms with their own computer room air conditioners (CRAC) and perforated tiles, and rooms sharing air columns with other rooms through louvered walls.

Air flow management is an important way to ease data center power and thermal problems very quickly. An air flow management solution can have several components:

Data center air flow and thermal efficiency. This means delivering the right amount of cooling air to servers and removing hot air with minimal mixing of cold and hot air or shorting (cold air returning to a CRAC without doing any work cooling a server).

Reduced heat generation. Reducing the intensity and number of heat sources leads to a corresponding reduced need for cooling. This can require an upgrade to more power-efficient platforms.

Consolidation. Moving two or more applications to a server, increasing the loading factor and reducing the total number of servers needed in a data center.

Virtualization. This can be considered a step up from consolidation where physical servers host one or more virtual machines in a highly automated environment.

Intel found inefficiencies in the use of the cold air supply. The modeling and root cause analysis identified a need for more cold air to support the projected server load created by the replatforming project.

Implementation

The Intel IT team suggested several options to help improve the data center's overall efficiency and provide for additional cooling capacity, dividing its recommendations into short and long-term improvements.

In the short term, the data center needed to:

Add blanking panels. This option was not feasible for all racks, but was still highly recommended to keep hot and cold air as isolated as possible. Investing in the panels will pay for itself-both in terms of reduced cold air requirements and ability to increase electrical loads of cabinets by adding additional compute capacity.

Eliminate cold air supply plenum leakage. The data center had numerous perforated tiles located in hot aisles or where there was no equipment. This reduced supply plenum pressure and efficiency of the cold air supply. It also adds to operating costs because more cold air is needed to maintain the existing equipment load.

Implement 25 percent flow perforated tiles. All perforated tiles in use were 7.5 percent tiles. The model predicted that hot spots would form at higher loadings due to insufficient air flow. The team recommended introducing 25 percent flow perforated tiles in specified areas to make it possible to maintain higher equipment loads.

Replace unused cut-out tiles not in use with solid tiles. A number of cut-out tiles were found to have no cables running through them, with some grouped together as an apparent way of building a resource pool. These tiles release substantial cold air from the supply plenum without cooling any equipment.

Install air leakage barriers for all cut-out tiles. This would significantly help curtail air leakage.

In the longer term, Intel recommended:

Installing a hot air return plenum. This would improve overall airflow design and allow for more efficient removal of hot air and additional load capacity while reducing the cost of cooling per kilowatt of load.

Removing inner-room walls. This would create a single large data center floor to help balance the cooling capacity across rooms.

Aligning racks to tile edges. This would increase the efficiency of the cold air delivery, particularly where two rows of racks are sharing the same cold aisle. The team recommended adopting a standard to align the fronts of racks to the edge of the perforated tiles.

After implementing all these recommendations, would the aging data center have the capacity to add the 300 new servers it needed? The answer was yes—and then some. To make an even greater improvement in the data center's performance, the Intel IT team recommended server virtualization, a more advanced form of consolidation that could reduce both the number of servers the data center needed and the resulting power/thermal load.

Conclusion

By coordinating application components, Intel was able to inject new life into a 20-year-old data center without an expensive infrastructure overhaul. Not only was the data center able to add the 300 new servers it needed to meet the goals of the SAP re-platforming project, it had the capacity to add even more servers in the future.

Repairing the data center's old, inefficient cooling delivery system and optimizing the layout more efficient one let the data center substantially increase its capacity while reducing operating expenses.

The project was so successful that the research team was able to find ways to free up enough power capacity for the initial 300-server requirement and then some-enabling the current infrastructure to host even more servers in the future.

Server Recycling Services

The above mentioned server refresh strategies all incorporated plans to replace old servers. Before undertaking any refresh plan, make sure to also specify how older servers will be disposed. Servers and data center equipment should not be sent to waste disposal areas if at all possible. Many states now consider computers to be hazardous waste, making their disposal costly. There are several organizations which can recycle older IT equipment.

Before disposing of a server, buy a disk drive data destruction program. Data destruction programs fill up the hard drive with random characters, wiping out files in the process. Formatting the hard drive isn't enough to stop dedicated thieves. Only a data destruction program can keep potential thieves away from passwords, financial records and other confidential business information.

The following list of companies offer recycling programs for free or at small nominal costs. This is not a comprehensive list, but a sampling. Be sure to check for local resources within your region.

Dell

Buy a Dell server or computer and Dell will recycle your old computer for free, regardless of its manufacturer. Dell also recycles any old Dell computers or products for free.

RECONNECT (*www.reconnectpartnership.com*) (specific cities within California, Michigan, New Jersey, North Carolina, Pennsylvania, and Texas only) is a comprehensive electronics recovery, reuse and environmentally responsible recycling partnership between Goodwill Industries and Dell, Inc. for consumers in participating communities.

For Recycling and Donation and Asset Recovery Services, see *www.dell.com.*

eBay

Rethink Initiative (*pages.ebay.com/rethink/*) provides information, tools and solutions that make it easy to find new users for idle computers and electronics, and responsibly recycle unwanted products.

Earth 911

Earth 911 (*earth911.com/electronics/*) is a comprehensive communication medium for the environment. Earth 911 has taken environmental hotlines, web sites and other information sources nationwide, and consolidated them into one network. Once you contact the Earth 911 network, you will find community-specific information on eCycling and much more.

Electronic Industries Alliance's Consumer Education Initiative

The Electronic Industries Alliance's eCycling Central Web site helps you find reuse, recycling and donation programs for electronics products in your state. *(www.eiae.org/)*

www.freecycle.org

A grassroots, community-based mailing list, Freecycle lets you post items you no longer want in the hopes somebody else will pick them up for free and give them a new life. Students, hobbyists, and repair technicians might still find some value in an old server.
(www.freecycle.org/)

Hewlett-Packard

HP offers a global product take back offering, where the company has aligned its trade-in, refurbishing and recycling operations to offer full asset-recovery services to commercial customers. These services match existing consolidated asset-recovery and recycling services offered by HP in Europe, Asia, Japan and the Americas.

- Product Recycling (including hardware, LaserJet supplies, and Inkjet supplies)
  (www.hp.com/hpinfo/globalcitizenship/environment/recycle/index.html)
- Trade-In Program
  (www.hp.com/united-states/tradein/home_flash.html)
- Hewlett-Packard/Compaq Asset Recovery Services
  (h20330.www2.hp.com/hpfinancialservices/cache/274694-0-0-225-121.html)

IBM

IBM accepts any manufacturer's servers or computers (including monitors, printers, and peripherals) from consumers and businesses. The program costs USD 29.99, including shipping. IBM's worldwide program saves anything refurbishable for philanthropic organizations and recycles or safely disposes of the rest. It's a great way to do one thing to help green the earth.
(www.ibm.com/ibm/environment/products/pcrservice.shtml)

Intel

Intel offers the Students Recycling Used Technology (StRUT) program. StRUT provides technology-based education for K-16 students through the process of refurbishing donated equipment for schools.

- Silicon Valley StRUT (*http://www.svstrut.org/cms/index.php*)
- Arizona StRUT (*http://www.azstrut.org/donate.html*)

- Oregon StRUT (*http://www.oregonstrut.org/*)

My Green Electronics

Provided by the Consumer Electronics Association, this site is a resource for consumers wishing to purchase green products and/or searching for local opportunities to recycle or donate used electronics.
(www.mygreenelectronics.org/)

TechSoup

TechSoup has compiled a comprehensive body of information to promote computer recycling and reuse. This site provides resources for those who would like to donate hardware, those who would like to acquire recycled hardware, and refurbishers.
(www.techsoup.org/resources/)

Summary

Server maintenance helps keep servers running with top energy efficiency. But for enterprise data centers, with thousands of servers, maintenance not only is impractical, but the required IT labor will cost significantly more than the server hardware or power costs. Large data centers are addressing this by analyzing server refresh cycles and implementing a shorter refresh cycle with optimum ROI.

For server refresh cycle analysis, a complete set of costs need to be included. The complete set should include server acquisition costs, deployment, power consumption, and IT labor related to provisioning, upgrading and troubleshooting tasks.

Results from Intel IT show the optimum ROI for servers occurs with a four year refresh cycle. Using average capital and power costs and assuming average IT labor costs, the on-going TCO for a x86 server starts rising in the fourth year of use and increasing more in year five. Analysis shows in an incremental USD 1,355 per server cost increase in year five when compared to operating costs in year three. A corporation with 1,000 x86 serves would experience an additional incremental cost of USD 48,000 retaining servers in production for five or more years.

Finally while not specific to data center facilities, another energy efficient measure for companies is in power management of the desktop PCs. Power management of desktop PCs can yield substantial savings. At many companies, PCs are left on overnight. By powering down PCs to a sleep state or turning them off, each PC consumes just three to five watts versus the 89 watts at idle. There are many available software packages that provide off-hour PC power management. A company with 50,000 PCs can realize a 40 percent energy cost reduction.

Chapter 11

Industry Vision and Recommendations

Man is the most extraordinary computer of all.
—John Fitzgerald Kennedy

The data center can be the corporate leadership for energy and economic efficiency. As this book has shown, there are many actions that can reduce power consumption today in data centers. But more can be done, and IT and data center management can set the lead for energy efficiency demand and new product creation. This chapter presents challenges and opportunities for improving energy efficiency in future products and data center analysis methods. As energy efficiency becomes more valuable, developers and system engineers have an opportunity to make increased energy efficiency a primary design objective for future components and systems. In addition to improving future products, new energy-efficiency standards, measurements and metrics will help universal adoption for a more complete characterization of data center and server energy behavior. Optimizing energy efficiency not only helps reduce energy costs for data center operators, it also benefits the environment and helps utility companies manage the cost and supply of energy for everyone.

Increased Energy Efficient Servers: Opportunities for the Computer Industry

This first section covers technology improvements to server architecture that yield better energy efficiency. By understanding what is possible, data center managers and operators can work with their vendors to deliver better systems with each generation. In addition, vendors will be able to identify the features and functions of products that would have increased value in the market. We explain the technologies in detail to aid in developing RFPs for energy efficient systems. This section begins with opportunities for components down on the motherboard, followed by options for server sub-systems.

Motherboard Components

A first step for improved energy efficiency is to extend power management down to motherboard components. To reach this goal, all hardware components within server, storage or network systems would be capable of reducing power consumption based on self-tuning intelligent features. Motherboard-level power management in servers can reach higher levels of integration and value in two ways: by sending outputs to baseboard management controllers (BMC) or other service processors and by integrating with standardized management protocols to system management consoles. Using standardized management protocols enables universal support by all management consoles and allows operators to fine tune their centers.

Servers spend most of their time at moderate utilizations of 10 to 50 percent and exhibit poor overall platform efficiency at these lower utilization levels. A great opportunity is for servers to scale their energy consumption with utilization. This *proportional computing* would enable additional energy savings, potentially doubling the efficiency of today's typical server. Some server processors already exhibit reasonably energy-proportional profiles, but most other server components do not.

There are significant opportunities for energy improvements in memory and disk subsystems, as these components are responsible for a rapidly increasing percentage of overall platform energy usage. Non-volatile memory technology, which consumes no power when idle, would bring significant value when incorporated into both the memory subsystems and within storage stacks. This would provide tremendous energy savings during low utilization or idle power server states.

Increasing Use of Thermal Sensors

Many servers today use three to five fans to keep components within a safe thermal range. Most servers implement a fan speed control to reduce fan power. But this is usually done to fulfill acoustic requirements. Most servers contain limited numbers of thermal sensors for use in optimizing fan speeds for optimum thermal management. As a result, system thermal design generally assumes a worst-case scenario to protect the motherboard components. This results in higher than necessary fan speeds accompanied by higher server power consumption.

To address this situation, consider the value of more thermal sensors. Having an adequate number of thermal sensors may eliminate practice of worst case scenarios and the associated wasted power consumption. If every critical component on a server motherboard had a built in thermal sensor, not only would accuracy increase, but the worst case cooling could be avoided. Reasonable accuracy for the thermal sensors is considered to be in the +/- 5°C range.

One of the common power wastes in data centers is over cooling. A simple, but highly valued solution would be to have a thermal sensor of the inlet air that is displayed on the front of every 1U rack server or blade. If each server and blade had a small LED reader displaying the temperature of the inlet air at the front server vents, this would provide an effective method for IT personnel to monitor server temperatures at a glance and adjust CRAC and air distribution units to higher efficiency. An accuracy of +/- 2° C of the inlet air temperature measurements would be useful for most data centers.

Platform Power Management

Another great opportunity for product developers is to embed power consumption thresholds and caps with corresponding manageability tools in all IT equipment. A dynamic power management scheme to cap server, storage arrays, and network equipment peak power draw to some predetermined value has clear benefits. Power capping and thresholds can act as a safety valve, protecting the power distribution hierarchy against overdraw. This would help data centers where applications are not characterized to see how much computational power, memory use, and disk access are required, or it could function as a safe fail for data centers that experience unanticipated load spikes. Capping power for even a small fraction of overall time can deliver noticeable energy savings and enable additional server deployments.

Server Power Supply Improvements

There are multiple opportunities to increase the energy efficiency of power supply units. First, many data centers would value units with increased efficiency at low utilization levels. A commodity server power supply unit has peak conversion efficiency of about 75 percent. The 80 PLUS specification stipulates power supply unit efficiencies must be over 80 percent for load levels over 20 percent for qualification. As of this writing, there are no guidelines for efficiency at low loads. Since servers spend much of the time at moderate utilization levels of 10 to 50 percent, an opportunity exists if power supply units could support higher efficiency at load levels as low as 10 percent. This high efficiency is especially critical for voltage rails that feed processors and memory subsystems.

In addition, there are opportunities for commodity DC-DC power supply units. The 80 PLUS specification helps by requiring increased efficiencies per utilization load of the server. Even though these new power supply units offer increased efficiencies, there still is waste in converting from AC to DC.

Data centers would value power supply units that support phase shedding based upon load. Use of multiple phases of conversion in a power supply unit is not very common. Use of multiple phases and powering down phases as the load reduces would help improve efficiency at low loads.

Data center managers are becoming increasingly aware of power consumption of the power supply unit itself. Most power supplies have built in fans which are always on. There would be business value if power supply fans incorporated speed control so that the fan speed and power consumption reduce dynamically with the load.

Just as everyone is aware of miles per gallon ratings for cars, data center managers are becoming increasingly critical of any wasted power with the data center.

As Figures 11.1 and 11.2 illustrate, a DC-DC power scheme can eliminate multiple points of conversion and power waste.

Increased Energy Efficient Servers: Opportunities for the Computer Industry **273**

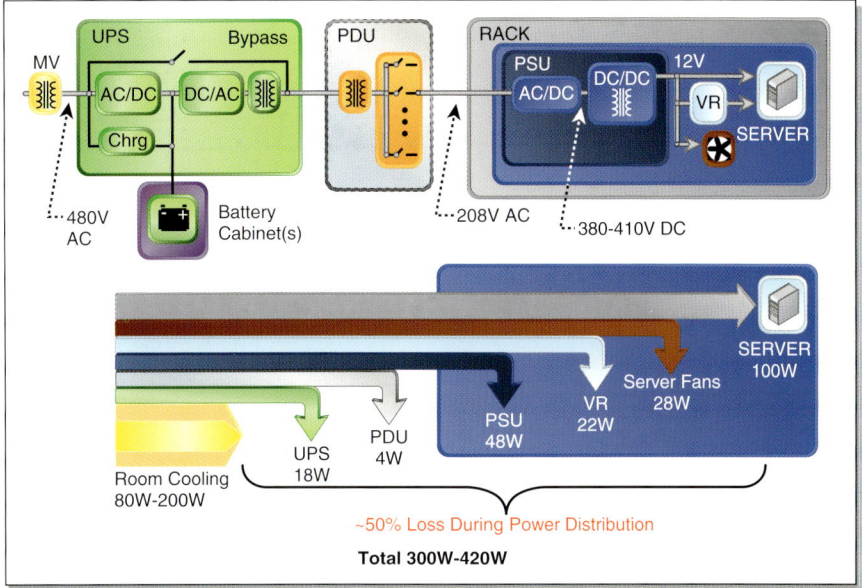

Figure 11.1 Data Center Power Losses
Source: Intel, 2008

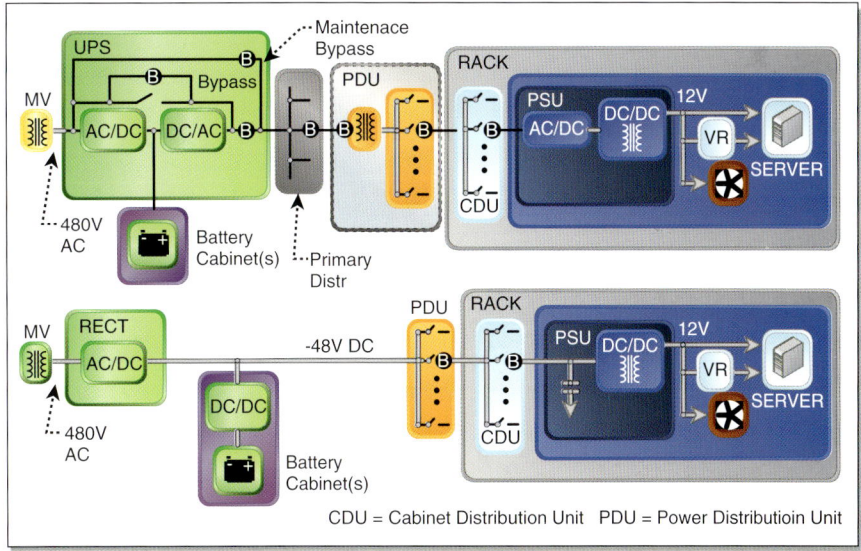

Figure 11.2 Lower Complexity with DC Power
Source: Intel, 2008

There is a growing business opportunity for both server manufacturers and power supply manufacturers to strongly consider changing from today's AC to DC power supplies and distribution systems to DC-to-DC power supply chains. In 2009, most power supplies in servers were AC-DC units, which are very inefficient and waste as much as 40 to 60 percent of power before even providing voltage to server components. In addition, DC power distribution is a convenient upgrade because most data centers already have DC running into their server rooms.

Another benefit of DC-DC power is modularity and ease of integration. Simplified distribution in DC-DC data center designs results in higher inherent availability and reduced maintenance complexity. If single-phase power loads are not balanced across all three-phases of the AC input source in a data center, harmonic issues arise and lower efficiencies can result. This balance is more difficult to achieve with AC-DC power supply units. AC systems also have more complex switchgear requirements and more circuit breakers in series. Complex paralleling requirements generally force AC systems to be less modular and restrict aggressive power-saving features. AC systems typically need 4 or 5 breakers after the power supply unit; DC systems typically need only 1 or 2 breakers after the power supply unit. Power supply vendors and server manufacturers could realize this growing business opportunity by expanding their product lines with DC-DC power supply units that have lower voltages for rack and blade servers.

While the 80 PLUS specification certainly helps improve AC to DC power supply efficiency, bulk rectification of AC to DC accompanied by DC power distribution and DC-to-DC power supplies is clearly the state of the art approach today. Power supply and data center equipment vendors have the opportunity to expand their product lines of DC-to-DC power system equipment to enable the transformation of data center design best practices. The efficiency opportunities tied to development in this area are relatively clear cut. However, it will take time for broad industry adoption and conversion of the existing data centers, servers, storage, and network equipment to this more efficient approach. Sunk capital considerations and the general lack of knowledge on design and operation of DC powered data centers and equipment are impediments.

USB Modifications for Increased Energy Efficiency

When bus master traffic is generated by a USB host controller on an otherwise idle system, the platform will immediately transition out of a low power state to process this traffic. Because this activity is a platform-

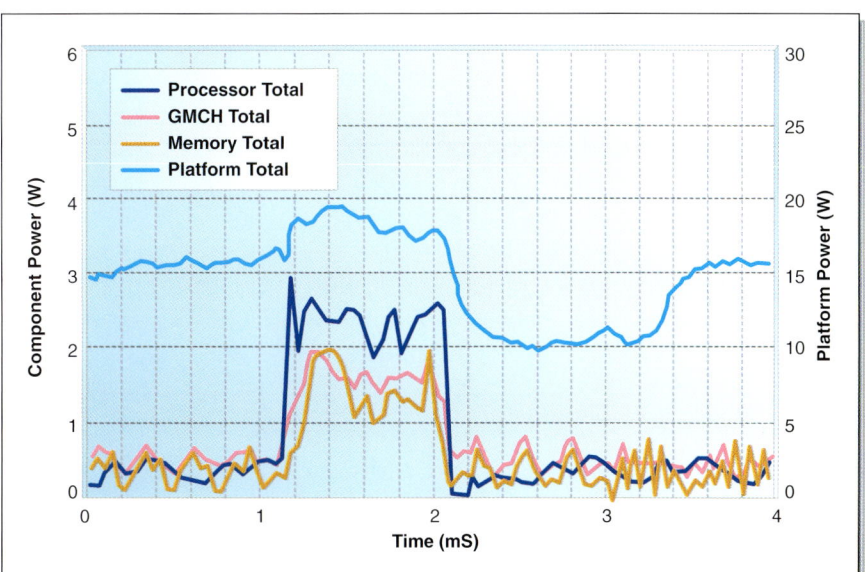

Figure 11.3 Platform Power Impact from USB-WLAN Polling
Source: Cooper et al., 2008

wide event, the resulting power impact can be large. Figure 11.3 illustrates a bus master transfer from a WLAN device fielding a keep-alive packet from an 802.11g access point. Although the actual transfer is short-lived, the component and platform power scales up dramatically to process this activity.

USB is based on an architecture that constantly polls devices. The polling times range from once every microframe (125 microseconds) for synchronous transfers to many times per microframe for asynchronous transfers. This nearly constant polling reduces a system's energy efficiency significantly. USB devices and architecture needs to be changed from the USB 2.0 continuously polled architecture to one where devices are only polled when needed.

In the short term, USB devices manufacturers could provide energy efficient products by supporting and using Suspend (L2) whenever the device is idle, occasionally waking to look for activity, incoming connections, or other device state changes. This is important as a energy efficient device should not continuously post periodic (and certainly not asynchronous) transfers when it is not active or actively connected.

The next generation, USB 3.0, implements a periodic polling transfer increasing system energy efficiency. Until widespread support of USB3 devices are in place, server manufacturers with USB 2.0 devices can improve energy efficiency by implementing a new low-power link state known as LPM L1. Supporting the L1 state requires modifications to both USB host controllers and devices. The L1 state is a new feature that augments USB 2.0 power management; it does not replace the existing L2 (suspend/resume) mechanism. Details on the LPM L1 state and recommended implementations can be found in the Intel Technology Journal at *www.intel.com*.

Controlling the Data Explosion

IDC research estimates that the digital universe, that is, the information that has been created, captured, or replicated in digital form, was 281 exabytes in 2007 (Gantz 2008).

In 2011, the amount of digital information produced in the year is forecasted to equal nearly 1,800 exabytes, or 10 times that produced in 2006. Figure 11.4 illustrates this explosive data growth. As mentioned in previous chapters, storage growth typically means increased disks and spindles which constantly consume power. The implications of this data explosion also translate into more and larger data centers. Data de-duplication and compression are recommended methods to minimize the

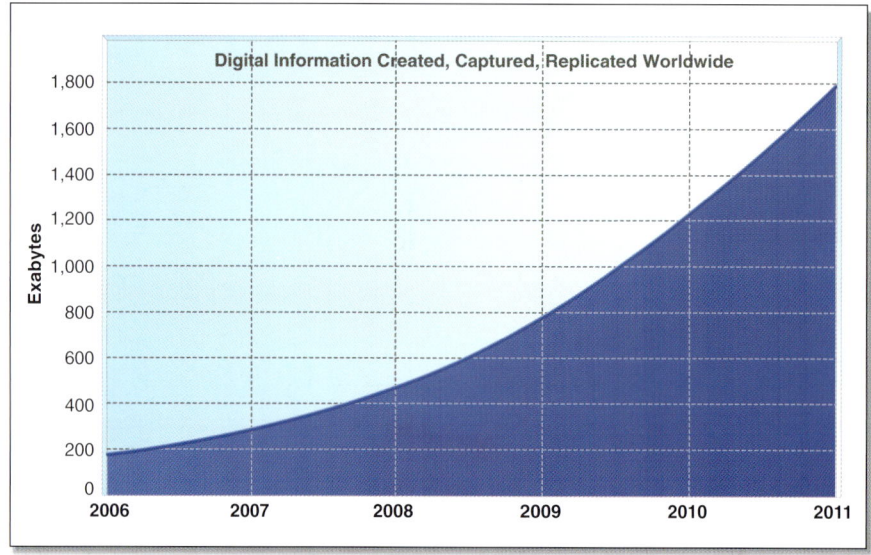

Figure 11.4 Exploding Storage Growth through 2011

Source: Gantz, 2008

amount of saved data. In 2008, data de-duplication solutions are focused on compression appliances for block-based storage systems. Because of the growing amount of file-based digital content, there is a growing opportunity for file-based compression solutions from storage vendors.

Future Energy Efficiency Standards: Power and Performance Metrics

Fair comparisons for data center and IT equipment energy efficiencies require a standardized set of performance and energy efficiency metrics accompanied by standardized methods for taking measurements. Without a standard set of metrics to understand the efficiency of their data centers, it will be difficult for IT operation managers to improve the performance-per-watt of their facilities and infrastructure. Making informed capital investment decisions related to data center capacity is challenging at best and without rationalized data it can be impossible. Standardized metrics provide a common way to benchmark against existing or legacy data centers as well as other organizations and industry norms.

Conventional models for estimating the electrical efficiency of data centers are grossly inaccurate for real-world installations. Many of the proposed metrics are static. They assume some steady-state aspect of the data center, for example, steady compute loads, steady number of servers, and so on. However, these do not match the dynamic nature of today's data centers.

Large data centers need dynamic system power characterization as a function of OS level resource utilization and generic performance metrics. This needs to be done across array structures, memory, disks, and networking equipment for power modeling under a variety of workloads. What is currently missing are power measurements and management for on-line workloads and to analyze large commercial workloads that take too long or are too complex to simulate.

Another problem with existing metrics is different vendors provide efficiency data for their systems using different methodologies. Data center managers need a well defined and objective set of methodologies which are repeatable and consistent. An example of inconsistency is how power and cooling equipment manufacturers provide efficiency data for their systems. For power equipment, efficiency is typically expressed as the percent of power out to power in. For cooling equipment, efficiency is expressed as the ratio of heat removed to electrical input power. Unfortunately, these individual values of efficiency often lead people to think that the efficiency losses of a data center can be easily calculated.

Listed below are a few recently proposed metrics that can accurately characterize performance and efficiency of data centers. These metrics will make a big impact if universally adopted and applied using a consistent methodology. They potentially address current gaps in data center and IT infrastructure power measurements and metrics. Universal adoption would greatly assist data center managers with identifying opportunities to be more energy efficient and enable benchmarking best practices. Without agreement on the methodology, application, and need for measurement over time, there will continue to be far too much opportunity for green marketing at the expense of real and measurable progress toward truly efficient IT infrastructure. If all vendors adopted these metrics, it would be a great step forward to aid power reduction with computing for all data centers.

Dynamic Deployed Hardware Utilization Ratio (DDH-UR). There is a static version of this metric (DH-UR) that measures the *Number of Servers Running Live Applications* divided by the *Total Number of Servers Actually Deployed*. A dynamic version of this metric analyzes the real-time utilization of hardware. It identifies how many deployed servers are actually doing work versus those that are sitting comatose. This is a valuable metric if it is used in conjunction with equipment that constantly optimizes how many servers are on and shuts down idle servers. A DDH-UR value of 1 implies that only required servers are actually powered-up and active. An energy efficient data center would have the goal to constantly minimize DDH-UR.

Dynamic Site Infrastructure Power Overhead Multiplier (DSI-POM). This is essentially the same metric as the Green Grid's PUE, but with dynamic measurement added. This metric is defined as the *Dynamic Data Center Power Consumption at the Meter* divided by the *Total Power Consumption at the Plug* for IT Equipment. The goal is to always drive toward a constant ratio, regardless of compute demand. DSI-POM improves when as compute demand falls, servers are retired and other support equipment (power handling, cooling) also shuts down, keeping the efficiency ratio balanced. The converse is also true. This is a metric that could be used to gauge the dynamic responsiveness of both facilities and IT infrastructure to demand.

Data Center Productivity (DCP). This metric is derived from dividing *Useful Computing Work* and dividing by the *Total Facility Power*

Consumed. The problem with this performance metric is there is no industry agreement on what constitutes useful work. Computing vendors and data center operators define useful computing work according to their own computing bias. A universal, standard definition and adoption of this metric would be an extremely useful tool for data centers because it would allow them to compare efficiency at the service level. In short, DCP is based upon a micro-economics model in which the cost of raw materials (for data centers, principally energy), sunk capital (facilities and IT equipment) and labor are compared to the value of the product produced (, internet content, competitive business advantage, accurate medical treatment) in order to determine optimal investments among alternatives.

Summary

When evaluating new capital investments for a data center, acquisition costs will always be important. But energy costs are quickly becoming a consideration for those data centers that are grappling with rising electrical bills or those that are located where there are limitations on the amount of available power.

As energy efficiency becomes more valued, many opportunities arise for vendors and system manufacturers. Some areas of growing market value are:

- Enablement of reduced power states for all components on server, storage and network motherboard components
- Implementation of thermal sensors for every critical component within servers and LED temperature readers at server air-intake vents
- Embedded remote power management capabilities on servers and other IT equipment with threshold settings (capping) over standardized management protocols
- DC-DC power supply units with energy efficiency at 10 percent utilization
- USB 2.0 devices that support suspend states to provide idle power savings followed by rapid adoption of USB 3.0 devices

Universal support for broad-based industry standards will provide a common language for everyone to work on energy efficiency. Gaps to current standards and metrics include: dynamic deployed hardware utilization ratio, dynamic site infrastructure power overhead multiplier and data center productivity.

Reducing power consumption has growing financial incentives for data centers to become green. Vendors and manufacturers can seize this opportunity by improving products with energy efficiency designs. Data center managers and technicians can help drive demand for energy efficient products by including questions about energy requirements in all requests for proposals. Finally, data center managers can personally drive demand by asking vendors what they're doing to improve energy efficiency in future versions of their products.

We expect that when we revisit the topic of reducing power consumption in servers and data centers in three years or so, that many of these advances will have taken place. While power consumption will likely continue to rise, we believe that we can reduce the rate of the increase. Hopefully this book will help IT organizations to do just that.

Appendix A

Energy-Efficient Server Maintenance

The problem with troubleshooting is that the trouble shoots back.
—Anonymous

Maintenance is sometimes thought of as boring and repetitive. The old adage "If it ain't broke, don't fix it" is followed by too many system administrators, especially those in small offices. However, preventative maintenance can uncover minor problems and keep the servers running at top performance per Watt.

The focus of this chapter is to provide some basics of server maintenance and best-practices to help maintain the energy efficiency state of server. This will include system management, recommended upgrades and troubleshooting server hardware problems to minimize power consumption. As with the majority of tasks and procedures in the IT world, there isn't an easy one-size-fits-all solution with maintenance, but there are some basic areas that are common among different types of x86 servers. Some key areas of maintenance are (in no particular order of importance):

- Establishing performance baselines and documenting the configuration
- System cleaning

- Corruption detection
- Backups, data and log file management

An unmaintained or poorly maintained server can develop problems which can eventually lead to poor application performance or even downtime and data loss. Server maintenance provides simple ways to mitigate the problems to keep a server running with optimum performance per Watt.

Server Maintenance to Maintain Energy Efficiency

Procedures and Schedules

An effective maintenance plan reflects the type of server environment in the data center. Environments that change or have problems frequently require more frequent maintenance. Some maintenance tasks are simple and should be performed on a weekly basis, others take more time…but they all help to keep things running smoothly and the reduced power consumption in the data center.

A maintenance plan begins by profiling and documenting configurations. Performance baselines should be set for all servers. When the server is in production, process performance information should be continually gathered to ensure that the server is still operating at efficient energy levels. Over time, as the retained set grows, specific hardware upgrades such as memory, will be required to maintain the optimal energy efficiency and performance per Watt. On-going performance monitoring and trend analysis against a baseline enables planning for hardware upgrades before they are actually needed.

All servers should be kept on a supported release for each OS/application/database as well as current with latest available fixes, patches, or upgrades. Upgrades fix known problems and keep the server operating efficiently. Keeping the server current helps ensure the server maintains its top performance per Watt and minimizes potential problems which may cause downtime.

Performance monitoring and tuning is an on-going task. It is not reasonable to simply tune a server once and then assume that it will remain tuned forever. Because the server workload mix changes over time, so will its energy efficiency.

Table A.1 shows a basic maintenance schedule. Following a schedule like this may be problematic for a data center with hundreds of servers, but it is valuable to understand recommended maintenance to know where problems can occur or how power inefficiencies can grow. An alternate method to server maintenance is to upgrade or replace servers every two to three years instead of a traditional five-year turn.

Table A.1   Maintenance Schedule

Schedule	Component	Maintenance Activity
Daily	Server	❏ Run a virus scan of the memory and HDDs
	HDD	❏ Create a differential backup
Weekly	HDD	❏ Create a full backup
		❏ Remove all .tmp files and clear C:\TEMP and C:\WINDOWS\TEMP
	Web Browser	❏ Clear browser cache, history and temporary Internet files
	Antivirus Software	❏ Update antivirus data files
	Database	❏ Perform maintenance procedures
Monthly	HDD	❏ Defrag the drive and recover lost clusters. Empty Recycle Bins.
		❏ Uninstall all unnecessary applications. Run a disk cleanup utility to remove unneeded files, such as temporary files, Internet content, and installation files.
	Server	❏ Monitor performance, check against baseline. Verify software and hardware configuration against documented known good configuration.
Yearly	Case	❏ Clean with compressed air to remove dust and other debris
As required	CMOS	❏ Record and back up CMOS setup configuration
	Database	❏ Run fix utility to clean any corrupted databases at server startup and as needed
	System	❏ Keep written record of hardware and software configuration of server

Spring Cleaning Keeps Servers Cool

Server components attract everything such as dust, dirt, lint and smoke particles. At least two fans are bringing air into the server to keep the internal components cool. Unfortunately, the air also contains dust and debris, which settles on the components, and can cause a variety of problems. Even the thinnest coating of dust will raise the temperature of the server components. The dust buildup causes overheating, which triggers baseboard management controllers to send alerts for extra cooling and resulting in extra data center power consumption.

The frequency of cleaning servers really depends upon the environment. However, on average for a clean, climate controlled data center, this procedure should be done once a year. The cleaning starts by checking the vents and grills for dust and debris. The more efficient the airflow, the cooler the server runs using less power and requiring less cooling of ambient air.

If the vents/grills show dust, they should be cleaned with compressed air or vacuumed. When the server case is open, the power supply case vents should also be checked for dust. Note: The power supply case itself should never be opened; power supplies can still carry a charge, even when the server is unplugged. Compressed air should be sprayed directly into the power supply vents from inside the case, so the grime exits out of the back of the case. A vacuum cleaner should collect this dust as it comes out before it recirculates through the data center CRAC units.

Server Maintenance to Maintain Energy Efficiency 285

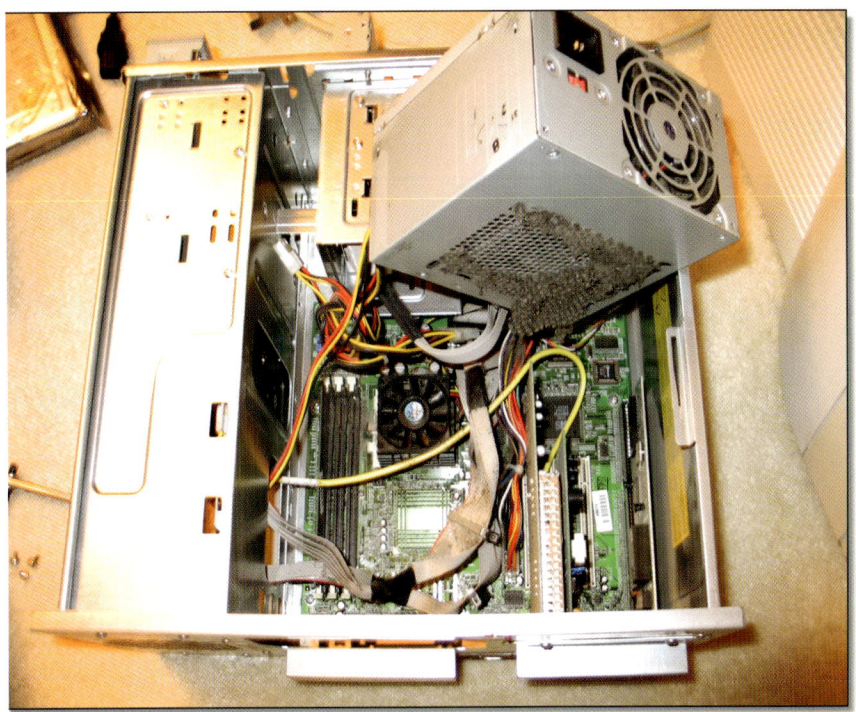

Figure A.1 Dusty Computer
Source: Around the Clock Information Systems, www.ACTIS.com, 2008

Dusty Add-in Cards Consume More Power

Over time, add-in cards can accumulate dust and debris on the connectors. Server and rack movements can cause them to unseat slightly. The add-in cards still may be functional, but consuming a bit more power than with proper seating. Also, cable changes could slightly move NIC cards. When performing maintenance, all cards should be checked that they are seated securely in their slots and screwed in tightly.

To ensure that you don't run into any of these problems, the following maintenance steps are recommended. Turn off the server, unplug it, remove the cover, and remove the add-in cards. Take a clean pencil eraser and rub it over the contacts on the part of the card that fits into the slot. Done in a slow and gentle manner, this can remove any corrosion or buildup of debris. Then reseat the card firmly and securely in its socket. Remember to leave empty slots between cards if possible, so as to optimize the cooling airflow within a server.

Data and Hard Disk Drive Maintenance

When a server crashes, the most effective way to recover the server and its data is to restore from a backup. The best time to make a backup/restore is when the server is properly configured and tuned for optimum performance per Watt. It is also good to know how effectively the server can be restored before actually needing it. If the server failure occurs and there isn't a backup, there most likely will be some data loss that could be very expensive for the business.

Loss of business data makes a very strong case for taking regular backups. Backups can be done in different ways. If full backups are done hourly or daily, the amount of data growth will require continual growth of storage arrays and the associated power use in the data center. An energy efficient method of performing backups is as follows:

1. Define a backup plan. Consider the following:
   - How critical is data?
   - How often does it change?
   - What are legal and regulative requirements?

2. Full backups should be done based on frequently accessed or changed data. To determine what should be backed up, consider how much data the business can afford to lose (, what is the cost of 1 day or 1 hour of data?)

3. If backups are needed more often than daily, utilize differential backups to complement the full backups. Less frequently accessed data should be moved to a MAID system and backed up once a week.

4. Archive older data to tape weekly. Once a month keep the tape heads in top shape by running a cleaning tape through the tape drive.

If there is a growing demand for more disks and storage arrays, remember that more disks equal more power consumption. Basic disk maintenance can clean up data and free up disk space, possibly eliminating the need to increase spindle count. Basic disk maintenance includes running a disk cleanup program with utilities such as defragmentation, deleting .tmp and .chk files, and checking the disks for errors. Some of these maintenance procedures can be scheduled to automatically run during off hours. Defragmentation and deleting the

.tmp and .chk files are good candidates for off-hours procedures in order to not impact business productivity.

Finally, the recommended maintenance procedure for RAID array systems, especially with large disks, is to perform bi-monthly consistency checks. A RAID array works because in the event of a failure of one drive, the missing data held on that drive can be obtained from the "parity data" on the other drives. If however, the parity data is not correct on the other drives, the whole RAID Array will cease to function. There is also the possibility that all of the data held on that whole RAID array will be lost. By scheduling regular consistency checks, should a single drive fail, the server will still be able to function normally until the failed drive is replaced.

Power Supply Maintenance

In addition to the inefficiency of an unmaintained power supply, a weak or faulty power supply can create a number of problems for components inside the server. Unexplained or intermittent memory or hard disk errors are commonly caused by a faulty or a failing power supply. Extended periods of low voltage can damage the hard disk drive as much as over-voltages can burn out the motherboard and memory. The symptoms of a faulty power supply can include things such as:

- Failure to power on or boot
- General instability
- Rebooting, either randomly or when the server is stressed
- Hardware failure, due to sudden power spikes/dips

Power supply maintenance involves nothing more than being sure the server is located in a place where air can ventilate through the system unit and that the fan in the power supply is operational. A visual check to the rear of the power supply can quickly identify if dust has collected in or around the fan. Use compressed air or a clean soft cloth to remove all excess dust. When performing a yearly cleaning of a server, take note of the power supply connectors for the drive. Be sure they are not damaged and tight if you have removed the connectors. This will allow the power supply to work more freely and maintain its power efficiency.

Figure A.2 Redundant Power Supplies
Source: Wikipedia

Preventive Maintenance: The CMOS and BIOS

Maintenance of the CMOS and BIOS involves monitoring the battery to have an idea as to when it should be replaced and making backup copies of the CMOS SRAM. The CMOS battery is mounted onto the motherboard and, just like all batteries, eventually these all die. Use a battery checker to check the battery level. When the battery for the CMOS fails, it could take hours to rediscover settings of the CMOS.

There are many good small software utilities on the market that can make copies of the CMOS and quickly restore the CMOS settings. Making copies of the CMOS should be done while the CMOS battery is working well. It is best not to wait until the server experiences boot-up problems to check the CMOS battery.

Operating System Maintenance

If the server seems to be running more slowly than in the past, then it is likely to be experiencing problems with its OS registry database. Even if you're extremely careful about how the server is used and you never download questionable files, it is inevitable over time that the server will accumulate unwanted registry entries, errors, and clutter. As previously mentioned, when a server is not performing optimally, it will also not be operating at top energy efficiency.

The most common causes of cluttered registers are the installation and removal of software, upgrades of software programs, application crashes, and online games. While many errors will go unnoticed, the more errors the server has, the higher the chances of energy inefficiencies and even potential downtime. There are good tools on the market that can scan, identify, and repair registry errors.

For Linux[†] and Netware[†] servers, the syslogs should be checked daily. If there's a problem, it will be in the syslog. When the servers are accessed by many technicians, it is important to look at the registries of critical servers monthly, looking for bogus software and services. The registry and syslog checks take only a few minutes, but they can definitely help to maintain servers on optimal performance per Watt configurations.

Database Maintenance

A poorly maintained database can develop problems of slow performance, increasing server and data center power consumption by requiring growth in storage disks to handle the unmanaged data growth. Key parts of database maintenance include:

- Eliminating index fragmentation
- Managing data and transaction log files
- Ensuring accurate, up-to-date statistics
- Detecting corrupted database pages
- Establishing a good backup plan

Eliminating index fragmentation

Index fragmentation—wasted space on data/index pages—can lead to the need for more pages to hold the same amount of data. Not only does this use up more disk space, it also means that a query needs to issue more I/Os to read the same amount of data. Moreover, all these extra pages occupy more space in the data cache, thus requiring more server memory.

Fragmentation can sometimes be prevented by changing the table/index schema. If prevention is not an option, fragmentation can be eliminated by rebuilding or reorganizing the index.

Along with index fragmentation is index scanning to keep a database performing optimally. Index Scanning maintenance procedure is valuable for maintaining energy efficiency because this speeds up index scanning performance. This procedure keeps the physical order of the index matching the logical order of the index. The operation also arranges the index pages in the same space allocated to the index. Pages that are left empty after the operation will be released, making the index more compact than it originally was and thus helping control disk demand.

Data and log file management

The settings related to data and transaction log file management should be checked. This involves verifying the data and log files are separated from each other and isolated from everything else as well. If this is not done, there is the potential for file fragmentation. In data files, excessive file fragmentation will contribute to poorly performing queries. In log files, file fragmentation will have a significant impact on performance, especially if auto-growth is set to increase file size as it is needed. Managing the data and transaction log files maintain optimum performance and also help control the demand for disks.

Statistics

The query decision-making process within databases utilizes statistics. These statistics describe the distribution of data values for columns within a table or index. Statistics need to be accurate and up-to-date for query process to be efficient, otherwise poorly performing query plans may be chosen. Poorly performing query plans increase database search times, making the server run at high utilizations for longer times, consuming more than average power.

The maintenance procedure for statistics is to keep them updated and accurate with the indexes. This can be automatically by turning on an "auto create statistics" database tool. If all indexes are rebuilt during monthly database maintenance, this auto-statistics tool will insure the server and database maintain energy efficient performance. For any indexes that were not rebuilt and for non-indexed columns, the statistics need to be updated manually to maintain minimum power consumption.

Corruption detection

Corrupted databases do not cause increased power consumption on servers, but the ineffective constant searching with corrupt data will. The overwhelming majority of corruptions are caused by the I/O subsystem. A common cause of corruptions is a temporary power failure where a disk drive does not complete the writing out of a database page. The result is an incomplete page image on the disk. This situation is called a *torn page*. Running a database page checksums tool can detect these types of corruption on a page. When corruption is found, the database should be restored to the last-known good backup. This will keep the server and database operating at top performance per Watt.

Backups

This brings us to the last section for power efficient database maintenance: the backup. Regular backups provide a single point in time to which the database can later be restored. A frequency should be chosen that reflects how much data or work the business is comfortable losing. If daily full database backups are chosen, this means the business might lose up to a day's worth of data in the event of a disaster. If daily backups provide too much risk for the business, consider differential backups. A differential database backup is based on a full database backup and contains a record of all the changes since the last full database backup. A sample backup plan could be for daily full database backup with differential backups every two hours.

In addition to database backups, a full recovery would include log backups as well. Maintaining a set of log backups with periodic full database plus differential database backups provides an unlimited number of points in time to recover and would provide the most safety.

Backups should be kept for a few days in case one of them becomes corrupt. The integrity of backups should be verified by using a backup database verify command or creating backups with the checksum option. In addition, for maximum energy efficiency, backups should be moved to tape rather than being housed on power hungry disk drive RAID systems.

Upgrading for Energy Efficiency

Determining When to Upgrade

The phrase "if it isn't broken, don't touch it" definitely applies to servers. There are times when upgrading a server can offer better performance and efficiency, therefore reducing the power usage of a server. Also, there are times when upgrading a server does not yield power or cost savings. The availability of newer technologies that typically offer better energy efficiency or lower power consumption are among the reasons to consider upgrading. Memory and SSD upgrades are worth the money.

Situations when upgrades should be considered include:

- When a new operating system is installed, as an upgrade of the operating system will typically require new hardware
- When wait times for compute transactions are noticeably long and business customers within the organization are complaining about response times.
- If there is no room for new applications. Remember, it is more energy efficient to consolidate servers and run applications on virtual managers. If hard disk drive space is limited for adding new applications, it is time to upgrade.

Upgrades should always be implemented one part at a time. After the upgrade, boot the server to check that everything functions correctly. If more than one part is installed at the same time, and the server does not boot up correctly, it will take more time to figure out which component is causing the conflict. Also, follow the safety recommendation of making a restore point before every upgrade. This allows a return to a functioning system while troubleshooting any new issues.

Here are some times and situations not to upgrade:

- Don't upgrade when a server part breaks while under warranty. Trying to fix or replace a part may void the warranty for the server.
- Avoid upgrading when there is a service deadline because upgrades often take twice as long as originally planned.
- Consider not upgrading when the server is old. Not all servers should be upgraded. If the server was purchased before 2004, no amount of money can improve its energy efficiency. Newer servers, are much more power efficient than older ones, and they

have significant performance headroom. Also, a newer server may actually cost less than trying to upgrade the older server.

Memory Upgrades: Lower Power, Better Performance

Upgrading memory improves performance, and it can also lower the power consumption from the memory subsystem. For upgrading memory, the lowest power choice comes from highest density DRAM configurations, with greatest capacity, low voltage components and DIMMs with power down features.

When considering upgrading memory in a server, remember less DIMMs = less power. Low power options should include highest density and capacity affordable. For example, a x8, 4Gb DDR3 DRAM 4GB capacity RDIMM would have lowest power/capacity of volume available DIMMs in 2008.

Figure A.3 Memory Upgrades for Improved Efficiency
Source: Kingston Technologies, 2008

If errors occur after a memory upgrade, such as a parity error message, begin by isolating the problem. Remove all but one pair of DIMMs, turn on the server and see if the error message reappears. If the server shows no problems, try reinserting the other memory modules, one pair at a time, and booting up the server after each addition. Eventually, the module that is causing the problem can be identified and replaced.

The following DIMM installation guidelines are recommended to minimize problems when adding additional memory to a server:

- Check to see if the server requires DIMMs to be installed in pairs.
- A DIMM installed on the same memory bank (DIMM pairs) must have the same part number.
- DIMMs installed in different memory banks can be of different sizes.
- If DIMM pairs are required, they should be installed evenly across processor memory channel.
- Check to see if the server requires DIMMs to be installed in decreasing capacity with the largest DIMMs installed in the banks furthest away from each processor.

Also, check that the memory clock speed matches the processor. Many times, processors have specific speeds if all four banks on a memory node are populated, and other speeds if two or fewer banks on a memory node are populated. Finally, note that some servers require DIMM fillers covering any pairs of empty DIMM slots.

Increasing Storage with Additional Hard Drives

If additional storage is needed, the low power recommendation is to consider SSDs or expand the NAS or SAN. This would be the most energy efficient method for increasing storage capacity. Storage power consumption increases as hard drive spindles increase. Before purchasing a new storage array, run disk tools and consider de-duplication or compression techniques to free up existing disk space.

Frequent Problems and Fixes

When a server starts to malfunction, sometimes it's obvious what the problem is, and other times it is not. Resolving a malfunctioning NIC card is as simple as replacing it. However, if the hard disk drive is intermittently producing read or write errors, the problem could be in the hard disk, power supply, memory, motherboard, cables, or software. Malfunctioning components or intermittent problems are a sign of power inefficiency. As with maintenance and upgrades, problems should be fixed to maintain top performance per Watt.

On servers, a majority of the problems are software related and can easily be solved by reconfiguring or reinstalling the software. Problems with the software typically show up almost immediately after the new software is installed. In fact, most problems on a server tend to happen right after new hardware or software is installed or reconfigured.

No general formula exists for solving all of the problems that can occur on a server, but there are general troubleshooting processes to isolate what might be causing the problem. The following sections contain a few of these processes as well as some helpful tips you can use to maintain an energy efficient server.

Troubleshooting Methods

One of the most overlooked tools in a server repair kit is a record of past problems, troubleshooting, installations, upgrades, and repairs that have been done on the server. This documentation can quickly solve a problem if it occurred before, and it can help identify which servers are problematic and are good candidates for quick replacement. The server record can also be valuable when dealing with warranty issues.

When problems appear, document whether it is the first time the problem has occured and what workload was being processed at the time. Can the problem be recreated? Were there any new hardware or software updates recently? Was anything happening in the environment, such as lightning storms or brownouts? This is all key environmental data that will help in isolating the problem.

Problem Determination Tips

Due to the variety of hardware and software combinations that can be encountered, troubleshooting often requires a call to a manufacturer's support center. The following information should be collected to assist the support center in problem determination.

- Machine type and model
- Microprocessor, memory or hard disk upgrades
- Failure symptom
    - Do diagnostics fail?
    - What, when, where, — single, or multiple systems?
    - Is the failure repeatable?
    - Has this configuration ever worked?
    - If it has been working, what changes were made prior to it failing?
    - Is this the original reported failure?

- Diagnostics version
  - Type and version level
- Hardware configuration
  - Print (print screen) configuration currently in use
  - BIOS level
- Operating system software
  - Type and version level

Troubleshooting the Processor

If a server's processor fails, it can only be replaced. However, most problems that appear to be processor problems are usually a problem with another component. What may show up as a processor problem is more likely a problem with the cooling of the processor (see Figure A.4) or the system, the power supply, or a compatibility issue between the motherboard and the chipset.

Figure A.4 Dusty Processor Fan

Source: Bryce Whitty, www.technibble.com, 2008

Common symptoms that a processor is about to fail include: inability to boot, operating system will not start, frequent crashes and POST parity errors in many devices. If you experience any of these systems, check the cooling on the processor and on the system. For energy efficiency, newer processors support low power states in addition to providing more power control over the memory. If the processor experiences problems more than a few times, the energy efficiency recommendation is to upgrade to a new lower power processor.

Troubleshooting Memory

Most memory problems happen just after new memory has been installed. Memory problems occur because of electrical problems on the motherboard. Troubleshooting memory problems is complicated because many FRUs give out symptoms that appear to be memory problems. For memory problems, the following should be checked:

- If new or additional memory was added to the server, the amount of memory installed may be more than the server or operating system is able to support. Check the server documentation for this. Also check that the BIOS CMOS settings are correct for the new amount and type of memory. Check the part numbers and speed of both the new and the old memory modules. Verify that the memory is appropriate for the motherboard, chipset and processor.

- Memory needs to be compatible and installed in complete banks. If slower memory is installed in one bank, all the memory will operate at the slower speed. The problem could also be that at least one memory module or chip is defective. Verify the memory was properly installed and configured in memory banks.

- Many memory problems are caused by the memory chips or modules not being properly installed in their sockets. It could be that a socket is bad, has a bent or broken lead, or just needs cleaning.

Troubleshooting Hard Disk Drives

When a hard disk error occurs, it could be a serious problem. This could signify more than the server not booting, but also a potential risk to losing data and programs. A hard disk problem can be caused by the hard disk drive, the hard disk controller, a SCSI host adapter, cabling or even the power supply.

- There are many items which cause failures in hard disk drives.
- The CMOS configuration is incorrect
- Hardware resource conflicts
- Boot partition is corrupted
- The hard disk may have a virus infection
- The hard disk cable may be bad or not connected properly
- Drive incompatibilities
- RAID configuration conflicts

The first step in hard disk drive troubleshooting is to create and verify a full backup of the hard disk before trying any problem isolation techniques. This is to protect the data if possible. The next step is to use BIOS tools and see if the controller can find the disk drive. If it can, then the problem is probably software related or partitioning of the disk. Try booting the drive or booting with a floppy disk then using partitioning tools to assess the disk problem. If the controller cannot find the disk, then the disk should be tried in another system or try a good disk in the problematic server. Other items to check include verifying good cables and connections, the power supply is supplying sufficient power, and the disk, BIOS and controllers are all configured correctly.

Should all above steps fail, then contact the drive manufacturer for data recovery or use a 3rd party tool to recover the data from the disk.

Troubleshooting the Power Supply

The power supply is the most failure-prone component in any computer system. A faulty power supply can cause other components in the system to malfunction and possible cause damage to the components by delivering an improper or erratic voltage. When the power supply begins to malfunction, one of the first signs is that the server will start rebooting at random or the screen will display error messages.

To troubleshoot a server's power supply, utilize a power meter to test each of the power connectors (+12VDC and +5VDC) for proper voltages. Power supply testers are widely available. These typically have a socket for each common type of power supply connector, and use several LEDs to indicate if the power supply is working. Check the power supply's documentation for information and make sure the power connectors are set to proper voltage levels. If the pins cannot be adjusted to the correct voltages, replace the power supply.

Power supplies can also fail when the electrolytic capacitors or internal cooling fans dry up and/or become defective. These are difficult to fix and the recommendation is to upgrade.

When upgrading, be sure to match the rating of the power supply to the server's requirements. For energy efficiency, only upgrade with 80 PLUS certified power supplies. Of all upgrades, an efficient power supply can cause the most power waste within the server.

Summary

Preventative maintenance allows servers to run cooler, quieter, and maintain a top performance per Watt. Ensuring that servers and databases remain energy efficient require a few *must do* tasks. Maintenance plans should reflect the type of data center environment. Clean, stable use of servers requires less maintenance than a server room where software and location of the server changes frequently.

Maintenance plans begin by documenting energy efficient configurations of servers. Server performance should also be documented to set an efficiency baseline. Ongoing monitoring can identify when a server starts varying from this baseline.

A basic maintenance plan should include daily virus checking and data backups, weekly disk and database maintenance, and yearly cleaning of server dust and debris. Dusty or improperly seated cards will start consuming more power than at optimal install state. Ongoing disk and database maintenance can help reduce or slow the demand for an increase in disks and spindles, thus capping demand for increased storage power.

Upgrades can help keep a server at optimum performance per Watt. As retained data sets, number of applications, or virtualization use increases, servers will definitely benefit from increased memory. DIMMs with the latest memory technology, density and large capacity draw the least power and can actually reduce a server's power draw. Upgrades should be performed one at a time and then checked to simplify troubleshooting of any possible new problems.

To speed troubleshooting, logs should be kept for each server of its issues, past troubleshooting, upgrades and repairs. If a problem is repetitive, this information can vastly speed repairs…or help assess if the server should be replaced. All server components can fail, but the power supply is most prone to failures. There are power supply testers on the market which can simplify the troubleshooting. When replacements are needed for any component, it is recommended to upgrade to a low power, increased efficiency part, such as newer processors, latest memory technology and 80 PLUS certified power supplies.

Appendix B

Energy Efficiency Measurement Templates

It doesn't work to leap a twenty-foot chasm in two ten-foot jumps.
—Proverb

U.S. Department of Energy Templates

The following tables are templates provided by the Department of Energy. They can assist in profiling a data center and developing benchmark measurements.

Table B.1   Data Center Assessment Inputs
Source: U.S. Department of Energy, 2008

	Initial Assessment Values
Overall Energy Management	
Environmental Conditions	
Air Management, CRAC / CRAH / AHU	
Central Cooling Plant	
IT Equipment Power Chain	
Lighting	
Other Electrical	

Table B.2 Data Center Assessment Inputs: Features

Source:U.S. Department of Energy, 2008

IT Equipment Power Chain	Assessment Values
What is the Utility input voltage?	
What is the UPS redundancy configuration?	
What is the power distribution configuration?	
What is the UPS load capacity?	
What type of UPS is being used?	
What is the UPS input current total harmonic distortion?	
What is the UPS input power factor?	
Number of transformers downstream from the UPS system?	
Number of transformers / PDUs upstream from the UPS system?	
Number of STSs downstream from the UPS system?	
What are the anticipated future IT loads?	
What is the stand-by power configuration?	
Is there co-generation?	
Do the servers have an efficiency rating?	
Is virtualization used?	

Table B.3 Data Center Assessment Inputs: Metrics

Source: U.S. Department of Energy, 2008

IT Equipment Power Chain				
Metrics	Unit	Data Required	Priority	Value
UPS load capacity	kVAkW	UPS rating	1	
UPS System Efficiency	%	UPS Output kW/UPS Input KW	1	
UPS input current THD	%	UPS THD measure at Input	1	
UPS input power factor	PF	UPS Power Factor measured at Input	1	
Transformer (upstream UPS system) Efficiency	%	XFMR Output kw/XFMR Transformer Input	1	
PDU (with built-in transformer) System Efficiency	%	PDU Output kW/PDU Input kW	1	
STS efficiency	%	STS Output kW/STS Input kW	2	
IT Peak Power Density (actual)	W/sf	IT Peak Power (actual)/DC Floor Area	1	
IT Peak Power Density (design)	W/sf	IT Peak Power (design)/DC Floor Area	2	
IT Rack Power Density (actual)	kW/rack	IT Peak Power (actual)/rack quantity	1	
IT Rack Power Density (design)	kW/rack	IT Peak Power (design)/rack quantity	1	

Table B.4 Data Centers: Data Collection Worksheet

Source: U.S. Department of Energy, 2008

ID	Data	Unit	Priority	Source Method	Measurement Frequency	Measurement Equipment	Guidance
General							
Annual Energy Use (NOTE: Include central plant energy used by DC, but exclude energy used for any offices, etc., that may be served by central plant)							
CRAC and AHU							
Economizer and Central Cooling							
IT Equipment Power Data							
Lighting Data							

Table B.5 Data Centers: Data Collection Worksheet
Source: U.S. Department of Energy, 2008

IT Equipment Power Data							
ID	Data	Unit	Priority	Source Method	Measurement Frequency	Measurement Equipment	Guidance
P1	IT Equipment Energy Use	kWh	1				
P2	IT Peak Power: Actual	kW	1				Use P4 or P5
P3	IT Peak Power: Design	kW	1				
P4	UPS Input	kW	1				
P5	UPS Output	kW	1				
P6	UPS Rating	kVA/kW	1				
P7	UPS Input current THD	THD%	1				
P8	UPS Input Power Factor	PF	1				
P9	Transformer (upstream UPS) input	kW	1				
P10	Transformer (upstream UPS) output	kW	1				
P11	Transformer rating	kVA	1				
P12	PDU Input	kW	1				
P13	PDU Output	kW	1				
P14	PDU Rating	kVA	1				

Table B.6 Data Center Assessment Efficiency Actions

Source: U.S. Department of Energy, 2008

	Efficiency Actions
1. Overall Energy Management	
2. Environmental Conditions	
3. Air Management and Air Handling	
4. Central Cooling Plant	
5. IT Equipment Power Chain	
6. Lighting	
7. Maintenance and Testing Management	

Appendix B: Energy Efficiency Measurement Templates

Appendix C

Resources for Energy Efficiency

It is our task in our time and in our generation to hand down undiminished to those who come after us, as was handed down to us by those who went before, the natural wealth and beauty which is ours.
—John Fitzgerald Kennedy

1. *www.7x24exchange.org*
   An association facilitating the exchange of information for "those who design, build, use, and maintain mission-critical enterprise information infrastructures.

2. *www.80PLUS.org*
   The 80 PLUS program is a unique forum that unites electric utilities, the computer industry and consumers in an effort to bring energy efficient technology solutions to the marketplace. It provides specifications for vendors of power supplies. It also provides listings of compliant products.

3. *www.acpi.info/*
   ACPI (Advanced Configuration and Power Interface) is an open industry specification co-developed by Hewlett-Packard, Intel, Microsoft, Phoenix, and Toshiba. ACPI establishes industry-standard interfaces enabling OS-directed configuration, power management, and thermal management of mobile, desktop, and server platforms.

4. *www.afcom.com/*
   AFCOM started as an association of "a handful of data center managers looking for support and professional education." AFCOM membership now includes "more than 3,000 data centers" worldwide. Their mission is to enable data center management professionals to share industry best practices by providing a forum for dissemination of critical information.

5. *http://tc99.ashraetcs.org/*
   ASHRAE Technical Committee 9.9 (Mission Critical Facilities, Technology Spaces and Electronic Equipment), is a technical committee that is concerned with all aspects of Mission Critical Facilities, Technology Spaces, and Electronic Equipment/Systems. This includes data centers, computer rooms/closets, raised floor environments, high density loads, emergency/network operations centers, telecom facilities, communication rooms/closets, and electronic equipment rooms/closets. ASHRAE book store publishes many books in the areas of designing and cooling data centers. In 2008, "High Density Data Center - Case Studies and Best Practices" was published. The ASHRAE TC9.9 committee will publish its next book in 2009, titled "Contamination in Datacom Equipment Centers".

6. *www.cee1.org*
   Consortium for Energy Efficiency (CEE): A nonprofit organization promoting energy-efficient products and services, CEE's board recently endorsed an exploration of efficient data center operations.

7. *www.cfroundtable.org*
   Critical Facilities Round Table. A non-profit organization dedicated to the discussion and resolution of industry issues regarding mission-critical facilities, their engineering and design, and their maintenance. They provide an open forum to share information and to learn about new mission-critical technologies, with the intention of helping members improve in technical expertise and develop solutions for the challenges of their day-to-day critical facilities operations.

8. *www.Climatesaverscomputing.org*
   Started by Google and Intel in 2007, the Climate Savers Computing Initiative is a nonprofit group of eco-conscious consumers, businesses and conservation organizations. The Initiative was started in the spirit of WWF's Climate Savers program which has

mobilized over a dozen companies since 1999 to cut carbon dioxide emissions, demonstrating that reducing emissions is good business. Their goal is to promote development, deployment and adoption of smart technologies that can both improve the efficiency of a computer's power delivery and reduce the energy consumed when the computer is in an inactive state.

9. *www.me.gatech.edu/CEETHERM*
   Consortium for Energy Efficient Thermal Management (CEETHERM): A collaboration of Georgia Institute of Technology and the University of Maryland to conduct "research on thermal and energy management of electronics and telecommunications infrastructure," CEETHERM operates a test-bed data center to test new power and cooling technologies and practices.

10. *www.datacenterdynamics.com*
    Data Center Dynamics: Hosts a conference and expo series for professionals involved in the design, construction and operation of 24/7 mission critical IT facilities in the world's top business cities. Also publishes ZeroDownTime magazine.

11. *www.datacenterknowledge.com/*
    A general data center site that offers good data center news reporting. Focus areas include energy related topics such as cooling and power distribution systems, and containerization.

12. *www.DRAMExchange.com*
    Similar to Price Watch, DRAM Exchange provides latest information on memory pricing and availability.

13. *www.ecoconsulting.com*
    With funding from a group of electric utility and energy efficiency organizations, industry experts from Ecos Consulting (Ecos) and EPRI have completed research into the energy efficient and power quality characteristics of power supplies utilized by high-density, rackable, and blade servers in data centers. Ecos has deep knowledge in power supply efficiency, specifically in the computing world both in the data center and all the devices connected to networks.

    Ecos delivers proven results for clients looking to reduce their energy use, manage their carbon emissions, or make their operations more environmentally sustainable. With over a decade of experience designing innovative and cost-effective ways to leverage market-based mechanisms for the benefit of the planet,

Ecos performs the research, develops the plans, and implements the projects that make the most significant impact on the vitality of both its clients and the world. Ecos has offices in Portland, OR; San Francisco, CA; Seattle, WA; and Durango, CO.

14. *www.ecsintl.com*
    The mission of Energy Control Systems is to provide cutting edge power quality solutions to customers, thereby increasing their overall profitability by decreasing overhead costs related to power quality issues. Through the past two decades, Energy Control Systems has eeevolved from a single product sales company to a multifaceted, multinational power quality solutions provider and product integrator. By utilizing a variety of technologies and products and combining them with 20 years of engineering and application expertise, we can effectively improve the efficiency of electricity usage within a facility.

15. *www.efficientpowersupplies.org*
    This Web site was created by EPRI and Ecos Consulting to initiate a global dialogue about energy efficient power supplies. Their focus is on the issue of energy consumption in the active or "on" mode of power supply operation.

16. *www.emersonnetworkpower.com*
    Emerson Network Power provides innovative solutions and expertise in areas including AC and DC power and precision cooling systems, embedded computing and power, integrated racks and enclosures, power switching and controls, monitoring, and connectivity. All solutions are supported globally by local Emerson Network Power service technicians.

17. *www.ENERGYSTAR.gov*
    This site contains the server and power supply specifications for Energy Star compliance.

18. *www.FormFactors.org*
    A site dedicated to specifications and testing of computer technologies. This site provides specifications and discussions for general technologies that are important to the design of PC systems.

19. *www.thegreengrid.org/home*
    The Green Grid is a global consortium dedicated to advancing energy efficiency in data centers and business computing ecosystems. In furtherance of its mission, The Green Grid is focused on the following: defining meaningful, user-centric models

and metrics; developing standards, measurement methods, processes and new technologies to improve data center performance against the defined metrics; and promoting the adoption of energy efficient standards, processes, measurements and technologies.

20. *www.lesswatts.org*
    Lesswatts is about creating a community around saving power on Linux[†], bringing developers, users, and sysadmins together to share software, optimizations, and tips and tricks.

21. *http://hpc.pnl.gov/projects/spraycool*
    Pacific Northwest National Laboratories (PNNL). PNNL is conducting research into energy-efficient liquid-cooling technologies for use in data centers, called the "Energy Smart Data Center" project. This DOE-funded research is publicly available. This project is supported by the U.S. Department of Energy-National Nuclear Security Administration (DOE-NNSA) Advanced Simulation and Computing (ASC) program to demonstrate advanced engineering and energy efficient electronics and concepts related to high performance computing.

22. *www.powersmiths.com*
    Powersmiths is a global leader in the manufacture of lean and green electrical power distribution systems. Powersmiths' products reduce electrical waste, improve power quality, provide fast payback and deliver lower lifecycle costs in non-residential buildings. In mission critical environments, Powersmiths' CSL-3 efficiency E-Saver-C3™ transformers and Energy Station™ PDUs have been demonstrated to significantly reduce electricity losses, resulting in direct energy savings and lower cooling costs. By generating electrical savings for customers, Powersmiths helps build a healthier more sustainable environment.

23. *www.PriceWatch.com*
    Price Watch provides availability and latest pricing on memory modules and DRAM.

24. *www.rfgonline.com*
    Since 1997, the Robert Frances Group (RFG) has assisted thousands of Global 2000, Public Sector, privately-held and Fortune 500 business and technology executives in making more informed decisions regarding the impact of technology on their enterprises. With a focus on the intersection of business and technology, RFG helps executives maximize their effectiveness by helping them

align IT efforts with corporate business strategies, drive revenues, improve processes and productivity, and reduce IT costs. RFG accomplishes this by working closely and directly with clients to evaluate hardware and software acquisitions including ROI and TCO analyses; help assess the impact of events, laws, and regulations; negotiate optimal contracts and optimize procurement management, improve human capital/workforce management, mitigate risks, transform data centers, and plan IT-empowered business strategies.

25. *www.snia.org/forums/green*

    The SNIA Green Storage Initiative is dedicated to advancing energy efficiency and conservation in all networked storage technologies and minimizing the environmental impact of data storage operations. SNIA's goal is to advance IT technologies, standards, and education programs for all IT professionals. Made up of some 400 member companies and nearly 7000 individuals spanning the global storage market, the SNIA connects the IT industry with end-to-end storage and information management solutions.

26. *www.ssiforum.org*

    Server System Infrastructure (SSI) organization. With blades representing the fastest growing segment in the server industry, SSI provides specifications which can help adopters take advantage of the modular platform opportunity. SSI has released a set of draft Modular Server Specifications, which are intended to help simplify and lower the cost of product development of modular, bladed platforms.

27. *www.uptimeinstitute.org*

    Uptime Institute has members from very large data centers. It sponsors benchmarking, the development of industry best practices and presents symposiums, seminars, certifications, and training for its member companies. The institute's website has a free library of white papers addressing energy efficiency, cooling, reliability, and best practices to improve data center uptime efficiency.

28. *www.solarenergy.org/resources/energyfacts.html*

    Solar Energy International (SEI) is a USA non-profit organization whose mission is to help others use renewable energy and environmental building technologies through education. SEI teaches individuals from all walks of life how to design, install and maintain renewable energy systems.

29. *www.facts-about-solar-energy.com/*
    This site provides research on Solar Power. It is a great starting point for someone thinking about using renewable energy resources to heat water or generate electricity.

30. *www.wikibon.org*
    Wikibon is a professional community solving technology and business problems through an open source sharing of free advisory knowledge. This site provides best practices, tips, project tools, help on RFP's, collaboration with peers and case studies.

Appendix C: Resources for Energy Efficiency

Appendix D

Performance Per Watt

If GM had kept up with technology like the computer industry has, we would all be driving $25 cars that got 1000 MPG.
— Bill Gates

Energy Benefits of Dual-Core Intel® Xeon® Processors

Relief has arrived for IT and facilities managers who need to pack more computing capacity into existing data centers, while simultaneously reducing total costs. For some time, Intel has been working to deliver new levels of energy-efficiency through silicon, processor, platform and software innovation. The results of these efforts are now clearly evident in the new generation of servers based on the Dual-Core Intel® Xeon® processor 5100 series (code-name Nehalem). These servers boost performance by up to 3 times and energy-efficiency by more than 3 times compared to previous generation, single-core Intel Xeon processor-based servers. They are delivering the best performance, price/performance and energy efficiency in their class, and can help IT organizations dramatically increase compute density, while reducing power and cooling requirements.

These processors also include silicon-level support for virtualization, another critical technology for optimizing data center power and cooling efficiency. By enabling multiple applications and operating systems (OSs) to be consolidated per server, virtualization can help IT organizations consolidate their server infrastructure, so there are fewer systems to power and cool-and more room for expanding compute capacity within existing facilities. These and other recent innovations are major steps toward increasing performance and energy-efficiency, but they are only the beginning. Intel researchers continue to push the limits of transistor density in next-generation process technologies, to deliver better performance and new capabilities, while simultaneously driving down power consumption. Intel is also delivering software tools, training and support that help software vendors and corporate developers optimize their software for multi-core processors and 64-bit computing. These are essential efforts, since optimized software can boost performance, while containing or even reducing power consumption.

To help server vendors and IT organizations balance power versus performance in diverse environments, Intel is offering several processor versions, including 65W processors for mainstream servers; 40W processors for ultra dense implementations, such as server blades; and 80W processors for implementations where absolute performance is most important.

Intel Core micro-architecture builds on the power-saving technologies Intel originally implemented in the Intel® Pentium® M processor for laptops. Many of those technologies have now been extended and optimized for Intel server processors, and integrated with a number of additional capabilities that help to deliver high performance per watt. As shown in Figure D.1, the combination of power saving technologies, new micro-architecture and advanced manufacturing technologies yields higher system performance per watt even while lowering the overall power consumption.

Key advances include:

More instructions per clock-cycle. Each core can process up to four simultaneous instructions, versus only three in previous generations. In addition, many common instruction pairs are combined into single instructions, to further improve processing efficiency.

Faster and more efficient data access. A more efficient memory subsystem and a multi-core-optimized, shared-cache architecture significantly accelerate data access, so multiple cores can sustain higher levels of productivity.

Energy Benefits of Dual-Core Intel® Xeon® Processors 317

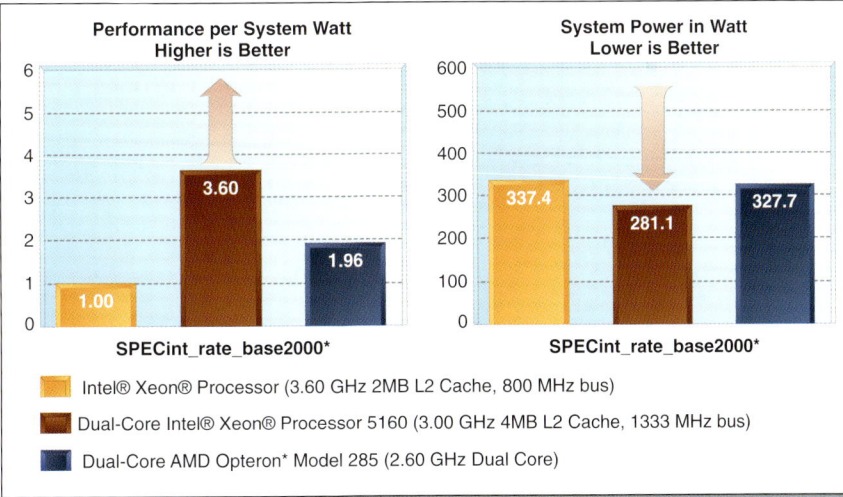

Figure D.1 Performance per Watt and System Power for Three Processors
Source: Intel, 2008

Faster execution of key instructions. The per-clock execution of Streaming SIMD Extension (SSE/SSE2/SSE3) instructions is effectively doubled, enabling a 4x increase in floating-point performance. This delivers critical speedups for a broad range of applications, including many security, financial, engineering and scientific solutions.

Dynamic power management. Power delivery to key processor subsystems is dynamically managed during runtime, to continuously optimize performance versus power efficiency as workloads vary.

For more information, read the Intel white paper: Inside Intel Core Microarchitecture: Setting New Standards for Energy-Efficient Performance.
*ftp://download.intel.com/technology/architecture/
new_architecture_06.pdf Multi-Core*

Intel has a long-term processor roadmap for delivering ongoing advances, and more than 10 processors with four or more cores are in development today. In all cases, there is an intense focus on ramping performance and energy-efficiency through both per-core innovation and multi-core integration. By increasing both per-core and multi-core performance, Intel will provide an optimized, energy efficient hardware platform for both current and emerging software applications.

Appendix D: Performance Per Watt

References

AFCOM. 2006. Five Bold Predictions for the Data Center That Will Change Your Future. AFCOM Data Center Institute.

ASHRAE 2005 Thermal Guidelines for Data Processing Environments *Mission Critical Facilities, Technology Spaces, and Electronic Equipment*. Atlanta, GA: American Society of Heating, Refrigerating, and Air Conditioning Engineers. *http://www.ashrae.org*.

ASHRAE Technical Committee 9.9. 2005. Equipment Power Trends and Cooling Applications. *Mission Critical Facilities, Technology Spaces, and Electronic Equipment*. Atlanta, GA: American Society of Heating, Refrigerating, and Air Conditioning Engineers. *http://www.ashrae.org*.

ASHRAE Technical Committee 9.9. 2008. Best Practices for Datacom Facility Energy Efficiency. *Mission Critical Facilities, Technology Spaces, and Electronic Equipment*. Atlanta, GA: American Society of Heating, Refrigerating, and Air Conditioning Engineers. *http://www.ashrae.org*.

ASHRAE Technical Committee 9.9. 2008. High Density Data Centers - Case Studies and Best Practices. *Mission Critical Facilities, Technology Spaces, and Electronic Equipment*. Atlanta, GA: American Society of Heating, Refrigerating, and Air Conditioning Engineers. *http://www.ashrae.org*.

ASHRAE Technical Committee 9.9. 2008. 2008 Environmental Envelope Guidelines: Expanding the Recommended Environmental Envelope (August 1). *http://tc99.ashraetcs.org/documents.*

Atwood, Don, and John Miner. 2008 Reducing Data Center Cost with an Air Economizer. Intel Corporation. Santa Clara, CA: Intel Corporation. IT@Intel Brief. (August). *http://www.intel.com/it/pdf.*

Avelar, V. 2006. Making Large UPS Systems More Efficient. American Power Conversion (APC). *www.apc.com*.

Blackburn, Mark. 2008. Five Ways to Reduce Data Center Server Power Consumption. The Green Grid. *http://doe.the greengrid.org*.

Cooper, Barnes, Paul Diefenbaugh, and Jim Kardach. 2008. Making USB a More Energy-Efficient Interconnect. *Intel Technology Journal 12:1* (February).

e! Science News, 2008. UC San Diego's GreenLight Project to improve energy efficiency of computing (July). *http://esciencenews.com.*

Eaton Powerware. 2007. Energy-Efficient Transformers Reduce Data Center Utility Costs (November). Doc. ID 6732. *http://www.powerware.com* .

Ecos and EPRI 2008. Efficient Power Supplies for Data Center and Enterprise Servers. Server Research Report (February). *www.80plus.org/documents/ServerResearchReportFinal.pdf.*

EPA Energy Star Program Report to U.S. Congress on Server and Data Center Energy Efficiency. 2007.

Fan, X., W. Weber, L. Barroso, and G. Bramlett. 2007. Power Provisioning for a Warehouse-sized Computer. *Proceedings of the 34th International Symposium on Computer Architecture* in San Diego, CA, Association for Computing Machinery (ACM), ISCA '07.

Filani, David, Jackson He, Sam Gao, Murali Rajappa, Anil Kumar, Pinkesh Shah, Ram Nagappan. 2008. Dynamic Data Center Power Management: Trends, Issues, and Solutions. *Intel Technology Journal 12:1* (February).

Gantz, John. 2008. An Updated Forecast of Worldwide Information Growth Through 2011. IDC. (March).

Gantz, John. 2008. The Diverse and Exploding Digital Universe. IDC white paper sponsored by EMC (March).

Greenberg, Steve, Evan Mills, Bill Tschudi, Peter Rumsey and Bruce Myatt. 2006. Best Practices for Data Centers: Lessons from Benchmarking 22 Data Centers. Proceedings of the ACEEE Summer Study on Energy Efficiency in Buildings. Asilomar, CA. ACEEE, August. Vol. 3. *http://eetd.lbl.gov/Emills/PUBS/PDF/ACEEE-datacenters.pdf*

Harris, Robin. 2007. Google's warehouse-size power problem. ZDNet (July 27).

Intel Corporation. 2008. Reducing Data Energy Consumption. A Summary of Strategies Used by CERN, the World's Largest Physics Laboratory. Santa Clara, CA: Intel Corporation. IT@Intel white paper, (August).

Intel Corporation. 2008. Dynamic Power Optimization for Higher Server Density Racks—A Baidu Case Study with Intel® Dynamic Power Technology. *http://communities.intel.com*

Intel Corporation. 2008. Reducing Data Center Energy Consumption. CERN white paper. (August). *ftp://download.intel.com/products/processor/xeon5000/CERN_Whitepaper_r04.pdf)*.

Kingston Technologies. 2005. Memory ranks and Intel E7320/E7520 chipset based servers (April).

Koomey, J. 2008. Worldwide electricity used in data centers. Environmental Research Letters, Vol. 3, No. 034008. (September 23).

Koomey, J. 2007. Estimating Total Power Consumption by Servers in the US and the World. Oakland, CA: Analytics Press.

Kumar and Dawson. 2007. Gartner paper G00153516.

Laverty, Denis. 2007. Calculating the Size of a Server Room Air Conditioner. *http://hvac-tqmcintl.blogspot.com/2007/12/calculating-size-of-server-room-air.html*.

Microsoft 2008. Energy Efficiency Best Practices in Microsoft Data Center Operations. *http://www.microsoft.com/environment/our_commitment/articles/datacenter_bp.aspx*

Mitchell-Jackson, J.D. 2001. Energy Needs in an Internet Economy: A Closer Look at Data Centers. University of California, Berkeley Masters Thesis. (July).

PowerSmiths. 2008. Opportunities for Transformer/PDU Energy Savings in Data Centers. (July). *http://www.docstoc.com/docs/3159789*.

Robert Francis Group. 2006. Demystifying Commodity and Blade Server TCO. Part Two: Numerical Analysis. (December). *www.rfgonline.com*.

Silicon Valley Leadership Group Case Study. 2008. Lawrence Berkeley National Laboratory (LBNL) Air Flow Management (March). *https://microsite.accenture.com/svlgreport/Documents/pdf/case%20study_LBNL.pdf*

The Green Grid. 2007. Data Center Power Efficiency Metrics: PUE and DCiE.

The Uptime Institute. 2007. Heat Density Trends in Data Processing Computer Systems and Telecommunications Equipment. Version 1.0. *http://uptimeinstitute.org*.

The Uptime Institute. 2007. Four Metrics Define Data Center Greenness. *http://uptimeinstitute.org*.

The Uptime Institute. 2007. The Invisible Crisis in the Data Center: the Economic Meltdown of Moore's Law. *http://uptimeinstitute.org*.

Torell, W. 2004. Calculating Total Power Requirements for Data Centers. American Power Conversion (APC). *www.apc.com*.

Turner, Vernon. 2009. Personal communication.

Turner, W. Pitt, John Seader, Vince Renaud, and Kenneth Brill. 2008. Tier Classifications Define Site Infrastructure Performance. Uptime Institute white paper. *http://uptimeinstitute.org*.

U.S. Department of Energy (DOE). DC Pro Development Team (LBNL, ANCIS, EYP Mission Critical, Rumsey Engineers, and Taylor Engineering). Data Center Tools Suite Assessment Tool Development: Electrical Example. *www.DOE.gov*.

U.S. Department of Energy, Federal Energy Management Program. *http://www1.eere.energy.gov/femp/procurement/eep_dist_transformers.html*

Verdun, Gary. 2008. The Green Grid Metrics: Data Center Infrastructure Efficiency (DCiE) Detailed Analysis, July.

Warmenhoven, Dan. 2005. Three Years Later, A Look at Sarbanes-Oxley. Forbes (July 27).

Ziff Davis Enterprise. 2009. Survey of IT decision makers. eWEEK (January).

Details on Demand Based Switching Benchmarks (Table 7.3.)

Performance tests were based on the following platform configuration: Intel® Server Board SE7520JR2 (Jarrell[†]); Dual Xeon® 3.60GHz processors; Lindenhurst[†] chipset; 4GB DDR2-400, dual ranked (Samsung[†]); Dual GB NIC on mother board; Single SCSI drive; Single PSU 600W; 9 system fans; Windows[†] server 2003 Enterprise Edition + Service pack Build 1247. CPU utilization was based on a Nocona[†] platform with DIBS OFF. All system power comparisons used the same number of engines for the WebBench workload.

Performance tests and ratings are measured using specific computer systems and/or components and reflect the appropriate performance of Intel products as measured by these tests. Any difference in system hardware or software design or configuration may affect actual performance. Buyers should consult other sources of information to evaluate the performance of systems or components they are considering purchasing. For more information on performance tests and on the performance of Intel products, visit *http://www.intel.com/performance/resources/benchmark_limitations.htm*.

References

Index

A

ACPI table 133, 135
acronyms used in this book
    ACPI - advanced configuration and power Interface 132
    AHUs - air handling units 198
    AMB - advanced memory buffer 37
    AMR - automatic meter reading 118
    ASHRAE - American Society of Heating, Refrigeration, and Air-Conditioning Engineers 83
    BMC - baseboard management controller 270
    BMS - building management system 121
    CAGR - compound annual growth rate 17
    CFM - cubic feet per minute 28
    CLTT - closed loop thermal throttling 37, 150
    DBS - demand based switching 7, 131
    DCiE - data center infrastructure efficiency 50, 51, 89
    DDH-UR - dynamic deployed hardware utilization ratio 278
    DH-UE - deployed hardware utilization efficiency 105
    DH-UR - deployed hardware utilization ratio 105, 278
    DIMMs - dual in-line memory modules 33–37, 85
    DRAM - dynamic random access memory 34
    DSI-POM - Dynamic Site Infrastructure Power Overhead Multiplier 278
    EIST - Enhanced Intel SpeedStep Technology 131
    FB-DIMMs - fully buffered DIMMs 4, 33, 37
    FDHS - full DIMM heat spreader 36
    GPU - Graphics Processing Unit 151
    HDD - hard disk drive 16
    IOPS - input/output operations per second 6
    iPDU - intelligent power distribution unit 78
    IPMI - Intelligent Platform Management Interface 85, 136

MAID - massive array of idle disks 7, 148
MRC - memory reference code 37
MTBF - mean time between failures 148
OCP - over current protection 155
OLTT - open loop throughput throttling 37
OOB - out-of-band 85
OSPM - OS power management 85
PMBus - power management bus 70
PUE - power utilization effectiveness 50, 51, 89
QPI - Quick Path Interconnect technology (Intel) 134
RDIMMs - registered DIMMs 34, 35
RMR - remote meter reading 118
RMS - root mean square 117
SCADA - supervisory control and data acquisition system 122–123
SI-EER - site infrastructure energy efficiency ratio 104
SI-POM - site infrastructure power overhead multiplier 105
SPEC - Standard Performance Evaluation Corporation 71
TDP - Thermal Design Power 71, 75, 130
UDIMMs - unregistered DIMMs 34, 35
UPS - uninterruptible power supply 83
WORSE - write-once-read-seldom-if-ever 148
WS-Man - Web Services Management 85
active and idle standby states 34
active idle 71
actual peak power vs. nameplate power 78
AFCOM
  predictions for power availability 22
AHU 186
American Society of Heating, Refrigerating, and Air-Conditioning Engineers (ASHRAE) 83
ammeter, defined 92
amps, defined 92
apparent power, defined 93
ASHRAE 55, 108, 200, 308
  data and temperature measurements 107, 107–108

automatic memory throttling 37

B

benchmarks
  designing 70
  determining system performance per Watt 71
    Black-Scholes 71
    SPECint*2006 71
  SPECpower 73
  SPECpower_ssj2008 71, 73, 86
  Thermal Design Power (TDP) 71
Black-Scholes workload 74
blade servers 17, 18
  cooling 30
blanking panels 188
British Thermal Units (BTUs), defined 92
business operations per second (bops) 74

C

C (CPU) states 132, 133, 158
ceiling plenum heights 8
Conduction 29
conduction area per fin 29
containerized data centers 9
convection area of heat sink 28
conventional CPU coolers 28
cooling 27
  measuring cooling efficiency 109–115
    air conditioning airflow efficiency (ACAE) 109
    cooling tonnage to BTU 110
cooling costs 20–22
cooling server components 27–31
  heat sinks 28
CPU utilization rate 79–81
CRAC 55, 56, 68, 107, 112–115, 186–188, 197, 202, 204
  calculation worksheet 113

D

data center infrastructure efficiency (DCiE) 50–51, 89

data center tiers 63
data centers
    availability 44
    data center infrastructure efficiency (DCiE) 51
    factors that can affect power consumption 52
    hot zones 21
    house load 51
    IT equipment power 50, 51
    IT load 51
    major elements of house load 52
    placement of servers 53
    power utilization effectivness (PUE) 51
    risk of interrupted operations 22
    total facility load 51
    total facility power 50, 51
    vena contracta effect 55
    wasted capacity due to poor layout and airflow design 22
DCiE ratios 90
demand based switching (DBS) 131–133
density in data centers 18
derating
    defined 94–95
    nameplate values 70
DIMMs 36
dynamic power monitoring 85

E

economizers 8
edge components 129
electric charge, defined 92
electrical power
    defined 92
    power (kW) vs. energy (kWh) 92
energy costs 93
Energy Star specification for servers 128
energy use of network equipment 17
energy-efficient operating systems 7
environmental impact 22
estimating processor power consumption 32

F

fans 28, 149–151
    power consumption 150
    used with heat sinks 27
formulas
    average power consumption 40
    estimating processor power consumption 32
    HDD power consumption 40
    three-year return on investment (ROI) 103

H

hard disk drive (HDD) heat dissipation 39
    calculating 40
heat distribution
    Watts per square foot 20, 21
heat pipes 151
heat sinks 27, 27–30
    fins 29
    performance 28
hot air return plenum 197
hot aisle/cold aisle layout 188
hot spots 18, 20
house load 43
    defined 46
    major elements 52

I

index fragmentation 290
Intel's 45nm technology 15
Intel® Core™ micro-architecture 15
Intel® Datacenter Manager 85
Intel® Dynamic Power Node Manager 85
Intel® multi-core processors 38
Intel® Pentium® 4 processor family 15
Intelligent Platform Management Interface (IPMI) 85
intelligent power distribution units (iPDUs) 78, 84
IOPS (input/output operations per second) 6, 91

K

kilowatt-hour, defined 92

L

Linpack benchmark 74
Linux† power management 160-162
liquid cooling 152, 199
lossless vs. lossy data compression 148

M

measuring
    average power 6
    server power consumption 6
memory
    and cooling 35, 36
    power consumption and workload 33
    RDIMM power consumption 35
    thermals 36
    Watts per DIMM 36
memory throttling 37
    and system performance 37
    closed loop thermal throttling 37
    open loop throughput throttling 37
metrics
    ASHRAE
        data and temperature measurements 107-108
    computational heat efficiency 110
    computational power efficiency 107
    CPU utilization 86
    data center infrastructure efficiency (DCiE) 98-102
    deployed hardware utilization ratio 6
    for cooling and air conditioning 109-115
        air conditioning airflow efficiency (ACAE) 109
        cooling tonnage to BTU 110
    hardware utilization ratio and layout efficiency 7
    input/output operations per second (IOPS) 91
    IOPS per kilowatt 6
    IT equipment power 99
    layout efficiency 6, 106
    marginal rate of return (MRR) 103
    performance per Watt 32, 86
    performance per Watt under load 71
    power distribution 86
    power usage efficiency (PUE) 98-103
    rack density 86
    return on investment (ROI) 91, 103
    revenue per Watt 6
    site infrastructure energy efficiency ratio (SI-EER) 104
    system performance per Watt 73
    total cost of ownership (TCO) 104
    total facility power 99
    Watts per rack 106
    Watts per square foot 106, 107
Microsoft† OS power management 158-159
motherboard components 270
MWAIT 133, 135

N

nameplate load 61
nameplate power vs. actual peak power 77
nameplate values 77-79
nanometers, in perspective 15
Node Manager 85, 135

O

on line transactionprocessing (OLTP) and TPC-C 74
optimizing applications 162-164
optimizing SAN infrastructure 8
OS power management (OSPM) 85
out-of-band (OOB) 85
over-clocking 27
overcooling 200

P

P (performance) states 131, 157
    Linux OS 160
peak power consumption 93
performance per Watt 32, 74, 86

placement of servers 53
platform 72
platform power capping 85
platform power consumption 72
power capacity costs 93
power consumed under load 71
power consumption by DIMMs 33–37
power management
    Linux† OS 160–162
    Microsoft† OS 158–159
    Sun OpenSolaris† OS 162
    tools for 82
Power Management Bus (PMBus) interface 70
power supplies 25, 38, 153–157
    and energy wastage 38, 41
    Energy Star requirements 75
power threshold alerting 85
power use effectiveness (PUE) 89
power utilization effectiveness (PUE) 50–51
processor power consumption
    formula for estimating 32
processors
    multi-core 31
    power consumption 31
proportional computing 270
P-state 8
PUE ratios 90
punch cards 16

R

rack servers 26
    cooling 30
raised floor considerations 8

S

S (system) states 132
Sarbanes-Oxley Act 16
server and storage efficiencies 8
server lifecycle and refresh 246–252
    five year TCO analysis with refresh 250
server memory requirements 137
server power consumption 271
server refresh 8

server workload throughput 72
servers
    and density increases 17
    and electrical power 25–41
    and U values 26
    blade 17
    built-in thermal sensors 81
    classes of 29
    cooling 30
    form factor and energy efficiency 26, 29–31
    hardware subsystems 81
    increase in number of x86 servers 14
    increase in total number 12
    maintenance 10
    methods for cooling components 27–31
    over-clocking 27
    performance per Watt 73
    processor power consumption 31
    rack 18
    risk of thermal failure 20
    tuning workloads 32
    volume, mid-range, and high-end 29
site infrastructure power overhead multiplier (SI-POM) 105
specification for 80 PLUS performance 75–76, 272
SPECjbb2005 benchmark 74
SPECpower benchmark 73
SPECpower_ssj2008 benchmark 71, 73, 86
Standard Performance Evaluation Corporation (SPEC) 71, 73
storage management practices 39
Sun OpenSolaris† power management 162
system performance per Watt benchmark 71, 73

T

temperature-based throttling 37
Thermal Design Power (TDP) benchmark 71, 75
thermal sensors 271
thin provisioning 8
TPC-C 74

U

U.S. Environmental Protection Agency (EPA)
    forecast for electricity demand 12
U.S. Health Insurance Portability and Accountability Act (HIPAA) 16
uninterruptible power supplies (UPSs) 83

V

vena contracta effect 55
virtualization 33, 62
voltage scaling 129, 131
Volt-Amps, defined 93

W

Watts
    defined 92
    Watt meters 73
Watts per square foot 20, 21
Web Services Management (WS-Man) 85
Windows 71

X

x86 servers 18
    and demand for power 12
    and growth of computing 11

Z

80 PLUS performance specification 71

Continuing Education is Essential

It's a challenge we all face – keeping pace with constant change in information technology. Whether our formal training was recent or long ago, we must all find time to keep ourselves educated and up to date in spite of the daily time pressures of our profession.

Intel produces technical books to help the industry learn about the latest technologies. The focus of these publications spans the basic motivation and origin for a technology through its practical application.

Right books, right time, from the experts

These technical books are planned to synchronize with roadmaps for technology and platforms, in order to give the industry a head-start. They provide new insights, in an engineer-to-engineer voice, from named experts. Sharing proven insights and design methods is intended to make it more practical for you to embrace the latest technology with greater design freedom and reduced risks.

I encourage you to take full advantage of Intel Press books as a way to dive deeper into the latest technologies, as you plan and develop your next generation products. They are an essential tool for every practicing engineer or programmer. I hope you will make them a part of your continuing education tool box.

Sincerely,

Justin Rattner
Senior Fellow and Chief Technology Officer
Intel Corporation

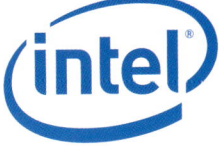

Turn the page to learn about titles from Intel Press for system developers

ESSENTIAL BOOKS FOR SYSTEM DEVELOPERS

Dynamics of a Trusted Platform
A Building Block Approach
By David Grawrock
ISBN 978-1-934053-08-9

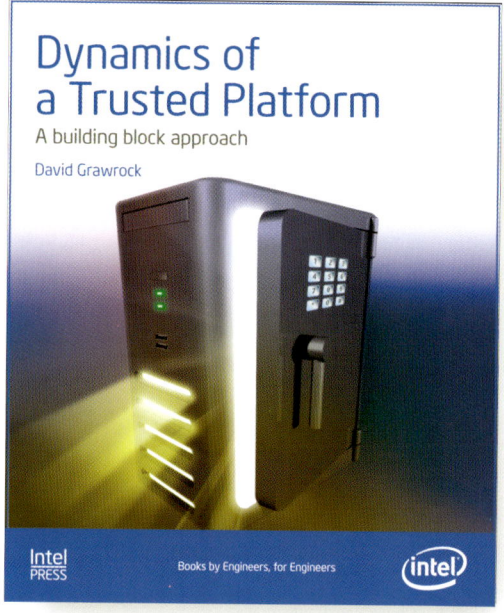

In *Dynamics of a Trusted Platform* David Grawrock has updated his highly popular *Intel Safer Computing Initiative* with new topics covering the latest developments in secure computing. The reader is introduced to the concept of Trusted Computing and the building block approach to designing security into PC platforms. The Intel® Trusted Execution Technology† (Intel® TXT) is one of those building blocks that can be used to create a trusted platform by integrating new security features and capabilities into the processor, chipset, and other platform components.

"The chapters on Anatomy of an Attack and System Protection present useful, practical information that will help familiarize a person with the impacts of protection (or lack thereof) of system components and resources. Treatment of the topic of measurement is particularly useful for system designers and programmers."
- *Amy C Nelson, Dell, Inc*

"David finds analogies in everyday life to clearly explain many of the concepts in this book. I would highly recommended *Dynamics of a Trusted Platform* for researchers, architects, and designers who are serious about trusted computing." - *Dr. Sigrid Gürgens Fraunhofer Institute for Secure Information Technology (SIT)*

"The opportunity now exists to start building trusted systems, making this book very timely. It would be foolhardy to start without a thorough understanding of the concepts; and this is what *Dynamics of a Trusted Platform* gives you. The building blocks described here are certainly able to imbue the infrastructure with a higher level of trustworthiness, and we may all look forward to the many benefits flowing from that." - *Andrew Martin Director, Oxford University Software Engineering Centre*

ESSENTIAL BOOKS ABOUT IT BEST PRACTICES

The Business Value of Virtual Service Oriented Grids
Strategic Insights for Enterprise Decision Makers

By Enrique Castro-Leon, Jackson He, Mark Chang
and Parviz Peiravi
ISBN 978-1-934053-10-2

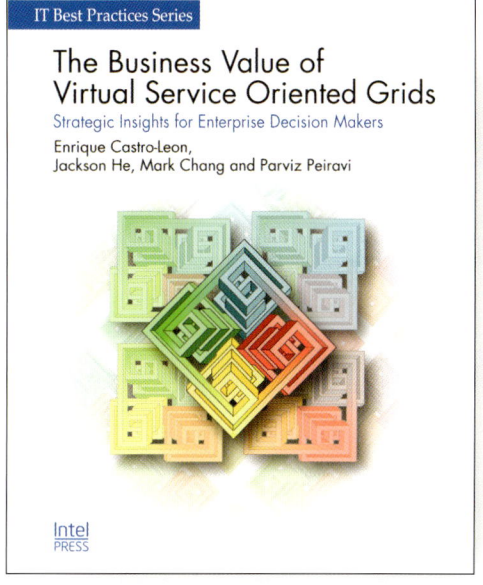

"In this book the authors track the trends, create new rules based on new realities, and establish new market models. With virtual service-oriented grids, the sky is the limit," writes Wei-jen Lee, a University of Texas – Arlington professor, about *The Business Value of Virtual Service Oriented Grids*, a new book published by Intel. The application of service-oriented architecture (SOA) for business will interest application developers looking for the latest advances in technology and ideas on how to utilize those advances to keep up in a global economy. *The Business Value of Virtual Service Oriented Grids* provides a framework that describes how the convergence of three well-known technologies are defining a new information technology model that will fundamentally change the way we do business. The first step, say the authors, is the development of new applications for the consumer market. However, even bigger is the development of new applications in a federated fashion using services modules called *servicelets*. These federated or composite applications can be built in a fraction of the time it takes to develop traditional applications. This new environment will lower the bar for applications development, opening opportunities for thousands of smaller players worldwide.

"We live in exponential times. . . . The economy is now thoroughly global. The Internet has replaced many of the middle layers of business, has enabled many to work from home or from a small company, and is revolutionizing the retail industries." writes Portland State University professor Gerald Sheble.

"The advent of SOA is going to impact information processing and computer services on a scale not previously envisioned." The speed-up in application development and integration will accelerate the deployment of IT capabilities, which in turn will have a consequential effect on the organization's business agility. Corporate decision makers will enjoy the ability to pick and choose among capital and operations expenses to suit their organization's business goals. The book describes the business trends within which this convergence is taking place and provides insight on how these changes can affect your business. It clearly explains the interplay between technology, architectural considerations, and standards with illustrative examples. Finally, the book tells you how your organization can benefit from *servicelets*, alerts you about integration pitfalls, and describes approaches for putting together your technology adoption strategy for building your virtual SOA environment using *servicelets*.

ESSENTIAL BOOKS ABOUT IT BEST PRACTICES

Service Oriented Architecture Demystified
A pragmatic approach to SOA for the IT executives

By Girish Juneja, Blake Dournaee, Joe Natoli, and Steve Birkel
ISBN 978-1-934053-02-7

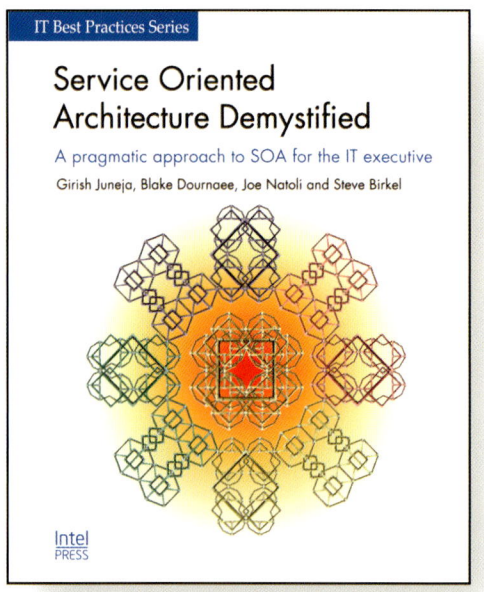

The authors of this definitive book on SOA debunk the myths and demonstrate through examples from different vertical industries how a "crawl, walk, run" approach to deployment of SOA in an IT environment can lead to a successful return on investment.

One popular argument states that SOA is not a technology per se, but that it stands alone and can be implemented using a wide range of technologies. The authors believe that this definition, while attractive and elegant, doesn't necessarily pass pragmatic muster. ***Service Oriented Architecture Demystified*** describes both the technical and organizational impacts of adopting SOA and the pursuant challenges. The authors demonstrate through real life deployments why and how different industry sectors are adopting SOA, the challenges they face, the advantages they have realized, and how they have (or have not) addressed the issues emerging from their adoption of SOA. This book strikes a careful balance between describing SOA as an enabler of business processes and presenting SOA as a blueprint for the design of software systems in general. Throughout the book, the authors attempt to cater to both technical and organizational viewpoints, and show how both are very different in terms of why SOA is useful. The IT software architect sees SOA as a business process enabler and the CTO sees SOA as a technology trend with powerful paradigms for software development and software integration.

SOA can be characterized in terms of different vertical markets. For each such market, achieving SOA means something different and involves different transformational shifts. The vertical markets covered include healthcare, government, manufacturing, finance, and telecommunications. SOA considerations are quite different across these vertical markets, and in some cases, the required organizational shifts and technology shifts are highly divergent and context dependent.

Whether you are a CTO, CIO, IT manager, or IT architect, this book provides you with the means to analyze the readiness of your internal IT organization and with technologies to adopt a service oriented approach to IT.

ESSENTIAL BOOKS ABOUT IT BEST PRACTICES

Managing IT Innovation for Business Value
Practical Strategies for IT and Business Managers
By Esther Baldwin and Martin Curley
ISBN 978-1-934053-04-1

Successful companies actively cultivate new ideas, put those ideas to work quickly and efficiently, and harvest the business value benefits of successful innovations. Discussions of innovation often focus on what a company offers, that is, its products and services. In *Managing Information Technology Innovation for Business Value*, Esther Baldwin and Martin Curley show how successful IT innovations pay back handsomely as well. Innovation is not just about what a company offers, innovation is also about how a company conducts business and how IT innovation can transform an organization into a significantly more efficient company.

Drawing on their experience with innovation in Intel's engineering operations, Baldwin and Curley emphasize that IT innovation does not require whole-scale invention. An innovative IT solution re-applied in a new context can provide even greater business value because the initial investment in developing the solution has already been made.

Managing Information Technology Innovation for Business Value includes examples and case studies from IT organizations as well as from Intel Corporation. It also includes assessment techniques, skill set descriptions, and a capability maturity framework to help IT organizations understand where they stand as innovators and what steps they can take to strengthen their competencies.

"Innovation is not just about new products and services. It's also about how an innovative organization conducts business practices and the invaluable role of IT in those processes. For innovation to 'stick' it must become a systemic mindset like quality and safety. *Managing Information Technology Innovation for Business Value* offers invaluable and fresh stories that can be applied to any size IT organization."
— *Charles Chic Thompson, Batten Fellow at the UVA Darden Business School*

"What can a small-medium business (SMB) learn from the IT experts at Intel? Some common-sense lessons on IT innovation management. Innovation can be incremental, for example, and a proven innovation can be re-applied over and over in new and different settings. That's a key message for those of us who serve the SMB market"
— *Mathew Dickerson, AXXIS Technology, Australia.*

ESSENTIAL BOOKS ABOUT IT BEST PRACTICES

Measuring the Business Value of Information Technology
Practical Strategies for IT and Business Managers
By David Sward
ISBN 978-0-976483-27-4

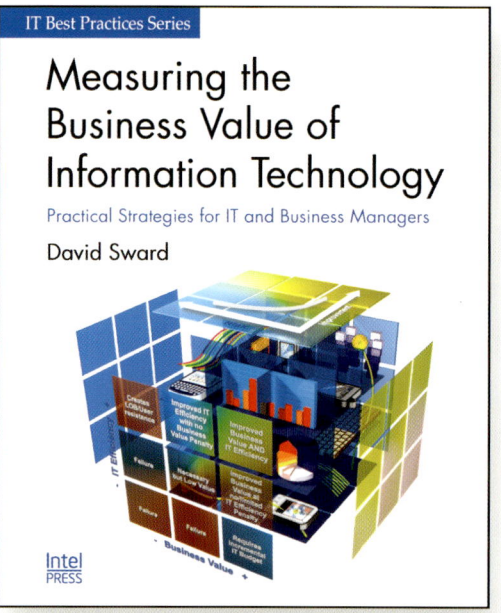

In today's fast moving competitive business environment, companies increasingly demand that IT investments demonstrate business value through measurable results.

Intended for IT professionals and consultants as well as business managers, this book covers one of the most important strategies any company can establish to help manage IT in the coming years. Namely, the creation of an IT Business Value customer focused approaches to determine the business value for any IT investment an organization may make.

Based on financial concepts and drawing on his background as a Human Factors Engineer, Sward makes the case that the process of establishing and running a business value program can ultimately create a new mindset for IT professionals. While Sward recognizes this will not happen overnight, he believes it serves to instill a belief that an organization can and will create a competitive advantage and increase shareholder value not by just deploying information technology, but by deploying the *right* information technology by linking IT to corporate objectives and focusing all efforts on the requirements of the end user.

"David Sward explains the why's, what's, and how's of IT value measurement, presents an intuitively appealing vocabulary, and offers an impressive portfolio of instruments to manage IT investments to produce measured business value."

—*Lars Mathiassen, Professor, Computer Information Systems, Georgia State University*

"Intel's IT Business Value program deserves to be widely emulated. David Sward was one of the program's founders, and he gives the inside details on how it was developed and implemented. This book should influence IT investment and management practices for years to come."

—*Robert Laubacher, Research Associate, MIT Sloan School of Management*

Managing Information Technology for Business Value
Practical Strategies for IT and Business Managers
By Martin Curley
ISBN 978-0-9717861-7-2

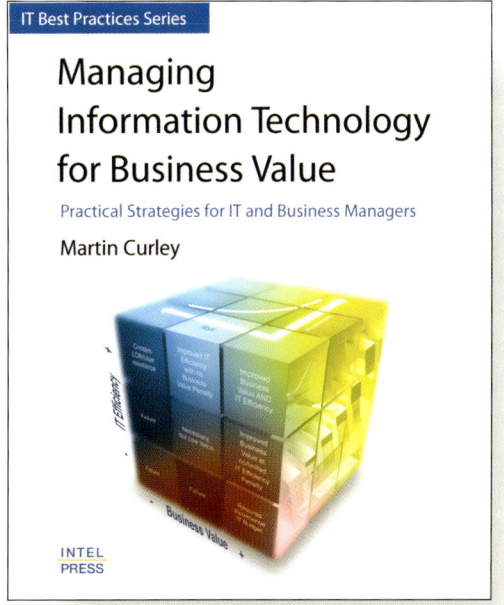

Managing Information Technology for Business Value is Martin Curley's call for IT and business managers to reformulate the way they manage IT. Traditionally, IT success has been measured in terms of IT parameters such as up time, capacity, and processing speed.

It is Curley's contention that if IT is to deliver business value, IT should be measured in core business terms---for example, customer satisfaction, revenue growth, and profitability. At a time when some corporations are reducing IT spending and once again looking at IT as a cost center, Martin Curley's Managing Information Technology for Business Value provides a necessary and timely counterbalance.

"Curley's book is required reading for all IT execs. Ignore this book at your peril."
-- Professor Paul Tallon,
   Carroll School of Management, Boston College

"Curley shines a light on the path ahead for ambitious users of IT. If you have any impact on how IT gets used in your organization, you owe it to your shareholders to read this book. It will impact your bottom line!"
   John Fleming, CEO, Enzo Consulting

"Martin Curley is a valued member of two very different communities---one populated by theorists who invent better methods to manage enterprises and the other populated by practitioners who put these methods to use."
-- Jeanne Ross, Principal Research Scientist, MIT Sloan Center for Information Systems Research

Special Deals, Special Prices!

To ensure you have all the latest books and enjoy aggressively priced discounts, please go to this Web site:

www.intel.com/intelpress/bookbundles.htm

Bundles of our books are available, selected especially to address the needs of the developer. The bundles place important complementary topics at your fingertips, and the price for a bundle is substantially less than buying all the books individually.

About Intel Press

Intel Press is the authoritative source of timely, technical books to help software and hardware developers speed up their development process. We collaborate only with leading industry experts to deliver reliable, first-to-market information about the latest technologies, processes, and strategies.

Our products are planned with the help of many people in the developer community and we encourage you to consider becoming a customer advisor. If you would like to help us and gain additional advance insight to the latest technologies, we encourage you to consider the Intel Press Customer Advisor Program. You can register here:

www.intel.com/intelpress/register.htm

For information about bulk orders or corporate sales, please send e-mail to **bulkbooksales@intel.com**

Other Developer Resources from Intel

At these Web sites you can also find valuable technical information and resources for developers:

www.intel.com/technology/rr	Recommended reading list for books of interest to developers
www.intel.com/technology/itj	Intel Technology Journal
developer.intel.com	General information for developers
www.intel.com/software	content, tools, training, and the Intel® Early Access Program for software developers
www.intel.com/software/products	Programming tools to help you develop high-performance applications
www.intel.com/netcomms	Solutions and resources for networking and communications
www.intel.com/idf	Worldwide technical conference, the Intel Developer Forum

6179-0134-3584-2595

If serial number is missing, please send an
e-mail to Intel Press at intelpress@intel.com

IMPORTANT

You can access the companion Web site for this book on the Internet at:

www.intel.com/intelpress/rpcs

Use the serial number located in the upper-right hand corner of this page to register your book and access additional material, including the *Digital Edition* of this book.